The remaking of social contracts

About the editors

GITA SEN is Adjunct Professor of Global Health and Population at the Harvard School of Public Health, and was until recently Professor of Public Policy at the Indian Institute of Management, Bangalore. She has been for many years a feminist analyst, activist and advocate on the political economy of globalization, and on sexual and reproductive health and rights. She is a member of DAWN's Executive Committee.

MARINA DURANO was a member of DAWN's Executive Committee from 2008 to 2011, working on gender issues in financing for development, including the examination of gender issues in international trade policies. She was a post-doctoral fellow at the Women's Development Research Centre (KANITA) of the Universiti Sains Malaysia, and is now an Assistant Professor at the Asian Center at the University of the Philippines–Diliman. She has a Ph.D. in economics from the University of Manchester.

About DAWN

DEVELOPMENT ALTERNATIVES WITH WOMEN FOR A NEW ERA (DAWN), founded in 1984, is a network of feminist scholars, advocates and activists from the economic South who work for economic and gender justice and sustainable and democratic development. DAWN provides a forum for feminist analyses and advocacy on issues affecting the human rights, livelihoods and development prospects of women, especially poor and marginalized women, in the South. It supports women's mobilization and building the capacity of young feminists to challenge inequitable power relations at all levels, and to advance feminist alternatives. DAWN draws strength from, and is committed to further empowering women's movements in the South to counter social, economic and political inequality, injustice and exclusion.

The remaking of social contracts

Feminists in a fierce new world

EDITED BY

GITA SEN AND **MARINA DURANO**

FOR **DAWN**

Zed Books | LONDON

The Remaking of Social Contracts: Feminists in a Fierce New World was first published in 2014 by Zed Books Ltd, 7 Cynthia Street, London N1 9JF, UK

www.zedbooks.co.uk

Designed and typeset in Calluna by illuminati, Grosmont
Index by John Barker
Cover designed by www.roguefour.co.uk

A catalogue record for this book is available from the British Library
Library of Congress Cataloging in Publication Data available

ISBN 978-1-78032-159-2 hb
ISBN 978-1-78032-158-5 pb
ISBN 978-1-78032-160-8 pdf
ISBN 978-1-78032-161-5 epub
ISBN 978-1-78032-162-2 mobi

Contents

Foreword

This book addresses some of the critical challenges of the fierce new world that marks the early decades of the twenty-first century. The complex interplay among the economic, ecological, political and social challenges of today have left the world lurching from crisis to crisis. This has had especially harmful consequences for people who are subordinated, oppressed and exploited, and threatens the very survival of our planet. Massive increases in inequality reflect a symbiosis between the extreme and growing wealth of some and deepening risks to the survival and livelihoods of many. The runaway celebration of greed in both North and South is matched by a reckless flouting of ecological boundaries, and rapid growth of militarism and conflict. Such challenges run counter to the deepened commitments to human rights and the upsurge in social movements that we witnessed in the last quarter of the previous century.

In an effort to address these complex issues, the United Nations is in the throes of a process to reach multilateral agreement on a new set of development goals after the time frame of the Millennium Development Goals (MDGs) ends in 2015. While many key global actors are caught up in the frenzy of negotiating the Post-2015 Development Agenda, it is important for civil society movements not to lose sight of the longer and larger perspective on growth, development and human rights, even as we speak out and advance our political critiques and alternatives in this global process of shaping the future of our earth and its peoples. This book is an attempt to address some of these larger questions. Its approach is based on DAWN's reflections on our thirty years of collective processes of feminist analysis, advocacy, popular resistance and movement building towards creating, together with other civil society allies, strong alternatives that will help move our world out of global gridlock.

The vigour and vitality that have driven the book to completion comes from activists, advocates and leaders of civil society movements and increasingly from a younger generation from the global South, who joined DAWN training sessions and organized discussions and debates and then later became members of advocacy teams at regional and global levels. It is on the young feminists – our DAWN alumni and associates as we call them – that we place our hope of sustaining DAWN's intergenerational politics of open debate and meaningful partnership. These are young women who we believe will shape and create a world truly committed to all human rights and to the human rights of all, regardless of class, caste, race, religion, ethnicity, age, sexual orientation and gender identity, abilities and citizenship.

We are grateful to the authors for their time, effort and commitment. The contributors are predominantly South-based feminists, allied with feminists from the economic North and with men advocating for fundamental change who share the vision and politics of DAWN. Through many years we have struggled together against neoliberal globalization, fundamentalisms and militarism on the streets as well as in the halls of inter-governmental negotiations.

We wish to thank Sonia Corrêa in particular for her vigorous engagement with the book in its initial phases of conceptualization and Seona Smiles for her support in the creation of the manuscript. We value our partnership with Zed Books, a friend of DAWN's through many years.

This book has been guided throughout by the DAWN Executive Committee and Global Board, and would not have been possible without the committed and hard work of the DAWN Secretariat. Last but not least, our appreciation goes to Gita Sen and Marina Durano for their guidance, persistence and focus that saw the book through to its completion.

JOSEFA FRANCISCO
DAWN GENERAL COORDINATOR
MANILA, PHILIPPINES

PART I

Introductory overview

Social contracts revisited: the promise of human rights

GITA SEN AND MARINA DURANO

This book has been a while in the making. Many of its authors have engaged over decades with the discourses and debates on development. They have also been involved in the practical politics of social mobilization and advocacy. Most would view themselves, as we the editors do, as part of broad social movements for economic, ecological and social justice. In particular, many are feminists (women and men) in the particular sense that has evolved through the analysis and practice of DAWN (Development Alternatives with Women for a New Era), the international network of researchers, activists and policymakers that came into being at the time of the United Nations Third World Conference on Women (Nairobi, 1984) and has been active since then in global and regional development debates. DAWN's approach from the beginning has been to recognize the connections between the different worlds of work, of reproduction, of interaction with nature, of social mobilization, within which we live. We are conscious that feminist thinking and practice have been shaped by the ups and downs of the development environment. Moving from the optimism about development of the 1960s and 1970s through the backsliding of the 1980s and 1990s, the world experienced an apparent resurgence in development thinking in the new millennium, but this was soon followed by current uncertainties and ambiguities, even as feminists and their allies struggle to challenge and transform that environment.

The book is the product of a collective attempt by DAWN and our allies to understand the complexities of our times, to challenge the webs of power and the many intersecting forms that social injustice takes; to spell out what it will take to resist and transcend the might of the juggernauts of globalization and reaction. Written by an international group of authors with diverse expertise in political economy, ecology, human rights and social change, the book attempts to weave these threads together to articulate a vision both multifaceted and interlinked. What drives that vision is our collective understanding of the world we live in, and our belief that changing this world is both essential and possible. This book explores, from a Southern feminist perspective, the potential of an interlinked approach to human rights for confronting and transforming the fierce world in which we live. We provide no blueprints. Indeed, we do not believe in them. We do value open questioning and debate, challenging ourselves to search for understanding of complex and difficult dilemmas in politically fraught terrains. This book is an attempt to open debates, not close them.

The first section of this overview provides a thumbnail sketch from this perspective of the period since World War II, paying particular attention to the emergence and fracturing of social contracts, the rise of social movements, and the promise of human rights. This sketch makes no claim to be comprehensive. It draws on some of DAWN's own experiences over the years, including issues we have had to confront and grapple with in that engagement. It also makes some analytical remarks about social contracts and the meaning of feminism. The second section orients readers to the different themes and dilemmas that are discussed in greater depth in the various chapters of the book, as well as in the short contributions in boxes found throughout.

A fierce new world, a fractured social contract

The early twenty-first century has been marked globally by the 'war on terror' and the financial and economic crisis. Beneath these headlines, however, lie other phenomena of no less importance – climate change, species die-offs and a host of related ecological crises, as well as a backlash against advances towards social justice and human rights for all. Even deeper beneath the surface lies the drastic transformation of the world of work towards flexibility and precariousness that shapes what is possible and probable by way of social policies. A fierce new world has been born – full of shaken premisses, complicated contradictions, serious fractures, severe backlash, broken promises and uncertain outcomes for the world's peoples. The period since World War II can be seen as having two parts: from 1945 until the early 1980s, and from the 1980s until 2008. These two sub-periods differ in multiple dimensions – the nature of global capital accumulation and political economy, the associated policies, social movements, and social contracts. The period since 2008 is one of great confusion and ambiguity with little clarity about future directions for global and national policies.

A word first about the way in which we use the term 'social contract' in this book. Definitions of the term from the seventeenth century on have entered political science textbooks, but they have also generated much criticism as being, among other things, rigid and patriarchal (Pateman 1988; Richardson 2007). We agree with much of this critique, and have had many internal debates about the value of the term given its troubled history. Nonetheless, we use it here to capture the recognition that social processes move in fits and starts, with turmoil and transformation being interspersed by short or long periods of stability, even stasis, when there is only slow or no change at all. Our usage is thus far removed from a notion of free and equal persons creating a society based upon rules to which all agree. Rather, it is embedded in the political economy of power and inequality at multiple levels and in varied forms. A social contract is a collective agreement that is built on and imbued with power; it may be imposed from above, fought over from below, and always holding the potential for change. But its fluidity is also interspersed with stability. Periods of stability in social contracts, local or global, are periods when our collective understanding of what is and what ought to be are stable and roughly in synchrony with each other; and when power structures and associated institutions are relatively steady.

In such times the main challenges to power remain within the boundaries of the system. Common normative understandings, as reflected in beliefs, social and political practices, and behaviours, reinforce the existing social order in different spheres – economic, political, legal, ecological, social, cultural and personal. Of course, there is no such thing as perfect stability. Internal contradictions lead to continuous pressures for change. Neither do the different spheres work synchronously. Thus, for instance, the demands for gender justice from women's movements may be far ahead of emerging changes in the political system. There is often not a single social contract in existence but multiple ones in different spheres that may or may not mesh smoothly with each other. Nevertheless, as we argue, the difference between periods of stable social contracts and periods of instability and transformation is not just of degree but of kind. What marks the difference is the breaking down of accustomed norms and beliefs, as people's lived realities conflict more and more with these familiar practices, to the point where there is a widespread sense that the contract is simply not working any longer.

Three characteristics of social contracts are important from this perspective. The first is that a social contract is not a teleology – 'rationality' discovering itself in some inexorable way. For instance, the inability of current political economic orders to effectively halt, let alone reverse, climate change is a good counter-example to any presumption of inevitable rationality. In fact, changes in social contracts may not even be progressive; witness the real risks to gender equality and women's human rights in the democratic churning of the so-called Arab Spring, or the current threats in the United States to overturn the advances made towards the civil rights of African Americans and the reproductive rights of women. Second, the norms that are part of our collective beliefs are as critical to holding up a social contract as the structures of material resources and political power. Indeed, there may always be inherent tensions between the real basis and functioning of power structures and what people believe about them. When such fissures widen into chasms, beliefs break down, as has happened in Greece where faith in the value of belonging to the European Union has practically collapsed in the face of massive unemployment and economic hardship. For this reason, movements for social change work at both the normative level and the level of institutions and power structures. Third, social contracts are always in a state of flux. The fracturing of existing social contracts can come from many sources: social movements, technological changes, institutional and cultural transformations, and of course economic and ecological pressures.

Our reading of recent history uses this open-ended and flexible meaning of social contracts to analyse both what is and what ought to be today from the perspective of social justice and human rights. From such a perspective, the two sub-periods after World War II (1945–80 and

1980–2008) offer a study in contrasts. During the roughly twenty-five years from the end of the war to the early 1970s, post-war economic growth, fuelled by the unravelling of colonial empires during the 1940s, 1950s and 1960s in Asia and Africa, created optimism about the developmental state and its potential to fight poverty and deprivation. The continuation of New Deal Keynesian policies and the Marshall Plan, together with the growth of the military–industrial complex (Eisenhower 1961), led to rapid job creation and expansionary social policies in the USA, Western Europe and Japan.

Demands for social and economic justice in the heyday of the first industrial revolution in the late nineteenth and early twentieth centuries had already led to the expansion of social democracy and the welfare state in Europe. After the war, these trends were picked up again and were fuelled further by the challenge posed by the creation of the Soviet Union with its underpinning normative premises of socialism. Despite anti-communist reaction within the United States and the bitter struggles over the Vietnam War, the 1960s and 1970s were a period of immense global optimism for progressive change towards greater social, economic and political equality and justice. This reached its apogee in the 1970s with the brave belief in the possibility of a New International Economic Order, espoused politically by post-colonial countries and the Non-Aligned Movement. Many states avowing socialism (whatever it meant) gained independence from colonialism in this period, although sometimes disguising one-party authoritarianism and bitter internal struggles over power and its spoils.

This period saw the rise of a number of social movements globally and nationally espousing the social, economic and political rights of people previously disenfranchised and marginalized on the basis of race, ethnicity and gender. There was also a thriving debate over the meaning and relevance of socialism among these new social movements. This expansive period saw women's movements in both South and North emerging as major social and political actors. The field of 'women in development' grew into a thriving arena of debate among academics, activists and policymakers; one that transformed rapidly to take on board the critique of both capitalism and socialism, and that brought new energy and ideas to the forefront of social movements (Beneria and Sen, 1981). The so-called personal sphere of domestic work and dual work burdens, of sex and reproduction, was recognized as political, a recognition backed by cross-national and cross-cultural political economy, history, anthropology and political science.

The publication of Rachel Carson's *Silent Spring* in 1962 had fired the first salvo against the belief in limitless growth without ecological boundaries. The Stockholm Conference on the Human Environment in 1972 questioned the local and global impacts of growth and development. Just as ecologists (Daly, 1991) argued that standard national income accounting excludes the contribution of natural capital to growth, feminists also pointed to the hidden tax (Palmer, 1991) that women pay through their unpaid work in caring for people (Waring, 1988), and the burdens that reproduction and control over sexuality place on their health and rights (Sen, 1984).

Progressive change was in the air, fed by beliefs in social justice, economic and political equality, and human rights, and substantiated by the expansive policies of the welfare and developmental states. Those expansive policies were supported during the 1970s by the World Bank under the rubric of basic needs (a concept first developed at the International Labour Organization) and 'redistribution with growth' (Chenery et al., 1974). Supported by expanding United Nations institutions, international norm-setting and governance increasingly began to cover workers' rights, development assistance, a more fair distribution of the benefits of trade and industrialization, as well as greater monitoring (if not actual control) of the activities of transnational corporations.

However, challenges to this optimism were also growing. Keynesian macroeconomics, built on the role of government in promoting growth of internal markets and expansion of the welfare state, came under increasing attack in the 1970s from the forces of financialization unleashed by the information technology revolution. These forces demanded greater openness to flows of money capital (and not only for commodities and industrial capital as in the Keynesian period), and, hence, for control of inflation and freeing of exchange rates. This meant, in turn, a push for fiscal tightening and curbs on government expenditure. By the mid- to late 1970s, prodded by the two oil crises of 1973 and 1979, the Keynesian social contract had begun to break down in the North. And with it, in the 1980s, went down the social contract of the developmental state in countries of the South.

The beginning of the second sub-period from the early 1980s to 2008 is associated with the coming to power of and deep collaboration between the financial elites of the USA and the UK through the Reagan–Thatcher years. As is well known, the era of financial globalization that followed imposed harsh conditionalities on government borrowing, limited government spending, unleashed the private sector, broke the power of labour unions, and eroded the welfare state in the North while decimating the developmental state in many countries in the South. The place of the developmental state has been filled by the private sector and public–private partnerships, creating growth booms in some instances and long periods of stagnation and even negative growth in others. Increasingly unfettered movement of financial capital meant that this period saw regular boom-and-bust financial bubbles even as hedge funds moved money daily in trillions across the globe. The untethering of finance from the world of industry and the removal of regulatory barriers to finance capital has meant great instability in the global economy as the financial and economic crisis of 2008 has shown (Stiglitz, 2003; Stiglitz, 2004).

By shrinking the welfare state and weakening labour laws, this period further increased labour market flexibility for capital, and led to massive inequality globally and within countries (Stiglitz, 2013). The emergence of a larger and larger 'precariat' (as Standing calls the increasingly permanent underclass of informal workers) has altered drastically the meaning of employment and social security, and drastically affects the hopes and aspirations of young entrants to the labour market. The rise of the World Trade Organization (WTO) to set the norms for a new era of expansive global trade enshrined flexible labour and cheap exports. The world's attention is drawn to BRICS (Brazil, Russia, India, China, South Africa) and the potential effects of these emerging markets on the global economic, financial and political scene, implying a new element of capitalist competition (O'Neill, 1981). Developments in emerging markets, in turn, spurred economic growth in Africa as the new BRICS multinationals search for cheap sources of minerals, energy and raw materials, replicating what their older Northern counterparts have done for over a century (Cheru and Obi, 2010). This period is replete with ironies, not least of which is the fear and chagrin among capitalist leaders in the North at being beaten in the game of capitalist competition by a country that still calls itself socialist: China.

In contrast to the growing earlier recognition of ecological limits to growth, the latter part of this period has seen continuing failures by governments to agree on such limits or to implement them effectively. On no issue is this failure so spectacular as in the problem of climate change, even as the earth tumbles towards catastrophic tipping points. Biodiversity and species losses come a close second in this failure, despite the existence of agreements.

Of great relevance has been the drastic change in norms and beliefs during this second sub-period. While the heyday of the welfare and developmental states had lauded equality of opportunity and even outcomes, and believed in the role of the state, the second sub-period rationalized the dismantling of state capacity and the shrinking of fiscal space on grounds of governmental inefficiency and 'rent-seeking'. Much less attention was paid to bribe-givers among private corporations than to bribe-takers within governments. The lauding of individual enterprise spilled over into accommodation, rationalization and sometimes enthusiastic embrace of corporate power, as in the Global Compact espoused by the United Nations, with little acknowledgement of a need to regulate let alone control that power. Development assistance has tended to move back from the solidarity principles enunciated in the first sub-period to 'donor fatigue', increased re-linking of aid to the donor's economic and especially corporate interests (a blatant return to 'tied aid'), and the rise of philanthro-capitalism (Edwards, 2010). Global regulation through norm-setting by UN agencies such as the World Health Organization (WHO) have become anathema to corporate interests – for example, baby food, tobacco and global pharmaceuticals companies. Agencies such as the WHO have seen their budgets shrink, forcing them to cut back on their activities and rely increasingly on the largesse of private unregulated funding.

The second sub-period also saw the rise of religious conservatism as the frontline of opposition to gender equality and women's human rights. It was the Reagan era in the United States that saw the consolidation of a new alliance within the Republican Party between economic conservatism, opposition to the civil rights of African Americans, and religious mobilization against gender equality and women's reproductive rights, culminating in the formation of the Tea Party in the last decade. While no such broad alliance has come into being globally, the same sources that have funded the Tea Party also support the global assault on sexual and reproductive rights. Heavily funded evangelicals, Mormons and other US groups have instigated and promoted anti-gay legislation and attacks in a number of African countries (Kaoma, 2009; Kaoma, 2012; Stan, 2013). They have made common cause with the Catholic, Islamic and Orthodox Church hierarchies against agreements on sexual and reproductive rights, gender equality, and the rights of young people at the UN, including at the Human Rights Council.

This regressive combination of neoliberal and religious fundamentalisms did not go without challenge. Social movements gained new momentum and vigour through the United Nations conferences of the 1990s. Desperation about the future of the planet drove many young people to the environmental movement. Women's movements mounted a robust attack on neoliberal structural adjustment almost from its inception (Sen and Grown, 1987). A very large number of the sessions at the NGO Forum during the Fourth World Conference on Women in Beijing in 1995 were on the harmful effects of neoliberally driven structural adjustment programmes on women's incomes, work burdens, health and education, as well as on the increase in violence against women. New identities emerged and claimed space – people with disabilities, indigenous people, LGBTIQ people; young people. Despite the shrinking state, these movements demanded justice and human rights, but, even as they grew, they seemed always to be outstripped by the hegemony of market ideologies and neoliberalism until the changes highlighted in the next section.

Social movements and human rights

Despite the hegemonic dominance of its ideology, all was not well in the world of neoliberal financial capitalism. The financial and economic crisis of 2008 marks a second fracturing of social contracts, this time of the more regressive beliefs and institutions of the sub-period from the 1980s onwards. The consequences of unregulated financial capitalism have become clear for all to see (Stiglitz, 2013). External and internal crises in varied forms and the resolutions to crisis in all their complexities have come to preoccupy all sovereign nations and the people they govern. Governments the world over are trying to address the causes and consequences of unfettered financialization leading to a series of banking and debt crises, of climate change rapidly heading towards the tipping point, the rise of religious chauvinism, and the resurgence of militarism and conflict. There is increased recognition in both South and North that government policies based on neoliberal fundamentalism are often themselves the problem, as they align with the powerful against the needs and best interests of the poor, the subordinated and the oppressed.

The rise of progressive social movements in the post-World War II era goes back at least to the global churning and open experimentation with new ideas, modes of living, and understandings of human rights in the post-colonial developmental period of the 1960s and 1970s in Asia, Africa, the Caribbean and the Pacific, during the struggles against dictatorships in Latin America, and against the Indo-China wars in the North. Movements for gender equality, for the civil and political rights of those discriminated against on the basis of race, ethnicity or caste, together with the environmental movements, matured in the 1970s.

By the 1980s, and in opposition to the neoliberal model of financial capitalism of the second sub-period, they had been joined by a number of other social movements – of indigenous people, of young people, of migrants, and of people with disabilities, as well as on the basis of sexual orientation and gender identity, to name some of the most prominent. As with all social institutions, progressive social movements have their conservative, middle-ground and radical variants. However, most of them drew energy from their opposition to the emerging social contract of the second sub-period after 1980, as well as from the deepening of norms and institutions for the protection, promotion and fulfilment of human rights.

The UN conferences of the 1990s – Rio on Environment and Development, Vienna on Human Rights, Cairo on Population and Development, Copenhagen on Social Development, Beijing on Women, among others – provided the sites for a major consolidation and clarification of a broad human rights agenda, including not only civil and political rights but also economic, social and cultural rights. For instance, the conferences at Vienna, Cairo and Beijing together affirmed a new and more expansive meaning for the right to health: for women and girls in particular, the right to health is not only about obtaining health services, or providing nutrition, clean water and sanitation. The right to health was affirmed to include the right to decision-making, control, autonomy, choice, bodily integrity, and freedom from violence and fear of violence.

Different social movements all have their particular focus, and connecting the dots is not easy as the relations among different movements across issues have not always been inclusive or harmonious. Thus, in the throes of the struggle for sexual and reproductive rights, the challenges of integrating global economic justice (the main concern of many South governments, and organizations) with gender justice (especially sexual and reproductive rights) became apparent (Sen, 2006). Religious conservative organizations, with support from the Holy See and some conservative governments, have taken advantage of these tensions to attempt to drive a wedge. While this has had some success with governments, it has not been particularly effective with progressive social movements.

There are many among different social movements, and notably in the women's movement, who have used their particular thematic focus not as a silo but rather as a lens through which to analyse the larger world, and to argue for change anchored in respect for human rights. DAWN views itself as being one such organization, working on four distinct but interconnected themes: the political economy of globalization, political ecology and sustainability, sexual and reproductive health and rights, and political restructuring and social transformation.

From the beginning, DAWN's approach to feminism has been based not on a calculus of identity alone but on the recognition that women's human rights are lost or gained in the midst of the interplay between the personal and the structural environment. For women as women, the politics of personal relations, of the body, of sex and reproduction matter greatly. The household and family relations are a critical site of gender power expressed in multiple dimensions. At the same time, women are workers juggling double and triple burdens under increasingly harsh conditions; are members of communities struggling for land and livelihoods; are agents in societies undergoing cultural transformations; are actors in economies shaped by globalization and militarism; and are parts of production systems unmindful of ecological limits. An approach to feminism that cuts across and is inclusive of these distinct yet interconnected spheres is still uncommon and calls for greater conceptual clarity. In the next section, we clarify the position that animates the essays in this book.

Feminism in an interconnected world

Three approaches to women's human rights exist today.

 ROLES AND IMPACTS

The first is an approach that explores roles and their consequential impact on women as producers, as consumers and as reproducers, without interrogating the power relations within which these roles are enmeshed. The approach focuses on women's practical needs and fails to challenge existing structures and hierarchies of domination and subordination that essentially define women primarily through their roles in the private sphere of the home – as reproducers, that is as weak and needing protection; or, paradoxically, as temptresses, that is as inherently sinful, evil or polluting, or through other similar culturally defined characteristics. With this approach, women usually are entitled to justice even within such a gender system or patriarchal order but only on terms circumscribed by those unequal norms. They have entitlements but not on equal terms with men, and only so long as they do not flout or transgress the norms themselves.

Conservative notions of justice (sometimes based on religious interpretation) often recognize the principle of equity (fairness) for women, but insist that women and men are inherently different (under male-dominated interpretations of holy books or supernatural codes), and therefore cannot be equal. Such notions are at odds in the most basic way with the core principles of equality and universality at the heart of the Universal Declaration of Human Rights (UDHR) and all other human rights treaties and agreements thereafter that form the basis of international jurisprudence. Thus, although the first approach may propose some useful measures to ameliorate the burdens placed on women by their norm-defined roles and may thus modify their negative impacts, it cannot transform existing power relations because the approach itself does not question them.

2 FOCUS ON GENDER POWER

A second approach recognizes and acknowledges women's subordination in a hierarchy of power relations underpinned by differential ownership or control over productive assets, incomes, tools, knowledge and access; reinforced by personal, political and juridical systems; and cemented by control over women's bodies. An important element is the idea of cooperative conflict (Sen, 1990) and how access to resources defines the different fallback positions of women and men in the household when negotiating over the allocation of tasks and responsibilities in familial and household maintenance. Differential access to land and other resources such as technology, credit and information; sex-based divisions of labour that assign 'caring' responsibilities to women and result in multiple work burdens; discrimination and bias in labour and other markets that create multiple barriers to income-earning options; and differential presence in public spaces – all compound the effect of discriminatory laws and biased legal systems, as well as low levels of presence and participation by women in legislative bodies, governments and judiciaries and other governance structures. Power within the household and in personal relations, and recognition of the exercise of power through violence, are central elements in this approach.

Sexuality and reproduction are viewed in this approach as crucial not only because they shape who controls women's and children's labour, but also because they are the sites of the most direct forms of control over human beings. We live in and through our bodies. We are deeply vulnerable in our bodies and can be controlled most directly through our sexuality and reproduction, including methods such as enforced childbearing and violence. Threats and fear of violence or the infliction of pain are not, however, the only ways by which control over the bodies of others is exercised, and bodily integrity and autonomy denied. The normative structures of the body deeply influence how we view ourselves and how others view us: too fat, too thin, too dark; impure while menstruating, 'unclean' if our genitals are not cut or mutilated; as bitches, as 'cunts' (a term used to refer to a body part as well as in a derogatory way to women as objects to be possessed, used and discarded), as sexual perverts – a seemingly endless list. For today's women, the norms of beauty intermingle with the structured disorder of romantic love, eroticism and desire, heterosexual norms, and the commercial drives of the beauty industry to create an often toxic mixture of control, self-regulation and subordination.

These methods of control intersect with cultural norms of behaviour and expectations in relationships that are idealized in popular beliefs and practices. The chaste and faithful girlfriend, the pliant wife, the obedient daughter-in-law, the responsible mother have as counterparts the virile male, the protective husband and the provisioning father. These norms are enforced by rewards and punishment that are both physical, whereby their flouting can lead to violence, disfigurement, rape or even death, and psychological, through expectations of acceptance, love, recognition, honour and social status.

The implications of these internalized norms for the structure of gendered power relations and different elements of subordination can be profound. For instance, conservative religious authorities (often male) may vary in their beliefs about sexuality depending on whether they are themselves required to be celibate or not. Fear of the disorderliness of sexuality and its ability to break through traditional power hierarchies can lead them to suppress, repress, deny and constrain sexuality to a limited functionality for purposes of human reproduction, the latter being the principal role assigned to women. Motherhood is deified but women are subordinate. Fear of the power of sexuality untied from reproduction leads them to oppose effective contraception, safe abortion, and all homoerotic relationships, practices and behaviour as dangerous disorders. Religious hierarchies that do not require celibacy may be less rigid, but they too tend to view sexuality as potentially dangerous to religious and social order, and women as well as LGBTQI people as threatening because of their sexual autonomy/power. Control over their presence in public spaces and women's subordination to men as their protectors and guardians are a consequence. Control over and subordination of women through sex and reproduction thus feed back into other spheres affecting their participation on an equal footing in economic, political and cultural life.

An approach focused on gender power can go much further and deeper than the first approach, which simply addresses differential roles and their impacts. When supplemented by an analysis of how gender power intersects with power in other spheres, this approach can become a powerful method for understanding and advocating against social inequality in many dimensions. These other spheres may be ascriptive, such as ethnicity, race, indigeneity, sexual orientation or caste, all of which also have historical and cultural underpinnings; may be personal but with social ramifications such as disability; or may be factors such as age, residence and migratory status that are not ascriptive but can be the basis of discrimination and bias. The structures of gender power and these other ascriptive or other bases of inequality each have their own history and relative autonomy while intersecting with others. Intersecting inequalities are undoubtedly more complex but they can in fact determine who is located in which position in different power hierarchies better than an analysis based on a single form of inequality (Sen et al., 2009).

But is a focus on power at the interpersonal level enough? Richer and more accurate as an intersectional analysis of gender power may be, the approach may still be limited if it remains at the level of personal and familial relations without interrogating power in other spheres that cannot be reduced to interpersonal relations. Despite its relative autonomy, interpersonal power is embedded in, or at least is in juxtaposition to, economic, ecological, political or other structures and processes. DAWN's own initial statement of position (Sen and Grown, 1987) challenged a liberal feminist focus on gender equality that did not recognize the influence of economic systems shaping development. As DAWN network members stated in multiple advocacy sites, 'do we need a larger piece of a poisoned pie?' Meaning thereby that a larger critique of development processes is needed to assess whether greater gender equality within them will actually be good for women. Thicker description and fuller understanding of the implications of development processes for women requires going beyond the previous two approaches while building on them to retain the insights of each.

3. THE INTERFACES OF MULTIPLE SYSTEMS OF POWER

The third approach includes, in addition to the previous two approaches, an interrogation of the economic and other power structures and processes that shape, modify and alter the environment within which power relations of gender, ethnicity, and other inequalities and social hierarchies are played out. Forces of trade, globalization, finance, climate change or militarization, to name some, are ineluctable shapers that govern how gender and other power relations are likely to work. Thus, for instance, it is well known that the globalization of recent decades has gone hand in hand with a significant increase in the proportion of labour that is 'flexible' – non-unionized, with few rights in the workplace, as well as suffering from poor wages and working conditions, creating the 'precariat' (Standing 2011). At the same time, young women in many parts of the world have been entering the industrial workforce in large numbers, for example in China, Vietnam, Bangladesh, Mauritius and many other countries. For these women, as Kabeer (2011) points out in her research on garment workers in Bangladesh, the ability to leave the patriarchal systems of rural households is undoubtedly liberating in the personal sense, although the work may be difficult or demeaning and throws them to the mercy of supervisors and employers in the textile industry's global commodity chain. When women workers are harassed sexually by bosses in these workplaces, or transsexual workers are fired because of their gender identity, is this an abuse of their sexual rights, or of their right to dignity as workers? Clearly both factors are at work and intersect in ways that cannot be well understood when presented as just one or the other. Sexual harassment or violence is undeniably an expression of interpersonal gender power, but it is shaped as well in this case by the forces defining the global commodity chain and the transformation of the labour process.

A number of other intersections between gender power and other power systems can be cited. One that has been extensively elaborated in the last two decades is the connection between gender relations and demographic processes (Presser and Sen, 2000). The emergence of gender equality and sexual and reproductive health and rights as a competing paradigm to earlier population-control approaches has radically altered the discourse, in addition to becoming the site of complex and multi-faceted power struggles.

Another example is from international trades where the growing tendency of powerful countries to push for bilateral and regional trade agreements in the face of the stalling of the Doha Round of multilateral trade negotiations has had many adverse consequences. Among them is the incorporation of onerous TRIPS-plus clauses on intellectual property, particularly but not exclusively affecting access to cheap generic medicines (Mabika and London, 2007; Love, 2011). The effects of this are to reduce the availability of affordable medicines for patients with life-threatening illnesses such as HIV/AIDS and cancer. As medicines become more expensive and difficult to access, gender power kicks in to affect who will get access and how. In addition to being affected as patients, women and girls are also affected as health-care producers because they are usually the primary health care-givers in the home, a consequence of the gendered division of care work (Grown et al. 2006).

Other similar intersections exist. Militarization and conflict lead inevitably to the breakdown of gender norms of what is acceptable behaviour. As generalized violence grows, so does sexual violence and the reaction to it through greater control over women's autonomy, as the experiences of women in Sri Lanka illustrate (ICAN 2013). Sexual violence may be used to humiliate and punish entire communities, as happened during the Balkan wars between the Serbs and the Croats, and in the state of Gujarat during the anti-Muslim pogrom in 2002.

Another crucial area is the extent to which ecological changes leading to land degradation and climate change affect women's ability to perform their tasks in the gender division of labour or to guarantee the food and other subsistence needs of their families. Disaster response and risk mitigation are also affected when acknowledging differential capacities across genders is combined with gender-blind approaches. The power dynamics within households and communities change as a result and can alter long-standing gender norms, which feeds back in turn to food and subsistence systems (UNDP, 2012).

It is apparent from this discussion that not only does understanding the dynamics of gender relations require an analysis of how they are shaped by political economy, ecology, militarization and conflict, and other systems and processes; the reverse is also true. Much public advocacy on macroeconomics, militarization or climate change, including by otherwise progressive advocates and analysts, is carried on without ever referring to gender power. Few analysts of the ongoing global economic crisis after 2008 invoke gender systems in their analysis, despite the fact that gender power determines who is affected, how they are affected, and how they cope, resist or organize for change. Few explanations of conflict refer to gender except when noting violence against women and girls as fallout. Climate change debates refer to gender – when they do – largely when examining consequences, but not when addressing the causes within production systems, consumption habits, and choice of energy sources and technologies, all of which are deeply gendered. Focusing on the interfaces of gender with other power systems and hierarchies involves recognizing the multidirectional causality within systems. For instance, one of the most enduring aspects of gender relations is the division of labour and women's responsibility for care work, including not only daily domestic work but also the care of children, older people and those who are ill or have disabilities. The dependence of health care and of social security systems on this typically unpaid work by women has been well noted by feminist economists over many decades. Government spending, budgets and macroeconomic policy ought to but almost never do recognize this hidden tax on women, even though they depend on it. Gendered divisions of labour affect the efficiency and productivity of economic systems in multiple ways that are as yet only partially recognized.

Gender systems typically govern, among other things, the physical mobility and autonomy of girls and women. Social control over sexuality and reproduction and the norms that govern them shape migration patterns and the structures of cities as well as of international and cross-border policies and politics. The rise of global communications and culture in recent times has shaped, like no other force, the beliefs, values and aspirations of young people about marriage, reproduction and sexuality, and has set off backlashes from conservative religious forces. Intergenerational differences, to which gender norms are central, shape labour markets, family formation, and demands for legal human rights and social policy responses. The impact of the 'culture wars' and the interplay of gender and age on the fiscal and other policies of the state and its approach to the protection and advancement of human rights need to be understood much better than they are at present.

Our argument above has important methodological implications for the chapters in this book. First, understanding the drivers of gender relations requires delving beneath gender roles and their effects on underlying power relations that govern the daily realities of people's lives.

Gender power relations intersect with class, race, ethnicity, caste and other markers of socio-economic inequality to create a complex lived reality. Second, forces of political economy such as globalization, military conflict and ecology are a significant influence on the environment for power relations such as gender, and thereby give them shape; but there are important ways in which gender power itself affects the dynamics of globalization, conflict or ecology, and these must be acknowledged and uncovered. Third, each of these sets of power relations has its own relative autonomy and must be analysed as such, along with the analysis of their interfaces. To put it sharply, gender power may not directly influence interest rates or the money supply, and hence one cannot attempt to 'add women and stir' to analyse every issue. One must nonetheless always ask the question whether it does or not. For instance, it is necessary to understand international trade in itself without trying to force-fit gender into every aspect of the analysis or cherry-pick only the gender-focused bits. However, it is equally important to have an analysis of women as producers and consumers, and of how gender power may not only be a consequence but a cause. The result can be a more fruitful and open dialogue and exchange between women's movements and other social movements to which women themselves often belong. Women themselves have expressed repeatedly in mobilization and advocacy meetings that DAWN has organized over the years that they do not want policy and programme silos that dissect their lives into fragmented airtight compartments. In the words of the old slogan, 'we want bread, but we want roses too!'

Towards a remaking of social contracts

This collection of essays covers a wide range of issues and debates that confront humanity at the turn of the twenty-first century. Additional to the essays is a series of short pieces in boxes, many of which were written by younger feminists. These boxes contribute to the identification and understanding of specific instances of confusion, contradiction and crisis that we call a fierce new world.

The essays in this book are a mixture of in-depth analysis of some of the issues raised above and proposals for the remaking of the broken social contracts of today. Part II is a series of critiques against the systemic reproduction of inequality. The challenges of responding to the global financial crisis arrive on the heels of market-oriented policy frameworks that have undoubtedly influenced late-twentieth-century economic reforms. The gendered impacts of the global crisis have been raised in this political context: that it impinges upon the time burdens of women; that women absorb care burdens even more as market-based services or public services become less accessible; higher unemployment rates, or women increasingly being marginalized into the informal sector, or worsening of working conditions. This describes the fate of women in every crisis. In Stephanie Seguino's 'Financialization, Distribution and Inequality', policies that will move the global economy to a sustainable path of improvement in living standards require that we work with a macroeconomic framework that enables greater equity with growth. Such a framework involves disciplining capital – not only financial interests but also footloose corporations and global producers that rely on outsourcing – so that firms align their profit interests with broader social and economic interests.

The reconfiguration and realignment of international political relations towards a multipolar world brings its own set of complexities to feminist challenges against unjust power structures. States and governments have attempted to assert a structure in global economic governance. Yet these new poles of accumulation and new centres of power, such as the large, middle-income countries, have not translated their actions into new directions and strategies for socio-political transformation. In Yao Graham and Hibist Wendemu Kassa's 'New Poles of Accumulation and Realignment of Power in the Twenty-first Century', the shifting balance of power between the declining imperial power (the USA), 'old' Europe, and the rising new poles of accumulation in the South on issues of trade and investment flows, regional power, aid politics, climate and reform of the international institutions – particularly the WTO, the UN and the Bretton Woods Institutions – is discussed. It uses the case of Africa to illustrate how cooperation and contradiction within the South play out. Oscar Ugarteche's 'The Modern Business of War' further argues that the growing illicit economies are not a marginal adjunct or by-product of the global economic order. Instead, declining productivity in the traditional leading economies of the world has led to economic policy impasses, growing militarization and 'illegalization' of the economy. Furthermore, as part of militarization, social repression is increasingly visited on poor, non-male and non-white peoples.

Where is the place for social reproduction in this fierce new world and how do we redistribute resources and opportunities? How do we put an end to the production and reproduction of inequalities by neoliberal policies? Aldo Caliari's 'The Convergences and Divergences of Human Rights and Political Economy' explores the human rights and political economy approaches to development, and argues that there is immense potential in their complementarities. However, both approaches have drawbacks from a feminist perspective and their synthesis is an urgent task for the feminist movement.

Part III tackles the issues of sustainability and climate change. In the many aspects of global environmental change, the impact on livelihoods and survival, and thus on women's work burdens, is very great. However, women are often framed as a vulnerable group in the discourse, thus masking their role as actors. What is needed is to recognize women as change agents engaged in struggles over fossil fuel exploitation, the reduction of pollution, and improving access to water, as these are linked to improvements in people's survival and well-being.

Although it has been explicitly recognized that historically industrialized countries have created the climate change problem, they have yet to assume the greatest share of responsibility for the resulting development dilemmas. This is apparent in the substance of intergovernmental discussions, which have not been about decisive changes in patterns of overconsumption and production, nor about long-term structural changes to the unsustainable nature of the neoliberal economic system. Rather, deliberations and negotiations emphasize ways and means to sustain the existing patterns and approaches to continue meeting the global resource needs of the North while they simultaneously push for technological and market-based solutions that privilege transnational corporations so that they can make the most out of the climate crisis. Also worrisome is the resurgence of Malthusian notions linking population stabilization and climate change, despite the fact that these connections have been challenged by feminists, most notably in the 1994 International Conference on Population and Development.

Anita Nayar's 'Climate Non-negotiables' outlines the policy responses to the convergence of those dilemmas. Market and technical 'fixes' to climate change, such as carbon trading, agrofuels, nanotechnology, geo-engineering and synthetic biology are at the centre of these discussions and are part of capitalism's response to the climate, food and fuel crises. The idea of re-engineering the planet used to be the stuff of science fiction, but a band of increasingly vocal scientists, venture capitalists, established corporations and other advocates is rapidly moving these controversial ideas from the margins to the mainstream of policy responses to climate change. Diana Bronson's 'Geoengineering: A Gender Issue?' is an exploratory essay suggesting directions for future research and reflection as well as strategic considerations for civil society movements – feminist, environmentalist, human rights – that must intervene on these questions in the coming years.

Reducing Emissions from Deforestation and Degradation (Redd) and the range of climate finance mechanisms are other attempts at seeking compromise solutions, but these will still fall short of shifting the international division of labour and the asymmetrical interdependence between the North and the South. Zo Randriamaro's 'Land Grabs, Food Security and Climate Justice' looks at aggressive land-grabbing operations in the African continent, either for speculative purposes or for securing food for land-scarce, capital-rich economies. The consequences for the food security of local inhabitants and for ecological balance pose serious challenges for handling risks and vulnerability. Twenty years after the Rio Earth Summit (United Nations Conference on Environment and Development) in 1992, feminist principles are again brought to the table to counteract apocalyptic scenarios that encourage resignation instead of promoting activism.

Part IV confronts fundamentalisms and attempts to decipher the complexity of biopolitics. The last decade has witnessed major steps forward in legitimizing a more holistic approach to 'development', which has led to efforts that address inequality and poverty through a multidimensional approach, taking into account empowerment, freedom, well-being and human rights of all people. The global women's movement can boast of important achievements in the area of human rights, where women's rights are increasingly recognized. At the global institutional level, the combined advocacy efforts of human rights defenders and women's rights activists have secured strong and consistent support for the principles of gender equality and women's human rights. In parallel, political and policy advocacy around reproduction and sexuality issues and related areas has become more visible at both national and global levels, as exemplified by the international debates on HIV/AIDS, reproductive and sexual rights and the articulation of human rights principles to tackle discrimination and violence related to sexual orientation and gender identity (Yogyakarta Principles, 2007; O'Flaherty and Fisher, 2008). Alexandra Garita and Françoise Girard's 'Negotiating Sexual and Reproductive Health and Rights at the UN' reminds us to continually secure full and equal participation in decision-making, as the work towards promoting and fulfilling sexual and reproductive rights is treacherous and complex.

Despite advances, many challenges remain to the implementation of the international conventions and consensus agreements on women's human rights. In addition, all too often human rights standards are applied as if they are gender-neutral, promoting thereby a conception of citizenship based on heteronormativity and the realities of elite males in a given society as the norms. For instance, African feminist activists and researchers contend that this dominant conception is not adequate for the African post-colonial context, where women's citizenship is still largely defined by ascribed social relations of subordination and their relations with the state are mediated by men, kin or communities. It is even more inadequate in the context of globalization where an 'internal patriarchal closing of ranks' occurs as social subgroups or communities strive for their specific interests and rights in relation to the broader national community. In such a context, women at the community level are often forced to accept community culture and values defined by subordination. Fatou Sow and Magaly Pazello in 'The Making of a Secular Contract' explore the difficulties in 'secularizing' the social contract through the lens of three major religions – Christianity, Islam and Hinduism. The revival of conservative religious and cultural values has serious implications in any reflection on the potential for a new social contract based on social justice and gender equality. Religious and cultural revivals often contribute to a backlash against emerging norms for women and gender equality.

These trends are compounded by the prolonged crisis of many nation-states in the Africa region, where women are particularly affected by the exclusions resulting from their fragmentation and capture by both national elites and external forces. On one level, state policies already reflect some elements of 'gender equality' frameworks, but on the whole these stop short of fully engaging with gender equality and, in particular, sexual and reproductive health and rights. Rosalind Petchesky's 'Sexuality as a Weapon of Biopolitics' argues that there is a need to start thinking through every domain or issue of political economy, markets, poverty, growth, militarization and climate change as profoundly gendered and sexualized from the start. Also the converse: that every domain of sexual and gender and reproductive politics has its deeply macroeconomic and development-related dimensions. A feminist politics relevant to the twenty-first century cannot take sexuality or gender out of political economy and development; nor can political economy and development be taken out of sexuality and gender.

Finally, Part V takes us to the complex act of building nation-states and the need to galvanize social movements. Peggy Antrobus and Gita Sen (2006) have raised questions that are even more crucial at this juncture of fractured social contracts: 'What is the social project of the global women's movements and is it larger than identity politics? Does the feminist social project go beyond the project of the movement for global economic justice? And if so, how?'

Debates on the role of the state and the relevance of sovereignty have become increasingly lively. Claire Slatter's 'The State of States' focuses on the struggles over the social contract in building and managing the nation-state under today's neoliberal globalization. She surveys the range of tensions confronted by feminists in the South today. Among these tensions, feminist politics must navigate formal democracy and authoritarianism, legislative reform and political extremism, the political conditionality of 'good governance' and widespread practices of corruption and fraud, private power centres and 'failed states', and citizen's rights movements as well as religion or ethnicity-based fascist forces intent on taking over the state.

It is not only about 'good' governance; there is also the question of secular governance. Amrita Chhachhi's 'Religious Fundamentalism and Secular Governance' argues that the distinction in practice is not so straightforward. Instead, if the intent is to undermine the basis of fundamentalist groups, the women's movement needs to focus on the creation of public spheres for deliberation that accommodates processes of democratization.

Contestations over the control of a state sometimes lead to conflict and war, whose nature has changed from predominantly inter-state to intra-state conflict, with civilians, mainly women and children, being severely affected. Conflict and attendant militarization lead to the suspension of law and order and accountable governance for military ends. Kumudini Samuel's 'Reframing Peace and Security for Women' points to the gendered nature of conflict and conflict resolution. This requires a nuanced understanding of aspects of masculinity and femininity that are reproduced and reconstructed in these settings.

Whether in the national, regional or global spheres, women's movements are still confronted with a daunting challenge, which has been articulated as follows by DAWN members: 'If a human rights framework is our core analytical tool, then we need to articulate clearly the connection between women's rights and the rights of others' (Antrobus and Sen, 2006). In pursuit of our transnational advocacies, how relevant is the United Nations as a multilateral site and for ensuring good global governance? Acknowledging the paradigmatic shifts induced by globalization, the decline of the nation-state and the reconfiguration of the geopolitical context, the UN as a multilateral site is being re-examined. Some suggest that the UN is no longer appropriate for both the revival of multilateralism and civil society engagement. It is a state-centred space that is highly politicized and heavily fragmented in its operations through a number of thematic 'silos', namely finance, security, trade, climate change and human rights. There appears to be a need for a new and people-centred space outside the UN, and correlatively an urgency to examine civil society as an alternative space given its potential for mobilization and putting forward propositions for alternatives. Against this backdrop of shifting contexts and the emergence of a fierce new world countered by a variety of movement activisms, Josefa Francisco and Peggy Antrobus's 'Feminist Activisms for New Global Contracts amidst Civil Indignation' draws attention to feminist movements negotiating for rights, inclusion and equal power in a dysfunctional multilateral system. Efforts at transnational inter-movement building, through global campaigns and knowledge-sharing, require feminist leadership to facilitate change for social transformation towards justice.

REFERENCES

Antrobus, P., and G. Sen (2006) 'The Personal is Global: The Project and Politics of the Transnational Women's Movement', in Srilatha Batliwala and David Brown (eds), *Transnational Civil Society: An Introduction*, Kumarian Press, New York, pp. 142–58.

Beneria, L., and G. Sen (1981) 'Accumulation, Reproduction, and Women's Role in Economic Development: Boserup Revisited', in E. Leacock and H. Safa (eds), *The Sex Division of Labour, Development, and Women's Status*, special issue of *Signs: Journal of Women in Culture and Society*, Winter, pp. 279–98.

Chenery, H., et al. (1974) *Redistribution with Growth*, Oxford University Press, London.

Cheru, F., and C. Obi (eds) (2010) *The Rise of China and India in Africa*, Zed Books, London.

Daly, H.E. (1991) *Steady State Economics*, Island Press, Washington DC.

Edwards, M. (2010) *Small Change: Why Business Won't Save the World*, Berrett Koehler, San Francisco.

Eisenhower, D.D. (1961) 'Farewell Address to the Nation', 17 January; www.information-clearinghouse.info/article5407.htm.

Grown, C., E. Braunstein and A. Malhotra (eds) (2006) *Trading Women's Health and Rights? Trade Liberalization and Reproductive Health in Developing Economies*, Zed Books, London.

ICAN (2013) 'What the Women Say. Elusive Peace, Pervasive Violence: Sri Lankan Women's Struggle for Security and Justice', *Brief* 8 (Spring); www.icanpeacework.org/wp-content/uploads/2013/06/Slanka-final.pdf.

Kabeer, N. (2011) 'Between Affiliation and Autonomy: Navigating Pathways of Women's Empowerment and Gender Justice in Bangladesh', *Development and Change*, vol. 42, no. 2 (March), pp. 499–528.

Kaoma, K. (2009) *Globalizing the Culture Wars: US Conservatives, African Churches, Homophobia*, Political Research Associates, Somerville MA.

Kaoma, K. (2012) *Colonizing African Values: How the US Christian Right is Transforming Sexual Politics in Africa*, Political Research Associates, Somerville MA.

Love, J. (2011) 'The Production of Generic Drugs in India', *British Medical Journal* 342: d1694.

Mabika, A.H., and L. London (2007) 'Zambia: The Right to Health and International Trade Agreements'; www.equinetafrica.org/bibl/docs/CBP14tradeZAMBIA.pdf.

O'Flaherty, M., and J. Fisher (2008) 'Sexual Orientation, Gender Identity and International Human Rights Law: Contextualising the Yogyakarta Principles', *Human Rights Law Review*, vol. 8, no. 2, pp. 207–48.

O'Neill, J. (1981) 'Building Better Global Economic BRICs', Global Economics Papers No. 66; www.goldmansachs.com/our-thinking/archive/archive-pdfs/build-better-brics.pdf.

Palmer, I. (1991) 'Gender and Population in the Adjustment of African Economic Planning for Change, *Women Work and Development Series*, vol. 19, ILO, Geneva.

Pateman, C. (1988) *The Sexual Contract*, Polity Press, Cambridge.

Presser, H., and G. Sen (2000) *Women's Empowerment and Demographic Processes – Moving Beyond Cairo*, Oxford University Press/International Studies in Demography, Oxford.

Richardson, J. (2007) 'Contemporary Feminist Perspectives on Social Contract Theory', *Ratio Juris*, vol. 20, no. 3 (September), pp. 402–23.

Sen, A. (1990) 'Gender and Cooperative Conflicts', in I. Tinker (ed.), *Persistent Inequalities: Women and World Development*, Oxford University Press, New York.

Sen, G. (1984) 'Subordination and Sexual Control: A Comparative View of the Control of Women', *Review of Radical Political Economics*, vol. 16, no. 1 (Spring), pp. 132–42.

Sen, G. (2006) 'Reproductive Rights and Gender Justice in the Neo-conservative Shadow', in T.D. Truong, S. Wieringa and A. Chhachhi (eds), *Engendering Human Security: Feminist Perspectives*, Women Unlimited, New Delhi.

Sen, G., and C. Grown (1987) *Development, Crises, and Alternative Visions – Third World Women's Perspectives*, Monthly Review Press, New York.

Sen, G., A. Iyer, and C. Mukherjee (2009) 'A Methodology to Analyse the Intersections of Social Inequalities in Health', *Journal of Human Development and Capabilities*, vol. 10, no. 3 (November), pp. 397–415.

Stan, A.M. (2013) 'Anatomy of the War on Women: How the Koch Brothers Are Funding the Anti-choice Agenda', 5 November; http://rhrealitycheck.org/article/2013/11/05.

Standing, G. (2011) *The Precariat: The New Dangerous Class*, Bloomsbury, London.

Stiglitz, J. (2003) *Globalization and Its Discontents*, new edn, Penguin, London.

Stiglitz, J. (2004) *The Roaring Nineties: A New History of the World's Most Prosperous Decade*, W.W. Norton, New York.

Stiglitz, J. (2013) *The Price of Inequality: How Today's Divided Society Endangers Our Future*, W.W. Norton, New York.

UNDP (2012) 'Gender, Climate Change and Food Security', Policy Brief 4; www.gender-climate.org/Content/Docs/Publications/UNDP_Policy-Brief-Gender-Climate-Change-and-Food-Security.pdf.

Waring, M. (1988) *If Women Counted: A New Feminist Economics*, Harper & Row, San Francisco.

Yogyakarta Principles (2007) *Principles on the Application of International Human Rights Law in Relation to Sexual Orientation and Gender Identity*; www.yogyakartaprinciples.org/principles_en.htm.

PART II

Governing globalization:
critiquing the reproduction of inequality

CHAPTER 1

Financialization, distribution and inequality

STEPHANIE SEGUINO

A distinguishing feature of economies over the past three decades has been the widening income and wealth gap both within and between countries (Galbraith, 2011). In addition to growing economic polarization, this period has witnessed a slowdown in economic growth rates except for some Asian countries, and greater limitations on the state's ability to promote rising living standards and social protection. Moreover, economies have experienced greater instability, with over a hundred financial crises occurring since 1980 (Eichengreen and Bordo, 2003).

The Great Recession, which began in 2008, is only the most recent disruption in an increasingly unstable global economy. Although the proximate cause of the Great Recession was the US financial crisis, prompted by the subprime mortgage debacle, its deeper roots can be traced to the widening income and wealth gap. Rather than hit the 'reboot' button in response to the crisis, there is both a brief space and a strong justification to rethink the previous path and to forge a new one. Policies that will move to a sustainable path of improvements in living standards require a macroeconomic policy framework that enables greater equity with growth.

This essay explores the role of inequality in contributing to the most recent global economic crisis, and the related tendency to 'financialization' – the increase in size and importance of an unregulated financial sector. It then discusses what an equity-led macroeconomic policy framework would look like, with suggestions for proposals not only to produce greater equality but also to reduce economic instability, while stimulating rising living standards.

The crisis is not just a *financial* crisis

Many analysts identify the immediate cause of the Great Recession as the meltdown of the subprime mortgage market in the USA. Facilitated by a period of financial sector deregulation, banks and investment firms seemed to run amok, with the development of exotic financial instruments and 'teaser' loans that bordered on predatory lending, which combined to produce toxic assets.[1] The period of deregulation that began in the 1980s ushered in a new era of finance, with banks shifting their focus to more speculative financial activities and away from the necessary, if unglamorous, day-to-day business of accepting deposits and extending loans to facilitate the firm investment and household consumption that fuel job growth.

Deregulation did not happen without a push from the financial sector itself. The accumulation of power and wealth by financial elites over the last two decades has been used to fund an anti-regulation lobby targeted towards policymakers and, as a result, regulatory agencies. The result has been tantamount to regulatory capture: public agencies charged with regulating in the public interest instead acted in favour of the financial sector, or turned a blind eye to the practices they were charged with regulating. A steady flow of new financial products that received little scrutiny or oversight by government regulatory agencies increased the availability of finance and expanded the pool of eligible, if not viable, borrowers.[2]

One clear lesson that emerges from this crisis is that economic behaviour is not always and everywhere economically rational. Lack of information and imperfections in quantitative human reasoning – for example, engaging in herd behaviour, believing that housing prices will continue to rise forever, and thus failing to identify an asset bubble for what it is – underscore the necessity to regulate markets, especially in finance.

While it may have been irrational for investors and homeowners to assume that housing prices would continue to rise indefinitely, the economic fissures that led up to the crisis were related to the growing inequality within and between countries over the past three decades. Focus on the malfunctioning of financial markets has obscured inquiry into the deeper systemic roots of the crisis.

TABLE 1.1 Global trends in income inequality

YEAR	GINI INDEX	RATIO OF INCOME SHARE
1820	43.0	3
1850	53.2	
1870	56.0	7
1913	61.0	11
1929	61.6	
1950	64.0	
1960	63.5	61
1980	65.7	74
2002	70.7	
2005		103

SOURCE Data on income shares are from UNDP, 2005 and 2008, cited in Ortiz, 2008; and Gini coefficients from Milanovic, 2009.

Table 1.1 provides data on inequality for the past two centuries, offering a historical perspective on trends. Two measures of inequality are represented here, the Gini index with a value of 0 for perfect equality and 100 for perfect inequality, and the ratio of income of the top 20 percent of households to the bottom 20 percent. The Gini index, representing a measure of global inequality in household incomes, rose 5 points between 1980 and 2002, a sizeable jump. Similarly, while the income of the richest 20 per cent of households was 74 times that of the poorest 20 per cent in 1991, by 2005 the ratio increased to 103. Whichever measure is used, the trend towards greater inequality is evident.

Of particular interest are the trends in inequality since the 1970s, marking the movement towards deregulation, privatization and liberalization – that is, neoliberal macroeconomic policies. Data from the International Labour Organization (2008) indicate that labour's share of income, the share of national income going to wage earners, fell between 1996 and 2006 in a number of industrialized and middle-income countries. These include most OECD countries and Brazil, India and the Russian Federation. Typically, a declining wage share is evidence that while labour productivity may be rising, workers are not in a bargaining position to claim a proportionate share of the additional income that their higher productivity produces. Also, when the labour share is falling, the profit share of income is rising.

Before turning to a discussion of the causes of growing inequality, the linkage between inequality and the financial crisis is briefly explained. Michael Kalecki, a contemporary of John Maynard Keynes, emphasized that an unequal distribution of income can have harmful macroeconomic effects on output and employment. Why is this so? Put simply, if income becomes concentrated in the hands of the wealthy, aggregate demand will fall, and with it, employment and output. This occurs because the wealthy tend to spend a smaller percentage of their income than lower-income households. A redistribution of income to the wealthy, then, results in higher saving rates and, as a result, a reduction in aggregate demand. In colloquial terms, 'without buyers, there are no sellers'. That is, businesses respond to slack demand (fewer buyers) by cutting back on production and laying off workers.

With the growth of inequality and thus inadequate demand, output and employment can only be sustained if households borrow in order to finance consumption; the USA is a case in point.[3] Or countries can pursue export-led growth strategies, with foreign demand for a country's goods substituting for domestic demand; many developing countries have adopted this approach. Neither of these strategies is sustainable in the longer term. Moreover, inequality can also result in too little investment in people in the form of education and health – both of which can limit a country's ability to raise its overall productivity, and thus its living standards, in the long run. An understanding of the current crisis then requires an analysis that identifies the sources of growing inequality within and between countries and traces the linkages of inequality to the global economic downturn.

Several factors have contributed to the intensification of global inequality over the past three decades. A key aspect of this process is the slowdown in wage gains and, in some instances, the decline in real wages. Several forces – economic and political – have reduced worker bargaining power and, as a result, held back improvements in wages. From the economic side, the twin policy shifts towards trade and investment liberalization have made it easier for firms to move production from high- to low-wage countries to reduce costs of production in order to bolster profits (Milberg and Winkler, 2007). Trade liberalization has allowed firms to then export their goods back to high-wage countries. But at least some workers in high-wage countries are worse off since their jobs have been exported (Goldberg and Pavcnik, 2007).

The negative effect of job losses spills over to depress the wages of workers in high-income countries who still have jobs. That is because a larger pool of unemployed workers makes it harder for employed workers to bargain for higher wages. With downward pressure on workers' wages, spending falls in rich countries. This of course lowers a firm's profits since profits are determined not only by the profit rate, which is the percentage firms can mark up the price of a good over its cost of production, but also by the volume of sales. With falling sales, or a slowdown in the growth of sales, corporations push on to set up production in ever-lower-wage sites as a means to buoy profits. Or they may reduce investment in productive capacity.

Another strategy firms, especially those in the USA and Europe, have adopted is to engage in offshoring, purchasing components from subcontractors located in countries with lower wage costs. This has led to a 'hollowing out' of manufacturing in rich countries. Increasingly, we are also seeing evidence of outsourcing of information technology (IT) services.

In both cases, firms have become more mobile, and with that mobility comes increased bargaining power to hold down or lower the wages of workers in both rich and developing countries. But it is those very same workers whom firms rely on to buy the goods they produce. Alas, with lower or stagnating wages, product demand falls.

A second factor contributing to growing inequality is the pressure on governments to reduce public-sector spending, especially on much-needed physical and social infrastructure such as roads, immunization, rural health clinics, agricultural extension and education. The impact of these trends is evidenced by the decline in global public investment as a share of GDP, which fell from 2.1 per cent in 1980 to 0.81 per cent in 2000 (Rathin, Heuty and Letouzé, 2009: 70).

The downward pressure on budgets in developing countries is in part attributable to the loss of tariff revenues as a result of trade liberalization.

Governments are also pressured to cut spending and lower budget deficits as a way to reduce imports, thereby rectifying trade imbalances, and attract foreign capital. Wealth holders, it is argued, are unwilling to invest in countries where inflation is too high since it erodes the real value of their holdings. Government budget deficits are seen by wealth holders as contributing to inflation, hence the pressure to cut spending. Cuts in government spending further depress aggregate demand with negative effects on employment, making it harder for workers to bargain for higher wages.

Yet another source of growing inequality and the resultant shortage of aggregate demand is the shift in policy framework among central banks. The focus of policy has shifted from price stability *and* full employment to an almost singular concern with controlling inflation. This is done by raising interest rates, which makes borrowing more expensive. As a result, private investment and consumer spending fall, depressing aggregate spending in the economy. With this, unemployment rises. Thus the focus on inflation targeting comes at a high cost in terms of employment.

The macroeconomic record of the past thirty years stands in stark contrast to an earlier time when wages rose along with GDP, the so-called golden age of capitalism from 1945 to 1973, and firms reinvested their profits in order to expand output to meet the rising demand for their goods. Simultaneously, firms hired more workers, creating a virtuous cycle of rising incomes for middle- and low-income families, increased demand for goods and services that benefits firms' sales and thus profits, and, as a result, rising employment.

In contrast to the earlier period of wage-led growth, the dampened demand and stagnating wages (and by definition, rising profit shares of income) observed over the past three decades have contributed to the lack of profitable opportunities for firms to expand output.[4] Moreover, increased risk has accompanied the process of globalization. This is due to volatility in exchange rates and financial markets due to financial liberalization, which makes physical investment in new factories and equipment less attractive (Stockhammer, 2010).

In response to this change in conditions, corporate strategies have shifted from 'retain and reinvest' (that is, retain profits) to 'downsize and distribute' (Lazonick and O'Sullivan, 2000: 18). The past decade and a half has been witness to a variety of mechanisms by which firms' profits have been funnelled out of the productive sector of the economy to the financial sector. Mergers and acquisitions have absorbed a large chunk of firms' profits. Share buy-backs, whereby firms repurchase shares from existing shareholders to concentrate ownership, have been one use of excess cash that firms decline to employ in expanding output.

In turn, shareholders have funnelled their increased earnings per share to financial markets, resulting in a flood of funds to the financial sector, which in some ways found itself in a situation akin to that of the big banks during the decade of the OPEC oil crisis. It will be recalled that the dramatic increase of oil prices in the mid-1970s left major banks awash with cash, so-called 'petro-dollars', which they then were propelled to lend to developing countries. The banks' tactics in lending petro-dollars led them to be labelled 'loan pushers' by some, reflecting the pressure they applied to sovereign governments to borrow and their willingness to lend to authoritarian leaders whose track record for using loan funds effectively was at best doubtful (Darity, 1988).

In the current period, the financialization of industrialized economies, which led to a surfeit of loanable funds in the hands of financial institutions – a surfeit we might label 'bubble dollars' – enticed banks and other financial institutions to develop exotic loans at teaser rates and other financial instruments to expand lending into the housing sector. Analysts have noted that many of the so-called subprime loans were 'predatory', a term that refers to loans made under unfair, deceptive or fraudulent conditions in the loan origination process, targeted to people of colour and single female heads of households (Dymski, 2009; Montgomerie and Young, 2009).

These were the very same households that were struggling to cope with declining economic conditions of low or falling real wages, higher health-care and education costs, and reductions in employer contributions to pension plans. Motivated by these economic stresses, many vulnerable families sought to refinance their homes as the housing bubble expanded, withdrawing the equity from homes in order to maintain their living standards. Many borrowers in the subprime crisis were not on a consumption binge; they were engaging in a coping mechanism to survive the declining fortunes of many middle- and low-income families in industrialized countries.

The financialization of the economy had other political economy implications beyond the housing bubble and subprime lending that ultimately
endangered the entire system. The growth of the financial sector and
redistribution of national income to the rentier class, the wealth holders,
translated into increased political power for that group. The increased
wealth of this sector funded lobbying efforts to convince government
officials to deregulate this sector and to provide less supervision and
oversight of financial activities. The repeal in 1999 of the Glass–Steagall
Act, legislation intended to create a firewall between everyday banking
activities and financially risky speculative activities in the USA, was only
the culmination of a long period of deregulation that began under the
Reagan administration.

Beyond the USA, financial elites have had influence at the International Monetary Fund (IMF), which has championed the elimination
of capital controls (the movement of finance across borders), thus leading
to increased global instability but also very large profits on speculation
for wealth holders.[5] At the same time, the IMF has pressured developing-
country governments to adopt 'independent' central banks – that is,
central banks liberated from pursuing government development strategies, such as targeting loans to strategic sectors of the economy or
employing asset-based reserve requirements to achieve employment and
investment goals. Instead, the IMF has used conditionalities on borrowing to require central banks in the developing world to pursue inflation
targeting, with the resulting negative employment consequences noted
above. This confluence of events – the financialization of economies and
deregulation – has thus been fuelled by growing inequality and in turn
propels the continued expansion of inequality. As a consequence the
global economy is more volatile. It is at the same time less secure due
to the downsizing of governments, and with it their ability to provide a
social safety net for those who are most vulnerable to economic volatility.

Explanations of the crisis that focus on the emergence of an asset
bubble, in this case a housing bubble, explain only why negative effects
of inequality were delayed. They fail to place sufficient emphasis on the
underlying problem, which is the negative effects of income redistribution
to the wealthy on economic growth and well-being, as well as overall
economic stability. The post-1973 period in industrialized countries can

be considered one of profit-led growth. That is, it has been a period of redistribution to profits that stimulated growth, but a growth that is distorted, only narrowly beneficial, and unsustainable. The 2008 crisis indicates exhaustion of that model.

A framework for transformational macroeconomic policy

This period of crisis in which mainstream economic theory has been called into question provides a critical moment to forge a new direction, both in theory and in policy. Feminist economists and activists, and, more generally, progressives in industrialized and developing countries have an opportunity to contribute to the definition of a transformational macroeconomic policy agenda.

The principles that guide such a framework should be sustainable and equitable growth[6] that promotes the expansion of 'green' jobs and earth-compatible sources of energy. Such an agenda would not only emphasize reductions in inequality and poverty, but also pay particular attention to race and gender inequality. Sustainable equitable growth requires a set of macroeconomic policies that create the conditions for wage-led growth. This can be defined as a set of macroeconomic conditions in which redistribution to workers and, in agricultural economies, to small farmers stimulates demand and, as a result, economic growth.

The liberalization policies of the last three decades have undermined the possibilities for wage-led growth. In part this is because as wages rise, firms can respond by moving across borders or outsourcing. Further, higher wages, especially in labour-intensive industries, are likely to lead to a decline in export demand, and thus employment losses. The downward pressure on wages in the current global macroeconomic environment has also hampered prospects for long-run growth, and thus rising living standards. Why is this so? First, by depressing wages and incomes of middle- and low-income groups, the ability of families to invest in children's well-being is lowered, and as a result children grow up with fewer skills and readiness to be productive citizens.[7]

Second, a firm's ability to rely on cheap labour, when coupled with the absence of labour regulation or other forms of regulation, makes it easier to take what is sometimes called the low road to competitiveness. That is, by shifting the burden of cost reduction to workers' compensation, the environment or governments, in the form of corporate tax reductions, firms are relieved of the obligation to compete on the basis of ingenuity and innovation, further slowing the rate of productivity growth and improvement in living standards.

Seguino (2007) provides empirical evidence of the depressing effect of firm mobility on productivity growth for a group of thirty-seven semi-industrialized economies over the period 1970–2000. This finding is consistent with the view that investment and trade liberalization, by increasing firms' mobility and reducing worker bargaining power and wages, has also made firms lazy, leading to a low-wage, low-productivity trap in a number of developing countries.

To exit the low-wage, low-productivity trap in which many countries find themselves requires policies and methods to discipline the financial sector. A number of progressive economists have advanced proposals for financial-sector reform. Here the focus is more broadly on defining an equity-focused development strategy and the requisite tools governments can avail themselves of to implement such a strategy.[8] Such policies, appropriately applied, can lead firms, both financial and non-financial, to align their profit goals with broad development goals.

Whatever the set of policies adopted, they must not only address the problem of a shortage of jobs, but also must assist developing countries to escape their inferior position in global commodity chains. Macro-level policies that shift the economy to domestic demand-led growth in place of reliance on exports, and thus global commodity chains, can enhance the possibilities for economic stability and wage-led growth. Clearly, many countries rely on exports to generate the foreign exchange to purchase much-needed imports. This is not to suggest, therefore, that an economy should close itself to international trade, but it should not serve as the primary source of employment generation. As a corollary, the promotion of import substitution would be required. Appropriately applied infant industry protections give domestic firms breathing space to catch up with industrialized countries, allowing them to move up the industrial ladder to production of higher value-added goods, which ratifies higher wages. Targeted credit is another tool for developing domestic productive capacity, but with an incentive structure that requires reciprocity from private firms – such as access to credit in return for achievement of performance goals, which could be investment, employment or export targets, for example.

More generally, rather than ends in themselves, export and import policies should form part of the toolkit to implement a country's industrial policy, the central goal of which would be to help domestic producers develop productive capacity and eventually compete in international markets (Memis and Montes, 2008). One of the benefits of this approach is that economies that produce higher value-added goods with a larger share of demand coming from the domestic market do not experience the negative effects of higher wages on employment that economies reliant on labour-intensive exports as a primary source of demand do.

Strategies in agricultural economies would differ from those in developing countries with larger manufacturing sectors. In sub-Saharan African countries for which agriculture is a large share of GDP, governments could use public spending to shift investment to the agricultural sector. Policies that promote greater access for women farmers to inputs and credit are likely to yield increases in productivity, expand output, raise incomes, and reduce reliance on imported food. This reduces pressure to export in order to earn foreign exchange to buy imports, and thus lessens the economic instability that comes with integration in global markets. It would also reduce the need for developing countries to hold such large foreign exchange reserves to protect against volatility in import and export earnings, thereby freeing up funds for public investment in the domestic economy.

For another example of how to rein in global commodity chains and multinationals, take the case of the Caribbean, a region for which tourism is a major source of foreign exchange. Multinational hotel groups, many of which rely on food imports to supply their chains, are a major source of investment in the tourism sector. Food supplies used in all-inclusive hotels, for example, are commonly flown in from the USA to the Caribbean, despite the fact that food could be purchased locally with a direct employment effect. Caribbean countries that agree to negotiate as a block with foreign-owned hotels could impose local content requirements as a condition for foreign direct investment in the region.

China, a country with a good deal more bargaining power than the small Caribbean countries, uses this power to shape foreign direct investment to promote technology transfer and target spending to key areas that meet the employment and technology goals of the Chinese government (Braunstein and Epstein, 2005). WTO restrictions place limitations on country-level collective bargaining, but in this era in which neoliberal policies have failed it becomes clear that it is time to challenge the WTO framework.

Equality-led growth also requires a reformed central bank, geared towards employment creation rather than inflation targeting. Most inflation in developing countries is due to supply-side bottlenecks – poor infrastructure, inadequate policies to smooth agricultural prices, insufficient investment in the agricultural sector, and a population that is poor and in ill health. Those problems, which can raise costs of production and thus contribute to inflation, are best remedied by the judicious use of fiscal, not monetary, policy.

Racial and gender equality must be addressed explicitly. Traditional macroeconomic policy can help to some extent by ensuring full employment. This would benefit women and ethnic minorities, who are frequently shoved to the back of the job queue, putting downward pressure on their wages and reinforcing negative gender and racial stereotypes. Gender and racial equality will be helped by moving the economy up the ladder to the production of higher value-added goods so that those lower on the social hierarchy are not saddled with bad jobs, reinforcing unequal norms and stereotypes.

In the end, there are no one-size-fits-all policies to achieve the goal of intergroup equality since the pathways by which inequality is reproduced differ between countries. Broadly speaking, however, affirmative-action policies to address the problem of job segregation, as well as state-level policies to redistribute the care burden more equitably from women to men and the state, are required.

Finally, attention must be paid to mechanisms that will finance development. A number of scholars underscore the importance of capital controls as a way to stabilize developing economies and, more generally, the global economy. Mechanisms to slow financial capital mobility can be constructed so as to serve as a pollution tax, thus inhibiting destabilizing

2. Igan, Mishra and Tressel (2009), indeed, provide evidence that lobbying lenders also engaged in riskier lending in the run-up to the 2008 crisis.

3. In the USA, household debt as a percentage of GDP almost doubled in just twenty-five years, from 49.8 per cent in 1979 to 94.0 per cent in 2005 (Palley, 2007).

4. There are varying perspectives on this point. Some observers attribute 'financialization' (defined as the increasing importance of financial markets, motives and elites in the operation of the economy) primarily to changes within financial markets. One such change is the increasing share of stocks held by institutional investors (rather than households), whose profit horizons are short rather than long term. According to Crotty (2005), a second fundamental change has been in management's reward structure from one that links CEO pay to the long-term success of non-financial corporations to one based on short-term movements in a firm's stock price. Whether the growth of inequality and its attendant effects on aggregate demand triggered shifts in the financial sector or vice versa is difficult to disentangle. A more likely explanation is that these trends are mutually causative, suggesting that it will not be sufficient merely to focus on rectifying imbalances in the distribution of income.

5. The IMF has recently considered a modification of its stance on capital account liberalization, although with serious constraints. Its plan would be to use loan conditionality to require borrowing countries to employ capital controls only as a last resort, after first trying other tools, such as raising interest rates and cutting government budgets, both of which are deflationary (that is, cause aggregate demand and output to fall).

6. Some might argue that rather than the pursuit of growth, a redistribution of existing income and wealth is sufficient to ensure broadly shared well-being. While this might be the case, the political limits of redistribution without growth are clear. Economic elites are more likely to resist efforts to reduce their absolute level of income and wealth than they are to oppose a growth strategy that leaves them absolutely no worse off, even if relatively worse off (as the incomes and wealth of the poor rise more rapidly). Moreover, economic growth is not of necessity resource-intensive. Growth in services is an example of a type of production that does not contribute so greatly to overuse of natural resources, as, for example, production of material goods might. Economic growth driven by R&D investments to identify new sources of renewable energy is another example.

7. A large body of evidence finds that inequality results in intergenerational poverty. For a particularly expansive discussion of these issues in a cross-country context, see Wilkinson and Pickett, 2009.

8. There are numerous role models that both developed and developing countries can pursue, one of the most salient being that of South Korea from 1965 to 1995 (Amsden, 1989; 2003).

REFERENCES

Amsden, A. (1989) *Asia's Next Giant: South Korea and Late Industrialization,* Oxford University Press, Oxford.

Amsden, A. (2003) *The Rise of 'The Rest': Challenges to the West from Late-Industrializing Economies,* Oxford University Press, Oxford.

Braunstein, E., and G. Epstein (2005) 'Bargaining Power and Foreign Direct Investment in China: Can 1.3 Billion Consumers Tame the Multinationals?', in W. Milberg (ed.), *Labor and the Globalization of Production: Causes and Consequences of Industrial Upgrading,* Palgrave Macmillan, Basingstoke.

Crotty, J. (2005) 'The Neoliberal Paradox: The Impact of Destructive Product Market Competition and "Modern" Financial Markets on Nonfinancial Corporation Performance in the Neoliberal Era', in G. Epstein (ed.), *Financialization and the World Economy,* Edward Elgar, Cheltenham.

Darity, W., Jr. (1988) *The Loan Pushers: The Role of Commercial Banks in the International Debt Crisis*, Ballinger, Cambridge MA.

Dymski, G. (2009) 'Racial Exclusion and the Political Economy of the Subprime Crisis', *Historical Materialism*, vol. 17, no. 2, pp. 149–79.

Eichengreen, B., and M. Bordo (2003) 'Crises Now and Then: What Lessons for the Last Era of Financial Globalization?', in P. Mizen (ed.), *Monetary History, Exchange Rates and Financial Markets: Essays in Honour of Charles Goodhart*, vol. 2, Edward Elgar, Cheltenham.

Galbraith, J.K. (2011) 'Inequality and Economic and Political Change: A Comparative Perspective', *Cambridge Journal of Regions, Economy, and Society*, vol. 4, no. 1, pp. 13–27.

Goldberg, P. K., and N. Pavcnik (2007) 'Distributional Effects of Globalization in Developing Countries', *Journal of Economic Literature* XLV, pp. 39–82.

Igan, D., P. Mishra and T. Tressel (2009) 'A Fistful of Dollars: Lobbying and the Financial Crisis', IMF Working Paper 09/287, IMF, Washington DC.

International Labour Organization (2008) *World of Work*, ILO, Geneva.

Lazonick, W., and M. O'Sullivan (2000) 'Maximizing Shareholder Value: A New Ideology for Corporate Governance', *Economy and Society*, vol. 29, no. 1, pp. 13–35.

Memis, E., and M. Montes (2008) *Who's Afraid of Industrial Policy?*, Discussion Paper, UNDP Regional Centre in Colombo, Asia–Pacific Trade and Investment Initiative.

Milanovic, B. (2009) 'Global Inequality and the Global Inequality Extraction Ratio: The Story of the Past Two Centuries', Policy Research Working Paper 5044, World Bank, Washington DC.

Milberg, W., and D. Winkler (2007) Financialization and the Dynamics of Offshoring in the USA', *Cambridge Journal of Economics* 34, pp. 275–93.

Montgomerie, J., and B. Young (2009) 'No Place Like Home? Gender Dimensions of Indebtedness and Homeownership', working paper, Centre for Research on Socio-Cultural Change (CRESC), University of Manchester, and Institute for Political Science, University of Münster.

Ortiz, I. (2008) 'Social Policy: The Way Forward', presentation at International Council on Social Welfare Conference, Tours, France, 30 June–5 July.

Palley, T. (2007) 'Financialization: What It Is and Why It Matters', Working Paper No. 525, Levy Economics Institute of Bard College, Annandale-on-Hudson NY.

Rathin, R., A. Heuty and E. Letouzé (2009) 'Fiscal Space for Public Investment: Towards a Human Development Approach', in R. Rathin A. Heuty (eds), *Fiscal Space: Policy Options for Financing Human Development*, Earthscan, London and Sterling VA.

Seguino, S. (2007) 'Is More Mobility Good? Firm Mobility and the Low-wage, Low-productivity Trap', *Structural Change and Economic Dynamics*, vol. 18, no. 1: 27–51.

Stockhammer, E. (2010) 'Neoliberalism, Income Distribution, and the Causes of the Crisis', Research on Money and Finance Discussion Paper No. 19, www.researchonmoneyandfinance.org/images/discussion_papers/RMF-19-Stockhammer.pdf.

UNDP (United Nations Development Programme) (2005) *Human Development Report*, New York.

UNDP (United Nations Development Program) (2008) *Human Development Report*, New York.

Wilkinson, R., and K. Pickett. (2009) *The Spirit Level: Why Greater Equality Makes Societies Stronger*, Bloomsbury, London.

BOX II.2 **Women's status and free trade in the Pacific**
LICE COKANASIGA

There are fourteen independent Pacific Island countries that include some of
the world's smallest microstates. The smallest is Niue with a population of
2,000 and the largest is Papua New Guinea with 6.3 million. Despite their small
sizes, or perhaps because of it, in 2001 these nations negotiated a free-trade
agreement known as the Pacific Island Countries Trade Agreement (PICTA).
We know that trade is important for the Pacific. But what kind of trade policies
should these countries put in place?

PACIFIC WOMEN AND FREE TRADE

As elsewhere, trade and economics are male-dominated areas. Naemeeh
Khan, an activist working with the Fiji Women Rights Movement, pointed out
in a consultation organized by DAWN and PANG: 'Within the governments,
the Ministries for Women, Welfare, Health, Education and those who provide
social services are not included in the formulation of (trade) policy.' Women
also have extremely low representation in national legislations with a mere 6.4
per cent of legislative seats (Houng Lee 2010). Jane Kelsey of the University
of Auckland issued this challenge during the consultations: 'We have to start
asserting that trade is not just men's stuff. It is treated conceptually as something that men do because women perceive the world differently. Are there
ways that we can think about trade from a feminist perspective that bridge the
economic and the social and also hope to bridge the local to the regional to
the global?'

Pacific women are subject to market asymmetries that work against them.
Anecdotal evidence suggests that even when women meet the eligibility criteria for borrowing, are perceived as too great a credit risk (Hutchens and
Bishop, 2008). As a result, they undergo inexplicably long delays in their loan
application process or are asked to identify male guarantors. In Fiji, between
4,500 and 5,000 women are currently employed in the textile industry. Their
income is estimated to positively benefit as many as 25,000 people (Rowland,
2009).

Land is sacred for the indigenous population in the Pacific, but how pre-
cious it is to women is often overlooked. There has been too much emphasis
on promoting commercial agriculture, resulting in the marginalization of
women not only from economic benefits but from their traditional roots, status
and authority. Women in the matrilineal societies of the Solomon Islands, for
example, were relegated to the role of mere advisers to men, who now control
decision-making over customary land management systems. Making matters

worse are foreign investors who prefer to deal with male chiefs when negotiating for corporate rights over land and forests.

RESISTING MORE FREE TRADE

Seeing that they were not part of this agreement and anxious about the commencement of free-trade talks between PICTA countries and the European Union in 2004, Australia and New Zealand negotiated PACER or Pacific Agreement on Closer Economic Relations (Kelsey, 2004). Today there are calls to negotiate a PACER Plus agreement. The Coordinator of the Pacific Network on Globalization, Maureen Penjueli, questions whether PACER Plus is 'all about the political priorities for Australia and has nothing to do with the Pacific...' The proposed reduction of tariffs through PACER Plus and the influx of cheaper Australian and New Zealand products will likely result in factory closures and significant job losses, most of which will be jobs currently held by women.

Pacific governments are urged to say 'no to PACER Plus' and to find alternatives to free trade in the Pacific. Before negotiating yet another trade agreement, countries need to assess the social and gender dimensions of trade policies through country case studies and by training policymakers and trade negotiators. Governments need to involve the NGO/CSOs, especially women's organizations, to provide a systematic gender analysis on the balance of costs and gains, and how governments may be able to address trade-related issues in ways that also promote gender, economic and ecological justice.

REFERENCES

AusAID (2008) 'Violence against Women in Melanesia and East Timor – Building on Global and Regional Promising Approaches', Canberra: AusAID, http://aid.dfat.gov.au/Publications/Documents/vaw_cs_full_report.pdf.

Houng Lee, G. (2010). 'Women's Legal and Human Rights', paper presented at the Secretariat of the Pacific Community 11th Triennial Conference of Pacific Women, Noumea, New Caledonia.

Hutchens, A., and S. Bishop (2008) 'Women in Business in Solomon Islands: Key Findings from April 2008 Scoping Mission', http://unpan1.un.org/intradoc/groups/public/documents/apcity/unpan038189.pdf.

Kelsey, J. (2004) 'A People's Guide to PACER: The Implications for the Pacific Islands of the Pacific Agreement on Closer Economic Relations (PACER)', Final Report Commissioned by the Pacific Network on Globalization, Suva.

Rowland, C. (2009) 'Pacific Trade: Trading Away Women's Rights?', Pacific Trade Fact Sheet No. 4, July 2009, Australian Civil Society Network on Pacific Trade.

Scollay, R. (2010) 'South–South and North–South Trade Agreements: The Pacific Islands Case', UNU–CRIS Working Papers W-2010/7, Bruges: United Nations University Institute – Comparative Regional Integration Studies.

CHAPTER 2

New poles of accumulation and realignment of power in the twenty-first century

YAO GRAHAM AND HIBIST WENDEMU KASSA

This essay focuses on selected countries in the economic South to illustrate the global and regional realignment of power. The countries are Brazil, China, India and South Africa. It is conceded that they do not make up the totality of the new poles of power. Russia, for example, is left out since it does not constitute a new pole of accumulation, despite the fact that it is important politically and economically due to its military power and its mono-cultural economy centred on energy exports to Europe.

The analysis charts the shifts towards new poles of accumulation from the North Atlantic through an exploration of trade and investment flows, regional power, aid politics and reform of multilateral institutions. There will also be an investigation of the issues of cooperation and contradiction within the South, particularly among these new poles. Africa will be examined closely to illustrate how these patterns are manifested. The central question is whether South–South cooperation will deepen in the coming years. More generally, there is also an examination of the direction of the evolving multipolar world. This is followed by an investigation of global power shifts and continuities in the economic model. In addition, the challenges posed for activism are examined.

The premiss is that the new powers in the global system represent new poles of accumulation. The accumulation model has been centred on the opportunities offered in the markets of the economic North with the rest of the globe as a secondary target. The accumulation model has also driven the shift of production, as well as the migration of technologies and jobs to these countries. Generally, the economic strength of these new poles of accumulation is that they are suppliers to the markets of the economic North.

The shift in economic power

The 2003 World Trade Organization (WTO) summit in Cancún was dominated by the quadrilateral group of trade ministers (also known as the Quad), which consisted of Japan, the United States (USA), the European Union (EU) and Canada. These countries were the dominant veto holders in the WTO. After Cancún, the Quad collapsed, and was replaced by the five interested parties (FIPs), which are the USA, the EU, Australia, India and Brazil. This reconfiguration represents an indication of the direction of the shifts in power.

A common attribute of these powers is their ability to produce industrial and agricultural products competitively for the global market while also competing among themselves for markets for their goods and investments, as well as markets and destinations for investments. There is no basic dispute among these powers and the old powers about the global economic system. However, there is a contestation about aspects of it. Crucially, this centres on how much leverage these new powers have and how governance of the model is set up.[1] The focus has, therefore, been on the domination of key international institutions at the UN, the Bretton Woods Institutions (BWIs) and the World Trade Organization by the North Atlantic powers.

According to the International Monetary Fund (IMF), the gross domestic product (GDP) at purchasing power parity in 2005 of countries in the economic South exceeded that of the economic North (IMF, 2011). Another study, which projects into the year 2020, predicts that China will become the largest economy in the world. This is expected to occur even though the USA, which is the highest consumer of Chinese exports, would gradually stagnate. India's per capita income is also expected to grow by 4 per cent annually (Cripps and McKinley, 2008). This provides a snapshot of the shifts in power. It also draws attention to existing consumption patterns, which highlight the ecological challenges of the economic model.

Regionally the shift in economic power is most starkly exemplified by changes in East Asia. Japan has been displaced by China as the regional economic power even though the former remains the region's technological leader, with China as the main workshop. China's leading role has involved a reconfiguration of economic relations into a hub with spoke linkages centred on China, with countries in the region acting as suppliers of various types of inputs to Chinese industry. As a result, China has become the workshop of the world. It is also the main financier of the deficits of the USA, as well as its biggest creditor (Hung, 2009: 16–17).

The wave of decolonization after the Second World War intensified calls and pressure for reform of the international system triggered by the Bolshevik Revolution of 1917. Since the Bandung conference of 1952 this demand has been mainly voiced by the non-aligned movement (NAM), which in diplomacy operates as the G77 + China. Although the NAM perceived the need for reform as a logical step in the rise of the then newly politically independent states, there was not enough economic muscle to support it. The striking aspect of more recent calls for reform by the new powers is that it is backed by the increased economic and political muscle of members of the NAM. The evolutions that we see now represent some movement forward from the days of the G77's call for a New International Economic Order (NIEO) in the 1960s and 1970s and the work of the South Commission in the 1980s. Even though current calls for reforms are backed by greater political and economic muscle, there are drawbacks. Whilst the demands for reform are piecemeal, the leading powers of the South have national agendas which compete against each other and also at times run counter to common South positions.

The reconstitution of the G8 into the G20, in the midst of the current economic crisis, is also a good illustration of some of the shifts that have already taken place. The G8 has always invited some powers from the economic South to participate in the forum. The creation of the G20 is the first institutional recognition of these new powers by the old ones. Despite this advance, there are still questions about what the G20 represents in terms of its democratic character, the power it is arrogating to itself and the kind of decisions it is taking. Alongside these concerns, there are outstanding issues like UN reform and the aspiration for Security Council membership by India, Brazil and South Africa (Funabashi, 2009: 8–9) and for reform of the BWIs, which are important issues for the new powers.[2]

Challenges and opportunities for South–South cooperation

As these shifts are taking place, elements of collaboration also persist. In these patterns it is possible to identify areas of both formal and informal cooperation, as well as some obvious contradictions. For instance the India, Brazil and South Africa forum (IBSA) is a particular formal expression of the new cooperation. At one level, this is described as an example of a new regionalism which is not geographically centred in contiguous countries, but is actually spread around the globe. The striking feature of this pattern is that it is an axis of countries of the South (Puri, 2007b: 2).

The G77, an aggregate of countries in the economic South, has been faced with growing divergence in power and interests among its members as the actual economic and political statuses of the countries within it have begun to escape the boundaries represented by that aggregation. Thus, even as it has remained important in some fora, its workings exemplify some of the contradictions within the South. Despite these challenges the G77 remains an important aggregating forum within which the countries of the economic South work together. In spite of the fact of intensifying tensions in the G77 the old G20 is still relevant in the WTO, but it is arguable that the creation of the FIPs has begun to stretch the existing contradictions. For instance, Brazil has been more interested in market opening than India. Notwithstanding this point of conflict, these countries are still able to find some accommodation. At the same time, the contradiction between the big Southern powers and the weaker countries is becoming somewhat sharper in the WTO.

The new G20 has been described as an attempt to accommodate the weight of the emerging powers within the existing architecture of global power without effecting a fundamental reform. The G20, therefore, represents a compromise which seeks to ensure that the growing power of these countries is absorbed into existing structures and symbolizes the acceptance of the evolving shifts in power. This process has been a source of some of the growing tensions and contradictions among the countries of the South. The compromises faced by these new powers seeking accommodation in the existing leading structures of global power have entailed the relegation of issues of common interest to the wider community of countries of the South, especially those of more importance for weaker countries than for the newly powerful. The new G20 differs from the original G20 in that it is grouped around the core of the G8. Moreover, it is dominated by NATO powers with a few developing countries. The operation of the G20, in important ways, is another challenge to the increasingly weak multilateralism centred on the UN.[3]

Countries of the South all want reform of the Bretton Woods Institutions but are not uniform in their areas of focus and emphasis. While the more powerful countries of the South are interested in voting reform, the smaller countries prioritize the removal of conditionalities, which remain some of their most important concerns. The growing power of both China and India are reflected in their emerging cooperation with the BWIs. India and the World Bank are discussing how India's experience of running the world's biggest railway network and passenger traffic could be usefully applied in other developing countries through the Indian Railway Company (IRC) acting as a lead in the privatization of railways in developing countries, particularly in Africa (Lamont, 2009). This will widen the investment opportunities for the IRC across Africa. China and the World Bank are also exploring how to relocate some light Chinese industry in developing countries, particularly Africa.[4] According to Deborah Brautigam (2010) 'China will push some of its labour- and energy-intensive industries to move to special economic zones in Africa because Chinese planners want industrialists at home to move up the value chain. Polluting industries such as leather tanneries and metal smelters are no longer tolerated in many Chinese cities.' This is a trend that is likely to increase as these emerging powers have greater influence over the use of the resources of the BWIs and as their contributions to the resources of the World Bank and the IMF increase.

The new powers in the south are all aggressively signing free-trade agreements (FTAs) and bilateral investment agreements around the world as they search for advantage against each other in the area of investments in addition to markets. Critically, they are competing for raw materials (Corkin, 2008: 129). The new scramble for Africa illustrates the cooperation and contradiction within the South (Habib, 2008: 24–7). The African region provides an illustrative case of what is happening within the coalition of the South. This is a region with 1 billion people, which, even though thirty-two countries are categorized as least developed (LDCs), still represents significant purchasing power, and which could become an even more important market as incomes and purchasing power increase.

The region also has significant amounts of raw materials, minerals, oil and gas, as well as forest products, to be exploited. In addition, the continent has a workforce which could be useful as a source of cheap labour as companies seek to relocate. Currently Africa as a continent has at least eight trade, investment and aid frameworks with other countries and regions. All these powers are seeking to have a framework which gives them some preferential access.[5]

India and China have more recently offered preferential trade access to their markets for certain commodities from African countries. This is competing in some ways with the Africa–EU EPAs and the USA's Africa Growth and Opportunity Act (AGOA) frameworks. China–Africa trade in 2010 exceeded $120 billion, up from over $91 billion in 2009, and China has removed duties on 60 per cent of imports from twenty-six sub-Saharan African LDCs. There are also links through investment flows. In spite of the great significance attached to Chinese investment in Africa, it is still some way behind Western flows. According to Broadman (2007: 93, 97), a 90 per cent share of FDI stock to Africa is from the North Atlantic countries. In 2004, Chinese investment in Africa represented only 2 per cent out of $45 billion of its total FDI stock, although it is growing fast. According to *The Economist* (11 April 2011), between 2005 and 2010 14 per cent of Chinese outward FDI went to sub-Saharan Africa. From 1995 to 2004, $2.6 billion of India's FDI flows, representing 16 per cent of the country's total, went to Africa.

China and India have also increasingly played the role of donor (Mc-Cormick, 2008). The challenge that African countries face is to make sure that China or any other country does not replicate the colonial experience. So far, the standard of exploitation has been set at a very low level by the West, which has been critically supported by the aid regime and also by the conditionalities supervised by the BWIs.[6]

In relation to Chinese expansion of investment, the perception of threat is mostly not expressed by Africans, but rather emanates from the West (Breslin and Taylor, 2008: 59). This alarm exists because, as the Chinese intensify their autonomous capacity to find destinations for investments, markets and inputs it improves their competitive advantage vis-à-vis the West (Breslin and Taylor, 2008: 63–5). The USA, for example, projects that 25 per cent of its oil imports will come from the Gulf of

Guinea by 2015.[7] Meanwhile, China imports 25 per cent of its crude oil from Africa (Broadman, 2007: 82–3).[8]

Natural resources represent the biggest area of competition in Africa among all major powers, old and new. FDI is significantly concentrated in countries with significant natural resource exports (UNCTAD, 2007: 12). This is the area where China, India, Brazil and South Africa are also active (Corkin, 2008: 129). For instance, China, as the world's leading workshop and a rapidly urbanizing and modernizing country, was largely responsible for the commodity boom between 2002 and 2008. This was because it was gobbling up large amounts of resources (Kaplinsky, 2008: 10). The discussion about interest in the natural resources in Africa has tended to centre greatly on China.

All of these trends pose challenges to African countries. What are the terms on which these firms are being allowed access to raw materials? Would it be on the same old colonial terms, or on different terms? The mining sector liberalization overseen across Africa by the World Bank and the IMF in the 1990s, which resulted in Western companies acquiring mineral assets at giveaway prices and on generous fiscal terms, are now widely seen by African governments and CSOs alike as inimical to the continent's development interests (Africa Mining Vision, 2009). The positive aspect of the entry of these new powers is that there are now options available, as opposed to the monolithic culture which was represented by Western transnational companies (TNCs). In the current conditions of the increase in options from the emerging powers, African governments are in a better position to negotiate. This competition not only offers options but potentially improves the policy space that African countries have, although it does not guarantee that new deals will be more beneficial than the old. It is a crack in the edifice into which feminists could insert efforts in the remaking of social contracts.

A common criticism of these new powers emanating from the West, governments, CSOs and media alike is that they have low standards of respect for human rights and the environment. There is evidence from a number of countries of Chinese firms treating workers poorly and being reckless on environmental issues (Lee, 2009). The Brazilian mining giant Vale has been accused by the international trade group ICEM of being hostile to unionization in its operations in a number of countries. Western expressions of concern about violations of human rights and environmental standards by Chinese firms operating in Africa are hypocritical since the long dominance of Western firms in Africa's economies significantly helped set low standards in the continent's extractive sectors (Breslin and Taylor, 2008: 68; Mohan and Power, 2008: 38). The record and legacy of Shell in the Niger Delta is only the most egregious of these violations. Western firms in Africa's extractive sector have long relied on support from host governments to suppress protests by affected communities and from their home governments for public relations and diplomatic support.

The policy environment within which new entrants are operating and benefiting was created by the liberalization of trade and investment regime, driven by BWIs. These institutions have created an extremely liberal climate that is open to all. It is unlikely that the expansion and benefit for firms from China, India and other countries of the South was a primary driver. This can explain to some extent why the arrival of the Chinese would trigger consternation regarding the liberalized regime, which Western companies have dominated. There is, therefore, a convergence of factors which demand that at this juncture the liberalized regime should be addressed. These centre on issues relating to the labour regime, environment, human rights and the complicity of companies and foreign governments with incumbent repressive regimes.[9]

In the case of Chinese firms, due to the fact that the labour regime in China is oppressive, there is a need for stronger pressures from unions within Africa. There is evidence that poor labour standards are maintained in most Chinese companies in Africa. It is also known that there are examples of countries where governments and unions have insisted on the observance of higher labour standards by Chinese investors. We cannot presume that the Chinese will impose lower labour standards in all cases (Baah and Jauch, 2009: 35–76).[10] But since unions tend to be weak in many African countries, the danger of this labour regime becoming the norm in the new powers is quite real. This means that insecure work, low wages and poor safety conditions are increasingly important issues. In the meantime Brazilian firms have attracted attention on account of the dispossession of large numbers of rural people from the substantial tracts of land they are acquiring across Africa for agricultural, especially biofuel, projects.

Compared to the Chinese, India has been particularly interested in industrial investments. This is probably due to the history of Indian manufacturing investment across Africa. As a consequence, not only do Indian companies have experience in that area, but this is backed by an interest in expansion. The Export–Import Bank of India and the Confederation of Indian Industry (CII) in 2005 organized a conclave on India–Africa trade and investment partnership to explore projects worth $5 billion. The following year another meeting covered projects worth $17 billion (Naidu, 2008: 120–24).

One potentially negative aspect is the impact of Indian and Chinese manufacturing exports on African firms producing for home markets and export, thereby undermining the development of indigenous manufacturing. Indeed imports from China are negatively affecting manufacturers of furniture, footwear, textiles and garments in a number of African countries. Furthermore, there are markets where African exports are in competition with exports from the new poles, especially China. In the US market African textile and garment exports grew under the preferential terms of AGOA. The ending of the Multi-Fibre Agreement in 2005 and quota-free access for all, including Chinese exports, has had a negative impact on African exports. Before this, textile manufacturing sectors grew rapidly in countries like Kenya, Lesotho and Swaziland. The end of the MFA and resultant competition in the US market resulted in the devastation of South African AGOA exports and reductions in Madagascar, Kenya, Lesotho and Swaziland (Kaplinsky, 2008). This means that the relationship should not simply be examined in terms of what is happening when the capital or investment from the new powers enters Africa, but also include the forms of competition that may be taking place in the global arena. This would provide a fuller picture of the consequences for African development.

The interest in minerals raises the spectre of the perpetuation of a dependence on raw material exports. A recent discussion in the African continent has focused on the commodity price hike from 2002 to 2008.[11] The concern is that as commodity prices went up, the gains to African countries were fairly minimal (Habiyaremye and Soete, 2010: 1–3). This was because the processing of resources was limited. The challenge of value addition has gained prominence as part of an attempt to reverse the years of deindustrialization. This process will depend on the terms for capital inflows which contribute to breaking the pattern of export of raw minerals and agricultural produce. This strategy will challenge all the countries that see Africa as a source of raw materials and have planned on that continuing to be the basis of the profitability of their processing and fabricating industries. Chinese strategy in Africa includes making massive investments in special economic zones (Davies, 2008: 136–7). African countries could negotiate terms for these zones that support processing, although it seems that so far the Chinese have been dominant in determining the conditions shaping their investments.

Developments in the climate change negotiations, starting with the Copenhagen conference, represent another expression of some of the contradictions within the South. As the new poles' economic scale and structure diverge from those of the majority of developing countries the impact of climate change and the issue of differentiated responsibility will contribute to an increase in tension. The attempts of the USA and the EU to change the terms of the Kyoto Protocol and de-emphasise differentiated responsibility runs against the interests of African countries but were supported by the Ethiopian prime minister Meles Zenawi at the 2009 Copenhagen Climate Change Conference. This exposes the fissures within the economic South (African Agenda, 2010: 4). This is a fault line that the Western countries will seek to exploit by offering aid to poorer, especially African, countries so as to cause splits in the G77, which will be to their advantage. Differences on the climate-change front could become a source of increasing weakening for the G77 in the years ahead.

In the area of South–South aid and development cooperation some evolution in aid mechanisms in the medium term can be anticipated. The attempts by the Organization for Economic Cooperation and Development (OECD) to bring China, Brazil and India into the Paris Declaration aid architecture is unlikely to work in the short run because the new poles stand to gain little from subordinating their aid policies and regimes to a framework dominated by the North Atlantic powers, which feel threatened by the increasing access and influence that China, Brazil and India are gaining in Africa with their particular uses of bilateral aid. However, as the aid from the South increases (McCormick, 2008), there will be pressure from recipient countries for better conditionality regimes. Recipient countries are likely to respond in the aftermath of a first flush of excitement in getting alternative sources of capital investment by paying more attention to the conditions under which the capital inflows come in. However, increases in investment flows are likely (Puri, 2007: 1–2). All of these developments would increase the pressure in Africa for frameworks of open regionalism; as the new powers offer preferential market access, they will also seek market and investment access agreements with other countries of the economic South.[12]

The development models in the new poles are the subject of increasing attention (Davies, 2008: 134–7). The role of the state in Asian economic transformation and the revival of state interventionism in the global North in the wake of the 2008 global crisis have brought the role of the state in the economy firmly back to the centre of development debates in Africa (ECA, 2011: 95–111). An aspect of this debate is focused on what kind of state is needed that can play a developmental role. Is it the authoritarian state which was very much at the centre of the Asian development model? The lessons from that experience show that a democratically accountable state is needed. Historically, this raises some important issues regarding the necessary type and scale of innovation facing African countries. Despite claims of revisionism in the West, state authoritarianism, at home in many cases as well as in colonies in other cases, was a key facilitator of capital accumulation and economic transitions. Even as the UK was opening up internally with the introduction of democracy in the nineteenth century, it was oppressing its colonies; and the authoritarian Jim Crow regime for blacks persisted in the USA from the end of the Civil War into the mid-twentieth century.

Challenges for activism

The challenges posed for activism by all of these factors are to be confronted in different countries as well as at the global level by the different social movements. The UN processes which have led to a number of important decisions about gender equality are to be noted. These advancements were achieved in the face of substantial opposition from all kinds of powers; progress was achieved as a result of activism. The work in and around environmental issues and the agenda for reform of global economic governance have been ensured by the substantial inputs made by the social movements.

Considering that there is an important connection between global power and the domestic political economy, it is vital to explore the link between the domestic situation of these new powers and the kind of challenges that activists will face. Each of the new powers offers us different scenarios. For instance, the Chinese export model has been strongly driven by an urban bias in relation to the countryside. This has led to the building of striking economic and social inequalities within the Chinese development model. All of these trends have been overseen and governed by an authoritarian state and politics, manifested also in the functioning of the labour regime (Hung, 2009: 13–14, 18; Breslin and Taylor, 2008: 66).[13]

Post-apartheid South Africa, on the other hand, has faced some con-testations over its position as a regional hegemon in Africa. Internally, South Africa has witnessed intense debate between elements that see expansion into Africa as a primary strategy and those that place emphasis on relations with the economic North and other powers of the economic South. This is still being played out in the constraints on South Africa's operations (UNCTAD, 2005: 16–17). Regionally, there has not been a complete acceptance of South African power because its firms are seen as taking advantage of their access to the continent without giving enough back.[14] In addition, South Africa has faced frustrations in the negotiations of the EPAs in the Southern African Development Community (SADC), es-pecially since Africa is seen as the turf of the old powers. The preservation of the essential elements for regional integration has been undermined by the pressure of the EU. The consequence has been the fragmentation of the SADC into different negotiating blocs.[15] Domestically, South Africa faces immense challenges as a result of the inequalities left by apartheid, which have not been resolved by the neoliberal economic agenda.

Although Brazil is a regional power its regional ambitions have had to contend with the USA as a powerful neighbour that has long seen all the Americas as its domain. In consequence, Brazil has constantly sought to find a balance between accommodation and asserting its independence in its dealings with the USA. In the region itself, there are pretenders seeking to challenge Brazil. Even though Venezuela and its allies do not pose a serious threat to Brazil, they still represent, at the very least, some irritation to the political left of Brazil in terms of regional power play. Brazil also faces domestic challenges. Despite advances made in the years of PT rule, Brazil is one of the most unequal societies in the world in terms of social class and race, with large numbers of urban poor and unemployed. Despite the fact that the country has an open political system with a left-leaning governing party, its police force has nevertheless had to engage in urban warfare in an effort to purge the cities of drug traffickers and other powerful crime groups (Morris, 2010).

All these configurations have a bearing on the likely evolution of the politics of these new poles. This puts emphasis on the capacity of internal social forces to exert an influence over them, as well as on the openings for collaborative relations between these internal social forces and those outside in any kind of global movement. The evolution of the emerging powers and their role in the global arena must be incorporated into the strategies developed by activists.

It is also important to consider how reform of the multilateral system would be shaped by a weakening of Western hegemony. It is likely that these old powers would accept some recentring, so long as it involved a greater role for them. This means that activists would have to persist in the struggle for a new and more democratic multilateralism centred on the UN.

The current trends of inequality in almost all of these economies mean that the agenda for working for a new economic model, with an emphasis on public spending, social investment and work security, remains important. This is because ultimately all the new powers have made their transition within the period of the dominance of neoliberal global economics, which has taken advantage of the domestic consequences of neoliberal policies. Moreover, the definition of corporate power that activists target will increasingly have to include corporate power from the South (Puri, 2007a: 1–2; Naidu, 2008: 122, 124).[16]

Conclusion

The predictions of global economic trends used in this essay are based on the assumption that the economic growth model will remain unchanged.

This raises the question of the climate agenda. If all the old and new powers grow between now and 2020 within this model, this process will be unsustainable. The recentring of power very much implicates the question of the burden of climate change and highlights how the governments involved perceive the link between the economic model and their power.

China is projected to be a leading global power by 2020. As a result there is particular interest in the direction of its evolution. Hung Ho Fung (2009: 17–16) describes China as the head servant of all the East Asian countries who are servicing Northern consumption. He questions whether China can be reconstituted economically and politically on the basis of changes in domestic consumption and to the growth model. This would ensure that the shifts between North and South actually decentre the world in a new way that creates fresh opportunities. However, this is obviously an issue that is burdened with some of the contradictions that make China the most striking exemplar of the problem posed by these new poles of accumulation.

NOTES

1. Funabashi (2009) explains that the economic crisis which accelerated the shift of economic power to the east did not require a change in the existing structures, '...but rather a reenvisioned process, with' a trilateral model with the U.S. – China – Japan. This model would ensure stability in the new world order (Funabashi, 2009).

2. The emergence of the original G20 in the WTO, with some of these new powers, was reinforced by groupings like the African group, the G33, the African Caribbean and Pacific (ACP) countries. This combination tilted the balance of power in the WTO at the 2003 Cancún Ministerial, resulting in the abortive end to the meeting. Before that it seemed the WTO was an unstoppable juggernaut.

3. For instance, almost all the G20 countries were not particularly keen for the UN to be at the centre of discussions on the economic crisis. However, many developing countries would have preferred a greater role for the UN in these discussions.

4. As China seeks to upgrade its technological capacity, it needs to offload some of the low-technology areas where Chinese capital will remain interested. For this to be possible, Chinese capital would need to relocate into new territories where cheap labour may be found.

5. These include the USA's AGOA, the EU–Africa frameworks, the Forum on China–Africa Cooperation (FOCAC), Africa–Brazil, Africa–Turkey, Africa–India and Africa–Russia frameworks. Although the relationships are actualized bilaterally, there is a tendency to sign the agreements at the multilateral level with the region as a whole vis-à-vis the other powers. The EU is seeking to transform the relation into free-trade agreements with African countries and regions.

6. Additionally, trade agreements such as EPAs and the AGOA and bilateral investment treaties play an important role in cementing this privileged access. African countries have to make sure that higher standards are set. In addition to this, the concerns about migration (which is not yet strong in South–South cooperation) combined with questions around environmental pollution, touch on how the development model affects the global commons. For instance, in South Africa the presence of a large

migrant population has unleashed xenophobic responses in recent years (Smith, 2008; Modi, 2003).

7. The creation of the Africa Command (AFRICOM) by the USA is very much connected with trying to position itself in relation to this scramble for resources (Bah and Aning, 2008: 118).

8. From 2000 to 2005, crude oil imports from African countries increased from $3.5 billion to $13.2 billion (Broadman, 2007: 82–3).

9. The US government and companies provide many examples of complicity with repressive regimes which are reliable suppliers of crude oil. The French also have similar relations with repressive regimes in Africa. This presents a challenge to ensure that there is not a replication of this pattern of politics by the new entrants.

10. In a report on construction firms in Ghana, the Ghana Trade Union Congress identified cases where Chinese firms had contravened labour laws by insisting on the classification of workers as casual workers, even after six months of continuous employment. This enabled the firms to deprive these workers of their rights as permanent workers. Poorer working conditions in these Chinese firms were attributed to the absence of unions. In another Chinese firm conditions of work were found to be almost equal to those in European firms.

11. For instance, from 2000 to 2007, Chinese share of global aluminum consumption increased from 13.0 per cent to 32.5 per cent. Other metals such as copper and iron ore (seaborne imports) increased from 11.8 per cent to 26.2 per cent and 15.6 per cent to 48.2 per cent respectively (Macquarie Commodities Research, 2008).

12. This has to be understood primarily within the sphere of the competition among themselves, and between the countries of the North and themselves for market access and investment destinations. It is, therefore, expected that FTAs, both within the circles of the new powers and with the North, will seek to carve out preferential arrangements with some of the weaker countries. This will be sweetened by aid packages.

13. This is despite the fact that the labour regime is increasingly coming under challenge from independent trade unions. This authoritarianism has been marked by of all kinds of discriminatory tendencies, including the collapse of the social security system in China, which has placed a lot of pressure on women working in the care economy. This has been pointed to as one of the reasons why an economic crisis in China would have some particularly grave aspects. The fact that India, which in comparison to China has a relatively more open political system, also faces an armed insurgency reflects some of its problems.

14. In recent years South African mining capital has expanded significantly across the continent. It uses its 'Africanness' as an opportunity for taking affirmative action on behalf of its companies' push to access the services sector across the continent.

15. The Southern African Customs Union (SACU), which is the older customs union of Botswana, Lesotho, Swaziland linked to South Africa, has also effectively been undercut by the EPA negotiations.

16. In these countries, 6 million workers were employed by TNCs from the economic South in 2005 (Puri, 2007: 1–2). CVRD in Brazil, for example, is the second biggest mining corporation in the world; its logic would be no different from that of any mining company looking for access to mineral resources. The Indian company Arcelor Mittal is one of the most aggressive TNCs in the world. It has a $900 million management contract in Nigeria and Liberia in iron ore reserves (Naidu, 2008: 122, 124). Recently, it had to renegotiate a deal in Liberia amidst a lot of criticism. This means that, essentially, the nature of capital remains the same. There is some minor fine-tuning, but its essential logic will not be affected by nationality. In the mining sector, the issues of human rights, livelihoods, benefits and the environment will remain.

REFERENCES

Africa Mining Vision (2009), *Africa Mining Vision: February 2009*, http://africaminingvision. org/amv_resources/AMV/Africa_Mining_Vision_English.pdf.

African Agenda (2010) 'Editorial: Cancún Climate Talks Saved, but Climate not Saved', vol. 13, no. 6.

Baah, A.Y., and H. Jauch (2009) *Chinese Investments in Africa: A Labour Perspective*, Africa Labour Research Network, Accra.

Bah, A.S., and K. Aning (2008) 'US Peace Operations Policy in Africa: From ACRI to AFRICOM', *International Peacekeeping*, vol. 15, no. 1, pp. 118–32.

Brautigam, Deborah (2010) 'Africa's Eastern Promise', *Foreign Affairs*, 5 January.

Breslin, S., and I. Taylor (2008) 'Explaining the Rise of Human Rights in Analyses of Sino-African Relations', *Review of African Political Economy*, vol. 35, no. 115, March.

Broadman, H.G., (2007) *Africa's Silk Road: China and India's New Economic Frontier*, World Bank, Washington DC.

Corkin, L., (2008) 'Competition or Collaboration? Chinese South African Transnational Companies in Africa', *Review of African Political Economy*, vol. 35, no. 115, March.

Cripps, F., and T. McKinley (2008) 'A Global Realignment by 2020: U.S. Decline, Emerging Economies Rise', *Development Viewpoint* 10, August, Centre for Development Policy and Research School of Oriental and African Studies, University of London.

Davies, M. (2008) 'China's Developmental Model Comes to Africa', *Review of African Political Economy* 35: 115, 134–7.

ECA (Economic Commission for Africa) (2011) *Economic Report on Africa 2011: Governing Development in Africa: The Role of the State in Economic Transformation*, Addis Ababa, Ethiopia.

Funabashi Y. (2009) 'Forget Bretton Woods II: The Role for U.S.–China–Japan Trilateralism', Centre for Strategic and International Studies, *Washington Quarterly*, vol. 32, no. 2, April.

Habiyaremye, A., and L. Soete (2010) 'The Global Financial Crisis and Africa's Immiserizing Wealth', *Research Brief* 1, United Nations University, Tokyo.

Habib A., (2008) 'Seeing the New African Scramble for What It Really Is: Reflections on the United States and China', in H. Edinger., H. Herman and J. Jansson, *New Impulses from the South: China's Engagement of Africa*, Centre for Chinese Studies, Stellenbosch University, South Africa.

Hung Ho Fung (2009) 'America's Head Servant: The PRC's Dilemma in the Global Crisis', *New Left Review* 60, November.

IMF (International Monetary Fund) (2011) *World Economic Outlook: Tensions from the Two-Speed Recovery Unemployment, Commodities, and Capital Flows*, April, IMF, Washington DC.

Kaplinsky, R. (2008) 'What Does the Rise of China Do for Industrialisation in Sub-Saharan Africa?', *Review of African Political Economy*, vol. 35, no. 115, March; http://dx.doi. org/10.1080/03056240802011360 (accessed 10 June 2009).

Lamont, J. (2009) 'World Bank Eyes India as Africa Rail Partner', *Financial Times*, www. ft.com/cms/s/0/723eb9ea-e28d-11de-b028-00144feab49a.html#axzz1LVTBYvIP.

le Pere, G., (2008) 'Prospects for a Coherent African Policy Response: Engaging China', in H. Edinger., H. Herman and J. Jansson, *New Impulses from the South: China's Engagement of Africa*, Centre for Chinese Studies, Stellenbosch University, South Africa.

Lee, C.K. (2009) 'Raw Encounters: Chinese Managers, African Workers and the Politics of Casualization in Africa's Chinese Enclaves', *China Quarterly* 199, September.

Manteaw, S. (2009) 'Ghana: China, U.S. Clash over Ghana's Oil', *Public Agenda*, 27 October; http://allafrica.com/stories/200910271136.html.

McCormick, D. (2008) 'China and India as Africa's New Donors: The Impact of Aid on Development', *Review of African Political Economy*, vol. 35, no. 115, March.

Macquarie Commodities Research (2008) 'Chinese Statistics and Metal Forecasting, Macquarie Capital Securities', April, www.icsg.org/index. php?option=com_docmantask=doc_downloadgid=73Itemid=62.

Modi, R. (2003) 'Migration to Democratic South Africa', *Economic and Political Weekly*, vol. 38, no. 18, pp. 1759–62.

Mohan, G., and M. Power (2008) 'New African Choices? The Politics of Chinese Engagement', *Review of African Political Economy*, vol. 35, no. 115, March.

Morris, H. (2010) 'Favela Urbanisation: Aim is to Bring Slums into the Mainstream', *Financial Times*, 6 May, www.ft.com/cms/s/0/a2bc15b4–571c-11df-aaff-00144feab49a.html.

Naidu, S., (2008) 'India's Growing African Strategy', *Review of African Political Economy*, vol. 35, no. 115, March.

Puri, L. (2007a) 'Going Beyond the Doha Negotiations: Promoting South–South Trade and Role of GSTP', UNCTAD statement, 9 August, New Delhi.

Puri, L., (2007b) 'IBSA: An Emerging Trinity in the New Geography of International Trade', *Policy Issues in International Trade and Commodities Study Series*, No. 35, UNCTAD, Geneva.

Smith, A.D. (2008) 'Is This the End of the Rainbow Nation?' *Guardian*, 25 May; www.guardian.co.uk/world/2008/may/25/southafrica.

Straw, J. (2006), 'Africa: A New Agenda', speech in Abuja, Nigeria, 14 February, www.britainusa.com/sections/articles_show_nt1.asp?d=9i=41058L1=41058L2=41058a=40982pv=1.

UNCTAD (2005) 'Case Study on Outward Foreign Direct Investment by South African enterprises', Trade and Development Board Commission on Enterprise, Business Facilitation and Development Expert Meeting on Enhancing the Productive Capacity of Developing Country Firms through Internationalization Geneva, TD/B/COM.2/77, December.

UNCTAD (2007) 'The Emerging Landscape of Foreign Direct Investment: Some Salient Issues', Trade and Development Board Commission on Investment, Technology and Related Financial Issues, Eleventh session, Geneva, 8–14 March.

CHAPTER 3

The modern business of war

OSCAR UGARTECHE

The militarization of the economy

Historically, it has been argued that war has been a solution to economic problems. It has reactivated failing economies while consolidating the political power of warmongering nations. This logic is the opposite of Bastiat's (1850) broken-window fallacy that argues that money spent on wars is not spent on something else, so there is no greater economic good from war but only profit for those related directly to the business of war. This argues that what is good for the military–industrial complex seems not to be so for the US economy, given that the greater the military expenditure, the greater both fiscal and external deficits become, while GDP growth does not necessarily respond.

What appears as the trigger for a new and greater military expenditure in the United States and a far more aggressive military presence is the result of the conclusions of the *Commission to Assess the Ballistic Missile Threat to the United States*,[1] also known as the Rumsfeld Commission, of July 1998. 'The Commission unanimously concluded three things: No. 1, the missile threat to the United States is real and growing; No. 2, the threat is greater than previously assessed; and, No. 3, we may have little or no warning of new threats.'[2] The fact that on 11 September 2001 the real threat came from five hijacked commercial airplanes and that no US intelligence service caught on to what was occurring for several minutes shows the weakness of security reasoning.

The Rumsfeld Report (1998) identifies a threat to the United States from Iraq, Iran, Libya and North Korea. If war is the means to impose our will on the enemy (von Clausewitz) then in the first decade of the

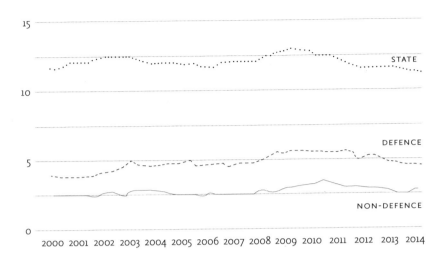

FIGURE 3.1 US budget: state, defence and non-defence expenditures, 2000–2014 (% of GDP)

SOURCE www.bea.gov.

twenty-first century the stated need for increased military expenditure in preparation for war against these four nations and in general against the threat of ballistic missiles from abroad is an expression of an imposition of US will through war.

It was to be expected that the end of the cold war would bring with it a reduced military presence generally, with the consolidation of the USA and the Pax Americana in a unipolar world. According to the Stockholm International Peace Research Institute (SIPRI, 2011) there was a doubling of US military expenditure between 1999 and 2009, from US$361 billion to US$687 billion (2009 constant dollars). So the end of the cold war at first brought with it a sharp reduction in outlays down from US$531 billion in 1988 to US$361 billion by 1999 (2009 constant dollars), and then a reversal. The level of US expenditure in constant 2009 dollars was 17 per cent higher in 2009 than at its peak in 1988 before the end of the cold war. This brought with it an increase in defence business, including the privatization of military force and the development of new unmanned war technology. The US government GDP shares as expressed by the Bureau of Economic Analysis (BEA) shows three trends reflecting public expenditure (see FIGURE 3.1): the upper line has a downward trend over the fifteen-year period 2000–2014, reflecting a reduction in state and municipal GDP; the second line, with an upward trend, is defence share, which grows from 4 per cent of GDP to 5.8 per cent in 2010 and then reduces to 4.4; and the last trend, with a stable line, is federal non-defence GDP on average.

The process of militarization of the US economy began at the end of World War II; hence Eisenhower's coinage of the term 'military–industrial complex' in his farewell address in 1961.[3] By that he meant the relationship between Congress, the Pentagon and the US defence industry with the aim of having wars for profit. This idea took on renewed strength at the end of the cold war. After 2001 a new military–industrial complex arose, supported by think-tanks like the neoconservative Foreign Policy Institute, the American Enterprise Institute and the Project for the New American Century (Daalder, 2002). Policymakers in the defence and security field came from these institutions and created the Bush doctrine of pre-emptive strikes. Pre-emption suggests striking first against a nation that is poised to attack (Gupta, 2008).

Among the most visible ideologues who made up the Project for the New American Century, founded in 1997 and part of the Bush administration, were Donald Rumsfeld, secretary of defense 2001–06; Richard Cheney, vice president 2001–08; Paul Wolfowitz, deputy secretary of defense 2001–05 and president of the World Bank 2005–07; Elliot Abrams, special assistant to the president and senior director for democracy, human rights and international operations at the National Security Council from 2001 to the end of 2002, when he was appointed special assistant to the president and the NSC's senior director for Near East and North African Affairs; and John Bolton, undersecretary of state for arms control and international security 2001–04 and ambassador to the United Nations 2005–06.

The Project for the New American Century is 'a think tank dedicated to the fundamental propositions that American leadership is good both for America and for the world; and that such leadership requires military strength, diplomatic energy and commitment to moral principle'.[4] This institution produced a report (Donelly, 2000) that called for an increase in defence spending for the coming decade in the face of a perceived reduction in military spending during the Clinton years.

What, then, is the price of continued American geopolitical leadership and military pre-eminence?

A finely detailed answer is beyond the scope of this study. Too many of the force posture and service structure recommendations above involve factors that current defence planning has not accounted for. Suffice it to say that an expanded American security perimeter, new technologies and weapons systems including robust missile defences, new kinds of organizations and operating concepts, new bases and the like will not come cheap (Donnelly, 2000: 81).

Bolstered by these arguments, defence spending began to escalate in 2001 before Bush's so called War on Terror became the Bush Doctrine. What should have been a focal front against a singular adversary became diluted and opened subsequent interventions on several fronts, namely Iraq, Afghanistan and Libya, all no-win situations. The Bush Doctrine is open-ended, implying that a US attack is justified if a nation or organization might pose a threat at some unknown future date (Hartung and Ciarrocca, 2003). As demonstrated in Iraq and Afghanistan, there was no threat: no weapons of mass destruction, no missile threat to the United States. This implies that a military threat was not the only consideration. What is clear is that, the economic crisis notwithstanding, the US military–industrial complex (Rundquist, 1978) has made substantial profits during the decade; more public spending has gone towards defence while less has been allocated to non-defence sectors (see FIGURE 3.1).

There are other neoconservative think-tanks such as the American Enterprise Institute, which defines itself as 'a community of scholars and supporters committed to expanding liberty, increasing individual opportunity, and strengthening free enterprise'.[5] The Heritage Foundation and the American Security Council are equally important members of this team of ideologically based institutions that, with support from both Republican and Democratic governments, supply the Defence and State Departments with specialists that could be perceived as developers of this new military foreign policy.

Friedman (2009) from Stratfor, a private intelligence firm aligned with this vision, suggests that the New American Century has begun. The conflict dynamics will be geared around secondary powers trying to contain and control the United States, with the latter, in turn, acting pre-emptively to prevent these coalitions from forming (Friedman, 2009: 5). The nature of the threat need not be military; any action that could be perceived as resulting in the weakening of American global power would be sufficient. Operation Desert Fox, in December of 1998, was aimed at degrading 'Saddam Hussein's ability to make and to use weapons of mass destruction. To diminish Saddam Hussein's ability to wage war against his neighbors. To show Saddam Hussein the consequences of violating international obligations.'[6] The choice of name is interesting as the original Desert Fox was the Nazi field marshal Rommel. In fact, given that there were no WMD, the Iran–Iraq conflict had already come to an end, and all of Iraq's bank accounts (Hufbauer et al., 1990) were frozen, Iraq was weakened in the face of a possible external occupation.

In this context, then, conflicts are not meant to win wars, but are first and foremost to make money for the defence industries and secondly to guarantee that power remains in US hands. In this new signification of war, what matters is not to win but to prevent the others from winning. So a losing war or one of attrition is positive as long as the enemy does not gain control over any aspect of the United States economy or in any way diminish its power. The most evident conflict over control is the energy industry. Those who control the oil could potentially control the United States and thus try to subjugate it to their own power; hence the wars in oil-producing regions.

According to Friedman (2009), the twenty-first century is the dawn of the New American Age that began with a group of Muslims striking at the United States in order to re-create the Caliphate, the great Islamic empire that once ran from the Atlantic to the Pacific. The United States responded by invading the Islamic world with a goal that was not victory in itself, but to disrupt the Islamic world and set it against itself. The business created and the profits accumulated with this logic have protected defence-related industries from the effects of both the 2000–2002 and the 2007–2010 recession, or, to take a longer view, from the first crisis of the twenty-first century.

Witness the Dow Jones Industrial Average, which showed a downward trend that began in January 2000 until it rebounded in March 2003. The explanation commonly given for this pattern is the increase in Chinese demand. However, given that Chinese demand had been growing since

TABLE 3.1 Top ten US defence industries, government contracts and PE ratios, 2002/2010

2002		CONTRACTS (US$ billion)	PE RATIO
1	Lockheed Martin	17.0	52.03
2	Boeing	16.6	11.37
3	Northrop	8.7	285.29
4	Raytheon	7.0	283.70[1]
5	General Dynamics	7.0	17.56
6	United Technologies	3.6	14.01
7	SAIC	2.1	n.a
8	TRW	2.0	50.95[2]
9	Health Net	1.7	14.75
10	L-3 Communications	1.7	n.a[3]
2010			
1	Lockheed Martin	14.9	8.90
2	Boeing	10.8	19.47
3	Northrop Grumman	9.9	9.96
4	General Dynamics	6.1	10.73
5	Raytheon	5.9	8.78
6	KBR Inc.	5.5	14.45
7	SAIC	4.8	10.60
8	L-3 Communications	4.2	8.97
9	Computer Sciences Corp.	3.4	8.44
10	Booz Allen Hamilton Inc.	2.8	6.29

[1] March 2003.
[2] Registered in the NYSE in 2004.
[3] Data not available through ycharts.com. It jumped to 8th place in 2010.

SOURCE PE ratios 2009, Bloomberg; Contracts, DoD Procurement and Personnel Statistics, http://siadapp.dmdc.osd.mil/procurement/historical_reports/statistics/p01/fy2002/top100.htm; PE ratios 2002, http://ycharts.com/companies/RTN; L-3 www.l-3com.com/about-l3.

TABLE 3.2 Old and new G7 countries: share of world total GDP (%)

Old G7	39.33	New G7	33.07
Japan	5.70	China	13.98
Germany	3.81	Russia	2.98
France	2.87	India	5.48
Italy	2.34	Brazil	2.91
USA	19.88	South Korea	1.97
Canada	1.80	Singapore	0.35
Great Britain	2.93	Indonesia	5.40

SOURCE IMF WEO, April, 2011; China includes Taiwan but not Hong Kong.

1990, the only element that can help explain the sudden change in March is the occupation of Iraq. In this sense, as a classical war, it should have resulted in an economic recovery. However, what occurred was that stock prices and stock exchanges recovered but the real economy did not. The stock prices of the largest defence industries enjoyed a boost after the 11 September attack:

> The big boost in the defence budget is good news for major Pentagon contractors, who were among the few companies to show increases in their stock prices when the market reopened after the September 11 attacks. Among the top gainers for the week of September 17–21, 2001, were military and space contractors like Raytheon (+37 percent), L-3 Communications (+35.8 percent), Alliant Techsystems (+23.5 percent), and Northrop Grumman (+21.2 percent).[7]

There was a real-estate boom associated with low interest rates, introduced shortly thereafter, but there was little or no actual growth, despite the increased military spending. One explanation might be found in global outsourcing. The restructuring of industrial production, in a post-Fordist global line of production, to different parts of the world based on production costs has led to a situation where increased US military spending has resulted in greater fiscal and external deficits in the USA

TABLE 3.3 Old and new G7 countries: basic data 2010

	Old G7	New G7
International reserves (US$ trillion)	1.8	4.5
GDP expected growth rate (%)	1.7	6.0
Public debt on GDP (%)	108	45.4
GDP per capita (US$ PPP)	37,336	19,400

SOURCE IMF WEO Report Database, April 2011; CIA *World Factbook*.

while increasing external surpluses and growth in other parts of the world. The other explanation would be the broken window fallacy: that the only profits are for those businesses directly related to war.

The defence industry in the United States is organized under the National Defence Industry Association, which claims to be the 'leading Defense Industry association promoting national security ... and the exchange of information between Industry and Government on National Security issues'.[8] It has 1,744 registered firms, the largest of which are shown in TABLE 3.1. All have very high price-to-earnings-per-share ratios (PE), indicating a very high market expectation regarding their profitability. Their PE ratios for 2002 are unusually high, as a result of extremely high share prices and very low earnings per share. This indicates that before the wars began the share prices of the listed firms were high in the expectation that they would become very profitable in the near future, but their earnings per share at the same time were low. At the end of the decade they were still have above-average PE ratios but were more in line with the rest of the stock market.

An aspect that might be taken into account in order to understand the new business of war is the change in the world power structure. The economy of the USA and of the G7 countries at the end of the first decade of the twenty-first century might not be as relevant for the world economy as it was at the beginning; hence the need for them to assert their military power. For 2010, the aggregate GDP of the new G7 countries

TABLE 3.4 GDP in US$, PPP projections

	2009		2010		2012		2017	
1	USA	14.12	USA	14.62	USA	15.82	China	18.87
2	China	9.05	China	10.08	China	12.43	USA	18.79
3	Japan	4.15	Japan	4.31	India	4.81	India	6.97
4	India	3.62	India	4.00	Japan	4.58	Japan	5.24
5	Germany	2.81	Germany	2.93	Germany	3.13	Germany	3.55
6	UK	2.13	Russia	2.22	Russia	2.48	Russia	3.11
7	Russia	2.12	Brazil	2.18	Brazil	2.43	Brazil	3.04

SOURCE IMF WEO 2011; 2017 projections made by Leonel Carranco/OBELA-UNAM.

reflects 84.1 per cent of that of old G7 countries (TABLE 3.2); International Reserves held are 2.5 times larger in the new G7 countries; the growth rate is 3.5 times faster; and publicly held debt, on average, is 42 per cent of that held by the old G7 countries (TABLE 3.3). By 2017 the world's seven leading economies will include only one Continental European country, and GDP per capita, on average, will reach the convergence point in a sixteen-year span if these growth assumptions hold (TABLE 3.4). There is agreement on this trend (Spence, 2011).

Our projections, using IMF (2011) data, show that by 2017 the USA will be the second largest economy; and, of the seven largest economies, Germany will be the only remaining European country on the list, and four of the seven will be Asian countries. The political significance of this is the loss of global market power of the richest economies, in spite of their having the highest incomes per capita and the highest standard of living.

Wages and social control, and the control of terrorism

The second problem has to do with economic reforms and globalization. From a positive economics point of view, after the Hayekian economic

TABLE 3.5 Wage bill as % of GDP, selected Latin American countries

	1980	2000	2009
Argentina	38.7	37.4	28.4[1]
Brazil	34.7	41.2	40.9[2]
Mexico	36.0	31.3	29.3
Chile	38.1	40.4	39.0
Colombia	41.6	35.5	32.7
Peru	29.7	24.4	22.0
Panama	51.1	37.8	29.8

[1] 2005 latest data.   [2] 2007 latest data.

SOURCE CEPAL: CEPALSTAT.

reforms known as TINA, people are working more and earning less everywhere in the world in an environment where there are fewer new jobs and
more informal-sector workers. Some of these are highly trained hi-tech
service-industry workers. Evidence from Latin America shows that the
total wage bill in GDP is sharply reduced and that economic growth
during the first decade of the century is not reflected in an improvement
in the wage bill. Exceptions are Brazil and Chile (see TABLE 3.5). This has
been attained through low-intensity democracies (Gills and Rocamora,
1992) – for example, Mexico, Argentina, Peru, Colombia during the 1990s
– while having as an escape valve the emigration of young professionals.
This might explain why social protest has been criminalized, leading
to increased homeland security in addition to the evident elements of
international terrorism (Correas, 2007). The reduction of the wage bill
on GDP and the criminalization of protests are worldwide trends that
correspond to the deregulation and flexibilization of labour (Taran and
Geronimi, 2003).

   The labour counter-revolution that occurred in the 1980s and those
human rights that materialized through the labour struggles of the

nineteenth and the early part of the twentieth century ended with the reduction of wages in the name of increased productivity and competition (Siebert and Addison, 1991). Aspromourgos (1987) and others have argued against this logic, which is supported by neoclassical theory. They observe that there has been a concentration of income and increased productivity at the expense of a reduction in the wage bill, while the quality of employment has deteriorated and skilled migration has sharply increased (Palma, 2009; Wickramasekara, 2003). Nevertheless, there is insufficient employment for the growing labour force, particularly in slow-growing emerging countries and in the old G7 countries. Income is so highly concentrated in 0.01 per cent of the world population (Palma, 2009) that the portion of GDP left for the rest of society is continuously shrinking.

The same trend seems to apply in the old G7 countries, with the added problem of wage competition from illegal migrants. This has not only restricted but has now criminalized the international movement of people (Guild, 2009; Medina, 1997). Therefore expenditure on territorial control of the borders has grown sharply in the old G7 countries. The US Department of Homeland Security[9] saw a fourfold increase in its budget, from US$14.3 billion[10] to US$55.1 billion (current US dollars), between 2002 and 2010.[11] This represents a sharper increase than the general defence budget in the same period.

The definition of unemployment varies. In the United States, for instance, a person is unemployed for a certain period of time while he or she seeks work and receives unemployment compensation. After that period, the person is no longer unemployed; they leave the workforce and are unaccounted for. In Mexico, in contrast, a person is employed if he or she has worked thirty hours a month over the past so many months. These two examples show how employment data do not really reflect the problems of the working population and its unrest.

The modern business of war

The second side of militarization has to do with the privatization of war. 'A private military company is a legally established international firm offering services that incorporate the "potential" to exercise force in a systematic way and by military or paramilitary means and/or the transfer or enhancement of that potential to clients' (Ortiz, 2007: 60). For example, US Training Center (formerly Xe Services and before that Blackwater USA) is one such firm. The firm billed US$1.5 billion between 2001 and 2009.[12] It has an aviation branch of its own. This case, made public in a 2010 *Vanity Fair* interview with the Center's CEO, shows the possibility of outsourcing conflicts; this has led to a very profitable and growing industry that contains officers and troops from such diverse corps as the Gurkhas from Great Britain, Mossad from Israel and top military teams in the US Army and Navy. Basic infantry are recruited primarily from developing countries where soldiers have done military service and received basic training. The industry web list[13] has forty-two entries that range from demining to basic security and air supplies.

PMCs, as private military companies are known, have the added advantage of reducing national army death tolls, given that private firms can hire nationals from anywhere and that they are not recorded as soldiers but as contractors. These private security firms are, in effect, paramilitaries or, as they were known before, guns for hire. They have no position; they have a contract. The best known case is the firm referred to above, US Training Center (formerly Blackwater and Xe). The withdrawal of US military personnel can be accompanied by the permanence or the growth of these private security firms, which essentially continue doing the same thing the army was doing previously in the same areas.

The case of Blackwater is important because it shows the power such firms may have. According to the company's web page (before it changed into Xe Services) it had three training centres and a 7,000-hectare training field; the CEO confirmed that it trained 30,000 soldiers a year. The firm maintained an aviation fleet, a naval fleet and an army of 100,000 soldiers ready to be called into action. These are new actors in the military–industrial complex, together with hi-tech designers of unmanned equipment. This can lead to war scenarios where US soldiers need not be present at all. The best business model is to obtain territorial control by flying in unmanned equipment – drones – first and then consolidate the position using a private security firm. This way all stakeholders make money and no US military lives are put at risk. It also saves the embarrassment of a prolonged war without a clear win.

Conclusion

The modern business of war is to wage wars not to win them; it is about their profitability as an industry. Second, having wars is to do with control. This requires not that wars be won, but that the other side does not take control of a resource that is strategically vital to the United States. Third, the game is to maintain power in a world where the old G7 countries are no longer the economic heavyweights in terms of GDP size. The USA and its allies are barely one-eighth larger than the new G7 countries, which are mostly Asian, except for Brazil. The world power structure is changing and the old actors are becoming aware that they are no longer the leaders, and are resorting to force rather than reason and leadership. The economic model imposed through Washington-based IFIs has brought with it massive unwanted migration, little new employment and a reduction of wages in GDP, together with massive income concentration through the financial sector. All of this requires militarized social control to quell protests, such as those in the streets of Paris in March 2006 or London in March 2012 from excluded people trying to enter the system.

The reasoning now is not to win wars but to have wars. This is the business of wars. Iraq was a good choice not because the conflict was meant to be won but because there will be a good security business there for the foreseeable future. It appears that the global economy has become militarized. Down the militarization road those who bear the greatest weight of this development are women, black people and children. These are the ones who suffer from the broken window and the distorted social contract.

NOTES

1. www.fas.org/irp/threat/missile/rumsfeld/execsum.htm.
2. www.fas.org/irp/congress/1998_cr/s980731-rumsfeld.htm.
3. http://mcadams.posc.mu.edu/ike.htm.
4. www.newamericancentury.org.
5. www.aei.org.
6. www.defense.gov/specials/desert_fox.
7. www.privateforces.com/index.php?option=com_content&task=view&id=67.
8. www.ndia.org/Pages/Default.aspx.
9. www.dhs.gov/files/bordersecurity.shtm.
10. www.dhs.gov/xlibrary/assets/FY_2004_budget_in_brief.pdf.
11. www.dhs.gov/xlibrary/assets/budget_bib_fy2010.pdf.
12. Adam Ciralsky, 'Tycoon, Contractor, Soldier, Spy', *Vanity Fair*, January 2010; www.vanityfair.com/politics/features/2010/01/blackwater-201001.
13. www.privatemilitary.org/private_military_companies.html.

REFERENCES

Aspromourgos, T. (1987) 'Unemployment, Economic Theory and Labour-Market Deregulation', *Australian Economic Papers*, vol. 26, no. 48, pp. 130–44.

Bastiat, F. (1850) 'Ce qu'on voit et ce qu'on ne voit pas', http://bastiat.org/fr/cqovecqonvp.html.

CIA *World Factbook*, https://www.cia.gov/library/publications/the-world-factbook.

Correas, O. (2007) 'The Criminalization of Social Protest in Mexico and Latin America', paper presented at the annual meeting of the Law and Society Association, Berlin, 25 July.

Daalder, I. (2002) 'Policy Implications of the Bush Doctrine on Preemption', Council of Foreign Relations, New York, www.cfr.org/international-law/policy-implications-bush-doctrine-preemption/p5251.

Donelly, T., et al. (2000) 'Rebuilding America's Defenses: Strategy, Forces and Resources for a New Century', a report of The Project for the New American Century, September, www.newamericancentury.org/RebuildingAmericasDefenses.pdf.

Friedman, G. (2009) *The Next 100 Years: A Forecast for the XXIst Century*, Random House, New York.

Gupta, S. (2008) The Doctrine of Pre-emptive Strike: Application and Implications during the Administration of President George W. Bush', *International Political Science Review* 29, March, pp. 181–96.

Gills, B., and J. Rocamora (1992) 'Low Intensity Democracies', *Third World Quarterly*, vol. 13, no. 3, pp. 501–23.

Guild, E. (2009) 'Criminalisation of Migration in Europe: Human Rights Implications', issues paper, EU Commissioner for Human Rights, www.commissioner.coe.int.

Hartung, W., and M. Ciarrocca (2003) 'The Business of War: The Military-Industrial–Think Tank Complex. Corporate Think Tanks and the Doctrine of Aggressive Militarism', *Multinational Monitor*, vol. 24, no. 12, January/February; http://multinationalmonitor.org/mm2003/012003.

Hufbauer, G.C., J.J. Schott and K.A. Elliott (1990) *Economic Sanctions Reconsidered: History and Current Policy*, 2nd edn, IIE, Washington DC.

IMF (2011) *World Economic Outlook*, April, www.imf.org/external/pubs/ft/weo/2011/01/weodata/index.aspx.

Medina, M.I. (1997) 'The Criminalization of Immigration Law: Employer Sanctions and Marriage Fraud', *Geo. Mason Law. Review*, vol 5, no. 4, Summer, pp. 669–731.

Ortiz, J.C. (2010) *Private Armed Forces and Global Security: A Guide to the Issues*, Praeger, Westport CT.

Palma, G. (2009) 'The Revenge of the Market on the Rentiers. Why Neo-liberal Reports of the End of History Turned Out to be Premature', *Cambridge Journal of Economics*, vol. 33, no. 4, pp. 829–69.

Rundquist, B.S. (1978) 'On Testing a Military Industrial Complex Theory', *America Politics Quarterly*, vol. 6, no. 1, January, pp. 29–39.

Siebert, W.S. and J.T. Addison (1991) 'Internal Labour Markets: Causes and Consequences', *Oxford Review of Economic Policy*, vol. 7, no. 1, Spring, pp. 76–92.

Taran, P., and E. Geronomi (2003) *Globalization, Labour and Migration: Protection is Paramount*, Perspectives on Labour Migration 3E, International Migration Programme, ILO, Geneva.

Spence, M. (2011) *The Next Convergence*, Farrar, Straus & Giroux, New York.

SIPRI (2011) *SIPRI Yearbook 2011*, Oxford University Press, Oxford.

United States Congress (1998) 'Report of the Commission to Assess the Ballistic Missile Threat to the United States', July 15, 1998, Pursuant to Public Law 201, 104th Congress, Washington DC.

Ward, B., and R. Dubos (1983) *Only One Earth: The Care and Maintenance of a Small Planet*, W.W. Norton, New York.

Wickramasekara, P. (2003) *Policy Responses to Skilled Migration: Retention, Return and Circulation*, Social Protection Sector, International Migration Programme, International Labour Office, Geneva.

World Bank (1999) *HIPC Definitions and Policies*, World Bank, Washington DC.

BOX 11.3 **Militarization, illicit economies and governance**
ADEBAYO OLUKOSHI

Several characteristics of contemporary globalization have contributed to and fuelled illicit economies. A major cause is the radical shift in the structure of rewards and penalties that undermine the real economy and long-term perspectives on its development, while encouraging and stimulating speculative activities and short-term approaches (Mkandawire and Soludo, 1999). Policies promoting one-sided and unidirectional trade and financial liberalization have contributed to this radical shift even as state controls are dismantled in favour of self-regulation by so-called markets (Harvey, 2003; Mkandawire and Soludo, 1999; UNRISD, 1995). Under-regulation has resulted in a proliferation of offshore banking opportunities, allowing for the tapping of hot money circulation for oiling illicit economies. The increased possibilities offered by cumulative technological revolutions for global economic transactions to be undertaken on several fronts simultaneously and in real time, and the absence of effective mechanisms for governing contemporary globalization to the benefit of all members of the international community, allow for untamed expansion of illicit activities (Trinkunas and Clunnan, 2010; Jung, 2003; Harvey, 2003; Naylor, 2002). Another factor is the erosion of the developmental state and, in particular, the consequent retrenchment of social policies. This has resulted in deep-seated and growing social inequalities that manifest in many forms and that have particularly penalized youth, women and the working poor (UNRISD, 1995). Illicit activities provide an alternative to joblessness and the absence of decent work. Cybercriminality, perpetrated by young, highly educated but perennially unemployed youth, has been a growing feature of the digital age. The activities of the cybercriminals go by different names in different parts of the world: 419ers, Yahoo Boys, Yahoo Millionaires. Urban lumpen culture has also been on the rise among youth, much of it centring around touting, extortion and pimping (UNDP, 2001; Jega, 2000).

Contemporary globalization has, furthermore, a distinct militarized character (Amin, 2003; Harvey, 2003; Jung, 2003;). Historically, the diversion of national productive capacities in support of increased arms production and related war efforts has also fuelled illicit economies. Today, the post-cold war peace dividend remains elusive in international relations. Armed conflicts – local, national and cross-national wars – continue unabated. Meanwhile, there is a need to wrestle with the political economy of new, unconventional wars. It is particularly challenging to look deeply into privatized security and its relations with a corporatized military and the provision of services adjunctive to the conduct of war, which are now integral to militarized globalization (Scahill, 2007; Singer, 2004; Mandel, 2002). In this realm, mercenaries are also miners and merchants in the global arms industry. What this means is that contemporary global illicit economies are driven by an assortment of players that include but also go beyond the old mafia clans to encompass a new generation of mercenaries, armed guerrillas, transnational smugglers, drug lords, money launderers, warlords, human traffickers and pirates (Trinkunas and Clunnan, 2010; Andreas, 2004; Standing, 2003; Jung, 2003; Naylor, 2002)

When conflicts and war are prolonged and cause the severe dislocation of 'normal' activities, illicit economies and the transactions within them reflect the state of crisis and the limitations of formal, licit economies and transactions in such situations. Similar to formal and licit economies, illicit economies are underpinned by complex relations of power and domination. In contemporary times, these power relations pose serious challenges to governance, democratization, citizenship and rights. Necessarily, they also pose challenges to long-standing struggles for gender equality.

While, for understandable reasons, the scale of contemporary illicit economies is difficult to gauge with accuracy, it is generally reckoned that since the end of the cold war they have grown at twice the rate of the global licit economy. Activity is conducted using all known economic channels, including cyberspace, where a thriving market in all manner of illicit goods has grown over the years. The commanding heights of the global illicit economies are dominated by men, and their ideological underpinnings are both macho and patriarchal. Their reliance on the threat and deployment of force and violence further reinforces their character.

The human costs of the expansion of illicit economies are many. They include, but are not limited to, the erosion of democratic governance, political stability and state legitimacy; the disruption of national development plans; revenue losses and leakages as well as corruption; the production and prolongation of armed conflicts; and the erosion of civic identities, labour standards and established human rights. The costs of illicit economies have extended to the realm of gender relations through violence deployed against women, the exploitation of divisions of labour that undermine gender equality, the increased commoditization of women and of womanhood, as well as the erosion of women's incomes and livelihoods. One of the clearest examples of this multidimensional process is the increased expansion in the cross-border/international trafficking of girls and women for sex work and other forms of labour under dehumanizing conditions (McCabe, 2008; Farr, 2004).

The taming of global illicit economies is inconceivable without a commitment to the retooling of the state's developmental capacity and regulatory powers. This, in turn, will require a recasting of the key pillars of neoliberal globalization to infuse it with a more developmental and democratic logic.

REFERENCES

Amin, S. (2003) The Alternative to the Neo-Liberal System of Globalization and Militarization: Imperialism Today and the Hegemonic Offensive of the United States, mimeo,
Dakar, February.

Andreas, P. (2004) 'Illicit International Political Economy: The Clandestine Side of Globalization', *Review of International Political Economy*, vol. 11, no. 3, August, pp. 641–52.

Farr, K. (2005) *Sex Trafficking: The Global Market in Women and Children*, Worth Publishers,
New York.

Harvey, D. (2003) *The New Imperialism*, Oxford University Press, New York.

Jega, A. (ed.) (2000) *Identity Transformation and Identity Politics under Structural Adjustment
in Nigeria*, Nordic Africa Institute, Uppsala.

Jung, D. (ed.) (2003) *Shadow Globalization, Ethnic Conflicts and New wars: A Political Economy
of Intra-State War*, Routledge, London.

Mandel, R. (2002) *Armies without States: The Privatization of Security*, Lynne Rienner, Boulder
CO.

McCabe, K. (2008) *The Trafficking of Persons*, Peter Lang, New York.

Mkandawire, T., and C. Soludo (1999) *Our Continent, Our Future: African Perspectives on
Structural Adjustment*, CODESRIA, Dakar.

Naylor, R.T. (ed.) (2002) *Wages of Crime: Black Markets, Illegal Finance and the Underground
Economy*, Cornell University Press, Ithaca NY.

Scahill, J. (2007) *Blackwater: The Rise of the World's Most Powerful Mercenary Army*, Nation
Books, New York.

Singer, P.W. (2004) *Corporate Warriors: The Rise of the Privatized Military Industry*, Cornell
University Press, Ithaca NY.

Standing, A. (2003) *Rival Views of Organised Crime*, ISS Monograph No. 77, Institute for
Security Studies, South Africa.

Trinkunas, H., and A. Clunnan (eds) (2010) *Ungoverned Spaces: Alternatives to State Authority
in an Era of Softened Sovereignty*, Stanford University Press, Stanford CA.

UNDP (2001) *Nigeria: Common Country Assessment*, UNDP, New York.

UNRISD (1995) *States of Disarray: The Social Effects of Globalization*, UNRISD, Geneva.

BOX II.4 Commodity exports and persistent inequality under Latin American progressive governments

NICOLE BIDEGAIN PONTE

In an increasingly multipolar world, Latin America and the Caribbean are often referred to as an 'emerging region'. It's a regional integration process that is intensifying with the creation of new institutions, exemplified by the Bank of the South. Though the region has learned to protect its members' economies from external volatility, it still has structural weaknesses. The region continues to rely on the export of primary commodities as a source of growth, which has been termed *primarisacion*. The prevailing high global commodity prices provide favourable terms of trade for the region's exports, but the region will be vulnerable to price fluctuations. The continuation of high prices can also discourage diversification and delay the development of knowledge-intensive sectors. Despite these disadvantages, Brazil's former president Lula da Silva spoke at the World Social Forum in Dakar of 'the benefits' of the agro-export model in Latin America in what seemed to be a kind of paternalist discourse addressed to Africa.

Latin America's share of global greenhouse gas emissions is produced by agricultural and livestock activity and reinforced by deforestation. The region's pattern of productive specialization in natural resources also entails a growing demand for energy, contributing to an increase in the emission of greenhouse gases: 'current production and consumption patterns rely heavily on fossil fuel' (ECLAC, 2010: 108). What is to be noted is the significant political resistance from the agricultural and livestock sector to discussing possible changes in this sector towards emissions reduction (Honty, 2007).

At the same time, the region has seen a reduction in poverty that has been sustained by increases in social expenditure. While 221 million people lived in poverty in 2002, by 2010 the number was reduced to 180 million. This downward trend, however, slowed in 2009 due to the global economic crisis. Despite progress in poverty reduction, Latin America and the Caribbean is still the most unequal region in the world. Besides being at a high level, inequality is persistent over time and reproduces itself in a context of low socio-economic mobility. The region's agro-export growth model possibly contributes to social rigidities. Uruguay's production of agrofuels, for example, is currently focused on ethanol from sugar cane, soybeans for biodiesel, and tree plantations to produce cellulose and ethanol. When the Argentinian government increased export taxes in the agro-exports sector, soy investors went to Uruguay and started buying and leasing productive land. Small farmers and rural workers feel they are being forced out as a result of the expanding foreign ownership of land. Advances in human development and poverty reduction are evident in many Latin American and Caribbean countries, but aggregate numbers hide important inequalities regarding territory, gender, ethnicity and race (UNDP, 2010).

Climate change makes more evident the need for new paradigms. This implies thinking about new forms of production, consumption, redistribution, generation and use of energy. It is important to move to an economic growth model based on low-carbon and cleaner sectors.

An important element to consider is the right to education and its potential role in the reduction of social inequality and elimination of intergenerational reproduction of poverty in Latin America. Access to education has an impact on the reduction of inequality. To achieve this, it is essential to broaden preschool education coverage and guarantee the entrance of boys, girls and teenagers into the education system. There is a need to promote the permanence of the educational process by guaranteeing access to lifelong learning and updating opportunities throughout life.

Latin America should improve participation in global negotiations related to climate change with its own regional agenda, in order to take on coordinated initiatives concerning economic–environmental improvement. This requires, in turn, that each country has a defined political commitment regarding the policies needed to deal with climate change. It is also important for young feminists and ecological and economic justice movements to work together to advocate for a transformative agenda. Spaces are needed for communication and mutual understanding among policymakers, feminists, and ecological and economic justice movements in the region.

REFERENCES

ECLAC (2009) *Climate Change and Development in Latin America and the Caribbean. Overview 2009*, coordinador Joseluis Samaniego, http://www.cepal.org/publicaciones/xml/8/38148/04_climate_change_overview2009.pdf.

ECLAC (2010) *Time for Equality: Closing Gaps, Opening Trails*, www.cepal.org/publicaciones/xml/1/39711/100604_2010-115-SES-33-3-Time_for_equality_doc_completo.pdf.

Filipini, A. (2010) 'Women and Climate Change in Cochabamba', www.climate-justice-now.org/women-and-climate-change-in-cochabamba.

Friends of the Earth International (2008) *Fuelling Destruction in Latin America: The Real Price of the Drive for Agrofuels*, www.foei.org/en/resources/publications/pdfs/2008/biofuels-fuelling-destruction-latinamerica/view.

Heinberg, R. (2010) 'The End of Growth' (Síntesis del libro accedida), www.energybulletin.net/stories/2010-11-12/end-growth.

Honty, G. (2007) 'América Latina ante el Cambio Climático', www.energiasur.com/cambioclimatico/ODGlbz4CambioClimaticoHonty.pdf.

Honty, G. (2011) *Cambio Climático: Negociaciones y Consecuencias para América Latina*, CLAES, www.energiasur.com/publicaciones/HontyCambioClimatico2011.pdf.

UNDP (2010) *Informe Regional sobre Desarrollo Humano para América Latina y el Caribe* http://hdr.undp.org/en/reports/regional/featuredregionalreport/RHDR-2010-RBLAC.pdf.

CHAPTER 4

The convergences and divergences of human rights and political economy

ALDO CALIARI

An assessment of the merits and demerits of both the human rights approach and what is cautiously termed a political economy approach to development – each of which is used by progressive activists to challenge neoliberal economic thinking – is a timely exercise. The current economic crisis – and its not coincidental occurrence alongside crises of food, energy, climate and care – poses the biggest opening since the late 1970s for such a challenge.

One purpose of such an assessment is to look into the solidity and integrity of these approaches as frameworks. Another and equally important purpose is also to evaluate them from the perspective of the feminist organizations and movements as they advocate for the advancement of gender justice. It will be shown not only that there are convergences and divergences between the two frameworks, but also, importantly, that both frameworks as tools for developing a progressive agenda for development and for gender justice are incomplete. There is certainly plenty of scope for a feminist analysis of both frameworks in order to identify their drawbacks. Furthermore, the assessment argues that there is immense potential in their complementarities. The chapter ends with the suggestion that a 'feminist' revision of both approaches – perhaps combined in a synthetic form – is an urgent task for the feminist movement.

The human rights approach to development

The existence of a close relationship between human rights and development seems to have been a matter of consensus already in the late 1980s. The Declaration on the Right to Development defined such a right as 'an inalienable human right by virtue of which every human person and all peoples are entitled to participate in, contribute to, and enjoy economic, social, cultural and political development, in which all human rights and fundamental freedoms can be fully realized' (Declaration on the Right to Development 1986, Art. 1). It further identified the 'failure to observe civil and political rights, as well as economic social and cultural rights' as obstacles to development that should be eliminated (Declaration on the Right to Development 1986, Art. 6.3).

That close relationship is also expressed in more recent documents. In his 2005 Report *In Larger Freedom* the UN secretary general chose to build on this relationship by stating that 'The notion of larger freedom also encapsulates the idea that development, security and human rights go hand in hand' (UN General Assembly 2005, para. 14), and that 'Not only are development, security and human rights all imperative; they also reinforce each other' (UN General Assembly 2005, para. 16). He went on to state that, 'Accordingly, we will not enjoy development without security, we will not enjoy security without development, and we will not enjoy either without respect for human rights' (UN General Assembly 2005, para. 17).

A closer look at the rhetoric reveals that the perceived connections between human rights and development may be less generally shared than it might appear. The existence of tensions becomes apparent in the attempt to address the following question: can human rights be achieved in the absence of development?

Human rights activists are prone to respond to this question affirmatively. The norms would certainly seem to support their claim. For instance, the Vienna Declaration and Programme of Action posited the idea that 'the lack of development may not be invoked to justify the abridgement of internationally recognized human rights' (Vienna Declaration 1993, para. 10). Accepting the contrary may be tantamount to giving states that have not achieved development a blank cheque to ignore their human rights obligations. Moreover, it would be unfair to countries that possess a very good track record regarding their human rights obligations in spite of very limited levels of development. For instance, the Social Watch Gender Equity Index 2009 shows Rwanda, one of the poorest countries – indeed one that qualifies as a 'least developed country' – in third place, ahead of countries such as Germany and Norway (Social Watch, 2009).

The global women's movement can boast of important achievements that have brought greater recognition of women's rights. The appointment of a Special Rapporteur on Violence Against Women and of a feminist to the post of Independent Expert on Cultural Rights, and the inclusion of women's rights issues in the outcome documents of most global processes, along with the establishment of mechanisms such as the Human Rights Council and its representatives at regional and national levels, are among the recent advances resulting from these advocacy efforts. The Financing for Development Conference called for a mainstreaming of gender at all levels (Monterrey Consensus, 2002, para. 64).

However, a human rights approach may well ignore the plight of women. The focus on the empowerment of women, and on civil and political rights, can obscure the more intricate cultural, social and economic dynamics that prevent women from effectively being empowered by what may be otherwise formally available legal human rights mechanisms.

One blind spot of the human rights framework is its state-centred nature, which by definition is meant to pose difficulties for feminist and other marginalized groups whose relationship to the state itself is not defined in a direct relationship but through a mediating construction, be it social, cultural or economic. In such a construct the state becomes the duty-bearer in opposition to rights holders, and in doing so leaves out of the picture those mediating constructions that are in what is considered the 'private' sphere (Binion, 1995). Take, for instance, the African post-colonial context, where women's citizenship is still largely defined by ascribed social relations of subordination, and their relations with the state are mediated by men, kin or communities. Another blind spot where the human rights framework is vulnerable to a feminist critique is its asymmetrical take on cultural difference. Patriarchal lenses are in some cases used to determine what is a human rights violation masquerading under a 'cultural' value or a 'voluntary acceptance' of cultural values by women in a certain community context (Binion, 1995).

The political economy approach to development

This essay sets out to contrast the human rights approach to development with what is cautiously termed a 'political economy' approach. There are several streams within political economy, which makes the task of generalizing about the features of 'a' political economy approach to development difficult. Nevertheless it is possible to note some key aspects that establish differences between these approaches (colonialism, dependency theory and structuralism, among others) and the human rights approach.

The political economy approach to development has helped to elucidate the processes behind the elite capture of the state and the state's subjection to external, if not imperialist, forces.

First, the political economy approach helps position in the debate the issue of the actual capacity that states have for promoting and fulfilling human rights. In particular, we owe to models of political economy valuable ideas with respect to a concept of development that addresses the dynamics of a nation-state attempting to develop in the context of the larger global economy where it belongs. Whereas the human rights approach has to be stretched to bring into its fold the actual power relationships within the state – the primary subject of its obligations – the political economy approach offers ready tools to make an assessment. Its assessment will be offered not as an add-on to the internal domestic dynamics of the state but rather as a central factor that influences all actors in the model and conditions their behaviour.

Second, the political economy framework is one that is more oriented to the dynamic of how development happens. By analysing the processes, in particular the historical processes, by which development has been achieved in different places, it fleshes out demands regarding the shape of the industrial, trade, investment, macroeconomic and other economic policies that go into such processes. This is quite different from the lack of concern that a human rights approach shows towards the detail of the economic policies by which development is to be achieved. Paradigmatic of this lack of concern is the well-known statement by the Committee on Economic, Social and Cultural Rights which established that the obligation to take steps 'neither requires nor precludes any particular form of government or economic system being used as the vehicle for the steps in question, provided only that it is democratic and that all human rights are thereby respected' (CESCR, 1990, para. 9).

This is important because human rights demands on economic policy issues are sometimes condescendingly dismissed by economic policymakers as well-intentioned but out of touch with the realities of limited resources. Political economists are more tuned into the practical challenges that policymakers face: limited resources for unlimited ends. Therefore they are more likely to think about trade-offs and practical policy solutions that cannot so easily be dismissed. They can build a critique that engages with economic policy while offering a progressive alternative to the sort of trade-offs that would be agreeable in a neoliberal model.

Critiques of the political economy approach

As is the case with the human rights approach, a political economy approach suffers from a number of drawbacks. Political economists, for instance, have extolled the virtues of developmental states for their successes in creating strategic approaches to industrialization and development. In certain schools of thought the focus is on processes of national development. It is expected that improvements in living standards and access to public services will reach everybody in the country as a result of development by some sort of 'trickle-down' mechanism. It is precisely the schools that shed better light on the international political economy that are more liable to disregard what happens within a given state and the internal power dynamics that may systematically prevent certain groups from benefiting from development. This is the chief concern of a human rights approach, which will carefully test whether the benefits of progress are reaching all, and in particular historically vulnerable or disadvantaged groups.

An exaggerated emphasis on and faith in the developmental state may carry the cost of ignoring the scope for unaccountable decisions from the state in its use of resources. The systematic distrust that neoliberal approaches place on the ability of the state to conduct strategic interventions on the economy may not be warranted. After all, the market, which such approaches offer as an alternative, has proved to be equally liable to make mistakes and is arguably less accountable.[8] Neither should this warrant, at least for progressive agendas, consent to any decision the state makes, simply on the basis that the state labels the decisions 'strategic'. In placing the sort of checks and balances that allow citizens to have an informed debate over the distributional consequences of possible strategic state interventions, and their conscious and open negotiation as part of a social contract, the principles of participation and accountability that a human rights approach brings can be most useful.

The political economy framework is very useful to untangle and chart the way to tackling the power dynamics that may be acting as obstacles to development. Unlike the human rights framework, however, it does not carry with it an institutional and legal structure that can empower individuals and social groups to make the claims that could overturn or change such power dynamics. Nor does it have the same claim and potential to capture the imagination of individuals and groups as the moral imperative that emanates from human rights norms. Focus on the developmental state can bar advocates from asking helpful questions about how the policies implemented by the state are affecting people's lives. There is satisfaction behind the invocation of outcomes as justification for a certain set of policies but with little being done to verify the realization of those outcomes.

In the last decade important achievements have been made by progressive movements that have framed this advocacy in a political economy approach. Notable are the debt relief campaign; the withdrawal of global investment rules in the World Trade Organization's Ministerial Conference in Cancún, in 2003; and the enshrining of the concept of policy space for the first time in a North–South declaration, at the UNCTAD XI Conference in 2004.

Certain versions of the political economy approach facilitate alliances with developing-country governments, as it is a framework that better speaks to their real concerns and power constraints. It takes the spotlight away from domestic dynamics that may enter into conflict with the interest of the ruling elites to focus on international ones. It also speaks to the practical problems that many of those countries face in their process to develop. These alliances raise important questions that haunt progressive activists. The unintended effect of building alliances that legitimize developing-country governments' concerns about such external constraints to development may be the legitimization of state practices domestically, including those that may be built on the oppression or the vulnerability and marginalization of large groups of the population, including along gender, class or ethnic lines. Easy answers are hard to come by, however, as it is undeniable that the external environment in which the nation-state operates in taking action towards the fulfilment of rights is crucial to the success of such action, and cannot in all fairness be just wished away.

The political economy framework, when supportive of notions of international power-sharing, can also alienate countries that, in most cases, once they have achieved an acceptable level of development, predicate for others a market-oriented model. This model permeates and shapes their prescriptions, supported in aid and trade policies, offering – to varying degrees – little space to trust the judgement of what they perceive as corrupt and incompetent developing-country governments to make calls on strategies for development. The political economy framework is also one that assumes that developed countries hold a position of greater power – and therefore greater responsibility – over global development outcomes.

Just as with the human rights framework, a hard feminist look at the political economy framework will surely find flaws in it. It is true that some political economy schools, by entering into the power analysis of economic development processes at the domestic level, have made an important contribution. Feminist economics has certainly brought a new lens with which to view the economic unit and the production and consumption processes, with outcomes that are certain to be reflected in a different economic model. Other formulations nonetheless would have gender take a backseat to other sources of oppression,[9] or are decidedly gender-blind, and in this regard arguably pernicious to a progressive feminist agenda too. The developmental states that are the principal paradigm for some advocates are not at the forefront of promoting human rights, especially women's human rights. It may even be argued that in these developmental states, social protection – critical from a feminist perspective – is seen, at best, as a logical result to follow from increases in living standards made affordable by wage and earnings increases. The global economic crisis has laid bare these weaknesses in social protection. As social protection is not seen as a focus of policy in its own right, it follows that unpaid burdens of care work are always an additional challenge to those brought on by deprivation.

Defining and taking up the challenge

As anticipated at the beginning, the counterpoint in the last two sections aims to support two conclusions. One purpose of such a counterpoint was to not just to show that there are convergences and divergences between human rights and political economy approaches, but to set the stage for discussion of the interesting complementarities that they offer. Feminist movements and organizations would be well served by taking note of such complementarities and using them as incentives to a deliberate theoretical effort to move towards a synthesis.

The complementarities have emerged in the text, but as proposals to motivate forward-thinking two specific agendas come to mind. One is the powerful outcomes that could result from combining the institutional approach that comes from the human rights framework – with its sense of entitlements – and the political economy approach that looks at the role of global economic policy and human rights. This combination could tackle the important issue raised by the neoliberal framework, which, in its disciplined effort to argue that its approach to economics is universally valid, has come to provide the basis for a global institutionality that refuses to allow economic policies to relate to non-economic considerations, such as human rights. The practical outcome has been that human rights considerations have become subservient to one particular approach to economics, one that has come to set the boundaries for the universe of economic policy tools that states are able to implement in order to fulfil their human rights obligations.[10]

A second agenda is the construction of a state that is both developmental and accountable. This is obviously a normative model, and as such runs the risk of being a utopia, but progressive thinkers cannot shy away from the challenge of reflecting on its feasibility and conditions of operation. What are the real constraints that states trying to construct a developmental identity may face? Are accountability, participation and transparency principles a threat to such construction – as they are often perceived, especially when powerful interest groups may avail themselves of such means to prevent reform and the building of regulatory and interventionist capabilities? Are there, on the contrary, conditions under which such principles can enhance the construction of such identity? Is the state condemned to ignore – and, thus, support the perpetuation – of male-led and patriarchal tendencies or can its developmental strategy and accountability features create a bridge to inclusion and the transformation of gender power relations.

A second purpose of the counterpoint was show that neither of the two approaches is inherently better observed through a feminist lens. This is even while agreeing, as this author does, that feminist economics has its own place as one of the streams of political economy. Consequently, the effort of synthesis proposed in the previous paragraph, if expected to be of service to a feminist agenda, should at the same time be continually oriented and checked against a gender and feminist assessment.

NOTES

1. See Chang, 2002 and Amsden, 2001 for a defence of this thesis, but also note World Bank, 1993 relativizing and challenging how relevant the role of the state was to such successes.

2. In the case of the East Asian Tigers, see Hoon, 2004, for instance, which provides an account of the Asian leaders' doctrine on human rights and the 'Asian values' argument that would justify sacrificing rights to achieve development. In the case of the industrialized countries' process of development, see Chang, 2002, which argues, for instance, that institutions prohibiting child labour were absent during the process of development of currently industrialized countries.

3. The open-ended Working Group on the Right to Development was established in 1998 by resolution of the Commission on Human Rights (1998). For the latest on the status of the efforts to develop the guidelines mentioned in the text, see Human Rights Council, 2009.

4. See below on the political economy approach to development.

5. Seymour and Pincus (2008) comment, regarding the objections to the human rights approach: 'The fulfilment of economic, social and cultural rights is hard to imagine without the prior achievement of development outcomes such as poverty reduction. But unlike the growth-oriented approach, recognition of these rights does not specify the means through which the rights can be realised. It merely states that [States Parties to the relevant treaties] must do the best they can with the resources available to them.'

6. See Vienna Declaration 1993, para. 5. ('All human rights are universal, indivisible and interdependent and interrelated.')

7. To be fair, the growing recognition of economic and social rights as rights with an equal weight and binding value as civil and political rights, and the growing acceptance of their indivisibility, are working to undermine the basis of such distrust towards the state, but it cannot be totally dismissed.

8. See Cornia, 1998 ('While it is obvious that the state … should not bite off more than it can chew, leaving to the market all activities the state is unable to manage is no guarantee of successful development. Where states are weak, markets also are often weak (i.e. incomplete, missing, thin, asymmetrically informed, etc.')

9. See, for instance, Hartmann and Markusen's (1980) critique of an approach that places class above gender in a hierarchy.

10. See for instance Stiglitz, Sen and Fitoussi, 2009, for a recognition of the existing rift between these two realms in their search for more relevant indicators of social progress.

REFERENCES

Amsden, A.H. (2001) *The Rise of 'the Rest': Challenges to the West from Late-Industrializing Economies*, Oxford University Press, New York.

Bell, D. (1996) 'The East Asian Challenge to Human Rights: Reflections on an East West Dialogue', *Human Rights Quarterly*, vol. 18, no. 3, pp. 651–67.

Binion, G. (1995) 'Human Rights: A Feminist Perspective', *Human Rights Quarterly*, vol. 17, no. 3, pp. 509–26.

CESCR (Committee on Economic, Social and Cultural Rights, Geneva) (1999) *Statement to the Third Ministerial Conference of the World Trade Organization*, E/C.12/1999/9, 26 November.

CESCR (Committee on Economic, Social and Cultural Rights, Geneva) (1990). The Nature of States Parties Obligations (Art. 2, par.1): CESCR General comment 3. Report on the Fifth Session (26 November 1–14 December 1990), Economic and Social Council, Official Records, 1991, Supplement No. 3, UN Doc E/1991/23.

Chan Yau Hoon (2004) 'Revisiting the "Asian Values" Argument Used by Asian Political Leaders and its Validity', Singapore Management University, http://works.bepress.com/changyau_hoon/4 (accessed 28 August 2011).

Chang, Ha-Joon (2002) *Kicking Away the Ladder: Development Strategy in Historical Perspective,* Anthem Press, London.

Commission on Human Rights (1998). Resolution 1998/72.

Cornia, G. A. (1998) 'Convergence on Governance Issues, Dissent on Economic Policies', *IDS Bulletin*, vol. 29, no. 2.

Declaration on the Right to Development (1986). A/RES/41/128. 4 December. 97th plenary meeting, Geneva.

ESCR-Net and Center of Concern (2010) Kuala Lumpur Guidelines for a Human Rights Approach to Economic Policy in Agriculture, www.escr-net.org/actions_more/actions_more_show.htm?doc_id=1431754 (accessed 28 August 2011).

Hartmann, H., and A. Markusen (1980) 'Contemporary Marxist Theory and Practice: A Feminist Critique', *Review of Radical Political Economics* 12, p. 87.

Human Rights Council (2009). 12th Session, *Report of the Secretary-General and the High Commissioner for Human Rights on the Right to Development*, A/HRC/12/29, 23 July, Geneva.

Jones, E. (1993) 'Asia's Fate: A Response to the Singapore School', *The National Interest*, Spring.

Mchangama, J. (2011) *The Right to Property in Global Human Rights Law*, Cato Policy Report, May/June.

Monterrey Consensus (2002), *Report of the International Conference on Financing for Development*, Monterrey, Mexico, 18–22 March, A/CONF.198/11.

Seymour, D., and J. Pincus (2008) 'Human Rights and Economics: The Conceptual Basis for Their Complementarity', *Development Policy Review*, vol. 26, no. 4), pp. 387–405.

Social Watch (2009) *Gender Equity Index 2009: No Progress There Where It Is Needed the Most*, www.socialwatch.org/sites/default/files/GEI2009_NoProgress_eng.pdf.

Stiglitz, J., A. Sen and J.-P. Fitoussi (2009) *The Measurement of Economic Performance and Social Progress Revisited*, www.stiglitz-sen-fitoussi.fr/documents/rapport_anglais.pdf.

Tay, S. and Goh Chien Yen (1999) 'Human Rights Revisited in the Asian Crisis', *Singapore Journal of Asian and Comparative Law* 3, pp. 26–57.

UN General Assembly (2005) *In Larger Freedom: Towards Development, Security and Human Rights for All*, Report of the Secretary General, A/59/2005, UN, New York.

Van Genugten, W., P. Hunt and S. Mathews, (eds) (2003) Tilburg Principles on World Bank, IMF and Human Rights, *World Bank, IMF and Human Rights*, Wolf, Nijmegen.

Vienna Declaration on Human Rights (1993), Vienna, 14–25 June 1993, U.N. Doc./CONF.157/24 (Part I) at 20 (1993).

Weede, E. (2008) 'Human Rights, Limited Government and Capitalism', *Cato Journal*, vol. 28, no. 1.

World Bank (1993) *The East Asian Miracle: Economic Growth and Public Policy*, Oxford University Press, New York.

PART III

Political ecology and climate justice: tackling sustainability and climate change

CHAPTER 5

Climate non-negotiables

ANITA NAYAR

We are witnessing a historic convergence of multiple global crises – financial, food, energy and climate – and vocal aspirations of the majority of citizens around the world who are no longer going to accept these outcomes. This is compounded by wars, increasingly militarized and repressive states, and a continuing lack of political will to fundamentally redress global problems at a global level. While industry and governments acknowledge some of these ongoing and latent crises, they have failed to recognize the interlinkages among them and the unsustainability of the capitalist model of production and consumption that lies at their core. These crises have also been exponentially exacerbated by the last thirty years of neoliberalism, which has progressively weakened the ability of states to meet their social obligations. The resulting grossly skewed distribution of wealth and the destruction of nature have never been more evident to the peoples of developed and developing countries (Wilkinson and Pickett, 2009).

Whether the present situation is characterized as a fundamental crisis of capital overaccumulation with multiple manifestations, or a converging series of structural economic, ecological and social crises, the present state of affairs cannot continue. There is mounting scientific evidence that the earth does have limits. Since the early part of this century the frailties of our planet caused by human activity have become ever more obvious and unsettling as the accumulation of greenhouse gases related to human activity have led to extreme weather and climate events causing, for example, more frequent and intense flooding, blizzards, heatwaves, droughts and wildfires (IPCC, 2011). According to the United Nations Environment Program, 1 in 4 mammalian species, 1 in 8 bird species, 1 in 3 amphibian species, and 70 per cent of all the world's plant species are now endangered (IUCN, 2010). Eminent scientists predict that global warming, along with deforestation, agriculture and urbanization, could drive half of all species on earth to extinction by 2100 (Whitty, 2007). Some 90 per cent of all large fish species have been driven toward extermination. Depleted water tables have become a global problem, and since 1950 the world has lost about one-third of its arable land and soil fertility, mostly in Africa, Asia and Latin America (McKibben, 2010).

Through the combined effects of climate change, overexploitation, pollution and habitat loss, we are near to or are tracking the worst-case scenarios from the Intergovernmental Panel on Climate Change and other predictions. Some impacts are showing up as predicted, but many are faster than anticipated, and many only just starting to accelerate (Nabulivou and Nayar, 2012).

Clearly the earth is tipping off balance and the crisis is escalating rapidly at a rate we cannot even begin to predict. What is known is that over the past two hundred years 20 per cent of the world's population (all in industrialized countries) are responsible for 75–80 per cent of the historical emissions that created the climate crisis, while 75 per cent of the effects of climate change will be felt in poorest countries (Klein, 2009). The poorest people and disproportionately women will suffer most and first from droughts, floods, sea rise, famines, water shortages and disease exposures, as well as related conflicts that will likely ensue.

We seem to be witnessing catastrophic climate change, which is being constructed as inevitable in the news media and elsewhere, alongside one of the most severe tests to capitalism as an economic system, yet we are failing to rise to these twin challenges. While some are in denial and others are taking advantage of the crisis or playing on people's fears, more need to question the very model of development based on the accumulation of capital and material goods with its social and political inequities, and envision sustainable alternatives. We need a shift in consciousness to realize the linkage between ecology and economy, as little if any progress can be achieved without addressing their interconnectedness.

This chapter offers a critical analysis of the main policy responses to global environmental crises, explores arguments for ecological justice, and calls for a recovery of feminist engagement, principles and alternatives.

Market 'fixes'

Although it has been explicitly recognized that historically industrialized countries have created the climate change problem, they have yet to assume the greatest share of responsibility for the development dilemmas that come with it. Instead they continue to deny their historical and current responsibilities and pass the burden of mitigation and adaptation on to developing countries. This is apparent in the substance of inter-governmental discussions, which have not been about decisive changes in patterns of overconsumption and production or long-term structural changes to the unsustainable nature of the neoliberal economic system. Rather, deliberations and negotiations emphasize ways and means to sustain the existing patterns and approaches to continue meeting the global resource needs of the North, while they simultaneously push for technological and market-based 'solutions' where transnational corporations are positioning themselves to take advantage and maximize their profits from the climate crisis.

Instead of finding alternatives to a global economic system with a production structure that depends on endless growth of consumption without regard for sustainability or equity, economists, traders and policymakers are recasting the climate problem into something that markets can handle.

While many now recognize that the Clean Development Mechanism (CDM)[1] adopted with the 1997 Kyoto Protocol is not working, the policy response seems to reinforce the same 'carbon market' to which it is linked. Market-based mechanisms such as carbon trading are being widely proposed, when there is no evidence that markets will actually protect ecosystems. Such schemes are about redistributing carbon emissions through trading, wherein companies or countries can offset their emissions by paying developing countries to store carbon. Simply put, every country gets credits for decreases of emissions and if a developing country is not using its credits an industrialized country can buy these from them and continue emitting the same amount of greenhouse gases. This model essentially privatizes the atmosphere and promotes the right to pollute.

To make matters worse, the financial services sector is now taking advantage of price volatility and uncertainty in the expanding carbon markets, incentivizing the management of risk through hedging services. As a result, the bulk of carbon trading is now taking place in the world of forwards, futures, options and swaps (Lohmann, 2006). This is similar to the speculative demand in agricultural commodities that played a significant part in the global food crisis (Wise and Murphy, 2011; de Schutter, 2010). Yet the global response to these crises does not seem to address the need to regulate speculation in such future markets.

Another scheme that governments are attempting to peg to carbon trading is REDD (Reducing Emissions from Deforestation and Forest Degradation in Developing Countries), which is portrayed as a quick 'fix' because 20 per cent of greenhouse gas emissions come from deforestation. However, in the equating of monoculture tree plantations with 'forests' we are seeing practices like land grabbing for agrifuel plantations or genetically engineered trees that may grow fast but destroy biodiversity and have a negative impact on available land for food production and other livelihood strategies. Further, REDD payments bypass those who cannot prove legal title to the land. It is cause for serious concern when money is poured into forests without attention to fundamental governance questions that take into account the rights of local communities. Plantations promote relationships among often repressive forestry departments, logging companies and traders while cutting out those who live in and around forests. The result is ecologically and socially harmful monoculture plantation projects being passed off as sustainable and economically beneficial.

If, like the CDM, the REDD scheme does not live up to its claim and if trees don't store as much carbon as we thought the net effect will be that global emissions will continue to rise and our commons (air, water, land, forest) will become commodities sold as carbon credits.

Technological 'fixes'

Market and technological 'fixes' to climate change, such as carbon trading, agrofuels, nanotechnology, geoengineering and synthetic biology, are at the centre of intergovernmental deliberations and are part of capitalism's response to the climate, food and fuel crises. The development of these new technologies is an attempt to maintain the structure of the predominant oil-based economy, continuing the pattern of the last generation of technologies that were offered as 'fixes', including the development of fossil carbon and the chemicalization of agriculture.

Yet these technologies, while posited as neutral solutions, are not in fact neutral in their design, implementation or effect due to pre-existing social, economic and political disparities. As a result, the manner in which these technologies are being introduced deplorably violates the precautionary principle, which requires a need to anticipate serious or irreversible harm without waiting for full scientific certainty of the damage.[2]

Capital-intensive and centralized technologies, which are corporate controlled and disrupt intricate ecological balances, are no 'fix' for today's multiple social, economic, ecological and political crises. They are part of the problem, not the source of solutions. When these technologies are placed within the political economy of interrelationships between industry, science, the military and weak government regulation, the resulting technocratic–industrial complex fosters the development of technologies that are likely to increase the existing imbalances between countries, undermine food sovereignty, result in the appropriation of biological resources and livelihoods of peoples, and disrupt the systems of ecological balances for the entire planet (ETC, 2003).

Financing the 'fixes' or fixing the finance

While corporations are well positioned to profit from these crises, industrialized countries have been very reluctant to promise any significant sums of money to finance mitigation and adaptation activities in developing countries. A 2009 UN report estimated the sum for climate financing at close to $US600 billion per year in new public monies, not through private investments, carbon trading or loans (UN–DESA, 2009). This is significantly higher than the $US100 billion recommended by the UN secretary general's High-level Advisory Group on Climate Change Financing, which took its cue from the Copenhagen Accord, a highly controversial political document that was 'taken note of' by parties to the UN Framework Convention on Climate Change (UNFCCC) in 2009. Meanwhile China has proposed that industrialized countries allocate 1.5

per cent of their GDP, while Bolivia has suggested the proportion should be set at 6 per cent, which is equivalent to average military spending worldwide.

Needless to say, so far climate negotiations are in a deadlock on commitments both to financing and to reducing emissions. Regardless of how much money is raised it remains unclear how these funds will be administered. The World Bank is positioning itself to become the 'environment bank' with a dual mandate on climate and development, continuing to disburse mostly loans, not grants, with conditionalities attached. The Bank has been given temporary control over the new Green Climate Fund established at the 2010 UNFCCC Conference held in Cancún, and many bilateral donors are entrusting their monies to various World Bank Climate Funds. This is alarming, given that these funds are completely at odds with the Bank's continued commitment to fossil fuel funding and failure to make a meaningful shift in its energy portfolio towards clean, renewable energy options (Macan-Markar, 2011).

Green or greed economy

All of the above plays into the United Nations Environment Programme's 'green economy' initiative – a centrepiece in the twenty-year review of the 1992 Earth Summit (Rio+20). It is based on the idea of 'decoupling' economic growth from increasing carbon emissions and rethinking traditional measures of wealth, prosperity and well-being (UNEP, 2011). In principle it sounds great, but as it is currently framed it prioritizes economic growth over ecology, essentially undermining sustainable development and the gains made twenty years ago, including the principle of 'common but differentiated responsibilities' and sustainable production and consumption (Dodds and Nayar, 2012).

The UN presented this initiative to corporate leaders at Davos as a path to meeting the Millennium Development Goals without compromising corporate profits. The claim made to Southern governments and civil society is that it will halve the human ecological footprint by 2050, eliminate poverty through green jobs, develop renewable energy, generate income through payment of so called 'ecosystem services', ensure social justice and be an engine of economic growth!

However, a number of South governments are not buying the promise of this framework. At the Latin America and Caribbean regional preparatory meeting towards Rio+20 countries expressed concern that the 'green economy' would lead to increased privatization and commercialization of natural resources like forests, land and water (Godoy, 2011). They were furthermore concerned that it can be used as a conditionality in trade whereby Northern countries can place trade restrictions on goods imported from Southern countries that do not meet 'green economy' standards. Industrialized countries, on the other hand, have embraced the framework with its focus on subsidizing jobs in the renewable energy sector and building so-called green infrastructure, but without any intention to transfer the technology and resources to the South to pursue this.

An additional complication are potential conflicts arising from obligations to international trade agreements, including those that make up the World Trade Organization, and multilateral environment agreements (MEAs) such as the Convention on International Trade of Endangered Species (CITES), the Montreal Protocol on Substances that Deplete the Ozone Layer, and the Basel Convention on the Control of Transboundary Movement of Hazardous Wastes, which has been the subject of negotiation under the WTO Doha Ministerial Declaration's paragraph 31(i). The scope of trade measures, including their flexibility and associated supportive measures, allowed under these MEAs is in question because of the divergence in clarity and flexibility across, at least, these three MEAs (Hoffman, 2003). In addition, Eckersley (2004) points to differences in dispute settlement between the two sets of international agreements. More specifically, the absence of rules exempting MEAs from a trade dispute challenge under the WTO creates an environment that limits the potential of trade instruments for environmental protection (Eckersley, 2004). On the other hand, governments of developing countries will continue to be wary of the use of standards that threaten the future of their development.

Be realistic, demand the impossible

The good news is that progressive social movements worldwide are rejecting their governments' fragmented responses and envisioning development alternatives that protect not only people's human rights but also the health of the planet. Demands for justice are growing louder, from earlier movements calling for environmental justice to more recent alliances for climate justice.

These calls for justice have moved the discourse beyond a scientific or environmental one towards the inequitable use of our commons and the adverse effects this has had on people and the planet. 'Environmental justice', for example, has been used for several decades as a political framework to respond to the disproportionately negative impacts of environmental hazards on marginalized communities, from adverse impacts on women's health, including rising levels of cancer, to political struggles over the targeting of minority communities as the sites for polluting and extractive industries.

The more recent framework of 'climate justice' challenges climate change analysis and policies that are driven by science and instead recognizes that climate change in fact emerged through economic and political systems. It addresses the historical responsibility of industrialized countries that contributed most to the problem to take the greatest responsibility now by not only drastically reducing their own emissions but also assuming the greatest burden of adaptation and mitigation costs. Today countries with the highest cumulative historical emissions from colonization and inequitable industrialization continue to deny their 'climate debt' and pass the burden of mitigation and adaptation on to developing countries (UN–NGLS, 2009).

One of the key demands of 'climate debt' is reparations from the North to the South via financing for adaptation, transfer of appropriate technology, and creating climate space (meaning greenhouse gas allowances) under the principle of 'common but differentiated responsibilities'. But as economies in the North continue to be in turmoil there is less and less public will to support ODA, much less a major climate debt reparations initiative to countries of the South. As the North owns the dominant share of environmentally sound technology patents it has no incentive to relax intellectual property rights to transfer these innovations to countries that would not otherwise be able to afford them. Meaningful financing and technology transfers as a form of economic redress/justice therefore seem unlikely, unless there is a major shift in awareness that the climate crisis is going to be so thoroughly catastrophic that it is in the interest of the North to immediately address it via these means. Whether or not demands for reparations will yield the positive changes that these movements aspire to, the call does provide an important framework for a common understanding of the historic and immediate injustices that created the climate crisis.

Climate debt also encompasses the idea that nature has rights, that people have violated those rights and must undertake legal and other measures to allow for the earth to regenerate. It remains to be seen whether and how the concept of rights should be extended beyond persons to inanimate nature. Further creating a normative frame of rights may translate into a legalistic system of laws resulting in a piecemeal approach to defending smaller territorial battles while climate change continues unimpeded. In the face of massive industry lobbying in the North and deregulation to attract investments in the South, the challenge is how to recover and protect the commons as public goods that are not subject to the excesses of the market.

What remains important, however, is framing climate change as a social justice issue, well beyond passive environmental preservation or simply measuring the 'state of nature' such as the extent of forest cover, the depth of the groundwater table, the number of endangered species, and so on. The struggle continues to further ground this framework and develop the necessary social agreements around different dimensions of the crisis, simultaneously encompassing principles of sustainability, human rights and equity.

Recovering feminist engagement

How are women's movements, especially from the South, engaging with these critical environmental debates of the century?

Feminist activism on ecological issues at a global level has been in something of a hiatus since the peak of engagement in the early 1990s. Prior to the 1992 Earth Summit, the Women's Environment and Development Organization was formed and played a key role in convening the first World Women's Congress for a Healthy Planet in Miami, with 1,500 women from 83 countries. The comprehensive Women's Action Agenda 21

that emerged served as the basis for feminist advocacy in the intergovernmental negotiations.[3] As a result, while the initial UN draft had only two
references to women, the final Agenda 21 contained over 172 references to
and an entire chapter on women.

Development Alternatives with Women for a New Era, a network of
Southern feminist scholar activists, participated actively in this advocacy
process, putting forward analyses on the systemic links between the
crises of debt, food, fuel and water, all leading to a 'crisis in reproduction' (Sen and Grown, 1987). In a series of case studies on the impacts
of environmental degradation on women's and local livelihoods, African
women identified food security and desertification as pressing issues;
Asian women saw poverty, deforestation, loss of biodiversity and natural
disasters as central; Pacific women saw nuclear testing as a primary
threat; and Latin Americans highlighted the increasing absence of clean
air, safe water, sanitation and imbalance of land settlements (Wiltshire,
1992).

DAWN challenged the prevailing myth that population growth is responsible for environmental degradation. This critique of population stabilization demonstrated that wealth inequities – leading to overconsumption
by some and the erosion of livelihoods for others – skewed the distribution
and use of resources. These consumption patterns have a stronger relationship to environmental degradation than population size per se.

In the years following this concerted engagement, women's movements
gained some further advances in the global policy arena, including in
1995 at the Fourth World Conference on Women, where one of the twelve
areas of concern focused on women and the environment, which was
absent from initial drafts of the Beijing Platform for Action. In 1994, at
the International Conference on Population and Development in Cairo,
UN member states concurred with feminists and rejected the notion that
overpopulation was a primary cause of environmental degradation and
instead named unsustainable patterns of consumption and production in
industrialized countries as a major factor. In Cairo feminists succeeded
in shifting the policy discourse from population control towards women's
sexual and reproductive health and rights.

The late 1980s through the 1990s also saw the emergence of several
analytical approaches to gender and the environment that were informed

by local-through-global activism. Ecofeminism was premissed on the notion that patriarchy and the domination of women are closely linked to environmental destruction and the domination of nature (Shiva, 1988). This message was influential in inspiring women all over the world to reflect on these connections and engage in defending environmental resources. However, the dualistic analysis posited by some ecofeminists that women have an inherently close connection to nature, whether based on biology or socially constructed, came under critique from a number of academics and activists.

Alternative perspectives put forward included feminist political ecology (FPE), which was framed by debates around alternatives to the dominant development paradigm that feminists articulated in the 1991 World Women's Congress for a Healthy Planet in Miami and thereafter. FPE drew attention to the structural forces that underpin environmental policies and practices and focused on the gendered differences in interests, knowledge, abilities, power relations over resources and labour, and political struggles on multiple scales from individual to global. Such analyses did not exclusively focus on gender but took an intersectional (alongside race, class, caste, culture and ethnicity) and interrelational (recognizing differences in times, places and social relationships) approach (Rocheleau et al., 1996).

While few activists engaged in gender and environmental issues carry the label 'feminist political ecology', this approach can be seen from the mid-1990s onward in a number of struggles over rights and resources in the context of economic globalization, including for example in mobilizations to resist the privatization of water, extractive industries, and industrial monocultures for food, energy and carbon sequestration.

However, in this millennium, with a convergence of the triple crisis of climate, finance and development, there appears to be less clarity of feminist interventions in global environmental policy debates. Despite women's leadership in community level resistance and sustainability movements, in global policy arenas, including the Rio+20 outcomes, women and gender tend to be 'added and stirred' in uncritically without a wider structural analysis that would take into account the issues raised above (Nayar, 2012).

Feminist principles and alternatives

Drawing on feminist principles, how can we elaborate on the demand for ecological justice towards alternative development policies? The following are seven points of entry from which to begin this conversation around what women's movements need to be mindful of and can advocate for.

We need to be wary of discourse that creates an inevitability of catastrophic climate change, leading to a sense of resignation that the planet is doomed. Most responses to these apocalyptic scenarios seem to offer another extreme based on fear – whether denialism promoted by neo-conservatives; climate manipulation by geoengineering scientists; population control by Malthusian environmentalists; 'salvation' by the religious right; or fascist tendencies to discriminate against women, sexual minorities, migrants and so on. These forces find it more expedient to plead the apocalypse than put into place equitable environment and climate policy.

We need to challenge the inevitability of these apocalyptic scenarios and fear-based responses. We may not have all the answers, but we need to be mindful that one of our challenges is to examine our assumptions of economic growth based on the limitless exploitation of natural resources and envision an alternative economic system that focuses on sustainability in terms of curbing overconsumption/production, underinvestment, excessive pressure on resources and the well-being of current and future generations (Sen et al., 2010). This will entail rewiring social, economic and ecological relations with principles of sustainability, human rights and equity.

First, to this end we can resist market-based mechanisms that privatize the atmosphere. Instead, we must massively scale up public investment in green energy to shift the world from fossil fuels to renewable and other low-emission technologies. A significant increase in government spending may seem like an unrealistic demand in the current global context. However, resources can be raised by imposing taxes on the wealthy 1 per cent of the population that is increasing the target of public protests by the 99 per cent. Such taxation would also begin to redress the dramatically increasing income inequality both within and across countries.

Second, we can challenge techno-fix responses to climate change such as agrofuels and geoengineering (large-scale manipulation of the earth's climate) that some governments are pushing given the failure of climate talks. Corporate science must be held accountable for their actions in these techno-fixes. Public discourse should be an integral part of the process of developing such technologies before making society bear the risks of their experiments. The precautionary principle must guide these activities, that is, proponents need to 'show no harm' until risks to the environment as well as social, cultural and economic impacts have been assessed.

Third, we can challenge extractivist economic policies based on the removal of large volumes of natural resources with high social and environmental impacts and essentially oriented towards global markets. While social and environmental safeguards are necessary in any extractivist undertaking, further transformations are needed towards a post-extractivist development model, based on renewable resource alternatives and socio-ecological justice (Gudynas, 2012).

Fourth, we can recover principles of sustainable development, sustainable livelihoods, and Common But Differentiated Responsibility in the policy discourse. Sustainable development demands that people should be the centre of development concerns and that environment protection is integral to any development process. This entails the eradication of poverty and the elimination of unsustainable production and consumption patterns as agreed to at the 1992 Earth Summit. It is not enough to have greener technologies that produce goods based on unsustainable patterns of consumption. Instead we need to rethink such consumption itself and figure out which goods and services are necessary and produced in a manner that limits the resource costs.

Fifth, we can defend the Multilateral Environmental Agreements (MEAs) and ensure that World Trade Organization (WTO) and bilateral trade agreements do not trump them. Instead of fulfilling its commitments to the MEAs, the North has turned to the WTO to obtain international rules that run counter to MEA principles. This seriously jeopardizes the multilateralism needed to meet the challenge of sustainable development.

Sixth, we can challenge the emergence of neo-Malthusian notions linking 'over'population with the energy, food and climate crises. A small but vocal camp of demographers, environmentalists and development analysts are relating world population projections with environmental ones and predicting a bleak future. They question the capacity of planetary resources to meet people's needs, including whether food production can keep pace with rising populations, citing projections of climate change, chronic water scarcity, less land under cultivation, and so on (Engelman, 2011). Such alarmist arguments do not take into account the considerably slower rate of population growth, with fertility rates close to replacement rates in most of the global South (Hartmann, 2009) or disparities in the distribution of resources and rates of consumption between and within countries or the impact of global commodity markets that are causing food and fuel prices to go haywire. The concern today should be less about the effects of population on the environment than with the impact of climate change on populations, including large-scale displacement, new infectious diseases, poverty and the destruction of ecological commons. What effects will these have on life expectancy, fertility and migration? Policy responses to such questions must be premised on the fact that unsustainable consumption and production in industrialized countries are a major cause of environmental degradation. Any action related to population must prioritize women's sexual and reproductive rights in the context of fulfilling sustainable livelihoods, basic needs (including reproductive health), women's rights, empowerment and political participation (Sen and Nayar, 2012).

Seventh, with the increasing severity of global environmental change there are massive impacts on livelihoods and survival of poor households across the economic South and thus on women's work burdens and rights. In much of the policy response to this women are framed as a 'vulnerable' group. We need to challenge this discourse of women as passive subjects, 'vulnerable' to 'disasters', and reclaim women's pivotal role in the productive economy given their gender-differentiated relationships to ecological systems as producers, workers, care-givers, consumers and conservers.

It is critical to interlink gender, economic and environmental justice. Ecological issues cannot be disassociated from women's rights and we need to continue to develop policies from women's experiences that challenge the unsustainable neoliberal economic system. Solutions to these crises call for radical measures. Feminists can contribute to the formulation of alternatives by building new solidarities across social movements to address these issues with the urgency that they deserve.

NOTES

1. The CDM and Joint Implementation (JI) are the two mechanisms that feed the carbon market. JI enables industrialized countries to carry out projects with other developed countries, while the CDM involves investment in sustainable development projects to reduce emissions in developing countries.
2. Principle 15 of the Rio Declaration states: 'In order to protect the environment, the precautionary approach shall be widely applied by States according to their capabilities. Where there are threats of serious or irreversible damage, lack of full scientific certainty shall not be used as a reason for postponing cost-effective measures to prevent environmental degradation.'
3. Themes included: Democratic Rights, Diversity and Solidarity; Code of Environmental Ethics and Accountability; Women, Militarism and the Environment; Foreign Debt and Trade; Poverty, Land Rights and Food Security; Women's Rights, Population and Health Biodiversity and Biotechnology; Nuclear Power and Alternative Energy; Science and Technology Transfer; Women's Consumer Power; Information and Education.

REFERENCES

de Schutter, O. (2010) 'Food Commodities Speculation and Food Price Crises: Regulation to Reduce the Risks of Price Volatility', Briefing Note 02, September 2010; www2.ohchr.org/english/issues/food.

Dodds, F., and A. Nayar (2012) 'Rio+20: A New Beginning', in *New Perspectives*, UN Environment Programme, Nairobi; www.unep.org/civil-society/Portals/24105/documents/perspectives/environment_papers_discussion_8.pdf.

Eckersley, R. (2004) 'The Big Chill: The WTO and Multilateral Environmental Agreements', *Global Environmental Politics*, vol. 4, no. 2, pp. 24–50.

Engelman, R. (2011) 'The Impact of Ecological Limits on Population Growth', *Guardian*, 14 October; www.guardian.co.uk/environment/2011/oct/14/1.

ETC Communiqué 78 (March/April 2003) *The Strategy for Converging Technologies: The Little BANG Theory*, ETC Group, Ottawa.

Godoy, E. (2011) 'Sustainable Development, Not Green Economy', Inter Press Service, 15 July; http://ipsnews.net/news.asp?idnews=56506.

Gudynas, E. (2012) 'Any Discussion of Development Models Must Simultaneously Discuss Alternatives to Extractive', interview by Nuria del Viso, FUHEM Ecosocial; www.fuhem.es//ecosocial/noticias.aspx?v=9183&n=0.

Hartmann, B. (2009) '10 Reasons Why Population Control Is Not the Solution to Global Warming', *Different Takes*, Winter.

Hoffman, U. (2003). 'Specific Trade Obligations in Multilateral Environmental Agreements and Their Relationship with the Rules of the Multilateral Trading System – a Developing Country Perspective', paper for the Sub-Regional Brainstorming Workshop on the Trade and Environment Issues Contained in Paragraphs 31 and 32 of the WTO Doha Ministerial Declaration; www.unctad.org/trade_env/test1/meetings/bangkok4/MEA-WTO per cent20relationship.pdf

IPCC (Intergovernmental Panel on Climate Change) (2011) *Special Report on Managing the Risks of Extreme Events and Disasters to Advance Climate Change Adaptation*; http://ipcc-wg2.gov/SREX.

IUCN (2010) IUCN Red List of Threatened Species, Version 2010.1; www.iucnredlist.org.

Klein, N. (2009) 'Climate Rage', *Rolling Stone*, 11 November; www.naomiklein.org/articles/2009/11/climate-rage.

Lohman, L. (2006) 'Carbon Trading: A Critical Conversation on Climate Change, Privatisation and Power', *Development Dialogue*, September, Dag Hammarskjold Centre, Uppsala.

McKibben, B. (2010) *Earth: Making a Life on a Tough New Planet*, Henry Holt, New York.

Macan-Markar, M. (2011) 'World Bank under Fire for Role in New Global Green Fund', Inter Press Service, 6 April; http://ipsnews.net/print.asp?idnews=55148.

Nabulivou, N., and A. Nayar (2012) 'Dawn Speaks Truth To Power At Rio+20', www.dawnnet.org/advocacy-cso.php?id=235.

Nayar, A. (2012) 'Normative Frameworks and the Integration of the Three Pillars of Sustainable Development', panel presentation at UN Women Leaders Forum at Rio+20 ahead of the Rio+20 UN Conference on Sustainable Development in Rio de Janeiro, Brazil.

Rocheleau, D., B. Thomas-Slayter and E. Wangari (eds) (1996) *Feminist Political Ecology: Global Perspectives and Local Experiences*, Routledge, London.

Sen, A., J. Stiglitz and J.-P. Fitoussi (2010) 'Report by the Commission on the Measurement of Economic Performance and Social Progress'; www.stiglitz-sen-fitoussi.fr.

Sen, G., and A. Nayar (2012) 'Population, Environment and Human Rights: A Paradigm in the Making', in *Powerful Synergies*, UN Development Programme, New York; www.undp.org/content/dam/undp/library/gender/Gender per cent20and per cent20Environment/Powerful-Synergies.pdf.

Sen, G., and C. Grown (1987) *Development Crises and Alternative Visions: Third World Women's Perspectives*, Monthly Review Press, New York.

Shiva, V. (1988) *Staying Alive: Women, Ecology, and Survival in India*, Kali for Women, New Delhi.

UN–DESA (2009) *The World Economic and Social Survey 2009: Promoting Development, Saving the Planet*, UN Department of Economic and Social Affairs, New York.

UN–NGLS (2009) *Climate Justice for a Changing Planet: A Primer for Policy Makers and NGOs*, UN–NGLS, Geneva.

UNEP (2011) *Towards a Green Economy: Pathways to Sustainable Development and Poverty Eradication*; www.unep.org/greeneconomy.

Whitty, J. (2007) 'By the End of the Century Half of All Species Will Be Extinct. Does That Matter?', *Independent*, 30 April.

Wilkinson, R., and K. Pickett (2009) *The Spirit Level: Why Equality is Better for Everyone*, Penguin, London.

Wiltshire, R. (1992) *Environment and Development: Grassroots Women's Perspective*, DAWN, Barbados.

Wise, T., and S. Murphy (2011) *Resolving the Food Crises: Assessing Global Policy Reforms Since 2007*, Global Development and Environment Institute and Institute for Agricultural Trade Policy, Medford MA.

BOX III.1 **Primitive accumulation revisited**

GITA SEN

One of the most powerful insights that political economy provides for our understanding of the world is the concept of 'primitive accumulation' – the forceful expropriation of resources and wealth and the separation of people from their means of production, consumption and survival. Marx analysed this in depth in the lead-up to the Industrial Revolution in Europe. The making of the industrial working class involved the forcible breaking over centuries of older entitlements to land and other resources, of long-held claims on subsistence, older guarantees of livelihood, and security provided by feudal relations. This was done through creating relations of private property where none existed before, reordering established property relations to the advantage of the wealthy and politically powerful, and rendering large sections of people partially or wholly destitute. It was often the insecurity created by the breaking of older relations that coerced ordinary people to submit to the travails of industrial discipline.

PRIMITIVE ACCUMULATION GOES GLOBAL

As we look at the global economy as it has evolved during the past three decades, it becomes clear that primitive accumulation is not some once-and-for-all, long-forgotten happening buried in the mists of early capitalism. Primitive accumulation recurs every time the resources of a new region of the world are eyed by the greedy, or when a new group of people is seen as a barrier preventing free access to such resources. The colonial period was one such time, when primitive accumulation went global. Today, with the promise of a major biotechnology revolution, and the multinational race to capture and privatize the rich biodiversity that has been the traditional common property of people in many parts of the South, we are seeing primitive accumulation occurring once again on a global scale. Land, seeds, plants, fauna, water are all being privatized by both domestic and multinational firms and prospectors on a scale never before witnessed.

As in previous times, the two main mechanisms through which primitive accumulation occurs are force and debt. Force comes into play if the prospective victim is seen as unlikely to go into debt – if you want her oil, roll in with tanks and depleted uranium bombs, and grab control. But debt is a marvellous mechanism because it usually makes the use of force unnecessary. If countries and people can be bribed, bullied, cajoled or confused into borrowing beyond their means to repay, and if the terms of repayment can be 'managed' so that repayment becomes an ever more distant dream, then countries and people can become like the Red Queen in *Alice in Wonderland* – running harder and harder to stay in the same spot. Their resources, their control over their means of livelihood, the security of their old age, their children's futures, and their ability to make decisions based on their own assessments of their needs and realities all become forfeit to the moneylender.

THE CORROSIVE POWER OF THE MONEYLENDERS

Traditional moneylenders always make sure that they retain control over four things: the size of the initial loan (the larger the better!), the rules of repayment (conditionalities of different kinds), the back-up of economic sanctions, and, if these don't work, physical force. It requires no great feat of imagination to see how remarkably similar is the functioning of the modern-day global moneylenders.

Periods of primitive accumulation are always accompanied by significant increases in wealth and income inequality of the kind we are now witnessing both between and within countries. I do not claim that all of the recent increase in inequality is the result of primitive accumulation. However, take India as an example, a country whose experiments with economic liberalization and privatization over the last decades have been lauded by the economic elite but which has also seen increasing destitution, deaths from starvation, suicides by debt-ridden farmers and traditional artisans, and a growing struggle for control over common property resources, biodiversity and water.

WOMEN TAKE THE BRUNT

Such periods hit hardest at the most vulnerable, and in particular at women who bear primary responsibility for the daily care and survival of families. The double whammy of the gender division of labour on the one hand, and of male bias and violence on the other, becomes particularly acute in such times. As common resources get privatized and commercialized, women's ability to care for families is stretched to breaking point. And their inability to 'manage' often becomes the excuse for violence against them.

Ironically, it is the last three decades that have seen the clearest public articulation and recognition of women's household work (the so-called 'care economy') and its dependence in much of the world on women's access to resources such as water and traditional common lands for food, fodder, fuel, medicines and seeds. There has also been a growing understanding of how gender relations of power not only constrain women's traditional role as 'carers' but also impact harmfully on their own lives and health, their control over childbearing, their ability to experience and express their sexuality, their right to live free of fear and violence. Unfortunately, the same agencies and governments that have helped to promote this understanding often turn a Nelson's eye to the worsening condition of women's livelihoods, and certainly refuse to acknowledge this to be a consequence of policies they espouse. This in turn provides an easy excuse for those countries and organizations that are opposed to the idea of gender equality or women's human rights.

Primitive accumulation has, however, another side that we are also witnessing today. While recognizing the destitution and misery it brings about, it is important not to romanticize the traditional relations that primitive accumulation tears asunder. Feudal and other pre-capitalist relations are often oppressive, coercive, exploitative and violent. While their breaking brings greater insecurity to livelihoods, it also holds forth the promise of newer, more equal relationships. Nowhere in the present time is this more clearly visible than in the transformation of gender, caste and ethnic or race-based relationships. Such changes can be, and often are, difficult, paradoxical and contradictory for women and other traditionally subordinate groups. Addressing the paradoxes honestly and effectively provides the greatest challenge today for organizations wishing to work for a more just and equitable world.

REFERENCES

Francisco, J. (2000) 'Gender Dimensions and Dynamics in International Lobbying on Trade and Development', *DAWN Informs*; www.dawn.org.fj.

Francisco, J., and G. Sen (2000) 'The Asian Crisis: Globalisation and Patriarchy in Symbiosis', *Social Watch* and *DAWN Informs*; www.dawn.org.fj.

Pettifor, A. (ed.) (2003) *Real World Economic Outlook – the Legacy of Globalization: Debt and Deflation*, Palgrave Macmillan, Basingstoke, ch. 13, pp. 130–32.

Sen, G., and S. Corrêa (2000) 'Gender Justice and Economic Justice: Reflections on the Five Year Reviews of the UN Conferences of the 1980s', in S. Corrêa (ed.), *Weighing up Cairo: Evidence from Women in the South*, DAWN, Suva, pp 265–72.

CHAPTER 6

Geoengineering: a gender issue?

DIANA BRONSON

In recent years, feminist scholars have revealed the myriad ways in which the modern scientific enterprise subjugates both women and nature. Within the Western philosophical tradition, nature is in fact conceptualized as female, and modern science articulates an ethic of control and domination over nature.[1] Central to this Enlightenment world-view are a series of binary concepts that emphasize sharp differences rather than similarities, overlaps or ambiguities: mind/body, reason/emotion, public/private, culture/nature, political/personal, male/female. The masculine bias in this mechanistic and dualist world-view was succinctly illustrated in the seventeenth century by Francis Bacon, who sought to extract 'the secrets still locked in nature's bosom'.

The accelerating power of science to affect nature in profound ways at this time of acute ecological crisis, from building artificial life forms from DNA molecules to re-engineering planetary systems and managing solar radiation, makes the questions of gender, nature and technology more urgent than ever. This is an attempt to tease out the links between an extreme area of scientific endeavour – geoengineering – and its relation to the mechanistic and masculinized world-view that dominates industrial civilizations.

There are many ways in which geoengineering discourse is profoundly gendered. Geoengineers tend to emphasize their ability to provoke changes in the climate and minimize the risk involved in such attempts. This raises the question of whether even risk assessment is gendered. Henwood et al. underline 'a longstanding and consistent finding ... that male respondents in quantitative risk perception surveys tend to express lower levels of concern when asked about environmental and technological hazards compared to women. This effect is empirically very robust, appearing across a range of studies asking about different environmental risk issues and using a variety of question sets.[2] Taking this finding seriously would mean ensuring that discussion about the risks of geoengineering technologies should at the very least be gender and geographically representative. This bottom line would completely change the tone of the discussion that has been under way for the past two years.

What is geoengineering?

> Geoengineering is the intentional, large-scale technological manipulation of the Earth's systems by artificially changing oceans, soils, and the atmosphere. Put simply, geoengineering is a technological fix on a planetary scale that can have devastating environmental, economic, and social impacts, particularly in the global South. Geoengineering is most often discussed as a response to climate change, although it has also been used for other purposes historically, including profit making and as part of a military strategy.[3]

The idea of re-engineering the planet used to be the stuff of science fiction. More recently, however, a band of increasingly vocal scientists, venture capitalists, think-tanks and other advocates – overwhelmingly male – is rapidly moving these controversial ideas from the margins to the mainstream. Furthermore, only a few years ago one could read the entire body of scientific literature on geoengineering during a transatlantic flight. Now, parliamentary and congressional hearings are coordinated across the North Atlantic and scientific gatherings where geoengineering is discussed are regularly held. It would now take several trips around the world to read the existing literature.

This essay begins with an overview of the main technologies that are being contemplated and summarizes some problems associated with them. This is followed by a discussion of some of the ways in which geoengineering has been marked by gender, examining elements of how and why it seems to attract a demographically skewed group of people: overwhelmingly white male scientists from industrialized countries.

There is nothing innately masculine about such a conception of technology, and it would be foolish to assert that women are in any way naturally less mechanistic in their relations with the natural world. Whatever gender differences have been found in attitudes towards engineering, science and technology and their relation to nature exist within a social context where gender differences are exaggerated, invented and used to perpetuate inequality. Furthermore, as many feminist scholars have pointed out, gender and technology are co-produced: that is, 'performed and processual in character, rather than given and unchanging and where the mutual sharing of gender and technology is seen as happening simultaneously, in a context of multiple, decentred agencies with no singular line of causation'.[4]

With no reliable empirical evidence on gender differences with regard to views on geoengineering,[5] this is an exploratory attempt to deconstruct geoengineering discourse from a gender perspective and argues that civil society movements – feminist, environmentalist, human rights – will need to intervene on these questions in the coming years. The point is to prevent a self-selected group of narrow scientific experts from the global North from standing in for a real global conversation where different views, experiences and visions of the future can be heard, understood and acted upon. Especially when the control of the global climate is at stake.

From engineering to geoengineering

Engineering is defined in *Webster's English Dictionary* as 'the application of science to the optimum conversion of the resources of nature to the uses of mankind'. Since 'geo' means earth, this optimum conversion implies planetary-scale interventions and risks. Not all people on the planet have a common view of how the resources of nature should be used, nor equal access to them. 'Mankind' in such a context is a loose and intellectually lazy notion, laden with the false universalism of the patriarchal mind. Geoengineering does not benefit 'mankind'. At best, it offers an appearance of a short-term remedy for those who caused the climate crisis and who do not want to pay for it. The majority of humankind has nothing to gain from a high-stakes gamble with Gaia,[6] no reason to trust the institutions likely to be charged with controlling the global thermostat, and, potentially, a great deal to lose.

Geoengineering is a dangerous and expensive distraction when compared to the urgent work that needs to be done on mitigation and adaptation. These technologies, by virtue of being large scale and highly centralized with significant commercial and military applications, are very likely to deliver inequitable outcomes. The illusion of a climate techno-fix just around the corner simply serves as an excuse for industrialized countries to continue avoiding the urgent changes required to reverse the climate's trajectory. Whether one uses as indicators the articles that have been published in both scientific and news media, the politicians who have shown interest, the respectability and solicitation of the scientists involved, or the private sector's involvement, the geoengineering field is rapidly growing and becoming more mainstream in North climate policy circles, particularly over the past two years.[7]

Geoengineering technologies

There are three broad categories of geoengineering strategies currently in research and development in Northern academic settings, funded by both public and private sources. They are solar radiation management involving reflecting sunlight back to space; carbon dioxide removal and sequestration; and intentional weather modification.[8]

MANAGING THE SUN

Solar Radiation Management (SRM) aims to increase the albedo (reflectivity) of the earth by reflecting more sunlight back into outer space, cooling the planet without changing the composition of greenhouse gases in the atmosphere. In other words, SRM technologies address the symptom of global warming without addressing the cause, which is increased concentration of greenhouse gases in the atmosphere. Very often, solar radiation management technologies are invoked as an emergency response measure, a high-risk Plan B rescue package that needs to be ready when a climate crisis hits – for example, a sudden release of methane or a rise in sea level. Examples:

- *Aerosol sulphates in the stratosphere* Pumping aerosol sulphates or other nanoparticles into the stratosphere to block a small percentage of sunlight, lowering the earth's temperature. Most scientists actively involved in the discussion regard this technology as the leading option and it received the most favourable rating in the 2009 landmark study by the Royal Society.[9]

- *Cloud whitening* Making clouds 'whiter' by using unmanned ships to spray seawater into the air. This would increase the clouds' condensation nuclei, reflecting more of the sun's rays back to space. Bill Gates has funded a research project that is developing a nozzle to deliver the sea water to the clouds for this purpose.[10]

- *Space sunshades* Launching trillions of small free-flying spacecraft a million miles above the earth. Made from a reflective mesh of aluminum threads and placed between the earth and the sun, these space mirrors would reflect the sun's rays away from the planet.

- *Albedo enhancement* Increasing the reflectivity of the earth's surface by planting whiter or shinier crops, painting roofs and roads, and covering desert regions with white material.

IMPLICATIONS Solar radiation management – the blocking or reflecting of sunlight – has the potential to cause significant environmental damage. This would include: changing weather patterns and reducing rainfall; disruption of food production; increased atmospheric pollution, negatively affecting health; damage to the ozone layer; altering the colour of our skies; undermining the natural adaptive capacity of species to environmental change; making solar power less effective; worsening ocean acidification by permitting higher CO_2 levels in the atmosphere; and, finally, provoking sudden climatic jumps if ever the technological intervention needed to be stopped.[11]

SRM technologies are primarily developed using computer climate modelling that seeks to simulate how the variables under consideration will react to technological interventions. Modelling is an inexact science and performs poorly on a series of rather critical factors: clouds, regional climate effects and precipitation to name a few.[12] There is currently a debate between scientists as to whether testing SRM is feasible without full-scale deployment. Some scientists argue that any test large enough to discern climatic effects is equivalent to deployment and therefore should never be attempted without international agreement. Others are anxious to move forward with real-world testing and warn against attempts to achieve international consensus on a regulatory framework.[13]

But the fundamental question in SRM of who controls the earth's thermostat remains unanswered. Who will make the decision to deploy when such drastic measures are considered technically feasible? How can the UN adopt rules to prevent dangerous experimentation, sanction any violations and ban attempts at unilateral deployment? In 2010, the Convention on Biological Diversity adopted a moratorium on geoengineering.[14] This was an important first step but it must be legally strengthened and rigorously enforced.

BURYING CARBON DIOXIDE

Carbon Dioxide Removal (CDR) and sequestration technologies take CO_2 out of the atmosphere and attempt to store it somewhere else. The main challenges of the removal part of the equation are cost, quantity and scale. The question of safe storage of carbon dioxide is more challenging, requiring the re-engineering of natural systems such as land, oceans and geological formations. Needless to say, this involves high risk, is hugely expensive and is uncertain in terms of duration. It also implies land use changes that could disrupt agricultural production and destroy rural and coastal livelihoods. Examples:

- *Ocean fertilization* Stimulating the growth of phytoplankton (algae) with iron or nitrogen in order to promote the absorption of CO_2 and its sequestration in the deep sea. While there have already been more than a dozen experiments in ocean fertilization, the Convention on Biological Diversity adopted a de facto moratorium on the practice in 2008. Meanwhile, the London Convention and Protocol debates what constitutes legitimate scientific research.
- *Ocean upwelling or downwelling enhancement* Using giant vertical pipes to bring nutrient-rich waters up to the surface in order to enhance phytoplankton production and the ocean sequestration of CO_2, promoted notably by the company Atmocean (www.atmocean.com).
- *Genetically engineered algae* Genetically engineering algae to cover urban buildings, open ponds or oceans to capture carbon dioxide. This solution is advanced by UK mechanical engineers.[15]

- *Direct air capture or synthetic trees* Extracting CO_2 from ambient air using chemical procedures, converting it to minerals or solids, and burying it in geological formations. Klaus Lackner and David Keith are prominent entrepreneurs in this field whose prospects of market success are not promising. The major challenges are costs and scale.[16]
- *Biochar* Burning huge quantities of biomass through pyrolysis (low oxygen) and burying the concentrated carbon in soil, a proposal backed by the International Biochar Initiative. As a geoengineering technology, biochar would need to be executed on such a large scale that the land, agriculture and food security ramifications would be tremendous.

IMPLICATIONS When deployed on a large scale, these technologies, which all attempt to remove carbon dioxide from the atmosphere after it has been emitted, can cause destruction or intentional modification of complex ecosystems and risk provoking unpredictable side effects. Each proposal has a slightly different set of concerns associated with it, although the duration and the safety of sequestration in land or sea (whether through biological or mechanical means) are common to all of them. Sequestering CO_2 in geological formations, for example, is extremely expensive, energy-intensive and not proven to be safe. Many of these techniques also require unsustainable inputs or land/ocean use changes that would negatively affect poor rural and coastal peoples with relatively sustainable lifestyles. Some of these land-based technologies could exacerbate food insecurity and land grabs, whereas those that rely on marine resources obviously directly intervene in the global commons.

CONTROLLING THE WEATHER

Often weather modification is not included in overviews of geoengineering but this oversight is in fact ahistorical, for the first attempts to modify the climate were experiments in weather control. And while they do not always aim for global changes, but rather seek to provoke regional or local effects, there are many similarities with what is commonly understood as geoengineering and the technologies have many of the same problems. Examples:

- *Cloud seeding for rain* has been used for forty years in more than a dozen countries, both as a military technique to make enemy troop movement difficult and to fight drought. Whether the technology of putting silver iodide into clouds actually works, and if so how, is not well understood. It has often delivered unpredictable results and has never been systematically successful.

- *Hurricane suppression or redirection* is another area under development, with patent claims already pending on technologies. The technology seeks to control the variables that lead to hurricanes, typhoons and other extreme weather events.

IMPLICATIONS Weather modification techniques that tinker with temperature locally and on a short-term basis are practised in dozens of countries. Cloud seeding is increasingly widespread and has been practised in many countries in a desperate attempt to avoid drought. But weather modification technologies have unpredictable and potentially devastating local and regional impacts, including conflict if one country or community is perceived to be 'stealing the rain' from another. James Fleming's *Fixing the Sky* provides a wealth of examples.

What's gender got to do with it?

A feminist perspective on science confronts us with the task of examining the roots, dynamics, and consequences of this interacting network of associations and disjunctions – together constituting what might be called the 'science–gender system'. It leads us to ask how ideologies of gender and science inform each other in their mutual construction.
Evelyn Fox Keller (1985)[17]

It is worthwhile for feminists to look more systematically at the different components of what makes geoengineering such a profoundly masculinist discourse without falling into the old essentialist trap of assuming that men and women actually think differently in some natural capacity. Theories that have tended towards essentialism[18] in characterizing the choices and views of women have rightly been criticized for underestimating/mischaracterizing/ignoring the social, economic and cultural determinants of women's epistemic positions as well as the complex differences that lie between diverse groups of women.

Twelve ways the geoengineering discourse is gendered

Just as we could expect to find sociological differences between the ways men and women of a similar background think about geoengineering, we should expect to find differences among women on this topic, depending on their class, location, access to technology, political views, experience of climate change, and a host of other factors.

The point of this section is to identify points of convergence and co-production between the dominant masculine gender identity and the enterprise of geoengineering. The points of co-production are grouped under three headings: assumptions and context; expression and language; and the political agenda.

ASSUMPTIONS AND CONTEXT

1. Geoengineering is being contemplated from an *epistemic position of privilege.* The key thinkers are receiving funding, prestige, or other benefits including contracts and patents from their contribution to technology development. They enjoy a sense of invulnerability to any ill effects from the technology and their main questions are about efficacy, not about legitimacy, ethics or precaution. Such positioning has also been culturally linked to a world-view that involves trust in institutions and authority, anti-egalitarian attitudes and disinclination to democratic decision-making.[19]

2. The *scientific solipsism,* or the failure to recognize that geoengineering is a discipline (to be generous) that has emerged in a certain geopolitical context: in industrialized countries historically responsible for the climate crisis and, having proved unable to remediate the problem using political means, have taken it upon themselves to find a technological solution. Science does not exist within a bubble and in a context of global inequality; it can be an instrument of domination.

3. Intentionally *controlling or dominating* the earth's climate systems is the express purpose of geoengineering. This is no longer the Baconian or Cartesian subtext that feminists need to decode.[20] Domination is explicit; it is intended; it is named. In this world-view, controlling the earth is possible and desirable, even necessary and exciting. As such, it reflects a durable cultural equation between masculinity and technology.[21]

4. Geoengineering research is characterized by *scientific hubris* and arrogance, with the planet itself reduced to a laboratory, a set of variables open to human manipulation or tinkering for which engineers hold a particular fascination. This blinkers geoengineers from taking a more critical or holistic view, or even understanding why some people oppose these extreme technologies.

EXPRESSION AND LANGUAGE

5. The construction of a *discourse of imminent catastrophe and inevitability* such that, over time, no other option seems realistic or responsible. This is a tactic that Naomi Klein deconstructed in *The Shock Doctrine*; a sort of collective shock therapy, ready to be imposed when the time is right. It only makes sense to geoengineer the planet if deep social change is impossible. Therefore people must be made to believe that it is too late for political or social change, too late for mitigation. Each time a new report on climate tipping points is published, triumphant told-you-so postings populate the geoengineering listservs.

6. The *explicitly masculine sexual metaphors are rampant.* My personal favourite: 'What distinguishes a big ass volcano is not just how much ejaculate it has but where the ejaculate goes' is how the authors of the best-selling *SuperFreakonomics* describe putting sulphates in the stratosphere, a leading SRM technology.[22]

7. The use of *sports metaphors*. Blue and red teams of scientists battle it out for the truth in an adversarial contest where some defend low-risk approaches against others who seek to make them fail.[23] But no one questions the foundational power of science and technology, or the rules by which they operate, or what the critical concept of 'peer review' might leave aside. Viewpoints that operate according to rules based on experience or tradition, or indigenous forms of knowledge – that are less concrete and more abstract – are ignored.

8. *Logos over pathos* The discussion around geoengineering is seen as one that is merely scientific, where rational discourse can prevail over softer ethical, religious, cultural or social objections to the proposition. Not only is the scientific discourse seen as separate from other considerations, it is regarded as superior, more legitimate, and the premiss upon which all other considerations should be based.

9. *Pragmatism* Geoengineering has proved to be a strategic and well-connected field of scientific enquiry with regard to identifying leaders and establishing partnerships. By expanding its influence in academic, corporate and political realms, in a few short years the field of geoengineering has moved from the margins towards the centre of climate-change response. Geoengineers project an image of scientific competence, even precaution, while opponents are characterized as romantic, ignorant, reckless and, worst of all, irresponsible.

10. *Opportunism and instrumentalism* Geoengineers will seize the opportunity – the algae, the clouds, the biomass, or a meeting, a government, a company – and disregard or underplay risks required to achieve their end: proof that we can intentionally manipulate the earth's systems. Imbued with the inflated sense of importance that comes from believing you are literally saving the world from climate catastrophe, geoengineers claim their opponents are the ones actually engaging in risky behaviour. When, for example, the ETC Group raised objections to geoengineering in the Arctic at the Convention on Biological Diversity, Stanford scientist Ken Caldeira claimed they were threatening biodiversity.[24]

11. *Research readiness* There is no geoengineering scheme that is ready for deployment. The call for action is really only a call for more research and development, for theoretical elaboration of technologies that may eventually be needed. This call for more research is all the more appealing since it unites geoengineers across disciplines, borders, economic sectors, technology and political persuasions. More research, therefore, sounds like an eminently reasonable call... unless of course research turns into deployment, as would be the case with testing aerosols in the stratosphere.

12. *The old boys' club* is alive and well. There is a handful of prominent women in the field but it is not unusual to see all-male meetings, all-male publications and all-male conversations. In recent parliamentary hearings held in the UK and the USA, the respective committees each heard from only one woman. All other witnesses who were called were white men from industrialized countries, each advocating more public resources to the field. In one survey of the media coverage of the issue, men provided 97 per cent of all commentary.[25]

The notion of dominating nature, of controlling the earth, itself tradition-ally perceived as female (as mother, as wild, as unpredictable), is deeply rooted in Western philosophical tradition, as many feminist authors have pointed out over the past thirty years. It is filled with the arrogance and hubris that boys are taught from the youngest age. Boys learn to tinker and engineer with tools and train sets, while young girls learn different and equally gendered and skewed roles in the Barbie/homemaking sphere. Sometimes, listening to geoengineers get excited about the potential climate leveraging geoengineering offers, one is reminded of small boys playing with a new set of Lego or video games. They are taught what has been called the existential pleasure of engineering, or the 'sensual absorp-tion, spiritual connection, emotional comfort, and aesthetic pleasures to be found in engineers' intimacy with technical artifacts'.[26] Except that tinkering in the computer-modelled world of climate engineering is much more dangerous than normal engineering pursuits.

Geoengineering governance

The international community is only beginning to come to grips with how to govern this controversial set of technologies, with heated debates under way in a number of international organizations:

- The 193-member Convention on Biological Diversity adopted a de facto moratorium on geoengineering activities at its meeting in Japan in October 2010. This decision is being followed up by a series of con-sultations and reports that will be influential in the years to come in deciding what will and will not be permitted.[27]
- The London Convention and Protocol on Ocean Dumping has also adopted strong statements against commercial ocean fertilization and has worked to define scientifically and legally what would constitute a legitimate scientific experiment. The Protocol could end up being influential in deciding the fate of many ocean-based geoengineering technologies, despite the fact that it has not been widely ratified (only thirty-five states).
- The Inter-governmental Panel on Climate Change (IPCC) is also in-volved in the debate, holding a closed-door experts meeting of all three working groups in Peru on geoengineering in June 2011. Their attempt

to put governance on the agenda of the meeting was contested by a large number of social movements and civil society organizations via an open letter.[28]

• Many other international bodies have the mandate to discuss geoengineering, most notably the Environmental Modification Treaty or ENMOD as well as the UN human rights system, but for a variety of reasons they have not yet been involved.

In the meantime, a small group of mostly male Northern-based scientists have been actively promoting a voluntary standards framework for research, rather than binding international rules. The UK Royal Society has initiated a multi-year project entitled the Solar Radiation Management Governance Initiative (SRMGI), and the Climate Response Fund brought together over 175 scientists in Asilomar, California, in order to establish voluntary research guidelines in 2010. These repeated invitation-only deliberations among a small group of Northern scientists in various luxurious settings have thus far failed to deliver anything of substance to a sceptical public. Women from the global South and indigenous peoples are rarely represented in such gatherings despite tokenistic efforts to improve the optics.

In the coming years there will be many opportunities to discuss how geoengineering should be governed, and whether the framework will be permissive or prohibitive. The scientists and industrialists engaged in the field are beginning to understand that the absence of clear rules will end up hindering their enterprise. They are therefore now trying to engineer that discussion in a way that suits their interests, primarily through the promotion of voluntary codes of conduct on research, established by the researchers themselves and ensuring that the discussion remains about scientific feasibility, not ethics or politics or equity. It is therefore wise for women from the global South, who have so far been completely excluded from the debate, to begin thinking about what a real discussion on geoengineering would look like, and to articulate collectively some demands for how this might go forward. In the meantime, a full test ban should be adopted.

As a conversation starter, ETC Group has argued that the international framework for discussing geoengineering should be:

- International, transparent and accountable, where all the governments of the world can freely participate; open to the scrutiny and participation by civil society organizations, indigenous peoples, women's rights advocates and social movements, especially those most directly affected by climate change; and accountable to UN member states.
- Free from corporate influence where private interests can use their wealth and power to determine favourable outcomes or to promote schemes that serve their interests.
- Respectful of existing international laws, including those protecting peace and security, human rights, biodiversity, national sovereignty, and those prohibiting hostile acts of weather modification.
- Mindful of concomitant crises, especially hunger, poverty, loss of biological diversity, ecosystem destruction and ocean acidification.
- Guided by precautionary principles and cognizant that neither the seriousness of the climate crisis nor a lack of scientific knowledge can be used to justify reckless and dangerous experiments.

But, even as geoengineering threatens to eat up the world's attention and resources, a new paradigm proposing a completely different relationship between humanity and nature, one that recognizes the rights of nature, is emerging. This less dualistic world vision honours our inherent connectivity, diversity and interdependence and requires a new humility towards the natural world of which we are a part. This vision, articulated by the government of Bolivia in international climate negotiations, seeks to end the impunity with which human civilizations have exploited nature's bounty, restoring some semblance of balance and integrity to our relations. And just as tens of thousands of civil society groups from all over the world gathered in Cochabamba, Bolivia, in 2010 to reflect together about this concept and begin drafting a Charter on the Rights of Mother Earth, an international campaign against geoengineering was launched: Hands off Mother Earth, or HOME – Our Home is not a Laboratory. While we should take care not to romanticize or oversimplify this emerging world-view, the emphasis on the social, the rejection of dualism, the deep questioning of our place in the universe, and the impulse to protect our home, Planet Earth, has something familiarly feminist about it.

Rasch, P.J., S. Tilmes, R.P. Turco, A. Robock, L. Oman, C.-C. (Jack) Chen, G.L. Stenchikov and R.R. Garcia (2008) 'An Overview of Geoengineering of Climate Using Stratospheric Sulfate Aerosols', *Phil. Trans. Royal Soc. A*. 366, pp. 4007–37, doi:10.1098/rsta.2008.0131.

Robock, A. (2008) 'Twenty Reasons Why Geoengineering May be a Bad Idea', *Bulletin of the Atomic Scientists*, vol. 64, no. 2, pp. 14–18, 59, doi:10.2968/064002006.

Rocheleau, D., B. Thomas-Slayter and E. Wangari (eds) (1996) *Feminist Political Ecology: Global Perspectives and Local Experiences*, Routledge, London.

Royal Society (2009) 'Geoengineering the Climate: Science, Governance and Uncertainty', RS Policy document 10/09, September, RS1636.

Sen, A., J. Stiglitz and J.-P. Fitoussi (2010) *Report by the Commission on the Measurement of Economic Performance and Social Progress*, www.stiglitz-sen-fitoussi.fr/documents/rapport_anglais.pdf.

Sen, G., and C. Grown (1987) *Development Crises and Alternative Visions: Third World Women's Perspectives*, Monthly Review Press, New York.

Shepherd, J., K. Caldeira, J. Haigh, D. Keith, B. Launder, G. Mace, G. MacKerron, J. Pyle, S. Rayner, C. Redgwell, P.Cox and A. Watson (2009) *Geoengineering the Climate: Science, Governance and Uncertainty*, Royal Society, London.

Shiva, V. (1988) *Staying Alive: Women, Ecology and Development*, Zed Books, London.

UN–DESA (2009) *World Economic and Social Survey 2009: Promoting Development, Saving the Planet*, New York; www.un.org/esa/policy/wess/wess2009files/wess09/wess2009.pdf.

UNEP (2011) *Towards a Green Economy: Pathways to Sustainable and Poverty Eradication (a Synthesis for Policy Makers*, www.unep.org/greeneconomy/portals/88/documents/ger/GER_synthesis_en.pdf.

Wilkinson, R., and K. Pickett (2009) *The Spirit Level: Why Equality is Better for Everyone*, Penguin Books, London.

Wiltshire, R. (1992) *Environment and Development: Grassroots Women's Perspective*, DAWN, Barbados.

Wise, T., and S. Murphy (2011) *Resolving the Food Crises: Assessing Global Policy Reforms since 2007*, Global Development and Environment Institute and Institute for Agricultural Trade Policy, Medford MA.

BOX III.2 **Green rhetoric in the Asian fiscal stimulus**

MARINA DURANO

Of an estimated US$1.5 trillion in fiscal stimulus commitments by Asia–Pacific governments, 19.9 per cent is classified by Robins et al. (2009) as 'green'. A large amount, however, is accounted for by China's spending on rail construction, which is its contribution to increasing energy efficiency. Support for renewable energy involves a much smaller amount that will be spent by South Korea, Japan and Indonesia.

Not only are the amounts minuscule; these plans are disconnected from the trends in resource material use in the Asia–Pacific region between 1975 and 2005. Estimates in Schandl and West, 2010, show that the Asia–Pacific region overtook the rest of the world in domestic material consumption, which is the estimated volume of material resources consumed by the world, by the turn of the twenty-first century. Construction materials overtook biomass as the biggest share of domestic material extraction measured in million tonnes, signifying the region's transition from an agrarian to an industrial society. The high infrastructure content of fiscal stimulus packages can only contribute to the intensification of construction materials extraction by the region.

Technological improvements are unlikely to slow down resource consumption. Resource efficiency trends indicate that as the world entered the twenty-first century, efficiency improvements through technological development declined rather than improved. It can even be argued that between 1985 and 2005 technology contributed to an increase in domestic material consumption (Schandl and West, 2010). Environmentalists looking specifically at technological efficiency and its relationship with economic growth insist on differentiating between 'relative decoupling' and 'absolute decoupling'. With relative decoupling, resource use and environmental impact will not rise as fast as GDP. Absolute decoupling is said to take place when resource use and environmental impact declines as GDP rises (Tienhaara, 2010).

If Northern deindustrialization and the consequent outsourcing through international production networks have resulted in the dumping of less efficient and obsolete production technology in developing countries, then additional policy measures are needed beyond the reliance on improving technological efficiency for resource use. Improvements in product standards are needed to secure not only environmental protection but also consumer safety. In addition, however, these standards must also be able to regulate the dumping of waste and polluting matter on developing countries on the grounds that these countries have 'comparative advantage' in 'waste management'. Moreover, the principle of 'special and differential treatment' in trade policies allows for a matching of production processes to a country's stage of development. This approach helps to avoid 'protectionist' stances that limit market access of developing countries – especially the small and medium-scale producers within them – due to an inability to keep up with new environmental regulations in export markets. Higher regulatory standards often imply higher capital requirements that developing countries simply do not have or will take time to accumulate.

The fiscal stimulus plans are unable to demonstrate either relative or absolute decoupling. Instead, there is an unrealistic reliance on technological improvements in the energy efficiency of consumer items such as home appliances, cars, as well as buildings (Tienhaara, 2010) given recent trends mentioned above. In the face of declines in resource use efficiency, the fiscal stimulus packages ignore the problem that the rate of growth of technological innovation is unlikely to be able to outstrip the rate of growth of economic activity. And to the extent that technological innovations bring down the cost of production, which is passed on as lower consumer prices, demand for these items will increase, contributing instead to resource-use intensification. Furthermore, the focus on energy efficiency has also marginalized proposals to reorient consumption away from overaccumulation towards less commodified lifestyles (Tienhaara, 2010). Consumption patterns, for example, need to move away from a tendency to use goods as markers of social status that, in turn, can contribute to a reduction in social inequality (Wilkinson and Pickett, 2009).

Clearly, fiscal stimulus plans will not be the vehicle for changes in consumption patterns, especially when these fiscal policies are motivated by a need to push up aggregate demand to mitigate the effects of economic recession. Declaring portions of the fiscal stimulus as green demands a demonstration that the stimulus can fulfil two roles, one of increasing demand and the other of reducing resource use. The contradiction is built in. And the green rhetoric becomes empty rhetoric.

REFERENCES

Khatiwada, S. (2009) 'Stimulus Packages to Counter Global Economic Crisis: A Review', Discussion Paper DP/196/2009, International Institute for Labour Studies, Geneva.
Robins, N., R. Clover and C. Singh (2009) 'Building a Green Recovery: Governments Allocate USD470bn and Counting...', HSBC Global Research Climate Change, London, May.
Schandl, H., and J. West (2010) 'Resource Use and Resource Efficiency in the Asia–Pacific Region', Global Environmental Change 20, pp. 636–47.
Tienhaara, K. (2010) 'A Tale of Two Crises: What the Global Financial Crisis Means for the Global Environmental Crisis', Environmental Policy and Governance 20, pp. 197–208.
Wilkinson, R., and K. Pickett (2009) The Spirit Level: Why Equality is Better for Everyone, Penguin Books, London.

CHAPTER 7

Land grabs, food security and climate justice: a focus on sub-Saharan Africa

ZO RANDRIAMARO

Competition for resources has led to aggressive land-grabbing operations in the African continent, either for speculative purposes or for securing food in land-scarce, capital-rich economies, spurred to a large extent by the convergence of energy, climate and food crises. The key driver of the scramble for land in African countries derives from the structural flaws in the global food system, whereby the vast majority of the billion people who suffer from hunger are food producers lacking decent livelihoods. Many of the land deals have been done in sub-Saharan Africa (SSA), where some 239 million people – one in every three – go hungry every day (FAO, 2008). The consequences for the food security of local inhabitants, especially women, and for ecological balance pose serious challenges for the handling of risks and vulnerability. While the urban and rural poor, who have to spend up to four-fifths of their income on food, are the most affected by hunger and food insecurity, women in poor net-food-importing countries bear the brunt of the impacts of hunger and food insecurity because of their ascribed gender roles as food providers and managers of food security at the household and community levels.

Linking hunger, food security and social reproduction from a feminist perspective

Agriculture is the mainstay of 60 per cent of the population, and provides 50 per cent of total exports and 20 per cent of continental GDP in SSA countries. The agricultural sector is dominated by small-scale farmers, with women making up at least 75 per cent of agricultural workers and accounting for some 70 per cent of food production, especially in the subsistence subsector. Despite this, food security in developing countries continues to be a challenge, aggravated by the combined effects of several factors. The most visible among these factors is the global food price crisis in 2007–08, which has increased the number of people in extreme poverty from 130 to 150 million (World Bank, 2009) and driven 115 million people into chronic hunger (FAO, 2009), mostly in the Low Income Food Deficit Countries (LIFDCs). According to a recent assessment, 'the proportion of people who suffer from hunger in the total population remains highest in sub-Saharan Africa (FAO, 2008). Most SSA countries are also net food importers (NFIDCs) depending heavily on imports from the international food markets to meet the needs of their peoples.

The Declaration of the 2009 World Summit on Food Security held in Rome one year after the global food crisis expresses concern about the inability of FAO member states to meet the commitments made during the previous World Summits on Food Security in 1996 and 2005 and the targets of the MDG 1 to halve the number of people living in hunger by 2015. It underlines that 'climate change poses additional severe risks to food security and the agriculture sector. Its expected impact is particularly fraught with danger for smallholder farmers in developing countries, notably the Least Developed Countries (LDCs), and for already vulnerable populations' (FAO, 2009: 2). This Declaration also states that 'the effects of longstanding underinvestment in food security, agriculture and rural development' (FAO, 2009: 1) are part of the underlying causes.

From a feminist perspective, it is important to take into account the gender dimensions of the causes and impacts of food insecurity and hunger, especially the distinct gender-based differences among the social groups that are the most affected. As Amartya Sen argues, 'this implies the need to view the food problem as a relation between people and food in terms of a network of entitlement relations' (Sen and Drèze, 1999: 159), and how these entitlement relations are shaped by patriarchal norms and practices, social inequalities, as well as inequitable global food and economic systems involving different agents with varying entitlements, as further discussed hereafter with a focus on the case of sub-Saharan Africa. A report submitted by the Special Rapporteur on the right to food, Olivier de Schutter, to the Human Rights Council, highlights five obstacles faced by women. The reality is that even before the recent food crisis, according to the FAO

(Pinstrup-Anderson 2007), women made up 60 per cent of the chronically hungry in spite of their central role in food production.

Most importantly, a feminist analysis of the causes and impacts of this situation should be contextualized in the political economy of the LIFDCs and net food-importing countries, and examine how food security and hunger are linked with social reproduction and care in the context of climate change.

Inadequate and inequitable responses to hunger and food insecurity

Hunger and food insecurity do not happen in a vacuum, but in a global food system which is an integral part of the global economic system, and which involves many players with different interests and unequal political and economic power – from smallholder farms and households to consumers in urban and rural areas, to various intermediaries, to governments and global corporations – as well as rules and institutions. Since the last major food crisis of the 1970s, the political economy of the global food system is characterized by increased corporate control over this system, which has gone hand in hand with an increase in the number of hungry from around 415 million in 1990 to 862 million at present (FAO, 2008).

This food system is characterized by (i) the growing concentration of a handful of firms in agribusiness, which enables these powerful players to affect prices, reduce competition and set standards within the agricultural and food sectors (Murphy, 2006; Vorley, 2003); (ii) the organization of a 'free global market' by these big players with the support of the power-holders in global governance; and (iii) the expanding use of science, technology and information, as well as laws, rules and regulations to control the risks faced by the different players and to protect their interests.

Underpinning this food system are the inequities in the existing global economic system and the organization of production and value chains at the global level, whereby most SSA countries are contained in the production of (non-food) primary commodities and the low-value-added end of global value chains, and are heavily dependent on food imports, especially cereals. These enduring inequities are combined with distorted trade policies that have continally subjected many SSA countries to import surges and price instability (HLTF, 2008).

At regional and country levels, as part of market-based reforms under structural adjustment programmes and agricultural trade liberalization under the WTO Agreement on Agriculture, the African countries concerned have applied reform measures that had negative impacts on food security and poor smallholders, such as the dismantling of marketing boards; the removal of guaranteed prices for farmers' products, along with agricultural subsidies and support; and the reduction of tariffs on food products (Khor, 2008; ActionAid, 2008). Because they overlooked women's unpaid work for social reproduction as well as the gender differences in constraints and opportunities between men and women in trade, what benefits these reforms had have mainly gone to men and have considerably hindered women's productive capacity and productivity (Randriamaro, 2006).

Trade reforms have made SSA countries particularly vulnerable to surges in food imports that are often subsidized by exporting developed countries. Compounded by the volatility of food prices, such surges have negatively affected the balance of payments of many LIFDCs and NFIDCs in Africa, where the total cost of food imports has more than doubled between 2000 and 2009 (FAO, 2009). Import surges have also increased food insecurity and devastated the livelihoods of smallholders, as many of them are no longer able to produce foodstuffs for the local markets (South Centre, 2009).

Land reform policy measures in general, in both investor and host countries, have been a determining factor of the land grabs: for instance, climate change mitigation policies and government consumption targets have increased interest in biofuel production in the European Union, while many host countries have implemented land reforms in order to attract foreign direct investment. A recent analysis of these land reforms suggests that these reforms mainly tend to take land away from the poor and to benefit the elite, through privatization and formalization of property rights, which simply amount to 'formalizing existing inequality, restitution without redistribution and other forms of counter reforms' (Borras and Franco, 2010: 116).

Against this backdrop, many African states largely lack the infrastructure and other resources necessary to respond adequately to the challenges of food insecurity, including more frequent and severe weather events. Despite the increased interest in agricultural development by governments, international lenders and foundations in recent years, investment in agriculture is still nowhere near the required level for addressing the needs of the millions of undernourished African people. Since the mid-1980s, the share of official development assistance (ODA) to agriculture in Africa has declined from over 16 per cent to just 4 per cent today (Worldwatch Institute, 2011). According to OECD statistics, during the year of the global food crisis in 2008, only US$1.7 billion was provided to support agricultural projects in Africa. The global economic downturn has made it difficult to raise the more recently pledged funding, and existing funding is hardly reaching poor African farmers.

Underlying the trends described above are persistent gender inequalities that have critical implications for food security, agricultural productivity and growth. While women constitute the large majority of the rural labour force, and dominate the subsistence subsector in most African countries, gender inequalities perpetuate their marginalization in access to productive assets such as land, agricultural inputs, labour, technology, credit, markets, information and decision-making, in spite of their multiple and central roles in food production, food security and natural resources management.

Land grabs and climate change: the scramble for Africa's land

Over the last few years, increased attention has been paid by the media, policymakers and social justice activists to the wave of so-called 'land grabs', whereby governments and corporations in capital-rich but land-scarce countries in both North and South have engaged in large-scale investments in land acquisitions to outsource food and energy in developing countries – including the African continent – more directly than through the global trading system. Together with climate change, this scramble for land runs a serious risk of perpetuating the inequities discussed earlier, and increasing the vulnerability of people in the concerned countries (Daniel, 2011).

While the land grabs show that the global food system is mainly organized for the interests of the most powerful players, the recent global food crisis has heightened the strategic dimensions of food. As noted in a *Financial Times* editorial, 'If food was ever a soft policy issue before, it now rivals oil as a basis of power and economic security' (Financial Times, 2009). Madagascar, Sudan, Ethiopia and Mozambique are among the main recipients of foreign direct investment in land in Africa, with an overall total of more than 803,414 hectares of land allocated to private companies between 2004 and 2009 (Cotula et al., 2009). The land-grabbing phenomenon adds another dimension to the complex setting of land claims in Africa due to the multiplicity of institutions and sources of political authority that underlie negotiations and bargaining over various claims to land use and ownership.

> If legal pluralism and institutional proliferation have confused contemporary claims to land access in Africa, they have also served to promote debate over how authority is acquired and exercised, and by whom. Such debates are a vital, if ambiguous, part of contemporary politics – creating space for negotiation over competing claims to property and power, and the meaning of Africa's history for ordering its political economies in the present. 'Negotiation' has been criticized, with reason, for blurring or even fostering inventions of tradition, or modernity, that legitimize expropriation, deter productive investment, and promote inequality and injustice. If ordinary people lack the means to take their cases to court, or gain the ear of the powerful, negotiations that exclude them are likely to reinforce established authority rather than challenge it. (Berry, 2002: 678)

Land grabs, climate change and food production

Wise and Murphy (2011) point to three areas that demand attention: biofuels expansion, food price volatility and land grabs. Africa is one of the world's continents most vulnerable to the effects of climate change, although its contribution to the problem is minimal, with less than 3.5 per cent of global emissions of CO_2. The historical responsibility of rich developed countries for the environmental damages that affect this continent has justified long-time demands for ecological and economic compensation.

More than 95 per cent of African agriculture is rain-fed, and is already highly vulnerable to climate variability leading to chronic food insecurity in many countries. At present, many rural communities are chronically vulnerable to food scarcity due to extreme weather events, such as extreme heat and irregular rainfall, which are becoming more severe and occurring more often, as already experienced by most African countries. The combination of greater climatic variability with a systematic warming trend is threatening food security and agricultural production. As a result, a decline in maize yields is anticipated in both West and Southern Africa (FAO, 2008). In Eastern Africa, Kenya is just emerging from a prolonged drought that curtailed growth and output of strategic sectors such as agriculture, which accounts for nearly a quarter of its GDP (Karanja, 2010).

With climate change, agriculture will become an even more pivotal sector in the African continent, while improving food security will be absolutely vital for its population, which is projected to double by 2050, to about 2 billion. The majority of poor African people depend heavily on climate-sensitive natural resources for rural incomes, employment and livelihoods. While the combined effects of changing weather patterns could devastate these poor local farmers, they have the least capacity and resources to cope with climate change impacts and to adapt effectively and sustainably. Climate change therefore represents a formidable challenge for the future food security of millions of African people.

Furthermore, the impacts of climate change on land and food production are intertwined with the consequences of development policies and political economy issues, including population pressures. Their combined effects increase land pressure and competition, resulting in greater vulnerability of poor smallholders in the absence of tenure security. Therefore land issues and policies are key considerations in addressing climate change, as its effects are felt not only through greater pressure on supplies of land – in terms of access and capability, land tenure and land use systems – but also through wider issues of governance of land resources and reforms.

In this respect, climate change is an important contributory factor to the host of governance issues at stake. In addition to tenure security, as mentioned earlier, the challenges involve the management of common property resources; land access and redistribution, including in regard to settlement demands from the increasing number of climate refugees and potential land conflicts; land use regulation and environmental protection; as well as the reform and development of effective land institutions (FAO, 2008).

In the context of climate change, the land grabs have gender-differentiated implications and impacts on local people. Chief among these is their loss of access to the resources on which they depend for their livelihoods and food security.

It has also been argued that some of the global initiatives to address climate change, such as the emerging carbon markets, may provide incentives for land acquisitions due to expectations of potential returns from long-term increases in land values on the part of investors. Thus, it has been suggested that carbon markets may be relevant for afforestation projects, including biofuel plantations and the Reduced Emissions from Deforestation and Forest Degradation (REDD) scheme negotiated as part of the post-Kyoto Protocol regime (IIED, 2009).

Women's rights activists have warned, however, that

> REDD+ as currently designed will contribute to a global land grab of communities' and Indigenous Peoples' lands and territories, which will particularly affect women. Industrialized-country governments and corporations will only pay for the preservation of forests if they get rights over the carbon in those forests in return. This will have a particular impact on women as their property rights are less secure. (Gender CC, 2010)

These concerns are justified by the challenges posed by the growing interest in purchasing forest land in developing countries as a means to offset carbon emissions, and in payments to governments to safeguard forest cover. In general, carbon forestry projects present potential threats to the lands and territorial security of social groups with insecure land rights. In particular, the customary ownership of these lands by indigenous and forest-dependent peoples is not recognized by governments, hence the high risk of expropriation through carbon forestry projects (Carruso and Reddy, 2005, cited in FAO, 2008). The risk is heightened by the lack of legal frameworks for carbon forestry and similar projects against deforestation (FAO, 2008).

Moreover, there is the worrisome record of existing carbon offset afforestation projects in countries such as Bolivia and Brazil, where some of these projects have undermined community land rights and participation. In such cases, 'local people were not properly informed, consulted or advised of the real net benefits they could expect, subjected to manipulative contracts and had their own access to land and natural resources curtailed, with some communities becoming indebted through failure to meet their obligations, or even removed from their land' (FAO, 2008: 45).

Land grabs and fuel production

The energy crisis has also increased global demand and financial incentives for biofuels, alongside speculation on agricultural commodities as expectations of rising rates of return in agriculture and land values have risen. In this regard, there had been much discussion in policy circles on the issue of 'available', 'idle' or 'waste' land, which is often presented as the main reason for the conversion of such lands to biofuel production. Subsequently, such concepts were used to justify land allocations to investors (IIED, 2009), even though they 'often reflect an assessment of the *productivity* rather than *existence* of resource uses: these terms are often applied not to unoccupied lands, but to lands used in ways that are not perceived as 'productive' by government' (IIED, 2009: 62).

The growing global demand for biofuels, combined with the high land requirement for their production, increases the pressure on these so-called 'marginal' lands, which represent a crucial part of the livelihoods and food security strategies of poor rural people. In particular, marginal lands provide key subsistence functions for women in many SSA countries, where they are often allocated low-quality lands (Lubbock, 1998; Dey Abbas, 1997, cited in FAO, 2008). For instance, in Burkina Faso 'women tend to be pushed to marginal plots as a consequence of environmental problems affecting the quality of agricultural land' (Saito et al., 1994, cited in FAO, 2008).

Policy responses to lands grabs and climate change: making matters worse?

The main policy responses to land grabs and climate change tend to exacerbate rather than mitigate their negative effects. A case in point is the large-scale production of biofuels in an attempt to switch away from fossil fuels, while addressing concerns about rural development and exports promotion. Most of the land deals involve the production of biofuels, which is among the main objectives of a number of investments in land.

The ongoing policy debate has focused on the pros and cons of biofuels for effective climate change mitigation, their contribution to the recent food price hikes, and their social and environmental impacts (FAO, 2008). The promoters of biofuel production affirm that

> biofuels can be instrumental in bringing an agricultural renaissance that revitalises land use and livelihoods in rural areas. Price signals to small-scale farmers could significantly increase both yields and incomes, securing real, long-term poverty reduction in countries that have a high dependence on agricultural commodities. Large-scale biofuels cultivation could also provide benefits in the form of employment, skills development and secondary industry. (FAO 2008: 6)

The critics of biofuels have underlined that the *sine qua non* condition for the realization of these possibilities is the security of land tenure for the local resource users who depend on land for their livelihoods (FAO, 2008). With respect to the sustainability of production systems, which is key to food security, these critics have also pointed out that investments in land for the production of biofuels are likely to undermine sustainable soil and water management, because they are associated with a short-term mining of soils and water through the cultivation of crops with high water or nutrient demands. Furthermore, feminist activists have called for attention to a number of gendered implications of biofuel production, which are likely to exacerbate ecological imbalances and to undermine food security as well as women's livelihoods and rights in rural areas where land traditionally used by women has been converted to energy crop plantations.

Since women are mostly involved in subsistence production for household consumption, biofuel production can impact household food security negatively. Moreover, both price and income effects resulting from increased global demand for biofuels can have gender-differentiated impacts on food access for net food buyers, urban and rural households. In the longer term, household food security will also be negatively affected by the loss of biodiversity and the likelihood of pest or disease problems associated with monocultural production.

The replacement of local crops with large-scale monocropping for the production of biofuels might lead to increased reliance by farmers on external inputs – with associated gender-related impacts – exposing such farmers to potential market shocks such as rapid increases in the prices of these inputs. More generally, large-scale plantations for the production of liquid biofuels require an intensive use of resources and inputs (water, chemical fertilizers and pesticides) to which poor smallholders in general and women farmers in particular traditionally have limited access. Therefore, richer male farmers are likely to benefit more than women farmers from biofuel production.

Rural women farmers' work burden and time budget can also be negatively affected, as a result of the additional workload resulting from the loss of agricultural land and biodiversity associated with biofuels production, combined with reduction of the time available to them to participate in decision-making processes and income-generating activities. In addition, women's participation in decision-making concerning household agricultural activities may be reduced, as the amount of land that they control declines.

Moreover, many rural women are likely to become agricultural labourers employed by the foreign companies engaged in biofuel production. In spite of the dearth of specific studies and data on the working conditions on energy crop plantations, empirical evidence shows that such companies tend to prefer women workers, who are considered a docile and dependent workforce that they are also able to pay less than their male counterparts (ILO/FAO/IUF, 2007), as already evidenced by the significant number of women workers in high-value-added agricultural exports production, such as the cut flowers industry. Furthermore, the piece rate work arrangements, where workers are paid on the basis of the number of pieces each worker manually cuts, that are commonly applied on biofuel plantations tend to discriminate against women, especially when they are drawn into unpaid work in order to help their worker-husbands meet production targets (Oxfam, 2007).

'Win–win' governance, ecological and gender justice

At a time when many initiatives to address global hunger and food security – such as the Obama administration's Feed the Future programme, the Global Agriculture and Food Security Program (GAFSP), the United Nations World Food Programme (WFP) and the Comprehensive Africa

Agriculture Development Programme (CAADP) among others – have proved their inability to reduce the number of undernourished people, the land-grabbing phenomenon is a cause for major concern.

After having initially referred to the land grabbing as a form of 'neo-colonialism', the head of the FAO now sees the transnational land deals as a means of economic development for poor countries, and this UN agency has developed Voluntary Guidelines for Responsible Governance of Land and Other Natural Resources. In the same vein, the International Fund for Agricultural Development (IFAD) and International Food Policy Research Institute (IFPRI) affirm that if the deals take into account the interests of both parties, including those of smallholder farmers, land acquisitions in poor countries can provide key resources for increasing agricultural productivity, provide jobs, boost export, bring in new technologies and needed infrastructure, and expand livelihood options for local people (Daniel, 2011).

At the continental level, the African Union has also developed a Framework and Guidelines for Land Policies in Africa in collaboration with the UN Economic Commission for Africa and the African Development Bank, while the G8 countries have demonstrated increased interest in promoting private investment in land, notably through the development of a code of conduct for investment that was adopted by the G8 leaders in July 2009.

At the country level, the sensitivity of the issue is such that in the case of Madagascar, policy discussions have focused on land reforms, especially on how to reconcile competing property regimes (individual titling vs community rights). In this regard, the transnational land deals are threatening the much-needed land reforms in the country, in the face of increasing poverty, mounting demographic pressure and resource depletion. Already the land deals have brought about social unrest and political instability, and are poised to increase conflicts over land in the country. For men and women farmers alike, food security and sustainable livelihoods are contingent on the effective implementation of equitable land reforms. Difficulties over the implementation of land reforms are due to the struggle to unpack how customary law, colonial legacies of alienation and the push towards agricultural commercialization are heavily intertwined such that tenure security remains uncertain for many

Africans (Berry, 2002). The stakes are higher for women as they are expected to benefit from the reforms that aim to give them more secure access to land without fear of harassment or eviction.

The growing support for large-scale land investments in policy circles tends to legitimize transnational land deals and to divert attention from the numerous risks and disadvantages facing small farmers – that is, between 70 and 80 per cent of the population in Africa. The predominant 'win–win rhetoric' ignores the history of foreign corporate agribusiness, which shows its negative impacts on rural socio-economic systems and livelihoods, including the 'de-peasantization of agriculture' (Bryceson, 1999, cited in Daniel, 2011) as a result of efforts to make rural areas more conducive to foreign investment.

The 'win–win' approach is based on the assumption that land deals will take into consideration the needs, capabilities and constraints of smallholder farmers, despite the fact that history provides ample evidence to the contrary. Moreover, it has been well established that women are the most affected by such changes, because of their vulnerable position. There is also ample evidence that women do not gain equally with men from any benefits that may come of such land deals, nor from large-scale intensive agriculture.

Daewoo and breadbasket deals

Following the global food crisis, which involved extreme weather events in major food-exporting countries, food security concerns in food-importing investor countries have led to 'breadbasket deals' such as the 99-year leasing of about half of the arable land in Madagascar to the Daewoo company from South Korea, which is the world's third largest importer of corn, with a population of some 50 million.

The protest against the land deal with Daewoo is evidenced by the contribution this dissatisfaction made to the fall of the former president Marc Ravalomanana. As a representative of Madagascar's Farmers Confederation (FEKRITANA) underscored, 'one of the biggest problems for farmers in Madagascar is land ownership, and we think it's unfair for the government to be selling or leasing land to foreigners when local farmers do not have enough land.... Our concern is that first of all the government should facilitate the access to land by local farmers before dealing with foreigners' (Shepard and Mittal, 2009).

There is no significant action at policy level for addressing the deleterious effects of climate change, which affect women disproportionately because of their crucial dependence on land for their livelihoods as well as for their central role in social reproduction. In the case of Madagascar, there is very little awareness that land deals are often done in violation of their right to property and right to food, which require that, at a minimum, land takings in contexts where people depend on land for their food security must be offset by alternative livelihood assets so as to ensure at least the same level of food security.

The overarching issue is that many African countries, including Madagascar, lack the mechanisms to protect the rights, livelihoods and welfare of those directly affected by land acquisitions. In most cases, the land deals in particular and investment agreements in general do not include provisions for including local people in decision-making, which increases the risk of them losing access to land and other resources. Due to pre-existing gender inequalities, rural women are excluded from decision-making on land ownership and have only insecure land rights. As such, they are the most affected by this regulatory failure, and highly vulnerable to dispossession.

The case of the land deal with Daewoo in Madagascar has spurred an ongoing policy debate on the pros and cons of such large-scale foreign investment in land, and the possible solutions. While many civil society organizations have clearly taken a position against the land grabbing, a predominant number of international institutions and policymakers are advocating for the need to turn the land deals into a development opportunity, so that the land grab becomes a 'win-win situation' for both investors and host countries. Chief among these is the World Bank and its affiliates (IFC and FIAS), which provide financial and technical support to investors and governments alike for improving the 'investment climate' in land markets.

With respect to the proposals from civil society, it should be noted that in the case of Madagascar, its mobilization around the land-grab issue has been initiated in the diaspora and remains weak because of the political context. Women's organizations have been particularly disconnected from the debate. Thus it comes as no surprise that their advocacy messages have focused narrowly on the need to ensure that women participate equally with men in land deals and the related outgrower schemes, and that they gain equally with men from the benefits. This points to the urgent need not only to unpack the land deals and their gender dimensions, but also to improve women's understanding of their interlinkages with broader issues of global governance and economic, social and ecological justice.

REFERENCES

ActionAid (2008) *Cereal Offenders: How the G8 Has Contributed to the World Food Crisis and What They Can Do to Stop It*, www.actionaid.org/sites/files/actionaid/hungerfree_cereal_offenders_report-_g8_and_food_crisis_2008.pdf.

Berry, S. (2002) 'Debating the Land Question in Africa', *Comparative Studies in Society and History*, vol. 44, no. 4, pp. 638–88.

Borras, S.M., and J. Franco (2010) 'Towards a Broader View of the Politics of Global Land Grab: Rethinking Land Issues, Reframing Resistance', ICAS Working Paper Series No. 001, Netherlands: Initiatives in Critical Agrarian Studies, Land Deal Politics Initiative and Transnational Institute.

Bryceson, D. (1999) 'African Rural Labour, Income Diversification and Livelihood Approaches: A Long-term Development Perspective', *Review of African Political Economy*, vol. 26, no. 80, pp. 171–89.

Carruso, E., and V.B. Reddy (2005) 'The Clean Development Mechanism: Issues for Adivasi Peoples in India', Forest Peoples Programme, Moreton-in-Marsh.

Cotula, L., S. Vermeulen, R. Leonard and J. Keeley (2009) *Land Grab or Development Opportunity? Agricultural Investment and International Land Deals in Africa*, IIED, FAO and IFAD, London and Rome.

Daniel, S. (2011) 'Land Grabbing and Potential Implications for World Food Security', in M. Behnassi, S.A. Shabbir and J. D'silva (eds), *Sustainable Agricultural Development: Recent Approaches in Resources Management and Environmentally-Balanced Production Enhancement*, Springer, Dordrecht and New York, ch. 2.

Dey Abbas, J. (1997) 'Gender Asymmetries in Intra-household Resource Allocation in Sub-Saharan Africa: Some Policy Implications for Land and Labour Productivity', in L. Haddad, J. Hoddinott and H. Alderman (eds), *Intro-Household Resource Allocation in Developing Countries: Models, Methods and Policy*, Johns Hopkins University Press for IFPRI, Baltimore MD, pp. 249–62.

Drèze J., and A.K. Sen (1989) *Hunger and Public Action*, Oxford University Press, Oxford.

Drèze J., and A.K. Sen (eds) (1990) *The Political Economy of Hunger*, 3 vols, Oxford University Press, Oxford.

FAO (2008) *The State of Food and Agriculture 2008*, Food and Agriculture Organization, Rome.

FAO (2009) *Crop Prospects and Food Situation*, No. 2, April, www.fao.org/docrep/011/ai481e/ai481e00.htm (accessed 25 January 2012).

Financial Times (2009) 'Fix the Land Deals', 29 March, www.ft.com/cms/s/0/96d3f1de-4a22-11de-8e7e-00144feabdco.html#axzz1kRorpndB (accessed 25 January 2012).

GenderCC (2011) 'Position on Women and REDD', www.redd-monitor.org/2011/03/11/on-international-women%E2%80%99s-day-an-invitation-to-sign-the-position-on-women-and-redd (accessed 20 June 2014).

HLTF (2008) *Comprehensive Framework for Action*, UN High Level Task Force on the Global Food Security Crisis (HLTF), New York.

IIED (2009) *International Institute for Environment and Development Strategy 2009–2014*, http://pubs.iied.org/pdfs/G02532.pdf.

ILO/FAO/IUF (2007) 'Agricultural Workers and Their Contribution to Sustainable Agriculture and Rural Development', International Labour Organization, Food and Agriculture Organization, International Union of Food, Agricultural, Hotel, Restaurant, Catering, Tobacco and Allied Workers' Associations, Switzerland.

Karanja, Wambui E. (2010) 'Effects of Climate Change on Women in Africa', *AU Monitor*, 23 April, www.pambazuka.org/aumonitor/comments/2690 (accessed 20 June 2014).

Khor, M. (2008) Trade: Africans Played PivotalRole at Turning Point of WTO Negotiations, *North South Development Monitor (SUNS)*, No. 6531, 5 August.

Lubbock, A. 1998 *Côte d'Ivoire: Securite Alimentaire et Problematique Hommes/Femmes dans La Region de Nord-Est*, International Fund for Agricultural Development, Rome.

Murphy, S. (2006) Concentrated Market Power and Agricultural Trade, in *Ecofair Trade Dialogue*, Heinrich Böll Foundation with Misereor, Berlin.

Oxfam (2007) 'What Agenda Now for Agriculture? A Response to the World Development Report 2008', Oxfam Briefing Note, Oxfam International, Oxford.

Pinstrup-Anderson, P. (2007) 'Still Hungry', *Scientific American*, September, www.gii.ncr.vt.edu/docs/SA.pdf.

Randriamaro, Z. (2006) *Gender and Trade: Overview Report*, Institute of Development Studies, Brighton, www.bridge.ids.ac.uk/reports/CEP-Trade-OR.pdf (accessed 23 February 2014).

Saito, K., H. Mekonnen and K. Spurling (1994) *Raising the Productivity of Women Farmers in Sub-Saharan Africa*, World Bank Discussion Paper 230, World Bank, Washington DC.

Sen, A., and J. Drèze (1999) *The Amartya Sen and Jean Drèze Omnibus*, Oxford University Press, New Delhi.

Shepard, D., and A. Mittal (2009) *The Great Land Grab: Rush for World's Farmland Threatens Food Security for the Poor*, Oakland Institute, Oakland CA.

South Centre (2009) 'The Extent of Agriculture Import Surges in Developing Countries: What Are the Trends?', South Centre Analytical Note, South Centre, Geneva.

United Nations Human Rights Council (2010) 'Report Submitted by the Special Rapporteur on the Right to Food, Olivier De Schutter, to the 16th Session. A/HRC/16/49 (20 December 2010)', UN, New York.

Vorley, B. (2003) *Food, Inc.: Corporate Concentration from Farm to Consumer*, Food Group, London.

Wise, T., and S. Murphy (2011) *Resolving the Food Crises: Assessing Global Policy Reforms Since 2007*, Global Development and Environment Institute and Institute for Agricultural Trade Policy, Medford MA.

World Bank (2009) *Global Economic Prospects: Commodities at the Crossroads*, World Bank, Washington DC.

Worldwatch Institute (2011) *State of the World 2011: Innovations that Nourish the Planet*, Worldwatch Institute, Washington DC.

BOX III.3 African feminist resistance and climate change politics

HIBIST WENDEMU KASSA

Today's generation of young people in Africa were born in a period of intensifying economic crisis. Young women in particular are living in an increasingly hostile world. They have not only had to come to terms with their multilayered identities (gender, ethnicity, sexual orientation and class) but must also confront a world of interlinked and multiple crises. These personal and global issues are not separate. Majorie Mbilinyi has described how African women have been identified by global capital as being potentially important allies as well as sources of resistance to the status quo (Mbilinyi, 2010). In my view, this is made possible because women play an important role in ensuring the stability of the current system through their care work in communities and households. However, it is precisely because women engage the system at the level of securing the survival of their communities that they are also a dynamic source of resistance. In these times of deepening multiple crises, the battle lines have already been drawn.

In 2008, the world was confronted with a global food crisis. According to the World Bank, FAO and the International Food Policy Research Institute (IFPRI) food prices rose by 83 per cent between 2005 and 2008 (181 per cent for wheat) and by 130 per cent between January 2002 and June 2008. The World Bank further states that 12 million people fell below the poverty line as a result of the food price increases (Golay, 2011). Several African countries were faced with food protests as a consequence. In Cameroon, at least twenty people were killed in the food protests of 2008. There were food protests in the Gambia, Senegal, Burkina Faso, Egypt, Algeria, Sierra Leone and Liberia. Women who were severely affected by the food crisis were part of these struggles. We must understand that the protests were not triggered by a fear of starvation, but out of a sense of exploitation (Fraser and Rimas, 2011). In other words, this was the struggle for justice!

Two years later, in Cancún, Mexico, where climate change talks were held in 2010, Africa was betrayed by its own leadership. Melez Zenawi, the Ethiopian prime minister, speaking for the African Union, argued for the discredited Copenhagen Accord to be the basis for negotiations. This betrayal was buttressed by Raila Odinga, prime minister of Kenya, who declared that $100 billion offered by the advanced capitalist states for all developing countries was sufficient. Africa originally demanded $600 billion (Okonjo-Iweala, 2011). The local–global connection goes back to Melez's first invitation to the 2005 G8 Summit in Gleneagles, which came soon after a controversial general election that led to a bloodbath of 190 women and men protesters.

This was not the first or the last betrayal. A few weeks after the talks in Cancún, the Tunisians and Egyptians expressed the bottled-up frustrations of young people, igniting revolutions. The food crisis and high unemployment rates were the triggers for the protests. Young women in these countries have organized and participated in these struggles on the streets, in online social networks and through traditional media outlets. Their issues of concern stem from their daily battles for survival. This time the protests succeeded in regime change.

This is a time which can offer opportunity for genuinely revolutionary political projects to be executed. Processes of struggle ensure that the dream of equality in diversity becomes a possibility. However, this can only occur if women, including young women, boldly own their struggles. Nowhere is such ownership more desperately needed than in Africa. Hope lies in the fact that social movements are already confronting the crises in their many facets and at at many levels. Platforms for dialogue and reflection can ensure that regional perspectives and experiences can be incorporated into building a knowledge base. Critical insights must be translated into less fragmentation within movements and an elimination of the false separation between the global and the local. In addition, it is my hope that the meaningful participation of young women will become integral to activism in Africa. Only through struggle can genuine social transformation occur. As Leon Trotsky observed, 'ideas that enter the mind under fire remain there securely and forever' (Trotsky, 2008).

REFERENCES

Fraser, E. and A. Rimas (2011) 'The Psychology of Food Riots, When Do Price Spikes Lead to Unrest?', Council of Foreign Affairs, 30 January 30, www.foreignaffairs.com/articles/67338/evan-fraser-and-andrew-rimas/the-psychology-of-food-riots.

Golay, C. (2011) 'The Food Crisis and Food Security: Towards a New World Food Order?' Graduate Institute for International Development Studies, Geneva, 22 February, http://poldev.revues.org/145.

Mbilinyi, M. (2010) 'Gender and Class in the Political Economy of Africa', TGNP, Presentation to African Activists School on Global Financial Crisis, Accra, August.

Okonjo-Iweala, N. (2011) Remarks to the African Union Summit, 3 February, available at http://web.worldbank.org/wbsite/external/news/0,,contentMDK:22820130~pagePK:34370~piPK:34424~theSitePK:4607,00.html.

Trotsky, L. (2008) *My Life*, Pathfinder Press, New York.

PART IV

Secularism and biopolitics: confronting fundamentalism and deciphering biopolitics

CHAPTER 8

Negotiating sexual and reproductive health and rights at the UN: a long and winding road

ALEXANDRA GARITA AND FRANÇOISE GIRARD

The twentieth anniversary of the Programme of Action of the International Conference on Population and Development (ICPD), held in Cairo in 1994, and the 2015 deadline set for realizing the UN Millennium Development Goals (MDGs) are rapidly approaching. How should women's health and rights activists, in the global South and in the North, assess the advocacy work undertaken at global level over the years to advance the Cairo agenda? Has the sexual and reproductive health community scored significant victories in these negotiations? Has it suffered losses, or missed key opportunities? And, with 2014–2015 looming, what's next?

Setting out at ICPD and Beijing

It is worth remembering how groundbreaking the paradigm shift from 'population control' to 'reproductive health and rights' achieved in Cairo, and strengthened at the Fourth World Conference on Women in Beijing a year later, truly was. At the ICPD, the brand new concepts of 'reproductive health', 'sexual health' and 'reproductive rights' were defined.[1] It was agreed that reproductive health required an integrated package of health services, from family planning to maternity care and including diagnosis of HIV, and that universal access to reproductive health should be provided no later than 2015. Governments concluded that unsafe abortion constituted a major public health problem and agreed to take (largely unspecified) measures to address it in circumstances where abortion was not against national law.[2] They explicitly recognized the rights of adolescents to reproductive health education, information and care.[3] Gender equality was acknowledged as a crucial determinant of sustainable development and of reproductive health, in addition to being a highly important end in itself.[4] Agreement on any of those subjects would have been nearly unimaginable just five years earlier.

But the ICPD Programme of Action did not stop at reproductive health; it recognized the interrelationships between consumption and production patterns, economic development, access to education, population growth, migration, demographic structure and environmental degradation. In the view of Sen and Corrêa, both gender justice and economic justice were advanced in Cairo.[5] In that sense, the PoA can legitimately be described as the blueprint for the eventual Millennium Development Goals (MDGs).

Five key elements made the ICPD outcomes possible; these are still instructive today.

First, progressive forces laid out the vision and the terms of the debate in Cairo. It was women's organizations from the global South and North, working and debating together over a number of years, that had developed these groundbreaking ideas. Activists were determined to ensure that respect for the reproductive rights of women would be the central concern, in order to end the abuses and coercion associated with 'population policy' focused on targets and quotas for family planning. Approaching women's health from the perspective of human rights – thereby building on the statement of the 1993 Vienna Conference on Human Rights that 'women's rights are human rights' – was essential to achieving Cairo. Activists lobbied their governments intensively to ensure this approach would prevail; several of them were in fact named as members of their official government delegations, which gave them unprecedented access and influence.

Second, by and large the population establishment, demographers, family planning groups and environmental groups from the North came into the negotiations opposing the new paradigm, for fear that it would dilute states' commitment to fertility reduction and population stabilization. Women's health and rights activists understood that they would have to strike an alliance with those constituencies in order to prevail over the Holy See's opposition; moreover, they believed that, if women were given options, and the information and means to decide freely on the number of their children, fertility rates would likely decline. The ICPD Programme of Action thus contains language that seems at times somewhat contradictory, outlining demographic and population stabilization concerns while also affirming the pre-eminence of individuals' and couples' right to decide the number and spacing of their children. The alliance was often uncomfortable and the strains continue to show to this day.

Third, the US government played a leading role in shaping the Cairo agenda and ensuring its adoption through skilful negotiation, outreach and use of its influence. The European Union, while supportive and essential to the eventual success, did not have the capacity to pull off the Programme of Action.

Fourth, the G77 negotiating bloc (all developing countries, sometimes joined by China) chose not to negotiate sexual and reproductive health issues as a bloc. This allowed for a diversity of views among developing countries, and for something more than the lowest common denominator. At the ICPD, the G77 acknowledged that it had initially been set up to address economic justice issues, and that it was not well-suited for addressing social issues such as sexual and reproductive health and rights. In fact, as soon became obvious, the growing diversity and divergence on economic issues *among* G77 members since the bloc's creation in the 1960s as an offshoot of the non-aligned movement also affected its ability and political will to negotiate on economic issues such as debt relief, Overseas Development Assistance (ODA) and fair trade.

And fifth, partly as a result of the above, attempts by the Holy See to forge an 'unholy alliance' with conservative Islamist countries were not yet successful. Adolescent sexuality, rather than abortion or contraception, proved to be the issue of concern to conservative Muslim states. As a result, the Holy See garnered support mainly from certain Catholic countries of Latin America (Argentina, Nicaragua, Guatemala and Honduras). However, the Holy See was able to present itself as champion of the South on economic matters, capitalizing on the non-sexual and reproductive health and rights issues that divided North and South governments in the negotiation, such as the right to development, ODA, trade policy, Structural Adjustment Programmes and the unsustainable patterns of consumption of the North.

Crucially, the ICPD Programme of Action was confirmed in Beijing a year later, proving that what had happened in Cairo was not an aberration.[6] Taking the agenda one step further, paragraph 106k of the Beijing Platform for Action called on governments to consider reviewing laws that punish women who had undergone illegal abortions. On sexuality, paragraph 96 asserted the right of women 'to have control over and decide freely and responsibly on matters related to their sexuality'. In Beijing, the Holy See was initially successful in establishing an alliance with certain conservative Islamist countries, by focusing on women's sexuality, adolescents and gender, rather than solely on abortion and contraception. The Holy See had not anticipated, however, the sophistication of Iran's delegation, with whom progressive states were able to negotiate paragraph 96. With the 1996 presidential elections looming, the US delegation adopted a more discreet profile in Beijing than in Cairo, while EU countries took on a more prominent role. The G77 again chose not to negotiate as a bloc on sexual and reproductive health, with South Africa and the Caribbean playing a leading role in maintaining and advancing the agreements. Once again, the terms of the debate in Beijing were mostly set by progressive forces, notably on the topics of sexual rights, sexual orientation, sexual violence and the human rights of women, with conservatives on the defensive. Nevertheless, the Holy See's surprise attempts to remove the word 'gender' from the document presaged future lines of battles.

Going uphill at ICPD+5 and Beijing+5

Five years later, at ICPD+5 and Beijing+5, the dynamics of the negotiations shifted significantly. The location – the UN headquarters in New York City – determined the content, players and the rules in new and unexpected ways. While the backdrop of the pre-Seattle World Trade Organization negotiations and Financing for Development conference should have dictated a sustained focus on development and trade issues, the prominent role of North American right-wing groups, who could access New York much more easily, caused attention to shift significantly towards sexual and reproductive health issues, relegating economic and other social issues such as migration, sustainable consumption and education to the back burner. This trend has persisted since that time whenever ICPD is up for review, and presents a challenge for the upcoming ICPD+20.

The conservative backlash against ICPD began in earnest at ICPD+5. New York-based diplomats, who negotiate multiple topics in any given month, did not always understand the importance of what had been agreed in Cairo. Technical experts from capitals did not attend in great numbers until the final meetings. Moreover, this being UN headquarters, the G77 began each negotiation speaking as a bloc on all issues, as is its custom in New York, obscuring the progressive views of many developing countries.

At ICPD+5, the G-77 thus sustained itself as a group through the preparatory meetings (PrepComs) and until near the end. Conservative Muslim and Islamist countries worked very closely with the Holy See throughout, notably Egypt, Libya, Sudan, Iran and Pakistan, resulting in a significant hardening of positions. In the last few days of the final negotiations, however, the G77 broke on adolescents and abortion. Peru and Brazil played a leading progressive role in reaching the eventual agreement[7] after many twists and turns. On the issue of abortion, the Holy See even saw, in the last hour, its ally Pakistan suddenly become the broker of paragraph 63, which called on health systems, 'in circumstances where abortion is not against the law', to 'train and equip health-service providers and ... take other measures to ensure that such abortion is safe and accessible. Additional measures should be taken to safeguard women's health.'

ICPD+5 also remedied one of the major defects of the ICPD PoA, namely the absence of time-bound targets and indicators to measure progress towards the ICPD goal of universal access to reproductive health by 2015. The ICPD+5 agreement focused on three targets: contraception, maternal mortality and HIV/AIDS.[8] These would be the direct inspiration for some the targets and indicators for MDGs 5 (achieving maternal health) and 6 (combating HIV and AIDS).[9]

At Beijing+5, the G77 broke much earlier on the entire sexual and reproductive health agenda, with Latin America (except Nicaragua, Honduras and Argentina) and the Caribbean setting up its own bloc on these issues, thereby loosening the hold of the Holy See on the region. Peru and Brazil again played a leading role. However, this was not sufficient to counteract the much more aggressive posture of the Holy See and its allies, who sought to set the terms of the debate early on with a renewed attack on 'gender' and attempts to insert into the text numerous paragraphs on 'the family' and 'motherhood'. Suddenly and unlike in Cairo, Beijing and even at ICPD+5, progressive forces found themselves on the back foot. The result foreshadowed what was to come during the Bush years – no significant new agreements on sexual and reproductive health (not even a repetition of paragraph 63 on abortion just agreed at ICPD+5), although the final document[10] did include groundbreaking new language on sexual violence, notably on combating honour crimes, marital rape and child marriage.

Throughout both negotiations, progressive US leadership on sexual and reproductive health and reproductive rights was once again crucial to fighting conservative attempts to undermine or qualify the previous agreements. The EU was consistently supportive, but, with the addition of new EU members, too often preoccupied with internal negotiations to reach out to other countries. While progressive Southern countries had hoped to obtain more on issues of economic justice in both negotiations, they did not hold reproductive health and rights and gender justice hostage to those agreements, and ultimately chose not to confront the USA and the EU on ODA, trade, unsustainable patterns of consumption and the like.

Running to stay in place during the Bush era

With the advent of the Bush administration in 2001, the balance of power significantly shifted in favour of conservative views on reproductive health (and many other subjects) at the UN, underscoring the crucial role and importance of US leadership up until that point. US government delegations now included UN lobbyists for the ultra-conservative Right to Life Federation and Family Research Council, and even a former adviser to the Holy See. The USA's rejection of multilateralism and efforts to overturn ICPD were bolstered by the continued intensification of conservative Muslim and Islamist positions at global level (notably Iran, Egypt and Sudan), whose governments had no qualms about working closely with the USA to attack sexual and reproductive health and rights.

The UN Special Session on Children, held in 2001–02, saw the first manifestation of this new and powerful alliance between the USA and conservative Islamists determined to scuttle any mention of sexual and reproductive health services and information for adolescents. Moreover, substantial pressure was applied on youth activists, notably via UNICEF, to drop or tone down the 'controversial' issue of sexual and reproductive health, for fear that a final agreement would not be ready in time for the heads of state coming to the Special Session. Youth and women's health activists were not deterred, but all they could achieve was a brief reference reaffirming ICPD and Beijing.[11]

Progressive governments and activists in the North and the South spent the next eight years in a mighty and sometimes surreal battle to prevent a rollback at ICPD+10 and Beijing+10 and in other UN conferences. That these progressive forces prevailed, time and time again, was important. Developing and developed countries that had previously relied on US leadership realized they would have to take a very public stand on reproductive rights and reproductive health services, unsafe abortion, and access by adolescents to information and services. The saving grace of ICPD+10 and Beijing+10 turned out to be the regional processes, attended by implementers and technical staff keenly aware of the content of sexual and reproductive health programmes, and therefore not inclined to agree to trade-offs with other issues. Regional solidarity and pride in the face of blatant attempts by the US delegation to intimidate developing countries played an important role, whether at the UN Economic and Social Commission for Asia–Pacific (ESCAP) or the Economic Commission for Latin America and the Caribbean (ECLAC). In addition, fewer North American right-wing groups made it to the regional venues, and those that did came across as out of place.

As one negotiation led to the next, it became clear to all that it was possible to hold the line and withstand US pressure, even in forums where delegates had not become inured to the hand-to-hand combat of ICPD. That being said, 2001–08 marked a period where it proved nearly impossible to move the reproductive health agenda forward at global level in terms of content, or to have meaningful discussions regarding progress (or lack thereof) in national level implementation. Each negotiation required great efforts merely to avoid a rollback of the existing agreements.

Meanwhile, the disappointing Financing for Development Conference of 2002 focused the attention and energy of key members of the G77 on issues of ODA, debt relief and equitable trade in global negotiations at the UN, leaving them less able to exert positive leadership on the Cairo agenda. In 2004 and 2005, notably, the G77 stayed as a bloc on sexual and reproductive health and rights, largely because there was no leadership in New York to break away. This allowed conservative elements like Egypt to take charge within the G77, reducing the bloc's positions to the lowest common denominator – just reaffirming ICPD and ICPD+5.

Further illustrating the 'running to stay in place' of that period, sexual and reproductive health activists had to devote tremendous energy and resources in the years 2000–2006 merely to restore universal access to reproductive health by 2015 into the MDG framework. The Cairo reproductive health goal was the only one of the signature goals of the great UN conferences of the 1990s to be left out, as such, of the Report (*We the Peoples: The Role of the United Nations in the Twenty-First Century*[12]) and draft Declaration crafted by Secretary General Kofi Annan's office for the 2000 UN Millennium Summit.

The Millennium Summit was prepared behind closed doors in the UN secretary general's office, without PrepComs or the participation or input of civil society and women's organizations. Granted, activists had just finished ICPD+5, were headed into Beijing+5 and did not pay much attention to the Summit and to the prospect that reproductive health could so easily be traded away, even as it was being reaffirmed. Early on in the process in 2000, Kofi Annan's staff decided (encouraged in this by certain conservative elements in the G77 – Sudan, Libya – and the Holy See) that including 'reproductive health' in the draft could derail a wide-ranging Declaration that raised issues dear to the secretary general's heart, such as increased ODA, debt relief, addressing the special needs of Africa, and UN reform. Instead of reaffirming the ICPD commitment to reproductive health, the Declaration instead focused on maternal health and HIV/AIDS, two of its components.[13]

Once the overall goal of ICPD was left out of the 2000 Millennium Declaration, it proved impossible to bring it back into the 2001 Millennium Framework,[14] which outlined the actual MDGs and their targets and indicators. A broad mobilization by the women's movement over the summer of 2001, with the support of concerned World Bank officials, was incapable of reversing the anti-Cairo momentum. The MDG Framework, in the end, picked apart the three targets of ICPD+5, with two of them (on HIV and maternity care) appearing as targets under MDGs 5 and 6. Contraceptive prevalence only featured as an indicator under MDG 6 on HIV and AIDS, malaria and other diseases – an odd placement.

These ongoing factors made it a particular challenge to negotiate a reference to sexual and reproductive health in the Political Declaration of the UN World Summit held in September 2005. The Summit sought to conduct a five-year review of the MDG agenda, as well as enact high-profile changes to the UN system (creation of the Human Rights Council, increased accountability and oversight of UN operations, establishment of a Peacebuilding Commission, streamlining and upgrading of the UN's structure on gender equality and women's empowerment) and tackle hot-button issues such as disarmament and the 'responsibility to protect' civilians in situations of genocide and crimes against humanity. Yet, sustained and intensive lobbying by women's human rights advocates in the summer of 2005 ensured that the ICPD goal was included in the final agreement.[15] This and extensive work with the Millennium Project (to ensure its conclusions made consistent reference to reproductive health as necessary for achieving the MDGs) paved the way for the retrofitting, in 2006, of the ICPD goal of universal access to reproductive health into the MDGs, as target 5b under MDG 5. Six years of persistent advocacy had been needed to achieve this, even after ICPD had already been reaffirmed in two previous Special Sessions of the UN General Assembly. The EU, notably the UK and the Netherlands, played a leading role in ensuring this result. Interestingly, the USA under ambassador John Bolton did not oppose paragraph 57g at the time, perhaps because of the many other battles it was waging over the text of the World Summit Declaration – many of them of its own making.

Finally turning a corner in 2009

Coming out of the Bush years, women's health and rights advocates from North and South, members of the LGBT community, HIV organizations, and reproductive health providers saw the 2009 Commission on Population and Development (CPD), which marked the fifteenth anniversary of ICPD, as a first opportunity to revive and advance previously agreed language on human rights, gender equality, and sexual and reproductive health. They were right.

In a preambular paragraph of the final CPD Resolution, governments expanded on the language of paragraph 96 of the Beijing Platform for Action by recognizing that it applied not only to women but also to men – thereby restoring the original intent of that paragraph as first introduced in Beijing.[16] This text, while not mandating specific action, nevertheless provided an important opening to combat the coercion, discrimination and violence that men – notably men who have sex with men, gay, bisexual and transgender men – also face with respect to their sexuality.

Further, the 2009 CPD Resolution contained the strongest language ever adopted on empowering young people. It reiterated their right to family planning, female and male condoms, sexual and reproductive health services, and 'comprehensive education on human sexuality' that teaches gender equality and human rights, without the usual restrictive qualifiers regarding culture, parental consent or age appropriateness. It also contained unprecedented action commitments by governments on integrating sexual and reproductive health information and services into HIV/AIDS plans and strategies; strengthened initiatives to increase the capacities of adolescent girls and women to protect themselves from HIV, principally through sexual and reproductive health services; and prevention education that promotes gender equality.[17] These were significant in the context of a global AIDS response which had been slow to prioritize actions to reduce girls' and women's vulnerability, to integrate HIV and reproductive health services, and to recognize that 'HIV education' also needs to deal with the underlying drivers of the epidemic such as inequality between men and women and unprotected sex. This paragraph later proved instrumental for the adoption in December 2009 by the UNAIDS Programme Coordinating Board of the Agenda for Accelerated Country Action for Women, Girls, Gender Equality and HIV (2010–14), the operational plan for its Action Framework on the same subject.[18]

Finally, the 2009 CPD Resolution was one of the first intergovernmental negotiations to prioritize sexual and reproductive health in health systems strengthening,[19] a key issue for implementation of global health initiatives at the country level. After several years wherein it had been impossible to reiterate agreements on abortion, this resolution also contains the agreed language from the Key Further Actions of ICPD+5 on access to safe abortion services.[20]

This was the first global negotiation in eight years to advance the language of Cairo and Beijing, similarly to those factors which had made ICPD possible – notably a US government recommitted to women's sexual and reproductive health and rights, skilled feminist activists on the delegations of several countries of the economic South (Uruguay, the USA, Mexico, Brazil, Peru, Zambia and South Africa) and the breaking up of both the G77 and EU blocs to negotiate nationally on sexual and reproductive rights issues. The more progressive members of these blocs (Brazil, Uruguay, Zambia and South Africa on the G77 side, Sweden and Denmark on the EU side) concluded that the only way to achieve a strong outcome was to break free of the more conservative members (Honduras, Egypt and Syria for the G77, and Poland and Malta for the EU).[21] This was an important development for the EU, which had not negotiated separately on these issues since Beijing itself. In subsequent negotiations of the Commission on Population and Development in 2010 and 2011, this phenomenon was amplified, with particular governments or subregional blocs (the Nordics; the Group of Latin America and the Caribbean; the Africa Group) negotiating separately from the G77 and the EU on sexual and reproductive health and rights. The growing influence and assertiveness of certain members of the G77 – notably the BRICs – and ever increasing diversity of interests within the group suggest that it may no longer be able to negotiate as one going forward. As noted earlier, this may play in favour of the sexual and reproductive health and rights agenda over time.

A different path: HIV and AIDS

The reproductive health community has had an often complicated and reluctant relationship with the issue of HIV and AIDS. While the ICPD PoA did recognize the impact of HIV and AIDS on women and adolescents, its main focus was general HIV prevention as part of reproductive health services, in the context of heterosexual relationships. ICPD+5 paid greater attention to the needs of adolescents, but its focus continued to be general HIV prevention, with the only mention of HIV treatment in a paragraph on prevention of vertical transmission of HIV.

During those very same years, the HIV movement was mobilizing to ensure access to universal, affordable life-saving anti-retroviral treatment, and to fight the severe discrimination and abuse experienced by persons living with HIV and by marginalized populations particularly affected by HIV and AIDS in concentrated epidemics, such as sex workers, men who have sex with men, transgender people and injecting drug users. These concerns were not taken on board by the reproductive health community with much alacrity. Conversely, reproductive health and women's health activists did not feel that the HIV movement paid sufficient attention to the increased vulnerability to HIV infection of women and young people in the general population and to the need to ensure that they have the necessary tools to prevent HIV infection, whether through HIV services in reproductive health settings – often their main point of contact with the health system – or through comprehensive sexuality education programmes.

Yet very few women's or reproductive health groups prioritized HIV and AIDS as a sexual and reproductive rights issue, and few of them participated in the 2001 United Nations General Assembly Special Session (UNGASS) on HIV and AIDS. Relatively few activists, it seems, had a foot in both the HIV and reproductive health movements in the global North and South.

The brutal fight reproductive health activists had to wage during the 2000s to protect the Cairo PoA may partly account for their lack of representation at board meetings of the Global Fund to Fight AIDS, TB and Malaria (GFATM), the large multilateral funding mechanism established in 2002. Beginning in 2006, some reproductive health groups chose, instead, to focus their attention on the Programme Coordinating Board (PCB) of UNAIDS, the inter-agency coordinating body in charge of HIV and AIDS in the UN system, which was then negotiating its strategy on the gender-sensitivity of the AIDS response.

Action at the PCB was chosen because UNAIDS provides guidance to countries (both UN country teams as well as national AIDS programmes, ministries of health and Global Fund implementers). This may have been, in retrospect, a less strategic choice, with much less funding at stake, and UN negotiating dynamics making it harder to identify 'win–win' solutions. The arrival of reproductive health groups at the UNAIDS PCB revived memories and concerns in both the HIV and reproductive health movements that the other side was not likely to support their priorities. The eventual UNAIDS Agenda for Accelerated Country Action on Women, Girls, Gender Equality and HIV was adopted in December 2009[22] after a long and bruising struggle about whether it should focus principally on directing HIV programmes and resources to meet the needs of women and girls and protect their human rights (as initially conceived by some women's groups), or also encompass other aspects of gender, such as the needs of men, boys and sexual minorities (as advocated by some HIV activists) *within the same strategy*. The women's groups prevailed, but at the cost of significant tensions and increased distrust between the communities.

By contrast, advancing policy on sexual and reproductive rights proved smoother at the GFATM, perhaps because from the beginning it was decided that there would be two separate but related strategies – one focused on women and girls, approved by the board in November 2008, and the other on sexual orientation and gender identities, adopted in November 2009. While many of its members are the same individuals who represent their governments on the PCB, the board of the GFATM operates largely as a corporate board, with no UN-style negotiations and relatively little governmental posturing in spite of often vehement disagreements. Three NGO representatives (out of twenty voting members) also sit on the board with full voting rights. Right from inception, the Bush administration adopted a largely pragmatic approach to 'controversial' policy matters on the board of the GFATM, and refrained from trying to impose the conditionalities on its GFATM funding that affected its bilateral PEPFAR monies, such as requiring that HIV prevention focus on abstinence-until-marriage or that implementing organizations be required to profess their opposition to prostitution.

Back at the UN, the old, bitter fights on reproductive health, sexuality and adolescent rights broke out again at the 2011 High-Level Meeting on HIV and AIDS in New York, which sought to galvanize political commitment towards achieving universal access to HIV prevention, treatment, care and support. A solid initial draft provided for prevention programmes based on comprehensive sexual and reproductive health services, as well as comprehensive education on human sexuality and promotion and protection of human rights in the AIDS response. By the sixth week of negotiations, it was clear that the Holy See, the Africa Group, the Arab Group (both led by Egypt), Russia (becoming increasingly conservative and vocally opposed to sexual and reproductive health and rights), Caribbean Community (CARICOM) and Iran were determined to remove any language on protecting the human rights of women and other vulnerable groups (men who have sex with men, drug users and sex workers) in the context of HIV, and insisted instead that what was needed was to 'eliminate unethical and unlawful behaviour.'[23] Although they did not secure such stigmatizing language, they did succeed in removing all references to human rights protections for these persons.

Meanwhile, countries with impressive national HIV programmes, such as Brazil and Thailand, chose to focus their energies on securing treatment and funding targets. The resulting language on trade-related intellectual property rights (TRIPS) will be important to enable greater access to HIV treatment for all.[24] Nevertheless, it was disappointing to reproductive health activists that these governments did not also champion prevention language on women's human rights and sexual and reproductive health services within HIV programmes as they would have at the CPD. The Declaration's references to women's and young people's health and rights are clearly insufficient thirty years into the AIDS epidemic, when nearly one-half of all new HIV infections occur among those aged 15–24, primarily young women in sub-Saharan Africa.[25]

Challenges and ways forward

The long and winding road of the ICPD comes to an important intersection in 2014/15, perhaps a crossroads. Important opportunities exist to further advance the sexual and reproductive health and rights agenda in creative and innovative ways, and for mobilizing multiple constituencies to secure implementation at country, regional and international levels.

The ICPD+20 review in particular, which is meant to be 'only' a review of progress and of implementation, must principally involve national and local implementers and advocates, instead of diplomats. The ICPD+10 process demonstrated that those who implement programmes and benefit from them will not easily cave in to pressures to remove crucial concepts and 'sensitive' words from documents, because they know what those concepts and words mean on the ground. If, as is usually the case, a declaration or resolution caps the process, it must reaffirm the ICPD agenda as well as expand it, notably on the areas most lagging behind in terms of funding and government commitment, namely adolescent access to sexual and reproductive health services and comprehensive sexuality education; contraceptive security; safe pregnancy and delivery; integrated HIV and SRH services; and expanding access to safe abortion services.

The UN is also expected to take stock of progress on the eight MDGs and possibly adopt a new post-MDG framework to eradicate poverty and ensure sustainable development. There are signs that the road to 2015 may be less bumpy than that to 2000. In January 2012, UN secretary general Ban Ki-moon released his 'Five-Year Action Agenda' on six major issues, namely sustainable development (including accelerating progress on the MDGs); climate change; human rights; security; countries in transition; and women and young people. Having perhaps drawn lessons from the MDG experience, the secretary general makes two important references to reproductive health in this Agenda:

> Fully implement the global strategy on women and children's health to save tens of millions of lives, including through the provision of reproductive health services to meet unmet global needs (section I.1 on sustainable development and the MDGs)

> Address the needs of the largest generation of young people the world has ever known by deepening the youth focus of existing programmes on employment, entrepreneurship, political inclusion, citizenship and protection of rights, and education, including on reproductive health (section V.4 on women and young people)

Given this early indication of high-level support, UNFPA, as well as the sexual and reproductive health community, feminists, young people and others, have a responsibility to ensure that this language is retained and adequately put forward as the negotiations ensue. In fact, women's health and rights activists have already signified their intention to recast sexual and reproductive health and rights in their proper, broader context within the development, human rights and environmental agendas.[26] A particular focus on ensuring that improvements are made in the overall well-being of human beings, particularly the poor, through policies and programmes that seek to achieve gender equality, health and human rights, is vital for progress towards sustainable development and for achieving the Millennium Development Goals.

The last twenty years have shown, if nothing else, that reproductive rights, gender equality, adolescents and young people, and women's human rights can easily 'disappear' without strong women's participation in political processes, as the 2000 Millennium Summit painfully demonstrated. Advocates should never underestimate the willingness and ability of conservatives of all stripes to make alliances to fight sexual and reproductive health and rights and women's rights, as did the USA, Egypt, Pakistan and the Holy See during the Bush years, or the tendency of even relatively friendly governments to shy away from these issues as too controversial or messy. Reproductive health and women's health activists must therefore never cease to demand full participation rights and access to decision-making venues. Supporting women's human rights activists, particularly younger generations of them, in ways that can help mobilize political commitment to and financial support for the issues that are most often stigmatized and considered by governments as unimportant, namely sexual and reproductive rights, is vital in the coming years. Thankfully, progress towards this has already begun.[27] The lives, health and rights of women, men, girls and boys are in the balance.

NOTES

1. UN, 1994, paras 7.2, 7.3, 7.6.
2. Ibid., para. 8.25.
3. Ibid., para 7.46.
4. Ibid., para 4.1.
5. Sen and Corrêa, 1999.
6. UN, 1995.
7. UN, 1999, document A/S-21/5/Add.1.
8. Regarding contraception, governments agreed to close the 'gap between contraceptive use and the proportion of individuals expressing the desire to space or limit their families' by at least 50 per cent by 2005, 75 per cent by 2010, and 100 per cent by 2050. With respect to maternal mortality, states agreed that countries should use the proportion of births assisted by skilled attendants as a benchmark indicator to measure progress (para 58). 'By 2005, where the maternal mortality rate is very high, at least 40 per cent of all births should be assisted by skilled attendants; by 2010 this figure should be at least 50 per cent and by 2015, at least 60 per cent. All countries should continue their efforts so that globally, by 2005, 80 per cent of all births should be assisted by skilled attendants, by 2010, 85 per cent, and by 2015, 90 per cent' (para 64). Regarding HIV/AIDS, states agreed that young people (15–24 years old) should be given specific attention – by 2005 at least 90 per cent, and by 2010 at least 95 per cent, of young people should have access to the necessary information, education and services. The HIV infection rates in young people should be a benchmark indicator, 'with the goal of ensuring that by 2005 prevalence in this age group is reduced globally, and by 25

percent in the most affected countries, and that by 2010 prevalence in this age group is reduced globally by 25 percent' (para 70).

9. The eight UN Millennium Development Goals are aimed at eradicating extreme poverty by 2015, with a focus on achieving universal primary education, promoting gender equality and empowering women, reducing child mortality, improving maternal health, combating HIV/AIDS, malaria and other diseases, ensuring environmental sustainability, and forging a global partnership for development.
10. UN, 2000a, document A/RES/S-23/3.
11. UN, 2002, document A/S-27/19/Rev.1, para. 37 (3).
12. UN, 2000b.
13. UN, 2000c, document A/RES/55/2.
14. UN, 2001, document A/56/326, Annex.
15. UN, 2005, para 57g.
16. UN, 2009.
17. Ibid., paras 13–19.
18. See UNAIDS, 2009.
19. Commission on Population and Development Resolution E/CN.9/2009/10; OP 9.
20. Ibid.
21. IWHC Analysis of the 2009 Commission on Population and Development. On file at IWHC, New York.
22. UNAIDS, 2009.
23. RESURJ Analysis of the 2011 HLM on HIV/AIDS, 11 June 2011. On file at the International Women's Health Coalition, New York.
24. UN, 2011.
25. UNICEF, 2011.
26. See 'Our Rights, Our Lives: Women Mobilize towards Cairo+20', a rallying call developed in December 2011 by IWHC, DAWN and RESURJ to mobilize the women's health and human rights movements, and particularly young people within them, to secure and advance the Cairo and Beijing goals; www.resurj.org.
27. Ibid.

REFERENCES

Komatsu, R., D. Lee, M. Lusti-Narasimhan, T. Martineau, E. Vinh-Thomas, D. Low Beer and R. Atun (2010) 'Sexual and Reproductive Health Activities in HIV Programmes: Can We Monitor Progress?', JECH Online.

Sen, G. and S. Corrêa (1999) 'Gender Justice and Economic Justice – Reflections on the Five-Year Reviews of the UN Conferences of the 1990s', paper prepared for the United Nations Development Fund for Women (UNIFEM).

IWHC, DAWN and RESURJ (2011) 'Our Rights, Our Lives: Women Mobilize towards Cairo+20', December, www.resurj.org.

UN (United Nations) (1995) *Report of the Fourth World Conference on Women*, document A/Conf. 177/20, UN, New York.

UN (United Nations) (1994) *Report of the International Conference on Population and Development*, document A/Conf. 171/13, UN, New York.

UN (United Nations) (1999) *Report of the Ad Hoc Committee of the Whole of the Twenty-first Special Session of the General Assembly*, July, document A/S-21/5/Add.1, UN, New York.

UN (United Nations) (2001) *Road Map towards the Implementation of the United Nations Millennium Declaration*, September, document A/56/326, Annex.

UN (United Nations) (2000a) *Further Actions and Initiatives to Implement the Beijing Declaration and Platform for Action*, June, document A/RES/S-23/3, UN, New York.

UN (United Nations) (2000b) *We the Peoples: The Role of the United Nations in the Twenty-first Century*, March, secretary general's report, A/54/2000, UN, New York.

UN (United Nations) (2000c) *United Nations Millennium Declaration*, September, document A/RES/55/2, UN, New York.

UN (United Nations) (2002) *A World Fit for Children*, May, document A/S-27/19/Rev.1, UN, New York.

UN (United Nations) (2005) *2005 World Summit Outcome*, A/Res/60/1, October, UN, New York.

UN (United Nations) (2011) UN, *Political Declaration on HIV/AIDS: Intensifying Our Efforts to Eliminate HIV/AIDS* 9 June 2011, A/65/L.77 (http://daccess-dds-ny.un.org/doc/UNDOC/ LTD/N11/367/84/PDF/N1136784.pdf?OpenElement).

UN Commission on Population and Development Resolution (2009) E/CN.9/2009/10; www. un.org/esa/population/cpd/cpd2009/CPD42_Res2009-1.pdf (accessed 14 February 2012).

UNAIDS (2009) *Agenda for Accelerated Country Action for Women, Girls, Gender Equality, and HIV*, Operational Plan for addressing the UNAIDS Action Framework: Addressing Women, Girls, Gender Equality and HIV; www.unaids.org/en/media/unaids/content assets/dataimport/pub/manual/2010/20100226_jc1794_agenda_for_accelerated_ country_action_en.pdf.

UNAIDS PCB (2009) 25th meeting, December, http://data.unaids.org/pub/InformationNote /2009/20091124_25th_pcb_genderoperationalplan_crp19_en.pdf.

UNICEF, *Opportunity in Crisis: Preventing HIV from Early Adolescence to Young Adulthood*, United Nations Children's Fund, Geneva, 2011.

CHAPTER 9

The making of a secular contract

FATOU SOW AND MAGALY PAZELLO

Relationships between religion, culture and politics are extremely complex in the contemporary context. Various actors use them to reshape the social contract between peoples, and between citizens and the state. They often join or confront each other at local, national and international levels. In most contexts, multiple social identities of class, caste, gender, religion, ethnicity and multiple relationships across groupings predicate not just the norms of social interaction, based on power and hierarchies, but also specific rights, responsibilities and obligations that fashion social contracts. Religion and culture appear to be the core elements of various current processes for restructuring and consolidating social and political power.

Considered as a dimension of private life in countries which claim to be secular, religion extends well beyond into public life and politics on a global scale. Religious revival is widespread in many societies and systems of beliefs. The former US president, George W. Bush, withdrew financial support to states and international organizations such as the United Nations Population Fund (UNFPA) because his neoconservative religious beliefs caused him to oppose abortion. Within the European Union (EU), some member states still demand that Christianity should be inscribed as a constitutive dimension of the European identity. Many of these states, if not their people, still express a strong resistance to the entrance of Turkey into the EU, on the grounds that it is a Muslim state, forty years after an undertaking that it might apply to join. Some Muslim states in Northern Nigeria used religion as a political tool in August 2002 when they enforced sharia laws in all courts, regardless of the faith that the plaintiff professed, even though this decision was declared unconstitutional by federal authorities in Abuja.

These are examples of a new relationship profile between religion and politics in a climate of rising radicalization within religious groups. These groups are imbued with a 'mission' to lead society and transform social contracts, based on a very particular view of the sacred. This view often diverges from some of the most basic interpretations of their own religion. They also try to subvert the concept of the state as an entity that in many instances has been formally independent of religion since the nineteenth century. In its place they want to impose a society that is based wholly on religious norms, which they themselves redefine.

Culture is used in parallel with religion to define identity and as a tool to reshape the social contract, as demonstrated significantly in the state of Gujarat in India. This state has a recent history of tension between Hindu and Muslim communities. Although on the surface this may appear to be a case of religious tension fomented by fundamentalist right-wing Hindu groups, known collectively as the Sangh Parivar, there is little of substance in the ideology or programmes of these groups that draws intrinsically from religious beliefs. Instead they base their ideology on particular and often questionable readings of history, cultural origins and nationhood in which Muslim invaders and contemporary Muslim communities are viewed as the other/the enemy. It could be argued that their beliefs are closer to classic fascist values than to religious fundamentalism. In Gujarat, these groups fomented and carefully engineered tensions that came to a head in the anti-Muslim pogrom of March 2002 and thereafter. While the situation varies across India, Gujarat provides useful insights on how right-wing forces can reorder relationships at the micro-level by altering social norms for particular groups of people, in this case the Muslim community.

It is impossible to ignore the revival of such religious and cultural values in any reflection on the potential for a new social contract based on social justice and gender equality. These religious/cultural revivals often contribute to a backlash against new norms for women and gender equality. While secularization of the law has helped the development of women's rights, especially after thirty years of major international conferences (on women, environment, human rights, population, etc.) under the aegis of the United Nations, these achievements continue to be challenged. Ecclesiastical authorities receive instructions from the

Vatican at major international conferences dealing with human rights, just as do mullahs from Iran, Saudi Arabia and Sudan. In India, the unleashing of violence and terror on the Muslim community and the consequent upheavals in their lives have led to a reordering of some of the gender-based contracts concerning men's control over women's lives and women's observance of social codes of dress and behaviour. The coming to power of a government with the dominant Hindu political party in the state of Karnataka has spread such gender-biased norms and practices to southern parts of the country, with the backing of the state and impunity for increasing violence against both Muslim and Christian communities.

The next section addresses the ways in which religion (Christianity, Islam and Hinduism), as well as cultural identity, has contributed to the mapping of a new social contract, especially regarding economic, social, political and reproductive rights, and the imperative for remaking a secular social contract.

Gender and secularism: history of a concept

The reference to secularism raises the question of the nature of relations between political and religious authority. It is no easy matter to define the term 'secularism' itself. The experiences in Europe – of France, Italy, the United Kingdom, Germany and Spain – are all very different from each other, even though the countries share the same Christian culture. The progressive secularization of their political institutions began at different times. But in many countries there are still official relations between church and state, and the preservation of laws inspired by religion. In addition, education and health often remain as privileged areas for the Church, with the support of the state authorities, whether these are regarded as secular or not. Taxpayers in Germany, Spain, Denmark, Finland and Italy still continue to pay taxes imposed by the state but handed over to the Church, usually based on religious/community membership.

French secularization is particularly remarkable, since this is the country that has worked the hardest to separate politics from religion in spite of its very deep Christian roots. The Church was at the heart of political power in monarchical France. It was the principle of sovereignty derived from divine authority that the French Revolution of 1789 wanted to abolish through the execution of Louis XVI and Marie-Antoinette. Napoleon Bonaparte embarked on the process of secularization and a break with the all-powerful monopoly of the Catholic Church. To this end, he signed a Concordat with Pope Pius VII in 1801 that provided for the regulation of religious life in France. This was the start of the movement towards state control, which also included Protestant communities and defined relations with the Christian churches (Catholic and Protestant), together with the rights of the state police. A more official statute was provided in 1808 for the Jewish religion, with the signing of a decree providing for its organization. Various revisions for this included providing greater freedom of movement and of trade that attracted an increasing Jewish population from Europe and North Africa. The law of 1905 ending the concordat system enshrined the break between church and state and established secularism as a political measure. It set up a new political arena where 'the Republican state, as an emanation of the democratic ideal, had as its ambition the replacement of the all-embracing function of the Catholic Church in its temporal capacity' (Bencheikh, 2005: 113). The inclusion of the words 'secular Republic' in the French Constitution dates from 1946, a principle that was adopted later on by Italy and Portugal (1976), Spain (1978), the Netherlands (1983) and Belgium (1993).

This attempt at recognition and regulation was not replicated for Islam, the religion of 'the natives of the colonies', until much later and in a completely different context. The French Council of the Muslim Religion was set up in 2003 to manage religious matters such as the building of mosques, the fixing of the dates of religious festivals, the training of imams, and so on. The many instances of social violence in France and of crises connected with ongoing conflicts in the Middle East, and the attacks of 11 September 2001 against the World Trade Center, influenced the decision to create this organization of the Muslim community, so as to be better able to control its movements and activities. This rapprochement was intended to help the decision to enact a law in March 2004 forbidding the wearing of any ostensible religious symbols or garb in state primary and secondary schools. This particular law was aimed in particular at prohibiting girls from wearing the veil in school.

The situation in some other European countries is more complex since secularism has not been part of their political traditions. The United

Kingdom, Germany and Denmark, for instance, were less concerned with secularism than with the protection of religious liberty. In the latter two countries, there is no formal constitutional separation between religious and political authority.

If secularism attracts so much attention, notwithstanding the different interpretations of what exactly it is, it is because it plays an essential role in current debates on democracy as a universal model of society. In the present situation of conflict between ideologies and religions, Western societies brandish it as a principle of democracy and consider how far it can be applied to countries with other religions, particularly Islam. So, 'are we moving towards a complete desacralization of the life of men organized in society, as many advocate?', in the words of Ghaleb Ben Cheikh, a Muslim theologian and chairman of the World Conference of Religions for Peace, on the occasion of the celebration of the centenary of the law separating church and state in France.

The reply to this perfectly legitimate question remains ambivalent, despite all that is said these days about secularization. Relations between modern states and their religious authorities remain close in varying degrees. This can be seen when one analyses all the controversies between civil society organizations, on the one hand, and states and religious authorities, on the other hand, concerning such sensitive questions as sexual freedom and orientation, contraception, abortion, ways of preventing HIV/AIDS, same-sex parenting, or bioethical subjects such as euthanasia, medically assisted conception, genetic testing, cloning, stem cell research, and so on. All these issues pose 'moral' challenges to peoples' identities, underlining the reciprocal influence of questions about identity and religion. Religion also has an intrinsic geopolitical dimension, as is underlined by Bencheikh (2005: 463). Besides the argument about whether Christian identity ought to be a qualification for membership of the European Union, there is the religious dimension of the Israel–Palestine crisis, which involves Israel proclaimed as a Jewish state in the face of Palestine, in a Middle East that has a Muslim majority. The coming to positions of power within the United States government apparatus of neoconservative groups ('neocons'), eager to support 'good against evil' since the events of 11 September 2001, was also significant in the geopolitical impact of such coalitions. The advent of the Obama administration in the United States has not reduced the growth of right-wing groups such as the Tea Party, whose ideologies include a potent mix of religious fundamentalism, opposition to gender equality and LGBTI rights, along with opposition to taxation and the welfare state.

Secularity does not, as argued above, automatically transform the gendered nature of religions. In the birth of the modern nation-state, religion partially left the public sphere but never left the personal/individual. It remained in the realm of family, communities and religious institutions, which provide social networks in a manner that the liberal secular state has not been able to. Related to that is the critical role religious institutions have played and still play in providing health and education services. Secular Europe continues to subsidize religious associations, schools and Christian missions. Some of its laws, particularly those concerning the family that have a fundamental impact on women's rights, have been of religious inspiration. The position of head of the family given to the man, the indissolubility of marriage as a sacrament, and the rejection of children born outside marriage are all based on patriarchal religious rules that are largely shared by the religions of the book (Judaism, Christianity and Islam).

These ambivalences in regard to the state–religion separation illuminate why conservative religious forces are now challenging the norms in this area. They are doing so because they perceive that transformations taking place in regard to gender and sexuality – through norms and rights – may in the long run transform the gendered and sexualized nature of religion itself. This means that their aim is not just to take over the state for the sake of political power. The takeover of the state and the retreat of gender- and sexuality-related norms are a means to preserve the status quo of the religious gender systems as they have been for the last ten millennia.

Fundamentalist movements: no room for transformation

Fundamentalism is a controversial concept. Fundamentalism is usually associated with other concepts such as fanaticism, indoctrination and radicalism, and also – to use less severe terms – with traditionalism and conservatism. *Intégriste* is a label in French regularly used to describe Catholic fundamentalists.

The fundamentalist image of Islam has been more present in the international media since the 1980s. The pictures of ayatollahs in turbans sitting in the Iranian parliament, of veiled women in the streets of Kabul, and of Algerian or Afghan mujahideen shown as symbols of freedom fighters of the Muslim world have been abundantly broadcast in the international media. However, it was American Protestants who first used the word 'fundamentalism', in the early twentieth century. They began to call themselves 'fundamentalist' to differentiate themselves from the 'liberal' Protestants, who they claimed had completely distorted the Christian faith. It was an attempt to return to the roots and to place emphasis on the 'fundamentals' of the Christian tradition. The origins of this movement lie in a dispute over the right to interpret the sacred texts.

No single community, social or cultural group, sect or religious movement can claim, however, to represent fundamentalists today. They consist of groups as heterogeneous as the fundamentalist Catholic movement of Archbishop Lefebvre, dissident member of the French clergy, the Pentecostals and Adventists of the United States, the Wahabis/Salafists of Saudi Arabia, the Muslim Brotherhood of Egypt, the Taliban of Afghanistan and Hassidic Jews. They share a similar vision of authority and power. They cultivate a religious idealism essential for maintaining their personal and community identity. They understand truth as one and revealed, and condemn their opponents as evil. Each of these groups practises 'the assertion of a religious authority (cultural/political) as holistic and absolute ... allows neither criticism nor reductions... [and] expresses itself in the collective demand that the specific precepts of belief and ethics deriving their source in the scriptures be publicly recognized and enforced by the law' (Lawrence, 1989).

The Network of Women Living under Muslim Law (WLUML) also acknowledges this search for power by fundamentalists in its plan of action, elaborated in Dhaka, Bangladesh. For its members, 'although the use of the term "fundamentalism" has been debated in the midst of WLUML during the years (some of us do not use it; others find that it is the one that is widely understood, the least shocking for indicating the phenomenon), we agree on the broad nature of the phenomenon to which we refer as fundamentalism, that is to say the use of religions (and often ethnicity and culture) to gain and to mobilize power' (WLUML, 1997: 5).

Fundamentalist movements are religious, political and social. They have a need for joint religious and political authority. Thus agreements exist between the church and the state in Latin America, between Islamic brotherhoods and governments in several African states, between fundamentalist groups and right-wing political parties such as the Bharatiya Janata Party in India. They exist even when the fundamentalists are not themselves in power politically, as they are in Iran or in the Gulf kingdoms. They may be on the fringes of politics, in permanent negotiation to acquire room for manoeuvring. Political power seeks the support of religious power, in return for spiritual influence. Fundamentalists can indeed be in opposition, as is the case with the Catholic Church in certain Latin American countries. This opposition can become violent and armed, as in the case of various Islamic armies in the Muslim world.

Whether they are in power or in opposition, fundamentalists condemn the progressive secularization of society and of the state. What fundamentalism authorizes is a redefinition of unchanging values that are sacred, or a conservative manipulation of values that makes any discussion difficult and any transformation impossible. This can be observed in the many debates on family issues. Muslims are very attached to the 'fundamental' principles of their faith, and do not fear the fundamentalist label, which is regarded as part of the usual Western prejudice against Islam, especially in the current period of secularist anxiety and anti-terrorist policies.

Beyond these fundamentalist extremist movements, there is a rampant everyday fundamentalism. It is the ordinary fundamentalism/radicalism of people who are no more than ordinary, but whose thinking, daily attitudes and behaviour have an impact on peoples' lives, and in particular on women's lives, that is even more insidious. It involves judgement on clothing, and on public and private conduct, which encounters disapproval and condemnation. This includes the obligation for women to wear the veil or longer skirts in public, the obligation for individuals to fast or not to eat in public at the time of Ramadan, to pray in an ostentatious manner in public, and so on. Any refusal to keep to these imposed codes of conduct can be the source of conflict and of violence. One remembers the lynching by Islamic groups in Algeria of women who refused to wear the veil, who lived as single women or who seemed too free, and of journalists and intellectuals judged to have too liberal a viewpoint. The ban on women wearing trousers or any Western clothes in President Mobutu's Zaire reinforced such a fundamentalist cultural order during his rule.

A gender problem

Fundamentalist religious leaders are vigorously active even in societies where democracy finds itself well consolidated; for example, the Catholic fundamentalists in France and England. They are also active in states whose constitutions define them as secular, for example, Brazil and Uruguay, where there is constant pressure from the Catholic Church to have the juridical and legislative sphere redefined on the basis of religious principles. They show great determination in their efforts to generate tensions between the state and religion and to build alliances to oppose the principle of secularism.

One of the best illustrations of this endeavour to assume the centre of power was the presidential election in the United States that gave George W. Bush his second mandate. An image spread on the Internet showing the political map of North America based on the results of the voting in the states, with the Republican-majority states marked as if they formed a new country, a nation called 'Jesusland' – a single image that sums up the kind of struggle, forces and strategies that accompanied the campaign to determine the choice of the occupant of the White House in the elections of 2004.

It is this interplay between religious and political forces that women's organizations experienced when they were negotiating women's rights as human rights during the various United Nations conferences of the 1990s. It is obvious that life experiences are extremely varied and complex throughout the world, but women share the experience of the current revival of fundamentalism, the reinforced constraints on their basic freedom as women, whatever their religion. It is only the forms, the level, the force and the coherence of these constraints that vary. Throughout the UN conferences, they were faced with many states' reservations on their rights, in the name of religion, be it Christianity or Islam. Indeed, the political alliance between the Vatican and some Islamic states has been a powerful force for backlash against gender equality and women's rights in various UN forums. Several issues have been at stake in this struggle for women's human rights. In recent years, the control of women's bodies has become a political project that has preoccupied the fundamentalists, whatever their religion. Family rights, health and sexual rights have been the most critical areas of contention. In the subsections below, we provide illustrations of how religious and political forces together shape the terrain for women's rights and gender equality.

Examples of fundamentalism contesting feminism

RECONFIGURING THE FAMILY

Islamic states, whether fundamentalist or not, have always demanded respect for Islamic values in managing the relations between men and women within the family. For example, Niger and Chad do not yet have secular family codes because of their attachment to sharia. A large majority of leaders in Muslim countries continue to elaborate and to revise family codes based on their interpretation of the sharia, while bringing in reforms of modern law. Senegal was the first Muslim sub-Saharan African country to have worked out a secular code that applied to all communities, in 1973. However, conflicts still continue between the formal position of the state and the views of fundamentalists and neo-fundamentalists,[1] who rely upon a literal interpretation of the Quran. Family laws are often at the centre of political controversies between fundamentalism and feminists.

Marriage and polygamy, filiation, divorce and alimony, and inheritance are the issues most often discussed, as stated in *One Hundred Steps* (*Cent une mesures*), a platform proposed by the Collectif 95 Maghreb Egalité (1995). This North African collective aims at reforming the family code and personal statutes in the Maghreb region, from Morocco to Egypt. In the preface of the publication, the collective argues that 'although the status and women's situation have registered some considerable changes, there remains a very strong social and political resistance while new threats against the gains and rights secured by women in Maghreb appear large on the horizon' (Collectif 95 Maghreb Egalité, 1995: 5). This action certainly played an important role in the reshaping of the Moroccan Moudawana (family law), by King Mohammed VI, in 2003.

There are still in force in the Muslim world legal provisions drawn from or inspired by religion (Koran, hadiths) that continue to maintain gender inequality at the level of state constitutions and diverse codes, and that form the main substance of traditionalist claims about the sexual, matrimonial and social behaviour of women. The extreme forms of Wahabite fundamentalism perpetuated in Saudi Arabia exclude the majority of women from economic and political activities. The Iranian Islamic Revolution played a decisive role in the present ascent of Muslim fundamentalism, and encouraged a number of Muslim countries to legalize the use of sharia as a fundamental law during debates on the discrimination against women, as in Northern Nigeria. Without imposing on them the wearing of the veil, they restored a patriarchal Islamic discourse whose terms had changed.

One of the fundamental principles denounced by religious Muslims is the very notion of gender inequality. For them, gender inequality is not at issue, because all believers – men and women) – are equal before God and there is no intercessor between believers and God. The exegetes underline the value and dignity that Islam has given back to women in Arab culture, which had previously killed them at birth and excluded them from inheritance. However, Sura 4, verse 34, of the Qur'an emphasizes:

> Men are the protectors and maintainers of women, because God has given the one more [strength] than the other; and because they support them from their means. Therefore, the righteous women are devoutly obedient and guard in [the husband's] absence what God would have them guard. As to those women on whose part you fear disloyalty and ill conduct, admonish them [first]; [next], refuse to share their beds; [and last] beat them [lightly]. But if they return to obedience, seek not against them means [of annoyance]: For God is Most High, great [above you all].

From this principle, questions of discrimination raised by the Convention on the Elimination of All Forms of Discrimination Against Women (CEDAW) were generally resisted, or at least evoked reservations over issues of gender equality before the law or over nationality, marriage, divorce and inheritance.

SEXUALITY AND REPRODUCTION

Disputes between fundamentalist religious forces and liberals in the United States have been evident for a long time, but outside the national context the ties between economic power, conservatives and the more radical religious leaders have not been seen so clearly. One example of this is the battle concerning the legalizing of abortion.

In the 1990s, religious extremists in the United States (where the practice of abortion is legal) did everything from keeping vigil at the doors of abortion clinics to murdering doctors and nurses. In Latin America, during the same period, the argument prevailed that interrupting pregnancy, when legal, was a birth-control mechanism that was imposed by the rich countries of the North on the poor countries of the South. This rhetorical argument, widely employed during the Pope's visit to Brazil in 1997, came straight from the propaganda of the North American anti-abortionists. Its extensive use was aimed at capturing the imagination of sectors of the left against the feminists, and it met with some success.

Numerous examples of opposition to sexual rights include the great commotion caused in the United Nations Commission on Human Rights by the Brazilian proposal for a Resolution on Human Rights and Sexual Orientation. Called simply the Brazilian Resolution, it met with a favourable response from many countries in informal negotiations but strong opposition from the bloc of conservative countries and the Vatican. The ambassador of Pakistan declared in the plenary that the proposal insulted the 1.2 billion Muslims in the world, since it was exclusively a cultural expression of the West because there were no homosexuals in Islamic societies. Pressure from the Vatican was put on certain Latin American countries to encourage them to vote against the proposal. An influential Brazilian bishop systematically attacked the proposal in the press, claiming that it was inimical to human rights, representing the destruction of the family and stimulating religious discrimination. Some religious websites in Portuguese even compared the Brazilian proposal to the atrocities committed by Hitler.[2] In the battle to have the resolution approved, the opposing bloc went so far as to request that the term 'sexual orientation' be deleted from the text. In the face of the resulting impasse and without any prospect of an immediate solution, the chair of the session strategically proposed that voting be put off until 2004.

Sexual orientation and the exercise of sexuality are not new themes in the arena of human rights and still less so in the sphere of multilateral negotiations at the United Nations. The International Conference on

Population and Development (ICPD) (Cairo, 1994) is important because one of its most significant achievements was to enshrine the phrase 'health and sexual and reproductive rights'. This phrase became established among the complicated set of contentious themes under discussion on account of the reaction these rights provoked among those who defended the principle of strict regulation of human sexuality. An example is the Vatican's insistence that sex should be practised solely for the purpose of procreation.

At the beginning of the twentieth century, Uruguayan legislation permitted abortion. In 1938, retrogression led to its re-criminalization. A recent proposal to legalize abortion was presented by the medical sector's representatives in Congress and supported by a broad alliance of progressive sectors, including several religions, feminists, trade unionists and jurists, who were alarmed at the increase in maternal deaths due to unsafe abortion in the country. Local anti-abortion advocates, articulated with groups in the United States and other countries in the region, started an intense campaign against the proposal. They sent intimidating faxes to Uruguayan parliamentarians during the voting in May 2004. This campaign, together with the Uruguayan president's loyalty to the Pope and the need for agreement to approve the national budget, led to the rejection of the proposal in the Uruguayan Congress.

Conclusion

These illustrations show that struggles for gender equality and women's human rights are highly complex in terms of their political and social manifestations. Yet common threads can be traced through the analysis of various forms of fundamentalism and their impact on women's lives. Many contemporary cultural and religious discourses aim to deprive and seclude women, as well as subjecting them to a cultural and religious order to which no man would subject himself. Women's bodies and rights are sites of their struggles. Control of women's bodies is a step towards the political control of society. The control of the state is the ultimate goal of fundamentalist groups and parties. Thus women's struggles for their rights are deeply enmeshed in the struggle for political power and the making and remaking of a secular social contract.

NOTES

1. The term 'neo-fundamentalists' refers to all the traditionalists who are outside fundamentalist movements, but who advocate a return to Islam in everyday life. It is they who really are in contact with people in everyday life. Their preaching overwhelms African radio.
2. www.jesussite.com.br/acervo.asp?id=836 (accessed 12 October 2006).

REFERENCES

Ahmed, L. (1992) *Women and Gender in Islam: Historical Roots of a Modern Debate*, Yale University Press, New Haven CT and London.

Antrobus, P. (2004) *The Global Women's Movement: Origins, Issues and Strategies*, Zed Books, London.

Armstrong, K. (2000) *The Battle for God: Fundamentalism in Judaism, Christianity and Islam*, Knopf, New York.

Abd al-Raziq, A. (1966) *Al-Islam wa usul al-hukm* [Islam and the Basis of Power], Maktabat al-Hayat, Beirut.

Bencheikh, G. (2005) *La Laïcité au regard du Coran*, Presses de Renaissance, Paris.

Benzine, R. (2004) *Les Nouveaux penseurs de l'islam*, Albin Michel, Paris.

Bouzar, D. (2004) *Monsieur Islam n'existe pas*, Hachette Littérature, Paris.

Callaway, B., and L. Creevey (eds) (1994) *The Heritage of Islam: Women, Religion, and Politics in West Africa*, Lynne Rienner, Boulder CO and London.

Chauprade, A. (2003) *Géopolitique. Constantes et changements dans l'histoire*, Ellipses Éditions Marketing, Paris.

Collectif 95 Maghreb Égalité (1995) *One Hundred Steps, One Hundred Provisions. For an Egalitarian Codification of Family and Personal Status Laws in the Maghreb*, WLUML, London.

Corrêa, S. (2004) 'A ameaça aos consensos do Cairo', Observatório da Cidadania, vol. 32, no. 4.

Corrêa, S. (2004) 'Religious and Secular Politics: Different Sides of a Single Thought', *DAWN Informs* Supplement, January.

Dayan-Herzbrun, S. (2005) *Femmes et politique au Moyen-Orient*, Collection Bibliothèque du féminisme, Paris.

DAWN Informs (2001) 'Between Globalization and Fundamentalism', November.

DAWN Informs Supplement (2004) 'The Faces of Fundamentalisms', January.

Ferreira, A. (2004) 'O Império Contra-ataca. As guerras de George W. Bush, antes e depois do 11 de setembro', *Paz e Terra* (Rio de Janeiro).

Imam, A. (2002) 'Of Laws, Religion and Women's Rights: Women's Rights in Muslim Laws', in *Islamisation in Secular Nigeria: Implications for Women's Rights*, WLUML, London, pp. 43–52.

Lamchichi, A. (2004) 'La Condition de la femme en Islam. Avancées et régression', in I. Taboada Leonetti, *Les femmes et l'islam. Entre modernité et intégrisme*, l'Harmattan, Paris, pp. 19–49.

Lawrence, B. (1989) *Defenders of God: The Fundamentalist Revolt against the Modern Age*, Harper & Row, San Francisco.

Maitland, S. (2000) 'Biblicism: A Radical Rhetoric?', in G. Sahgal and N. Yuval-Davis (eds), *Refusing Holy Orders: Women and Fundamentalism in Britain*, WLUML, London.

Marty, M., and R. Scott Appleby (eds) (1991) 'Conclusion: An Interim Report on a Hypothetical Family', in *Fundamentalisms Observed*, University of Chicago Press, Chicago and London, pp. 814–42.

Marty, M., and R. Scott Appleby, (eds) (1991–95) *The Fundamentalism Project*, 5 vols, University of Chicago Press, Chicago and London.

Mazrui, A. (1997) 'Islamic and Western Values', *Foreign Affairs*, vol. 76, no. 5, pp. 118–32.

Moghissi, H. (1999) *Feminism and Islamic Fundamentalism: The limits of Postmodern Analysis*, Zed Books, London.

Mukherjee, V.N., 2004. 'The Rise of Hindu Fascism in India: Challenges for Feminist Politics', *DAWN Informs*, pp. 7–8.

Ng, C. (2004) 'An Unholy Alliance: Malaysian Women Engaging with the State', *DAWN Informs* Supplement, pp. 5–6.

Pazello, M. (2004) 'Interesses comerciais, políticos e religiosos no caminho dos Direitos Humanos', *Observatório da Cidadania*, pp. 28–31.

Ramadan, T. (2001) *Islam. Le Face à face des civilisations. Quel projet pour quelle modernité?* Éditions Tawhid, Lyon.

Renaut, A., and A. Touraine (2005) *Un Débat sur la laïcité*, Stock, Paris.

Simmons, G.Z. (2003) 'Are We up to the Challenge: The Need for a Radical Re-ordering of the Islamic Discourse on Women', in O. Safi (ed.), *Critical Islam*, One World Press, London.

Sow, F. (2003) 'Fundamentalisms, Globalisation and Women's Human Rights', in C. Sweetman and J. Kerr (eds), *Reinventing Globalisation, Gender and Development*, OXFAM/AWID, London.

Sow, F. (2005) 'Les Femmes, l'État et la mosquée', in M. Gomez-Perez (ed.), *L'Islam politique en Afrique subsaharienne*, Karthala, Paris.

WLUML (Women Living under Muslim Laws/Femmes sous lois musulmanes) (1997) *Plan of Action*, WLUML, Dhaka

WLUML (Women Living under Muslim Laws/Femmes sous lois musulmanes) (2003) *Knowing Our Rights: Women, Family, Laws and Customs in the Muslim World*, WLUML, London.

WLUML (Women Living under Muslim Laws/Femmes sous lois musulmanes) (1996) *Femmes, lois, initiatives dans le monde musulman, Femmes, lois, initiatives dans le monde musulman*, WLUML, Grabels.

WLUML (Women Living under Muslim Laws/Femmes sous lois musulmanes) and Feminist International Radio Endeavor (FIRE) (2003) 'Women's Peacecast V: In Search of Justice, Human Rights and a Just Peace', WLUML Occasional Paper No 13, London.

BOX IV.1 **The abortion debate in Latin America and the Caribbean: one step forward, two steps back**

ERIKA TRONCOSO

Women in Latin America do not have much choice when it comes to the biological fact of pregnancy: the only countries that allow women access to voluntary, legal and safe abortion services are Cuba, Puerto Rico and Mexico, though in Mexico City alone. On the other hand, in five countries of the region (Chile, Dominican Republic, El Salvador, Honduras and Nicaragua) abortion is fully criminalized, even in instances where the woman is in a life-threatening situation and in therapeutic cases. The laws of other countries of the region allow abortions on specific grounds and for specific reasons, such as rape and risk to health (Center for Reproductive Rights, 2012). However, safe and legal access to an abortion is not truly guaranteed due to the absence of protocols, an insufficiency of advice to women regarding their reproductive rights, restrictive interpretations of the law and several other barriers preventing women accessing the information they need. In 2011 Chile, Argentina and Uruguay had open discussions in their parliaments to increase access to abortion, but to little effect.

As has been observed many times, legal restrictions do not prevent women from having abortions in the event of unwanted or unintended pregnancies. It is estimated that between 3.9 and 4.2 million abortions take place every year in the region (WHO, 2008). It is difficult to estimate the number of unwanted pregnancies. According to recent estimates from Colombia in 2009, unwanted pregnancies account for 61 per cent of all pregnancies (Guttmacher Institute, 2011). Despite the figures, some advances had been made in terms of regional and global support to loosen restrictions on abortion. For instance, the Inter-American Commission on Human Rights, during its regional hearings on reproductive rights in March 2011, emphasized that the current legal framework in the region is contrary to women's rights enshrined in international treaties that countries had already signed. The recommendations of the UN Special Rapporteur on the Right to Health on October 2011 echo this fact.

In those places where women's access to safe, legal abortions has been guaranteed, the role played by pro-choice civil organizations that promoted parliamentary and social debate, and eventually the passing of the law, cannot be overlooked. Such is the case of Mexico City, where the commitment of the Ministry of Health, plus the support of several pro-choice non-governmental organizations, made possible both the decriminalization of abortion in the city and meaningful access to services, both public and private. Between April 2007 and January 2011, more than 50,000 women had access to legal, voluntary and safe abortions in Mexico City Ministry of Health facilities (Mondragón y Kalb et al., 2011) and an unknown number likewise in private facilities (Schiavon et al., 2010). A very different situation exists in Nicaragua, where due to the criminalization of abortion, all women – even those with life-threatening conditions such as ectopic pregnancy – are deprived of quality care because health-care providers are unable to act. This situation has led an indefinite number of women suffering from unnecessary health risks; some women may have even died on account of this legal framework (Gómez and Blandón, 2007).

Another situation is observed in certain countries where, despite popular support for the decriminalizing of abortion, such as in Uruguay, or the active work of NGOs involved in the issue, as in Brazil, the personal religious beliefs of certain dignitaries, the upper classes and the Catholic Church have prevented advances towards decriminalization. The social and political power of the most conservative sectors of society, ranging from individual players to bishops, has strengthened; indeed it might even appear that an entire regional strategy is in place for the cohesion of these sectors, which are not only against abortion but also against other statements of individual freedom on the part of citizens, such as same-sex marriage and the use of birth-control (see Catholic for Choice Opposition Watch). One of the most dangerous aspects of the strengthening of right-wing groups is the disinformation they impose on societies. Among the arguments used to oppose birth control are some that have been scientifically proven to be false, such as the assertion that breast cancer is a possible side effect. Women have even been given fliers with misleading or false information about abortion procedures.

Given these scenarios, in Latin America and the Caribbean the debate over women's right to choose has continued to be polarized between progressive and oppositional sectors. Located in the middle of this discussion are the majority of the population, who lack easy access to unbiased information, which is vital given the resources and power wielded by the opposition. In order to further the progress of democratization in the region, engaging in the abortion debate is a pressing task for the whole of society.

REFERENCES

Center for Reproductive Rights (2012) http://worldabortionlaws.com (revised 12 January).
Gómez, S., and M. Blandón (2007) *The Faces Behind the Figures: The Tragic Effects of the Criminalization of Therapeutic Abortion in Nicaragua*, Ipas Central America, Managua.
Guttmacher Institute (2011) *In Brief. Facts on Inintended Pregnancies and Induced Abortion in Colombia*, Guttmacher Institute, 2011.
Mondragón y Kalb, M., A.A.,Ortega, J.M.,Velazquez, C.D. Olavarrieta, J.V. Rodríguez, D. Becker and S.G. García (2011) 'Patient Characteristics and Service Trends Following Abortion Legalization in Mexico City, 2007–10', *Studies in Family Planning* 42, pp. 159–66.
Schiavon, R., M. Collado, E.,Troncoso, J. Soto, G. Zorrilla and T. Palermo (2010) 'Characteristics of Private Abortion Services in Mexico City after Legalization', *Reproductive Health Matters*, vol. 18, no. 36, pp. 127–35.
WHO (World Health Organization) (2008) *Unsafe Abortion: Global and Regional Estimates of the Incidence of Unsafe Abortion and Associated Mortality in 2008*, 6th edn.

BOX IV.2 **MDGs, SRHR and poverty-reduction policies: evidence from a DAWN project**

BHAVYA REDDY

There has been great concern over whether the Millennium Development Goals (MDGs) have been a step forward or a regression from the more complex and integrated approaches to development agreed to by governments during the UN conferences of the 1990s.

DAWN's project on Nigeria, India and Mexico analysed the extent to which the MDGs agenda is integrated into policy frameworks and debates, has favoured the adoption of Sexual and Reproductive Health and Rights (SRHR) policies, or fostered the strengthening of pre-existing SRHR initiatives. The project illuminates the many challenges faced, while recognizing the gains made.[1]

In Nigeria, the MDGs agenda is strongly integrated into government structures, policymaking and programmatic action, leveraged by state-level debt relief gains. India represents a mixed picture, with very limited usage of MDG discourse in policy and a disjunction in targets and indicators. Yet several issues championed by the MDGs are addressed by national and state policies and programmes. In Mexico, as in India, the MDGs have not formally entered national policy discourse, but in this case appear to have had negligible policy impact.[2] National aggregates, however, show the country having achieved some MDGs, with government criteria for poverty, health and education exceeding the scope of MDG indicators.

Poverty-reduction strategies have typically not gone deep enough to address the intersections of poverty, gender and SRHR. Among dominant approaches to poverty reduction for women adopted by governments – reservation for women in social welfare programs; targeted income-generating programmes for women through self-help groups (SHGs); and women as beneficiaries of conditional cash transfer (CCT) programmes – CCTs have shown greater steps towards the inclusion of SRHR. While CCTs primarily focus on compliance with maternal and child health services in exchange for cash payments, Mexico's Oportunidades includes mandatory attendance of family planning and SRH workshops for women and youth. Nigeria's CCT programme In Care of People (COPE) identifies women-headed households, women with vesico-vaginal fistulae, and PLWHA not only for cash payments but for skills training and start-up funds for income-generating activities. In India, SHGs often include village health workers. Tamil Nadu state has engaged with these groups on promoting HIV/AIDS awareness. But SHGs largely remain a missed opportunity for engaging with broader areas of SRHR.

FRAGMENTATION OF SRHR

Although all three countries – Nigeria, India and Mexico – have shown results from their commitment to the ICPD, SRHR as enshrined by the ICPD has been compromised in multiple ways in the past decade. Nigeria is a signatory to the 2005 Continental Framework on SRHR and exhibits a rich SRHR policy environment, yet SRH components of the MDGs have seen greater programmatic action. In India, though the decriminalization of sex work and same-sex relations indicate progress in sexual rights,[3] a comprehensive SRHR framework is not upheld by any policy or programme but is caught between two silos – maternal health and HIV/AIDS. Mexico also has increasing focus on maternal health, largely because of fiscal restrictions in the course of health-sector reform.

Access to safe and legal abortion remains a critical concern for the three countries. India has a comparatively liberal legal framework for abortion but access to safe services and post-abortion care is far from universal. In Mexico, despite a long-running battle for abortion rights and first-trimester abortion being legalized in the Districto Federal, conservative religious forces have strengthened and legal restrictions remain for most of the country. In Nigeria an estimated 20,000 women die of complications due to unsafe abortion annually (SOGON, 2004), yet conditions for legal abortion are restrictive and safe services scarce.

Adolescent health and rights is another SRHR area poorly addressed. Though Mexico has been implementing preventive and promotive SRHR programmes for young people, adolescent SRH services have received stringent cutbacks due to fiscal belt-tightening. In India and Nigeria adolescent SRHR policies and programmes have been developed, but, with little political priority and strong resistance from conservative forces, are poorly implemented.

CONCLUSIONS

Poverty-reduction strategies have generally failed to address adequately the relationship between poverty and health, and sexual-reproductive health and rights more specifically. In India and Nigeria, HIV/AIDS, compared to other areas of SRHR, is better linked to poverty alleviation. In all three countries maternal health initiatives have received considerable political backing and programmatic focus, yet the contribution of unsafe abortion to maternal mortality and morbidity has been marginalized. With nearly 30 per cent of the populations in these countries aged between 10 and 24 years (PRB, 2013), the health needs and rights of young people also need greater programmatic attention.

NOTES

1. This box is based on research published as DAWN, 2012.
2. In 2009, Chiapas, Mexico's poorest state, amended its state constitution to incorporate the MDGs (UNDP, 2010), and has been carrying out a MDG adoption strategy in its State Development Plan, but there is little evidence of this coherence nationally.
3. The ruling to decriminalize sex work has since been overturned by the Supreme Court of India, making same-sex relations illegal again.

REFERENCES

DAWN (2009) 'Positioning Sexuality in Holistic Development through Inter-linkages' (excerpt from Angela Collet's presentation), UNRISD NGO Consultation, Geneva, 12–13 January.

DAWN (2010) 'MDG 5 Maternal Mortality: In Need of Rescuing from the Depths of a Silo', Statement by DAWN, 22 September, www.dawnnet.org/feminist-resources/content/mdg-maternal-mortality-need-rescuing-depths-silo.

DAWN (2012) *Breaking through the Development Silos: Sexual and Reproductive Health and Rights, Millennium Development Goals and Gender Equity. Experiences from Mexico, India and Nigeria*, DAWN, www.dawnnet.org/feminist-resources/sites/default/files/articles/breaking_through_the_development_silos.pdf.

Khanna, R., A. Pradhan and L. Priya (2012) 'Coherence or Disjunction? MDGs, SRHR, Gender Equity and Poverty in Gujarat and Tamil Nadu', in DAWN, *Breaking through the Development Silos: Sexual and Reproductive Health and Rights, Millennium Development Goals and Gender Equity. Experiences from Mexico, India and Nigeria*, pp. 64–151.

PRB (2006) World's Youth 2006 Data Sheet, Population Reference Bureau, www.prb.org/DataFinder/Topic/Rankings.aspx?ind=19fmt=19tf=4loct=3notes=True (accessed 29 August 2011).

PRB (2013) The World's Youth: 2013 Data Sheet, Population Reference Bureau, www.prb.org/pdf13/youth-data-sheet-2013.pdf.

Raufu, A. (2002) 'Unsafe Abortions Cause 20 000 Deaths a Year in Nigeria' *BMJ* 325 (7371) (Nov 2), p. 988.

SOGON (Society of Gynecology and Obstetrics of Nigeria) (2004) *Status of Emergency Obstetrics Services for Safe Motherhood in Six States of Nigeria*, project report submitted to MacArthur Foundation, Chicago, May.

Surma, N., and M. Okpe (2012) 'Sexual and Reproductive Health and Rights, Poverty and the Millennium Development Agenda in Kaduna State', in DAWN, *Breaking through the Development Silos: Sexual and Reproductive Health and Rights, Millennium Development Goals and Gender Equity. Experiences from Mexico, India and Nigeria*, pp. 152–203.

Troncoso, E. (2012) 'MDGs and SRHR in Mexico's Social Programs: So Near and Yet So Far', in DAWN, *Breaking through the Development Silos: Sexual and Reproductive Health and Rights, Millennium Development Goals and Gender Equity. Experiences from Mexico, India and Nigeria*, pp. 36–63.

UNDP (United Nations Development Programme) (2010) 'Mexico's Poorest State Tackles Extreme Poverty through Budget Shifts', http://www.undp.org/content/undp/en/home/presscenter/articles/2010/09/22/mexicos-poorest-state-tackles-extreme-poverty-through-budget-shifts.

CHAPTER 10

Sexuality as a weapon of biopolitics: rethinking Uganda's anti-homosexuality bill

ROSALIND P. PETCHESKY

Framings: intersectionality and biopolitics

This essay is an argument for viewing social and development conflicts through a double lens, integrating the perspective of Foucauldian bio-politics with that of feminist intersectionality.[1] These convergent perspectives direct us to see controversies over sexuality and gender, particularly in a globalized world fraught with catastrophes, as inseparable from macro-economic and militarized power relations, and such power relations in turn as laden always with contests over the meanings and lived realities of sexuality, gender and race. What I call a deep intersectional approach invites us to conceptualize every domain or issue of political economy – markets, poverty, growth, militarization, climate change, as well as most problems in public health – as profoundly gendered and sexualized from the start; and, conversely, to understand every arena of sexual, gender and reproductive health politics as having deeply macroeconomic and development-related dimensions (see Corrêa, Petchesky and Parker, 2008; Crenshaw, 1991; Harcourt, 2009; Mohanty, 2003; Petchesky, 2003). Influenced by moves in queer theory, intersectional analysis also calls into question a regressive gender binarism (the ubiquitous 'women and men'), recognizing instead the multiple expressions of masculinity, femininity and hybridity that travel across diverse bodies and intersect with race and ethnicity in historically and geographically specific ways (see Butler, 2004; Currah, Juang and Minter, 2006; Puar, 2007). A language and politics that erase gender-nonconforming people become particularly exclusionary in the midst of disasters and armed conflict zones, where privileged victim status is routinely conferred on legible 'women and children'.[2]

I will explore these complex relationships by examining a recent case study: the Anti-Homosexuality Bill in Uganda and the complex politics and local and transnational debates surrounding it. Ultimately I will argue that the Uganda case raises troubling dilemmas for transnational sexual rights and gender justice activists. It demonstrates the difficulty, if not impossibility, of engaging in defence of sexual rights and human rights more broadly in any pure or 'neutral' terms; the dangerously thin line between solidarity and protection on one side and corporate profiteering and militarization on the other. And it points to the centrality of sexualized, racialized – and sometimes dead – human bodies as both the objects and the subjects of transnational biopolitics waged in the name of human rights. All this suggests that we have to complicate even further the usual ways of thinking about current crises in sexual politics by paying attention to the heavy layerings of temporality. For we find the present scenarios in such crises almost invariably haunted by the past – by vestiges of colonialism, slavery, sexual predation, and old wars fought in new guises.

Before moving to the Uganda scenario, let me recollect some of the ideas of French philosopher Michel Foucault that seem directly pertinent to thinking about the transnational dimensions of catastrophe, sexuality and public health. In the 1970s Foucault introduced the concept bio-power, or biopolitics, into the lexicon of theorizing about power and governance.[3] He posited that somewhere around the late eighteenth and well into the nineteenth century in Europe (and in the colonial regimes Europe imposed on the third world) there was a shift in the techniques of power from the classical, juridically based modalities of sovereignty – which worked mainly through the 'right of the sword' and 'power over death' – to forms of governance that took charge of 'life itself' (Foucault 1978: 135–9; 1984: 63). The primary focus of what Foucault called 'governmentality' became not only enhancing life but managing it, regulating it, calculating and quantifying it, normalizing it, and organizing it into a whole network of sciences and knowledge regimes, or 'disciplines', claiming their own truth and wielding their own methods. Biopower took two forms as it developed in the nineteenth century: first *disciplinary* techniques that act directly on individual bodies, to render them docile, or obedient or 'normal'; and later *regulatory* processes directed at populations – their movements, size, hygiene, sanitation, housing, birth rates, longevity, disease and epidemics – in short, the whole sphere of 'apparatuses', and the discourses and knowledges they produce, that would become the domain of public health and order and render them distinctly modern (Foucault 2003: 239–49; 1978: 139–41).

Although Foucault notoriously ignored gender, biopolitics as a conceptual frame has obvious relevance to feminist thinking about the body, sexuality and health as a gendered experience and has influenced a wide range of feminist scholars (see Butler, 2004; Cooper, 2008; Corrêa, Petchesky and Parker, 2008; Luibhéid, 2002; Puar, 2007; Shalhoub-Kevorkian, 2009). Especially appealing to feminists is Foucault's insistence that the new apparatuses or 'truth regimes' of biopolitics – some directly tied to the state and statist institutions and others (for example, the medical and psychiatric professions or the pharmaceuticals industry) operating around or outside it – are inseparable from power. There is nothing disengaged, neutral or 'objective' in the knowledges and techniques that biopolitics deploys; on the contrary, whether directed at individual bodies or populations and 'general biological processes', they '[act] as factors of segregation and social hierarchization, ... guaranteeing relations of domination and effects of hegemony' (Foucault, 1978: 171).

By the second half of the nineteenth century and throughout the twentieth, when the politics of life (migration, settlement, fertility, marriage, disease, etc.) became ingrained in state practices and nationalisms, these techniques became the vehicles for racism and genocide. While Foucault's main focus in probing the racism inherent in biopolitics was the Nazis in Europe, he was also acutely aware of colonialism as the laboratory where biopolitical techniques originated and of racial divisions and stereotyping, in both Western and post-colonial contexts, as their continued effects. In one of his 1976–77 Collège de France lectures, he makes this brief observation: 'Racism first develops with colonization, or in other words, with colonizing genocide. If you are functioning in the biopower mode, how can you justify the need to kill people, to kill populations, and to kill civilizations? By using the themes of evolutionism, by appealing to a racism' (Foucault, 2003: 257). Biopolitics and necropolitics are revealed as two sides of a coin. Killing or letting die certain groups, the 'degenerates', 'will make life in general healthier and purer' (2003: 255).

Critics have argued persuasively that Foucault's thoughts about co-lonialism and racism are fleeting at best, and in any case he failed to apply them to the experience of the colonized or the legacies of 'coloniz-ing genocide' in the post-colonial world, particularly sites of militarized occupation (Stoler, 2005; Mbembe, 2003). Achille Mbembe and Nadera Shalhoub-Kevorkian both argue that 'late-modern colonial occupation' in places such as the West Bank and Gaza combines 'the disciplinary, the biopolitical, and the necropolitical'. They suggest that Foucault underes-timated the extent to which technologies of war, terror and violence are central to 'the management of multitudes' in late modernity, whereby 'brutal attempts to immobilize and spatially fix whole categories of people' become intertwined with attempts to secure the health of the occupiers (Mbembe, 2003: 34, 12, 27). Shalhoub-Kevorkian describes how 'the multilayered effect of the biopolitical deployment of bodies in a militarized space' is also heavily gendered, when women's bodies become 'weapons' to deliver colonial assertions of power and 'the incapacitation of Palestinian males' (2009: 118–21). This is an important expansion (not a refutation) of biopolitical theory. But, as we shall see, the conversion of biopolitics into necropolitics and the militarization of rescue operations may occur in situations that fall short of full colonial occupation or war.

Two other important elements in Foucault's conceptualization of bio-politics bear emphasizing here. First, at the very centre lies *sexuality* – not simply as a dimension or subfield of biopolitics but rather at its core. 'Sexuality represents the precise point where the disciplinary and the regulatory, the body and the population', meet, Foucault writes (2003: 251). Surely the politics of HIV and AIDS prevention, family planning, sex education, and harm reduction in drug treatment programmes make this intersection clear. Second, biopolitics also intersects with all the regula-tory mechanisms beginning in the eighteenth century related to the flow of goods, capital and labour. That is, the politics of markets, trade and the liberal (laissez-faire) and neoliberal doctrines they would engender are inseparable from those that regulate the flow of people, bodies, miasmas, sexual encounters and cultures of sexual expression. Not by accident did Foucault's lectures of 1977–78 focus on the relations between population, territory and security; and those of 1978–79, titled *The Birth of Biopolitics*, concern the origins and diverse trajectories of neoliberalism (Foucault,

2007, 2008). Securitization of bodies and borders, and the pathways, pathogens and substances that penetrate them, not only serves global capital but also develops its own logic in the division and hierarchical ordering of human, and all, life. These complex interconnections materialize in the politics of sexual regulation in Uganda during 2009–12, so I turn now to that case.

Re-examining Uganda's anti-homosexuality bill

The nefarious 'anti-homosexuality bill' tabled in December 2009 by David Bahati, a little-known member of the Ugandan parliament, has been widely publicized. After a series of submissions and retractions, it was reintroduced for the third time in February 2012. Although homosexuality is already illegal in Uganda, the new bill would go much further, imposing harsh prison sentences or even the death penalty in certain cases on anyone accused of being lesbian, gay, bisexual or transgender as well as some HIV+ persons. It also specifies criminal penalties for anyone who knowingly fails to report such persons – for example, doctors and other medical workers, human rights defenders, teachers and family members (Gettleman, 2010). In the United States, the popular Rachel Maddow Show, a news commentary programme on the cable news network MSNBC, reported every night for two weeks on what she called Uganda's 'Kill the Gays Bill' (Maddow, 2009), and similar reports appeared on CNN and other news outlets. In addition, commentary about the bill and its tragic aftermath went viral on social networking and other Web 2.0 Internet sites (Nyong'o, 2011). Many observers in cyberspace have seen this bill as the most draconian example of what Nigerian sexual rights activist Cesnabmihilo (Dorothy) Aken'ova refers to as 'the wind of state homophobia [that] has swept over the African continent' (Aken'ova, 2010) – a trend towards the criminalization of non-conforming genders and sexualities that was certainly not confined to Africa but rampant in many other countries and regions as well.[4] They have pointed to the rash of hate crimes, illegal detentions, beatings, 'correctional' rapes of presumed lesbians, and raids on LGBTI and human rights organizations that have accompanied these homophobic legislative campaigns wherever they occur (LeGendre, 2010).

From outside the continent, an initial barrage of protests from human rights, HIV/AIDS and other public health groups raised the alarm about the adverse public health consequences of such legislation as well as its obvious human rights violations. They were joined by a chorus of leaders from Western donor countries, whose influence for a while seemed to blunt the bill's worst provisions, without however achieving its withdrawal. In response to United States and European (especially Swedish) pressure, President Museveni made a number of gestures in January 2010 signalling his non-support of the bill and telling parliament to 'go slow' (Branch, 2010). WikiLeaks cables later revealed a more complicated message to United States government officials 'that in the African context, homosexuality is not a human rights issue ... [but rather] a disorder and not something to be promoted or celebrated'; that the United States should not 'push' Africans too hard on this issue but should leave the bill 'to die a natural death' (*Independent*, 2011).

Yet by October and November of 2010, the global LGBTI movement's worst nightmares had come true, when a local newspaper calling itself *Rolling Stone* published a series of articles denouncing Ugandan homosexuals with headlines that read 'Homo Generals Plotted Kampala Terror Attacks', 'Hang Them; They Are After Our Kids!!!!' And '100 Pictures of Uganda's Top Homos Leak', along with photographs and, in some cases, even addresses of Ugandan gay activists and human rights defenders (Civil Society Coalition, 2010, 2011a; High Court of Uganda, 2010). Expressing poignant faith in the mechanisms of civil rights and the law, three members of the Civil Society Coalition on Human Rights and Constitutional Law filed a complaint with Uganda's High Court asking for a permanent injunction to restrain *Rolling Stone*. One of the three plaintiffs was David Kato, a leading gay rights activist in Uganda who had spoken out publicly against the anti-homosexuality bill, calling it 'profoundly undemocratic and un-African', and whose name and photograph were among those published in *Rolling Stone*.

On 30 December 2010 the Court issued its ruling granting the injunction and agreed that the publications were in violation of 'fundamental rights and freedoms', including gay persons' 'right to human dignity' and 'to privacy of the person and their homes' (Civil Society Coalition, 2011a; High Court of Uganda, 2010). Yet less than four weeks later, David Kato was bludgeoned to death in his home (Rice, 2011; ILGA, 2011; Human Rights Watch, 2011). Also troubling and sad is that, while the language of the Anti-Homosexuality Bill expressly names and condemns transgender people, transgender expression and rights were almost entirely silenced in statements of those opposing the bill as well as the December 2010 ruling of the Uganda High Court. Exclusions appear to reproduce themselves like Russian dolls.

When we look more deeply and broadly into the politics of homophobia in Uganda we find it sits on top of a number of geopolitical, imperialist and macroeconomic fault lines – forces that surpassed the Internet in globalizing the Uganda sexuality crisis. The first of these is what we might call *evangelical neocolonialism* – the machinations of a United States-based network of operatives on behalf of Christian homophobic piety throughout Africa, Southeast Asia, Eastern Europe and Latin America. Uganda's particular status as the poster child for the George W. Bush administration's abstinence-oriented PEPFAR (President's Emergency Plan for AIDS Relief) policy is well known (Corrêa, Petchesky and Parker, 2008: 36–8). It is true that Uganda's HIV prevalence rate dramatically declined during the decade of the 1990s – due to a variety of factors, including that so many people died without treatment. But the combination of more recent availability of free anti-retroviral treatment (which some experts believe has led to complacency about sexual behaviour and prevention) and Uganda's fervent embrace of the Abstain–Be Faithful–Use Condoms (ABC) approach (with a de-emphasis on either comprehensive sexuality education or aggressive condom distribution) has meant that prevalence levels have now begun to rise again. This increase is strongest among married heterosexual women, who constitute 57 per cent of all newly infected adults (Avert.org, 2011; UNAIDS, 2010).

But evangelical colonialism in Uganda is two-pronged, involving not only acceptance of ABC and Bush's PEPFAR policy but also the clandestine love affair between local Ugandan politicians and visiting right-wing Christian evangelicals from the United States, selling their message of the dangers of homosexuality and the importance of their brand of 'family values'. In March of 2009, the year before Bahati introduced his anti-gay bill in parliament, a team of American evangelical preachers – most prominent among them the long-time Christian right-wing preacher and attorney

Scott Lively – went to Kampala claiming to be able to 'cure' homosexuality and defeat its alleged danger to African children and families.[5] These so-called 'experts on homosexuality' gave a series of talks to civil society groups, including teachers, politicians and police officers, and consulted directly with the legislators who drafted the bill. Globe-travelling sexual conservatism in the name of Jesus apparently met a receptive audience in Uganda. According to one *New York Times* reporter, visiting preachers were welcomed with 'proposed virginity scholarships, songs about Jesus playing in the airport, "Uganda is Blessed" bumper stickers on parliament office doors, and a suggestion by the president's wife that a virginity census could be a way to fight AIDS' (Gettleman, 2010).

What we have here quite obviously is a classic re-enactment of collusion between missionaries and complicit native elites, a pattern that has centuries-old roots in Western colonialism and neocolonial projects. Notwithstanding the American evangelicals' public disclaimers that killing homosexuals was not what they had in mind, their direct hand in inspiring and building a constituency for homophobic legislation is hardly in doubt (Maddow, 2009; Burroway, 2011). Further, like that of Christian missionaries before them, their message plays into local homophobia and heteronormative codes reinforced through the history of colonial subjugation, while homophobia in turn provides a convenient diversion from the bad sexual behaviour of married men, whose wives are becoming infected with HIV at growing rates. Yet the irony goes almost unnoticed that African politicians, echoing their evangelical allies, call homosexuality 'an immoral Western import', but not the neoliberal economic policies that impoverish local growers and traders, nor Christian evangelical neocolonialism and its crony, patriarchal marriage.[6] Indeed, one may ask whether homophobia is the real 'immoral Western import'. Feminist anthropologist Sylvia Tamale of Makerere University made this point sharply in her public testimony before parliament opposing the bill. Contrary to the false assumptions of the bill's drafters concerning homosexuality in Africa, Tamale informed parliamentarians that 'homosexuality was not introduced to Africa from Europe', but rather 'Europe [exported] legalized homophobia to Africa' through colonial anti-sodomy laws (Tamale, 2010).

A second set of forces we must take into account in analysing Uganda's Anti-Homosexuality Bill as a focal point of biopolitics involves Uganda's

positioning in the global economy, the dynamics of international development, and superpower rivalries. An important part of this context are
robust economic growth rates on the continent as a whole, a surge in
foreign direct investment since 2000, rising commodity prices (especially
for natural resources like oil, gold and diamonds), and increased Chinese
activity in financing infrastructural projects (Dugger, 2010). On the
surface, in response to worldwide protests and media exposure President
Museveni said he would oppose the anti-homosexuality bill and warned
its sponsors that at stake were 'not just our internal politics' but also 'our
foreign policy interests'. Presumably he was worried about foreign donors
like the Swedes, the British and, particularly, the United States (Branch,
2010).[7] But, far from being a friend to gays and lesbians, Museveni has
a record of egging on the homophobic hysteria in his country, telling a
public youth forum that he had heard 'European homosexuals are recruit-
ing in Africa' (Allen, 2009).

While he may try to appease foreign donors, the Ugandan president
has more pressing areas of interest that he would rather keep far away
from parliamentary scrutiny. Among other things, he has been engaged
in a campaign to court Chinese aid and investments in infrastructure and
the energy sector. According to a recent report by McKinsey & Company's
Global Institute, 'China has provided more financing for roads, power,
railways and other infrastructure [in Africa] in recent years than the
World Bank' (Dugger, 2010). The discovery of sizeable oil reserves – *The
Economist* calls it 'one of the most spectacular recent finds' – in Uganda's
Albertine Lake region has provoked a scramble of foreign bidders, resulting in a pending deal involving a consortium of Irish and French
companies and the China National Offshore Oil Company (*Economist*,
2010; AllAfrica.com 2009, 2010). How convenient for Museveni to distract
domestic legislators (who, like many Africans, are wary of China's influence in the region), tying them up in a debate over 'African family values'
and the evils of homosexuality while keeping control over trade and
economic development policies firmly in his own hands.

Economics also plays a hidden but powerful role on the domestic
front in configuring the biopolitics of sexuality in Uganda. Systematically
knocking down every premiss of the Anti-Homosexuality Bill's sponsors about who or what, exactly, is undermining African families, Sylvia

Tamale argues: 'the re-criminalization of homosexuality is meant to distract the attention of Ugandans from the real issues that harm us' and truly threaten African families – above all, the economic crisis, lack of jobs, food insecurity, and rampant domestic violence and child sexual abuse (Tamale, 2010). As if to fully confirm this analysis, within a few weeks after it was announced that the bill would be permanently shelved (see below), students and other protesters launched a series of violent demonstrations at Makere University and in the streets of Kampala against the Museveni government. Their main complaints? Not sexual outlaws but rather rising food and fuel prices and the lack of jobs for young graduates (Kron, 2011a).

Adding another layer to the complexity, a thorough study of sexuality policies in Uganda would need to consider how the crisis in food and jobs traces back to economic reform and structural adjustment programmes initiated in World Bank and International Monetary Fund Loans; the emphasis of these programmes on agricultural production for export, 'reorganization of market structures through liberalization', and raising prices; the Museveni government's desire to accentuate its standing as a 'stable' global trading partner (see Baffoe, 2000); and the gendered consequences of these policies as they impact on women and men small farmers and traders in Uganda. In other words, I am arguing not only that homophobia becomes a decoy to divert popular attention from state and global neoliberal policies, but also that such policies are an integral piece of sexual biopolitics and need to be rethought through that lens.

On the level of diplomatic rhetoric, in 2010 United States President Obama and Secretary of State Clinton loudly denounced the anti-gay bill as 'a very serious potential violation of human rights'. In April that year the United States Senate Foreign Relations Committee passed a resolution condemning Uganda's bill, declaring that 'such laws undermine our commitment to combating HIV/AIDS globally by stigmatizing and criminalizing vulnerable communities' (Allen 2009; LeGendre 2010). Six months later, British prime minister David Cameron threatened to cut development aid to 'countries that persecute homosexuals', followed in December 2011 by the Obama administration issuing an unprecedented memorandum to all heads of executive departments and agencies on 'International Initiatives to Advance the Human Rights of Lesbian, Gay, Bisexual, and Transgender

Persons' (Kron, 2012; Presidential Memorandum, 2011). Without naming Uganda or any specific countries, the memorandum urges US agencies 'to strengthen existing efforts to effectively combat the criminalization by foreign governments of LGBT status or conduct and to expand efforts to combat discrimination, homophobia, and intolerance on the basis of LGBT status or conduct'. It signals that foreign assistance funds will be aimed at civil society groups engaged in efforts 'to build respect for the human rights of LGBT persons' and sets up a standing group within the US State Department 'to help insure the Federal Government's swift and meaningful response to serious incidents that threaten the human rights of LGBT persons abroad'. In what appeared to be a carefully orchestrated public event following the memorandum's release, Secretary of State Hillary Clinton spoke at the United States Mission to the United Nations in Geneva to announce the new US policy, suggesting that, henceforward, US foreign assistance would be conditional on countries' respect for LGBT human rights. A group of fourteen LGBT activists from Africa, Asia and Latin America – including one leader of Uganda's Civil Society Coalition on Human Rights and Constitutional Law – had been brought to Geneva to applaud this turn in United States policy and its hopefulness for the future of LGBT rights (Capehart, 2011.)

Below I will consider the ways in which homonationalist diplomacy, including aid conditionality, becomes a form of biopolitics in a neo-liberal global landscape. For the moment it is sufficient to point out that, despite these significant political and rhetorical moves on the part of the Obama administration, at no time has the United States government actually imposed economic sanctions or withheld financial assistance from Uganda, which might have threatened its trade and strategic relations with a major East African ally and thus put it at a disadvantage in its economic and geopolitical rivalry with China in the region. Echoing the story of Brazil's withdrawal of its famous resolution on sexual orientation in the United Nations Human Rights Commission in 2004 when it feared jeopardizing its trade relations with Arab countries, foreign trade and geopolitics hide behind the scenes in this case as well (see Corrêa, Petchesky and Parker, 2008).

Moreover, entangled with United States economic interests in Uganda are, as always, its military and strategic interests. In July of 2010, two major bombings were carried out in Kampala by a Somalian Islamist group, al-Shabab, reportedly linked to al-Qaeda. The blasts killed over seventy civilians (including one United States aid worker and many foreign tourists) who had assembled to watch the World Cup Final on television, reminding the world that the United States-led 'war on terror' still governs much of its foreign policy and, in a newly configured pattern of imperialism, may engage even non-Muslim, supposedly peaceful, African countries. Uganda, as the United States ambassador in Kampala put it, is 'a close ally in the fight against terrorism', maintaining 3,200 troops in Somalia and thus serving as a key proxy for the United States in its strategic battles there. In recent decades it has received millions of dollars in United States military assistance to fight insurgents in the Congo, Central Africa and Somalia (Kron and Ibrahim, 2010). For Uganda, the trade-off appears to be exposure of its citizens and visitors to risks of attack by Islamic terrorists in return for bargaining power in its international trade relations and virtual impunity in its domestic trampling of sexual rights. Indeed, this context sheds new light on the dubious *Rolling Stone* headline of November 2010, 'Homo Generals Planned Kampala Terror Attacks'. In whose interests does homosexuality become a scapegoat and pivot of a diversionary tactic to obscure accountability for the real dangers of entrapment in the snares of global militarism? The insertion of sexual politics into military and security agendas could not be starker, while the probability that security politics will always trump any 'swift and meaningful response' by Western governments to homophobia and transphobia abroad is undeniable.

At the same time, it would be a mistake to portray Uganda as simply a pawn in the US-led 'war on terror'. Uganda and its various regimes, from Idi Amin to Yoweri Museveni, have been, like many African governments, thoroughly militarized and embroiled in armed conflicts on the continent for decades – conflicts that are fuelled by the global traffic in small arms and its primarily Western-based purveyors (AFJN, 2009; Schroeder, 2004). Museveni's career in particular has been one continually buoyed by military, counter-insurgency and anti-terrorist methods and discourses.[8] From his guerrilla training with FRELIMO in Mozambique as a young man; to his participation in the civil war and National Resistance Army in the 1980s; to his assumption of the presidency in 1986 and the beginning of a twenty-five-year armed conflict with the Lord's Resistance Army (LRA) in the Acholi region of the north; to the rapid escalation of this conflict into a regional war encompassing the Democratic Republic of Congo (DRC, formerly Zaire), Central African Republic, Sudan and Rwanda; to the involvement of Ugandan forces in Somalia, Museveni's hold on power has relied on an aura of sustained armed conflict and the use of military courts and accusations of terrorism to suppress political opponents.

Certainly the LRA has posed a severe threat, terrorizing civilians and kidnapping and brutalizing tens of thousands of children during the course of the war. But the Ugandan government's militarized response has also been brutal. In 2005 the International Criminal Court in The Hague found its forces guilty of human rights abuses and of the plundering of resources in its 1999 invasion of the DRC. In the mid-2000s the government herded almost a million displaced people into IDP camps in the north, where, according to United Nations reports, 'poor health and sanitation conditions, lack of access to education, and high levels of sexual and gender-based violence' are rampant. Children in these camps are compelled to trade sexual favours to 'camp middlemen in order to avoid being passed on to armed [LRA] groups' seeking boy combatants and girl sexual and domestic slaves (Kälin, 2007; UNFPA, 2006). A subsequent study found poorly trained staff and inadequate health services for survivors or those at risk of gender-based violence, particularly youth, in northern Ugandan IDP camps. Uganda's law making abortion illegal even in cases of rape renders this situation even more desperate (Henttonen et al., 2008).

Probing still deeper, we encounter the race–ethnic as well as gendered dimensions of militarism in the Museveni regime's application of biopolitical governmentality. Mahmood Mamdani's historical analysis of the civil war and genocide in Rwanda in the 1990s makes compelling arguments to show that this horrific conflict originated in an internal Ugandan crisis over citizenship – a 'politics of indigeneity' as a means of defining 'the postcolonial subject' that derives directly from 'the colonial inheritance' (Mamdani, 2001: 166, 181). That policy favoured 'indigenous Ugandans', attempted to exclude squatter refugees (mainly Rwandan Tutsis[9]) from grazing land and citizenship rights more broadly, and finally led to the formation of the Rwandese Patriotic Front (RPF) and its 'armed repatriation from Uganda' in 1990. Although Museveni loudly denied claims by his opponents that he was privileging the squatters, Mamdani finds clear evidence that his government gave material support to the RPF in exchange for a promise of 'no return' from Rwanda and thereby participated in the exclusion and racialization of Tutsis (Mamdani, 2001: 176–84, 268).

What Mamdani fails to mention, and feminist analysis would reveal, is that militarized ethnic exclusions are always at the same time ways of reconstituting gender: asserting nationalist (indigenous) political leaders as dominant men, while spatially dividing refugee/ethnic minority populations into masculinized repatriation fighters and feminized and infantilized captives of displaced-person camps – or bare life (Giles and Hyndman, 2004; Agamben, 1998). Reflecting on empirical research done in northern Uganda in the early 2000s, Dubravka Zarkov comments on the ways in which men who experience a sense of ethnic exclusion and loss of status do so through the prism of gender, normative masculinity, and attempts to restore their manhood through increasing militarization and violence:

> When men of a specific group are excluded from achieving prescribed norms of masculinity, it is not only their tribal identity, but also their identity as men, that is threatened. This inevitably brings the militarization of masculinities, and the normalization of violence as a means of achieving manhood. (Zarkov, 2008: 11–12)

The politics of sexuality and gender become the most useful distraction from issues of economic injustice and the militarism that undergirds it because they have affective power. They arouse passions about individual bodies and identities through norms of true 'manhood', 'womanhood' and moral virtue; as well as about collective bodies and identities via post-colonial rejection of all that is labelled 'Western' in the name of true 'Africanism' and 'Ugandan' (or Islamic, or Nigerian, or Christian) virtue. In this way, biopolitics has both disciplinary and regulatory effects, working simultaneously to imbue fear and hatred into individual bodies/psyches and to construct homophobic societies. At the same time, neoliberal economics and the militarized security state are themselves steeped in the biopolitics of sexuality, gender and race. We see this starkly in the Uganda case in the hysterical blaming of 'homo generals' for the al-Shabab bombings, in the military conscription and racial marking and exclusion of Tutsi refugees, and in the expulsion and sexual and gender-based violence imposed on those in camps. Militarization, racialization, and sexual and gender economies weave tightly together in the production of biopolitics as a 'general strategy of power'.

Sexuality politics as decoy

On 22 March 2011, as I was presenting this paper to a conference of students and faculty in Toronto, two key and possibly related events occurred that would seem to alter the import of the Uganda case. That day the Ugandan minister of information appeared on television to announce that President Museveni's administration had determined that the Anti-Homosexuality Bill 'was redundant in consideration of existing laws already criminalizing homosexuality' as well as a new and pending Sexual Offences Bill, and therefore would be shelved (Levesque, 2011).[10] The very same day, at a meeting of the United Nations Human Rights Council in Geneva, an unprecedented eighty-five countries from all the world's regions signed a joint statement calling on states 'to end violence, criminal sanctions and related human rights violations based on sexual orientation and gender identity, and [urging] the Human Rights Council to address these important human rights issues' (ARC International et al., 2011).

In May and June of 2011, nearly the same scenario unfolded again. Another lobbying campaign to pass the Anti-Homosexuality Bill resulted in its being briefly 'unshelved' (Kron, 2011b), which created waves of panic on the Internet, followed by a fizzling out of the lame-duck session of parliament without any action on the bill. About a month later, the Human Rights Council, with the encouragement of many civil society groups, passed a historic resolution '*expressing grave concern* at acts of violence and discrimination, in all regions of the world, committed against individuals because of their sexual orientation and gender identity' (UN, 2011). Presented in eloquent terms by South Africa, the Resolution on Human Rights, Sexual Orientation and Gender Identity' passed by 23 votes to 19, with those in favour including mainly Latin American, European, and some Asian countries along with the USA; and those opposed being mainly Islamic countries and members of the Africa Group, including, not surprisingly, Uganda.[11] Then, within less than six months, the British and United States governments publicized their new international LGBT human rights policy, featuring at its centre the carrot-and-stick power of foreign aid. The response of politicians in Uganda played out a predictable backlash scenario. In February 2012 the anti-homosexuality bill was reintroduced in parliament, this time with a life-imprisonment penalty replacing the earlier death penalty provision. A few days later, Uganda's state minister for ethics and integrity shut down a conference organized by FARUG (Freedom and Roam Uganda), a leading LGBTI rights organization, saying: 'I have closed this conference because it's illegal. We do not accept homosexuality in Uganda. So go back home' (Ssebuyira, 2012). But, of course, as David Kato's fate reminds us, home is hardly a refuge from homophobic violence.

How should we read this extraordinary roller coaster of events? Clearly, pressure had been building even within the African region, but also as a result of years of relentless lobbying by international human rights NGOs for recognition of sexual orientation and gender identity as protected human rights categories (Corrêa, Petchesky and Parker, 2008). At the same time, as a number of Ugandan and transnational advocates stressed, the recurring attempts to pass the bill have served as an unmistakable diversionary tactic intended 'to blind the world to everything else that is going on in Uganda right now'. This included the assault on democracy and freedom of speech in April and May 2011, tear-gassing and firing on peaceful protesters, several deaths and hundreds of injuries as a result, and above all the escalating food and jobs crisis in Uganda that triggered the protests in the first place and persist to this day (Civil Society Coalition, 2011b; Gunther, 2011; IGLHRC, 2011; Statement of African Social Justice Activists, 2011).

I shall return to the vexing problem of *sexuality as a decoy* and what it signifies for sexual rights activism below. For now it is sufficient to say that this back-and-forth, advance and retreat movement of the Ugandan Anti-Homosexuality Bill in relation to international and local dynamics suggests that recognition at the level of international human rights discourse is a normative achievement whose effects are mainly discursive, possibly resulting in a shift within law and, above all, giving activist groups rhetorical weapons with which to continue struggles for greater sexual freedom and gender justice. But such norms do little to change the material realities of a biopolitical landscape in which homophobia and transphobia continue their peculiar dance with neoliberal trade, investment and military policies, and evangelical neocolonialism and its local co-conspirators still menace the lives of sexual and gender nonconformists, whether in public or private space. This tells us that the hidden fault lines of biopolitics require more grounded, structural and intersectional forms of opposition.

Resisting biopolitics

How might we imagine democratic, social-justice-based approaches to sites where sexual hysteria and macroeconomics converge? How can we counter the prevalence of militarized neoliberal biopolitics in such crises? In conclusion I want to address the role of transnational human rights activists and solidarity campaigns in responding to the biopolitics of sexuality, development and militarism. Are transnational activist campaigns, however well intentioned, integrally bound up in global biopolitical governmentality? Do they sometimes produce their own forms of paternalism, anti-colonial backlash, local disempowerment and racist stereotypes? And what strategies might help to avoid these minefields?

In a provocative article, Tavia Nyong'o presents a critical assessment of what he calls the 'fantasy of virtual participation' that pervades the volley of transnational Internet activity opposing homophobia and transphobia, particularly in Africa. Drawing on the work of Jodi Dean and Slavoj Žižek, Nyong'o makes two important and related arguments worth the attention of transnational sexual rights activists. First, Nyong'o suggests that new, instantaneous communication technologies – Twitter, Facebook, petition campaigns transmitted through electronic media – help to incite 'fantasies of spurious proximity and connectivity' that give us the illusion, and the affective satisfaction, of being directly involved in political action in an 'elsewhere' across the globe: 'the effect of such activist urgency ... is often to elevate the transmission of affect over the accomplishment of political objectives, reducing politics to what Dean calls a fantasy of participation' (Nyong'o, 2011: 46). Coupled with the frequent unreliability of Internet information and, one might add, its filtering through emotive images and condensed rhetorics, we become even more inclined to 'attach ourselves to intensities that seem plausible insofar as they conform to our imaginary structures' (42). Thus, another lesbian murder, another transphobic hate crime, another homophobic website or headline, morph into 'the wind of state homophobia [that] has swept over the African continent'. This affective intensity is problematic in at least two ways – first, in so far as it substitutes virtual connectivity for real action on the ground and possibly even pre-empts or disempowers local activist organizations; and, second, in so far as it occurs 'within a media context that frames contemporary sub-Saharan Africa as a charnel house of horror' and thus reinforces racist tropes of Africa as the site of darkness, violence, and barbarism (41).

A second argument Nyong'o makes involves a critique of human rights and humanitarian discourses deployed by transnational advocates as reducing Africans to the status of helpless victims and perpetuating the arrogant assumption of Northern-based NGOs 'rescuing Africans from their death driven impulses': 'If Africans are the permanent targets of humanitarian intervention, who repeatedly have to be rescued from the worst they are about to visit upon themselves, then they cannot become visible as agents of a transformational critique of globalization, or of the impoverished, exploited position they have been assigned within it.'[12] Neither does he spare Africans themselves from this critique, citing what he calls the 'neoliberal pervert' with her 'room full of computers and cell phones' who, every bit as much as her counterpart across the globe, invests in a particular way in the present economic and political order that presents itself as the only alternative (56). The important point of which Nyong'o reminds us is that neoliberalism – including the commerce of transnational communication, its replication of shopping for a desired outcome, and the focus on single issues as virtual commodities of desire – has become 'increasingly deterritorialized'; there is no neat divide here between 'North' and 'South' or between the subjectivities of differently located 'global activists'. But are there also distinct differences of power and location?

To avoid the pitfalls Nyong'o warns against, it seems to me that transnational sexual rights activists, especially those based in the global North but also the South-based queer and feminist subjects who often get pulled into legalistic and neoliberal frames, need to embrace two critical strategic positions. First, transnational campaigns are most effective when undertaken in full partnership with, and under the guidance of, local groups working on the ground whose knowledge, courage and expertise are often formidable even if their resources are small. In Uganda, groups like Sexual Minorities Uganda (SMUG, www.sexualminoritiesuganda.org) and Freedom and Roam Uganda (FARUG, www.faruganda.org) have developed far-reaching visions of a mission not only to fight against discrimination and inequality at home but also to challenge the neoliberal agendas of Northern governments, however couched in pro-LGBT human rights rhetoric. In order to have a vocal public presence and impact on policies, leaders of FARUG and SMUG have spoken out, at considerable personal risk (witness David Kato), in local media and international gatherings – and, yes, through electronic media. For example, in November 2010 FARUG transmitted an international 'Call to Action' for groups to protest the Ugandan government's cancellation of a conference on sex workers' human rights organized by the pan-African women's organization Akina Mama wa Afrika, based in Kampala. Demonstrating a clear perception of the links between erotic and economic justice, FARUG named the government's ban 'an injustice, a violation of [sex workers'] political and civil rights as well as of the right to work of these young women' (FARUG, 2010).

Given the authoritative location from which FARUG speaks, as well as the overtly hostile environment in which its members manage to survive, many Western-based NGOs have learned to see such calls to action as coming not from helpless victims needing 'rescue', much less from plugged-in Africans participating in neoliberal 'circuits of power' (Nyong'o, 2011: 56), but from courageous and resourceful political leaders. A politics of solidarity recognizes the distinct leadership position of such groups in struggles to gain respect and dignity for sex workers across the globe. It responds to appeals to build 'stronger partnerships with mainstream human rights and women's rights organizations' and for technical and financial support to build communications and strategic capacity and secure safe office and living spaces (FARUG, 2011), not with missionary illusions, but with a sober understanding that empowered LGBTI groups in Africa are an important bulwark against evangelical neocolonialism and militarized neoliberal capitalism everywhere. A very promising example of such partnership is the lawsuit that SMUG filed in March 2012, in conjunction with the US-based Center for Constitutional Rights, against the notorious Christian evangelist Scott Lively (see above) and his campaign of persecution against LGBTI persons in Uganda. Using the Alien Tort Statute that allows foreigners to sue US nationals in US courts for wrongs committed abroad, this lawsuit both focuses on the re-sponsibility of American evangelicals for the hateful anti-homosexuality bill in Uganda and positions local Ugandan activists as drivers of this human rights strategy.

Countering prevailing forms of biopolitics also requires a second and related strategic position: that of broad-based, multi-issue alliances. At the forefront of such strategies should be building strong coalitions between sexual rights advocates and economic and social justice groups that oppose distorted neoliberal development policies and the continued militarization of the African continent as well as militarized forms of humanitarian intervention and corporate investment in disasters. At stake here are the security and free expression of sexual minorities, which actually are exposed to greater menace and intimidation when LGBTI politics are isolated under a glaring global media spotlight. The Civil Society Coalition on Human Rights and Constitutional Law in Uganda made this point very directly in a 'Guidance Note' it issued to its 'inter-national partners' in November 2011. 'International partners [should] note that it is counterproductive to single out the Anti-Homosexuality Bill over all the other bills and human rights violations currently taking place in Uganda', the Civil Society Coalition wrote:

> in case a partner wishes to speak out loudly about the bill, then the message should condemn human rights violations in general including continuing restrictions to freedom of expression and assembly, and the worsening economic conditions and corruption scandals [in Uganda]. (Civil Society Coalition, 2011c)

Nowhere does this intersectional perspective become more urgent than in response to the issue of aid conditionality attached to violations of sexual and gender rights abuses. Self-righteous United States and British pronouncements of determination to cut off foreign assistance to countries that commit such violations, or even to give special support to

local gay rights organizations and leaders, while engaging their governments in neoliberal trade policies and arms deals, easily stir accusations
by local politicians of Western neocolonialist interference (see Kron,
2012; PRA, 2012). Sexual rights discourse and movements become tainted
by such 'homonationalist' diplomacy, which becomes a tool of the neoliberal state to elevate its hegemony and human rights credentials (possibly winning gay and lesbian votes at home) while never challenging
the priorities of global militarism and capitalist growth. Again, African
activists have taken the leadership on this question. In response to Prime
Minister David Cameron's threat in 2011 to cut off aid to 'countries that
persecute homosexuals', a statement by around 140 African social justice
organizations and individuals took a strong and principled stand that
might serve as a model for activists in the North in confronting their
own governments.[13] Pointing out that such policies create 'the real risk of
a serious backlash against LGBTI people' on the continent and actually
may harm those they profess to protect, the statement argues that

> Donor sanctions are by their nature coercive and reinforce the
> disproportionate power dynamics between donor countries and recipients.
> They are often based on assumptions about African sexualities and the needs
> of African LGBTI people. They disregard the agency of African civil society
> movements and political leadership. They also tend ... to exacerbate the
> environment of intolerance in which political leadership scapegoat LGBTI
> people for donor sanctions in an attempt to retain and reinforce national
> sovereignty.
>   Further, the sanctions sustain the divide between the LGBTI and the
> broader civil society movement. In a context of general human rights
> violations, where [heterosexual] women are almost as vulnerable as LGBTI
> people, or where health and food security are not guaranteed for anyone,
> singling out LGBTI issues emphasizes the idea that LGBTI rights are special
> rights and hierarchically more important than other rights. It also supports
> the commonly held notion that homosexuality is 'unAfrican' and a western-
> sponsored 'idea' and that countries like the UK will only act when 'their
> interests' have been threatened.
>   ... aid cuts also affect LGBTI people. Aid received from donor countries
> is often used to fund education, health and broader development. LGBTI
> people are part of the social fabric, and thus part of the population that
> benefit from the funding. A cut in aid will have an impact on everyone, and
> more so on the populations that are already vulnerable and whose access
> to health and other services are already limited, such as LGBTI people.
> (Statement of African Social Justice Activists, 2011)

The intersectional analysis embedded in this statement also shows clearly the ways in which a sexual rights politics tethered to neoliberal policy agendas reflects biopolitics at its most insidious. In contrast, the Statement of African Social Justice Activists presents a hope and vision of 'new ways of engaging', ones 'that affirm peoples' differences, choice and agency throughout Africa'. To become reality, such multiple, or 'polyversal' (Eisenstein, 2004), visions cry out for similarly polyversal coalitions, partnering global, regional and local organizations across many fields of activism.

Ultimately, single-issue politics have deadly consequences. Homosexuality and gender nonconformity become available as decoys to deflect from systemic crises, as in the case of Uganda's on-again, off-again Anti-Homosexuality Bill, precisely because they are seen, by advocates as well as opponents, as isolated and disconnected from the conditions of economic distress, militarism, trade inequities and structural violence. Conversely, the militarization of humanitarian relief efforts and the conversion of armed conflict zones into impoverished, dangerous, semi-permanent camps, can become an 'economic and political order that presents itself as the only alternative' (Nyong'o, 2011) only when their catastrophic effects on gendered and sexual bodies disappear from view. Opening up the panorama of these complex intersections is dangerous but, at the same time, the only way forward to a politics that moves beyond rhetoric and legalism towards social transformation.

Coda

The Ugandan parliament passed the Anti-Homosexuality Bill in December 2013. Then, on 24 February 2014, after weeks of manoeuvring back and forth, President Yoweri Museveni signed the bill into law. The final version omits the death penalty but is nonetheless draconian, presenting the possibility of life imprisonment for 'repeat offenders' and HIV-positive individuals and threatening those found guilty of 'aiding and abetting homosexuality' (presumably LGBTI organizations, AIDS support groups, human rights groups, parents and teachers who fail to report gay and lesbian youth, doctors and nurses, etc.) with up to seven years in prison (Cowell, 2014).

At the time of writing, the immediate national outcome has been an avalanche of mob violence, threats, intimidation, harassment, beatings, arrests and a fever of homophobic hysteria in the press. In a furore recalling the 2010 attacks in *Rolling Stone*, the Kampala-based newspaper *Red Pepper* published front-page photos of local LGBTI activists it labelled 'Homos' along with their addresses, putting the lives and safety of not only these persons but anyone perceived to be gay or lesbian at grave risk. The slogan 'We are all David Kato' has now come true for Ugandan sexual and gender nonconformists.

The international outcry of protest against Museveni's move was instantaneous and resounding. Prominent voices speaking out against the law for its blatant discrimination and violation of basic human rights included those of Archbishop Desmond Tutu, US President Obama and Secretary of State Kerry, UN Secretary General Ban Ki Moon and Special Rapporteur for Human Rights Navi Pillay, World Bank president Jim Yong Kim, the British foreign secretary and his counterparts in Scandinavia and other European countries, and of course countless human rights organizations and sexual and gender rights NGOs across the globe. SMUG leader Frank Mugisha met directly with top State Department officials to appeal for help in assuring the safety of the Ugandan LGBTI community and its members. The governments of Denmark, Norway and the Netherlands quickly cut or redirected existing aid commitments to Uganda. World Bank president Kim warned of the dire consequences that discriminatory laws will have for local economies: '(preventing) productive people from fully participating in the workforce' and 'discouraging multinational companies from investing or locating their activities in those nations'. In direct response to the Anti-Homosexuality Law, the World Bank 'indefinitely delayed a decision on a $90 million health care loan to Uganda' (Kim, 2014; Feder, 2014).

Should we expect any of this to have a significant impact on sexual politics in Uganda and elsewhere? In the short run, probably not, for the reasons and global conditions that likely motivated Museveni to sign the law. On the surface, evangelical neocolonialism once again enters the picture in the early 2014 scenario. Justifying his action by citing alleged 'scientific evidence' that homosexuality has no genetic basis and is a product of cultural imperialism, Museveni once again revealed the influence of US-based right-wing evangelical Christians, who invoke pseudo-science in their war against abortion, gays and lesbians, and non-traditional families and gender expressions. But, as Scott Long has urged, even on an ideological level we should be careful not to pin all the blame on 'Western evangelicals' to the exclusion of 'other factors (for instance, the way that "tradition" has become a source of political legitimacy in many African societies post-structural adjustment)' (Long, 2014; *The Economist*, 2014). Museveni was surely encouraged to sign the Anti-Homosexuality Law by the action of his counterpart in Nigeria a month earlier; in January President Goodluck Jonathan signed into law the Same Sex Marriage Prohibition Act, with provisions similar to the Uganda law and similarly horrific consequences for Nigerian LGBTI citizens. But lest we re-enact the racist stereotypes embedded in the mantra of a 'wave of African homophobia', we should recall that the Indian Supreme Court shocked the world by reinstating Section 377 of the Indian Penal Code just two months earlier, a fact not lost on President Museveni; and that not only 38 out of 54 African countries but 81 countries in all the world's regions have laws criminalizing homosexuality grounded in an imagined 'tradition' – despite, all too often, their historical roots in colonialism.

Underneath these ideological trappings lurk, as I have argued, a host of national and geopolitical fault lines for which sexuality functions as a kind of decoy. Both the national and the global conditions have shifted since 2010, but the dynamics are similar. First, Museveni is motivated by domestic political concerns – the recent weakening and fragmenting of his political party, the National Resistance Movement; the continued economic and infrastructural problems and budget deficit; and his own ageing, which makes his reputation as heroic freedom fighter irrelevant to younger voters. Standing up to Western neo-imperialism by castigating homosexuality as a 'Western import' not only arms him with the weapon of 'anti-colonial populism' but also helps shore up his power vis-à-vis the 'religious conservatism that can unite people across Uganda's heterogeneous regions, ethnicities and religions' (Shepherd, 2014; Kaoma/PRA, 2014) And once again it serves to divert attention from ongoing economic and social problems in Uganda.

Second, the changing global geopolitical context makes protestations by donor organizations and Western governments sound rather hollow.

Caught in the contradictions between their purported commitments to human rights and their interest in maintaining good trade relations and military ties in the region (see above), they are unlikely to deploy sanctions that have teeth. Moreover, Presidents Museveni and Jonathan gain credibility for their posture as champions of African national sovereignty against Western arrogance and imperialism from the shifting 'balance of power between African states and the donors'. In the past few years, African countries have found their position bolstered by their substantial natural resources and growing economic ties to countries like China, Malaysia and Russia whose aid does not come tied to human rights conditionalitites; whereas persistent economic crises and military misadventures have weakened the global power position of the United States and Europe (Shepherd, 2014; Kaoma/PRA, 2014).

In this very overloaded context, transnational activists find themselves caught in a double bind not so different from that of the self-righteous Western donors. If they protest too furiously and start calling for sanctions, aid cuts and the like, they reinforce the accusations of neocolonialism and outside interference in national affairs. If they do nothing, they betray their commitment to solidarity and supporting human rights defenders across the globe – and risk contributing (by inaction) to the oppression, abuse and murder of their colleagues abroad. All of this current debacle simply confirms, however, the two principal arguments that I made in the article before the Anti-Homosexuality Law was passed: (1) that sexual politics must always be understood in their complex relation to deep geopolitical and economic forces and never be seen in isolation or as 'single issues'; and (2) that Northern-based human rights activists must continue to act in solidarity with groups in the global South, including Africa, but always taking guidance and leadership from those working on the ground. In this respect, it is heartening to see a new set of 'Guidelines to National, Regional, and International Partners on How to Offer Support Now that the Anti-Homosexuality Law Has Been Assented To', issued by the Uganda Civil Society Coalition on Human Rights and Constitutional Law in early March 2014. Calling on such partners to continue speaking out against the law, to hold demonstrations before Ugandan embassies in their countries, and to protest arrests and harassment consequent upon the law, the Guidelines also stress in no uncertain terms the importance of broadly framed political strategies. Campaigns targeting Uganda (or other countries), they insist, should not focus exclusively on 'LGBTI rights' or sexual rights but should 'draw international public attention' to a whole range of related issues, including 'corruption, human trafficking' and 'the suppression of media freedom and civil society space' (Civil Society Coalition, 2014). Like the 2011 Statement of African Social Justice Activists, these Guidelines call for intersectional politics and polyversal coalitions. They suggest that 'we' – particularly those of us situated in spaces of relative privilege and safety – need to listen more, pontificate less, and see more complexly. In the long run, this work is much harder than a click on Twitter.

NOTES

1. Many thanks to DAWN for providing the stimulating space where this paper originated, at the DAWN Development Dialogues in Mauritius in January 2010. Thanks also to Sonia Corrêa, Zillah Eisenstein, Yao Graham and Andrew Park for very useful comments and suggestions, and to Ying Huang, my research assistant at Hunter College, CUNY, New York, for technical help.

2. It seems important to clarify the particular way in which I am using the concept of 'intersectionality' in this writing and building on its original meaning. Originally developed by Crenshaw (1991) and other women of colour feminist theorists in the 1980s and 1990s, the intent was to expand narrowly framed identity politics into a more comprehensive view of the multiplicity of identities and subjectivities, particularly for women of colour. Here I am attempting to take intersectional perspectives to another scale by positioning subjectivities within the larger economic, social and political contexts that produce them. Deep intersectionality refers not only to the multiple, multi-sited identities and positionings of political actors but also to the matrix of conditions and forces that construct political events and further complicate subjectivities. (Thanks to Zillah Eisenstein for pushing me to think more about this.)

3. At the beginning of his first Collège de France lecture in 1978, Foucault defined 'bio-power' as 'the set of mechanisms through which the basic biological features of the human species became the object of a political strategy, of a general strategy of power' (Foucault, 2007).

4. Alerts about bio-policing of and hate crimes against sexual minorities in Iran, Jamaica, Indonesia, Turkey, South Africa, the United States and elsewhere have appeared on many listservs and the websites of organizations such as the International Lesbian and Gay Human Rights Commission (www.iglhrc.org), AVAAZ (www.avaaz.org), the Coalition for Sexual and Bodily Rights in Muslim Societies (www.csbr.org) and Human Rights Watch (www.hrw.org). See also Lee, 2011 on Malaysia, Turkey, Australia, India and the USA.

5. Since the early 1990s, Lively has been involved in strident anti-gay activism both within the United States and in Latvia, Russia, Moldova and Uganda. His speeches and writings propagate the view that homosexuality is rooted in child sexual molestation and that all gays – among whom he includes transsexuals and the entire range of nonconforming gender and sexual identities – are insatiable sexual predators always on the lookout for vulnerable children. In 2009 he told his Uganda audiences that 'the goal of the gay movement is to defeat the marriage-based society and replace it with a culture of sexual promiscuity', linking 'the gay movement' to AIDS. This is particularly ironic, since AIDS in Uganda, as in most of Africa, is predominantly a heterosexually transmitted disease. For an excellent profile of Lively and his doings, see Burroway, 2011.

6. Lively's 2009 speech before members of the Ugandan parliament accused 'European and American gay activists' of 'external interference' in Ugandan affairs by trying to 'homosexualize that society' (Burroway, 2011). Christian evangelism apparently escapes this accusation in its claim to follow the teachings of Christ rather than Satan.

7. According to Andrew Park, during the lead-up to the November 2009 Commonwealth Heads of Government Meeting (CHOGM) in Trinidad and Tobago, devoted mainly to climate change, certain member states also put pressure on President Museveni to temper the anti-homosexuality politics that were festering in Uganda (pers. comm.).

8. Information on Uganda's militarization comes from the following sources: World Vision, 'Crisis in Northern Uganda', www.worldvision.org/content.nsf/learn/globalissues-uganda; www.GlobalSecurity.org; BBC News, 'Timeline: Uganda', 29 April 2011, http://newsvote.bbc.co.uk/mpapps/pagetools/print/news.bbc.co.uk/2/hi/africa/country_profiles/1069181.stm?ad=1; Richard Dowden, BBC News, 30 September 2010, http://news.bbc.co.uk/2/hi/programmes/from_our_own_correspondent/9045342.stm.

9. Many of these Rwandan Tutsis, or Banyarwanda, were descendants of refugees from earlier decades and had fought alongside Ugandans in the National Resistance Army that installed Museveni as president (Mamdani, 2001).

10. The Sexual Offences Bill covers a very wide range of acts, including, among others, rape, prostitution, incest, and the ill-defined category 'unnatural offences' (*Uganda Gazette* vol. 104, no. 2, 14 January 2011).

11. Among African members, in addition to South Africa, only Mauritius supported the resolution; Burkina Faso and Zambia abstained; and Angola, Cameroon, Gabon, Ghana, Mauritania, Nigeria, Senegal and Uganda, plus all the Islamic states currently on the Council, voted against (see ARC International, 17 June 2011). A resolution has more force under international law than the joint statement passed in March.

12. One problem with Nyong'o's analysis is his continual confusion of human rights and humanitarianism, ignoring that these are two very different regimes in international law, with very different rules, systems and mechanisms. Another is that he conflates all human rights advocacy into a single, stereotyped mould, ignoring the multiple ways in which human rights has become a dynamic discursive field for a wide variety of marginalized social movements – transgender people, Dalits, sex workers, indigenous peoples – claiming their agency, not their victimhood (see Corrêa, Petchesky and Parker, 2008: ch. 7).

13. The very interesting and now widely used concept of 'homonationalism' as a deployment of LGBT rights in the service of national aims was first introduced by Puar (2007).

REFERENCES

AFJN (Africa Faith and Justice Network) (2009) 'Impact of Small Arms Proliferation on Africa', 2 June, http://afjn.org/Focus-campaigns/militarization-us-africa-plicy/105–commentary.

Agamben, G. (1998) *Homo Sacer: Sovereign Power and Bare Life*, trans. D. Heller-Roazen, Stanford University Press, Stanford CA.

Agamben, G. (2005) *State of Exception*, trans. K. Attell, University of Chicago Press, Chicago and London.

Aken'ova , C. (2010) 'Draconian Laws against Homosexuality in Africa', *Sexuality Policy Watch*, Newsletter No. 8, March, www.sxpolitics.org.

AllAfrica.com (2009) 'Uganda: Museveni Hails China Over Aid', *New Vision*, 9 November, http://allafrica.com/stories/printable/200911100266.html.

AllAfrica.com (2010) 'Uganda' Big Companies Press Museveni for Oil Deals', *Independent* (Kampala), 9 February, http://allafrica.com/stories/printable/201002120276.html.

Allen, M. (2009) 'US Assails Uganda Plan to Toughen Antigay Law', *Wall Street Journal*, 18 December.

ARC International (2011) 'Historic Decision at the United Nations: Human Rights Council Passes First-Ever Resolution on Sexual Orientation and Gender Identity', press release posted on SOGI (Sexual Orientation and Gender Identity) List, 17 June.

ARC International et al. (2011) 'UN Human Rights Council: A Stunning Development Against

Violence', joint press release posted on 22 March, www.arc-international.net/global-advocacy/statements-resolutions/sogi-joint-statement-03-2011.htm.

Avert.org (2011) 'HIV and AIDS in Uganda', www.avert.org/aids-unganda.htm (accessed 7 June 2011).

Baffoe, J.K. (2000) 'Structural Adjustment and Agriculture in Uganda', Working Paper 149, March, International Labour Organization, Geneva, www.ilo.org/public/english/dialogue/sector/papers/uganstru/index.htm.

Branch, G. (2010) 'Uganda President: "Go Slow" on Anti-Gay Bill', *Global Post*, 15 January, www.globalpost.com/dispatch/africa/100114/uganda-anti-gay-bill-museveni.

Burroway, J. (2011) 'Lively's Lies: A Profile of Scott Lively', *The Public Eye*, vol. 26, no. 1, Winter/Spring, www.publiceye.org/magazine/v27n1/ScottLively.html.

Butler, J. (2004) *Undoing Gender*, Routledge, London and New York.

Capehart, J. (2011) 'Clinton's Geneva Accord: "Gay Rights Are Human Rights"', *Washington Post*, 7 December, www.washingtonpost.com/blogs/post-partisan/post/clintons-geneva-accord-gay-rights-are-human-rights/2011/03/04/gIQAPUipcO_blog.html.

Center for Constitutional Rights (2012) 'Ugandan LGBT Activists File Case against Anti-Gay U.S. Evangelical in Federal Court', 14 March, press release; press@ccrjustice.org.

Civil Society Coalition on Human Rights and Constitutional Law (2010) 'Protecting the Rights of Sexual Minorities: Civil Society Coalition Welcomes High Court of Uganda's Decision', *New Vision*, 8 November; www.ugandans4rights.org.

Civil Society Coalition on Human Rights and Constitutional Law (2011a) 'Civil Society Coalition on Human Rights and Constitutional Law: Court Rules that All Ugandans Have a Right to Privacy and Dignity', *New Vision*, 3 January; www.ugandans4rights.org.

Civil Society Coalition on Human Rights and Constitutional Law (2011b) 'Is Uganda's "Kill the Gays" Bill Being Used to Blind the World?', 9 May, www.ugandans4rights.org.

Civil Society Coalition on Human Rights and Constitutional Law (2011c) 'Guidance Note to Coalition International Partners on the Way Forward on the Anti-Homosexuality Bill in Uganda', 16 November, www.ugandans4rights.org.

Civil Society Coalition on Human Rights and Constitutional Law (2014) 'Guidelines to National, Regional, and International Partners on How to Offer Support now that the Anti-Homosexuality Law has been Assented To', 3 March, www.ugandans4rights.org.

Cooper, M. (2008) *Life as Surplus: Biotechnology and Capitalism in the Neoliberal Era*, University of Washington, Seattle and London.

Corrêa, S., R. Petchesky, and R. Parker (2008) *Sexuality, Health and Human Rights* Routledge, London and New York.

Cowell, A. (2014), 'Uganda's President Signs Antigay Bill', *New York Times*, 25 February.

Crenshaw, K. (1991) 'Mapping the Margins: Intersectionality, Identity Politics, and Violence against Women of Color', *Stanford Law Review* 43, pp. 1241–99.

Currah, P., R.M. Juang and S.P. Minter (eds) (2006) *Transgender Rights*, University of Minnesota Press, Minneapolis.

Dugger, C.W. (2010) 'Report Offers Optimistic View of Africa's Economies', *New York Times*, 24 June.

Economist (2010) Editorial, 'Oil Discovery May Turn into Curse for Uganda Government', *The Economist*, 31 March.

Economist (2014) 'Right Cause, Wrong Battle: Why the World Bank's Focus on Gay Rights is Misguided', *The Economist*, 12 April.

Eisenstein, Z. (2004) *Against Empire: Feminisms, Racism and the West*, Zed Books, London and New York.

FARUG (Freedom and Roam Uganda) (2010) 'Call To Action: Uganda: Government Should Break the Chains of Injustices against Sexual Minorities and Lift Decision to Ban Sex Workers Human Rights Workshop', 20 November, posted on sogi-list@arc-international.net, 19 November.

FARUG (Freedom and Roam Uganda) (2011) FARUG website, www.faruganda.org/index.php?option=com_content&view=article&id=2&itemid=2 (accessed 8 May).

Feder, J.L. (2014) 'World Bank review team to recommend approving loan to Uganda despite Anti-Homosexuality Act', 22 April, buzzfeed.com/lesterfeder.

Foucault, M. (1978) *History of Sexuality*, Volume I, Pantheon, New York.

Foucault, M. (1984) 'Truth and Power', in *The Foucault Reader*, ed. P.Rabinow, Vintage, NewYork.

Foucault, M. (2003) *'Society Must Be Defended': Lectures at the Collège de France, 1975–1976*, Picador, New York.

Foucault, M. (2007) *Security, Territory, Population: Lectures at the Collège de France, 1977–1978*, Palgrave Macmillan, New York.

Foucault, M. (2008) *The Birth of Biopolitics: Lectures at the Collège de France, 1978–1979*, Palgrave Macmillan, New York.

Gettleman, J. (2010) 'Americans' Role Seen in Uganda Anti-Gay Push', *New York Times*, 4 January. Giles, W., and J. Hyndman (eds) (2004) *Sites of Violence: Gender and Conflict Zones*, University of California Press, Berkeley and London.

Goodstein, L. (2012) 'Ugandan Gay Rights Group Sues U.S. Evangelist', *New York Times*, 15 March.

Gunther, S. (2011) 'Why Uganda's Anti-Homosexuality Bill Is Still a Threat', American Jewish World Service (AJWS), New York, 9 May, posted on sogi-list@arc-international.net.

Harcourt, W. (2009) *Body Politics in Development: Critical Debates in Gender and Development*, Zed Books, London.

Henttonen, M., C. Watts, B. Roberts, F. Kaducu and M. Borchert (2008) 'Health Services for Survivors of Gender-Based Violence in Northern Uganda: A Qualitative Study', *Reproductive Health Matters*, vol. 16, no. 31, May.

High Court of Uganda (2010) Court Ruling: Miscellaneous Cause No. 163 of 2010, *Kasha Jacqueline, David Kato Kisuule, Onziema Patience* vs. *Rolling Stone Ltd., Giles Muhame*, Kampala, 30 December.

Human Rights Watch (2011) 'Uganda: Promptly Investigate Killing of Prominent LGBT Activist', press release, 27 January, www.hrw.org/lgbt.

IGLHRC (International Gay and Lesbian Human Rights Commission) (2011) 'IGLHR Shocked at Possible Passage of Ugandan Anti-Homosexuality Bill – Rights Protections for All Ugandans Precarious', press release, 6 May, posted on sogi-list@arc-international.net.

ILGA (International Lesbian and Gay Association) (2011) 'ILGA Condemns David Kato's Murder Urging Uganda Authorities to Ensure Safety LGBTI Community', press release, 26 January, posted on sogi-list@arc-international.net.

Independent (2011) 'Unexpected Consequences', *Independent* website, 3 March, www.independent.co.ug/society/society/3985?task=view.

Kälin, W. (2007) *Report of the Representative of the Secretary-General on the Human Rights of Internally Displaced Persons*, United Nations Human Rights Council, 4th Sess., Doc. No. A/HRC/4/38.

Kaoma, K. (2014) *American Culture Warriors in Africa: A Guide to the Exporters of Homophobia and Sexism*, Political Research Associates (PRA), Somerville, MA.

Khanna, A. (2011) 'Aid Conditionality and the Limits of a Politics of Sexuality', 31 October, http://participationpower.wordpress.com/2011/10/31/aid-conditionality-and-the-limits-of-a-politics-of-sexuality.

Kim, J.Y. (2014) 'Discrimination By Law Carries a High Price', *Washington Post*, 27 February, www.washingtonpost.com/opinions/jim-yong-kim-the-high-costs-of-institutional-discrimination/2014/02/27/8cd37ad)-9fc5-11e3-b8d8-94577ff66b28_story.html.

Kron, J. (2011a) 'Pulling Out All the Stops To Push an Antigay Bill', *New York Times*, 14 April.

Kron, J. (2011b) 'Protests in Uganda over Rising Prices Grow Violent', *New York Times*, 22 April.

Kron, J. (2012) 'Resentment Toward the West Bolsters Uganda's New Anti-Gay Bill', *New York Times*, 29 February.

Kron, J., and M. Ibrahim (2010) 'Somali Militants Claim Credit for Uganda Attacks', *New York Times*, 13 July.

Long, S. (2014) 'Unintended Consequences: How Interntional Advocacy Against the Anti-Gay Bill in Uganda Became Self-Defeating', 27 February, email, sogi-list@arc-international.net.

Lee, J.C.H. (2011) *Policing Sexuality: Sex, Society and the State*, Zed Books, London.

LeGendre, P. (2010) 'Planned Rally Could Inflame Intolerance against Ugandan LGBTI Community', *Huffingtonpost* website, 28 April, www.huffingtonpost.com/paul-legendre/planned-rally-could-infla_b_555637.html.

Levesque, B. (2011) '"Kill The Gays" Measure In Ugandan Parliament Shelved – for Now', LGBTNATION website, 26 March, www.lgbtqnation.com/2011/03/kill-the-gays-measure-in-ugandan-parliament-shelved-for-now.

Luibhéid, E. (2002) *Entry Denied: Controlling Sexuality at the Border*, University of Minnesota Press, Minneapolis.

Maddow, R. (2009) 'Uganda Be Kidding Me', *YouTube* website, www.youtube.com/embed/GynDWIAnrlM (accessed 2 December 2009).

Mamdani, M. (2001) *When Victims Become Killers: Colonialism, Nativism, and the Genocide in Rwanda*, Princeton University Press, Princeton NJ and Oxford.

Mbembe, A. (2003) 'Necropolitics', *Public Culture*, vol. 15, no. 1.

Mohanty, C.T. (2003) *Feminism without Borders: Decolonizing Theory, Practicing Solidarity*, Duke University Press, Durham NC and London.

Nyong'o, T. (2011) 'Queer Africa and the Fantasy of Virtual Participation', *Women's Studies Quarterly*, vol. 40, nos 1 and 2.

Petchesky, R. (2003) *Global Prescriptions: Gendering Health and Human Rights*, Zed Books, London.

PRA (2012) 'Has Supporting Gay Rights Become Political Suicide in Africa?', Political Research Associates, 7 March, pra@publiceye.org.

Presidential Memorandum (2011), 'International Initiatives to Advance the Human Rights of Lesbian, Gay, Bisexual, and Transgender Persons', The White House, Office of the Press Secretary, 6 December, /www.whitehouse.gov/the-press-office/2011/12/06/presidential-memorandum-international-initiatives-advance-human-rights-1.

Puar, J.K. (2007). *Terrorist Assemblages: Homonationalism in Queer Times*, Duke University Press, Durham NC and London.

Rice, X. (2011) 'Ugandan Gay Activist David Kato's Funeral Marred by Angry Scenes', *Guardian*, 28 January, www.guardian.co.uk/world/2011/jan/28/gay-activist-david-kato-funeral/print.

Schroeder, M. (2004) 'The Illicit Arms Trade', Issue Brief #3, Federation of American Scientists (FAS), www.fas.org/asmp/campaigns/smallarms/IssueBrief3Arms Trafficking.html.

Shalhoub-Kevorkian, N (2009) *Militarization and Violence against Women in Conflict Zones in the Middle East*, Cambridge University Press, Cambridge.

Shepherd, B. (2014) 'The Politics of the Anti-Homosexuality Legislation', Chatham House, 24 February, https://www.chathamhouse.org/media/comment/view/197622.

Ssebuyira, M. (2012) 'Ethics Minister Shuts Down Gay Rights Conference', *Sunday Monitor*, 14 February, www.monitor.co.ug/News/National/-/688334/1327440/-/boqolnz/-/index.html.

'Statement of African Social Justice Activists on the Threats of the British Government to "Cut Aid" to African Countries that Violate the Rights of LGBTI People in Africa' (2011), distributed on SOGI list (sogi-list@arc-international.net), 28 October.

Stoler, A. (2005) *Race and the Education of Desire*, Duke University Press, Durham NC and London.

Tamale, S. (2010) 'A Human Rights Impact Assessment of the Anti-Homosexuality Bill', *AllAfrica Global* website, 14 January, http://allafrica.com/stories/201001140884.html.

Uganda Gazette (2011) Bills Supplement No. 1, *The Sexual Offences Bill, 2011, Uganda Gazette* vol. CIV, no. 2, 14 January.

UNFPA (United Nations Population Fund) (2006) *State of World Population 2006: A Passage to Hope, Women and International Migration*, United Nations Population Fund, New York:

UN (United Nations) (2011) General Assembly, Human Rights Council, 17th Session, Follow-up and implementation of the Vienna Declaration and Programme of Action, 17/... Human rights, sexual orientation and gender identity (resolution), A/HRC/17/L.9/Rev.1 (15 June).

UNAIDS (2010) *UNAIDS Report on the Global AIDS Epidemic 2010*, Joint United Nations Programme on AIDS, Geneva.

WILPF (Women's International League for Peace and Freedom) (2011) 'Women Say Stop the War – End Sexual Violence in the Democratic Republic of Congo', http://Congoaction-now.weebly.com/women-say-stop-the-war.html (accessed 21 June 2011).

Zarkov, D. (2008) 'On Militarism, Economy and Gender: Working in Global Contexts', in D. Zarkov (ed.), *Gender, Violent Conflict and Development*, Zubaan/Kali for Women, New Delhi.

BOX IV.3 **HIV and SRHR**

RODELYN MARTE

Worldwide, HIV is the leading cause of death and disease among women of reproductive age (WHO, 2009: 10). At the end of 2009, 53 per cent of the world's 33.3 million people living with HIV were women and girls. The percentage of women living with HIV varies. It is higher in the sub-Saharan Africa and the Caribbean and lower in other regions (UNAIDS, 2010: 10). As with other marginalized groups, the often disadvantaged social and economic status of women causes them to experience the impact of HIV disproportionately.

The global response to, and politicization of, the AIDS epidemic has gained ground in the past twenty years. Activists have been asserting that only by addressing the issues of gender equality, economic justice and human rights can the epidemic be dealt with effectively. Maintaining support for this assertion is becoming more critical in the current era of diminishing funding for health and a crowded space for public and political attention among different development issues (Germain et al., 2009).

STAKING WOMEN'S CLAIMS WITHIN AIDS RESPONSES

The limited resources for HIV are most effective through responses aligned to country-specific epidemic transmission dynamics (Sarker et al., 2009: 20). This approach facilitates demanding women-responsive AIDS programmes in regions such as Southern and Eastern Africa, where HIV transmission occurs mainly through unprotected heterosexual sex, as well as to newborn and breastfed infants. This demand is becoming more difficult to voice in many countries in Asia and the Pacific, Latin America and the Caribbean, Middle East and North Africa and West Africa, where the epidemic is concentrated among particular vulnerable populations. Who is and who is not part of a vulnerable population or key affected group is heavily debated within the AIDS community. In countries with concentrated epidemics, key affected populations usually include people living with HIV (PLHIV), sex workers (SW), men who have sex with men (MSM), transgender people (TG), people who use drugs (PUD) and, recently, 'young key affected populations' (young KAP). Who makes the list effectively translates into who gets prioritized in AIDS funding and programming. Except for sex workers, where women predominate, women often don't make the list.

Although women-centred HIV prevention programme frameworks exist, these frameworks also need to be continuously questioned. Currently, the emphasis is on conducting HIV tests among pregnant women in antenatal clinics, which means that women who are not pregnant are left out of the screening programme. It also reinforces notions that children's health is more important than that of their mothers, since the primary objective of antenatal testing services is to prevent transmission of the virus to infants. Hence there is an implied disregard for the inherent value of women's lives (ICW, 2008; ITPC, 2009).

An expansion of gender-responsive programme approaches for key affected populations should be called for. Women-specific concerns related to gender-based violence, violations of sexual and reproductive rights, and criminalization of sex work and drug use need to be articulated in these approaches as well as in the broader discourses on human rights approaches to HIV. The protection of the human rights of key affected populations is increasingly acknowledged by HIV programme planners, implementers and development partners in the response to AIDS as a critical factor in effectively addressing the epidemic (UN, 2001: paras 16, 58–61; 2006: paras 11, 15, 29; 2011: paras 39, 77–85).

Efforts at inter-movement collaborations and dialogues within the HIV community need to be supported and sustained since much remains to be accomplished. This involves addressing power relations between women and men, among women, among men, among transgender people and across these diverse sexualities in order to build genuine solidarity and understanding. There is a responsibility on the part of women's groups to support more inclusive gender frameworks.

REFERENCES

Germain, A., R, Dixon-Mueller and G. Sen (2009) 'Back to Basics: HIV/AIDS Belongs with Sexual and Reproductive Health', *Bulletin of the World Health Organization*, vol. 87, no. 11, pp. 840–45.

ICW (International Community of Women Living with HIV/AIDS) (2008) 'HIV Positive Women, Pregnancy and Motherhood', ICW Briefing Paper, London.

ITPC (International Treatment Preparedness Coalition) (2009) *Missing the Target 7 – Failing Women, Failing Children: HIV, Vertical Transmission and Women's Health*.

Sarkar, S., N. Menser and W. McGreevey (2009) 'Cost-Effective Interventions that Focus on Most-at-Risk Populations', Working Paper, Results for Development, Washington DC.

UN (United Nations) (2001) General Assembly Special Session, *Declaration of Commitment on HIV and AIDS*, UN, New York.

UN (United Nations) (2006) *Political Declaration on HIV/AIDS*, General Assembly, UN, New York.

UN (United Nations) (2011) *Intensifying Our Efforts to Eliminate HIV and AIDS*, General Assembly Special Session, UN, New York.

UNAIDS (2010) Joint United Nations Programme on HIV/AIDS, Epidemic Update, in *UN-AIDS Report on the Global AIDS Epidemic 2010*, UNAIDS, Geneva.

WHO (World Health Organization) (2009) 'Adult Women: The Reproductive Years', in *Women and Health: Today's Evidence Tomorrow's Agenda*, WHO, Geneva.

BOX IV.4 **Sexuality and human rights in Brazil: the long and winding road**

SONIA CORRÊA

Realizing human rights in relation to sexuality is a complex and contradictory process. Over the last three decades, Brazil, for example, has experienced positive cultural transformation, as well as legal and policy reforms favourable to sexual rights. Yet these gains were not set in stone and the 2000s have seen flagrant policy regressions.

Sexuality has always been indelibly fused with Brazilian culture, embedded in structural violence, class and racial inequalities and deeply imprinted by hetero-procreative religious and secular norms. Contemporary claims related to sexuality, human rights and reproduction took form in the early days of democratization that would put an end to the military regime (1964–85). Since then feminists, advocates of LGBTI rights and prostitutes' groups have claimed for citizenship rights to encompass gender and sexuality. In the early 1980s, progressive revisions were proposed to Civil Code provisions on marriage and the Penal Code articles on abortion, while policy frameworks for sex education and women's health were also reshaped (Vianna and Carrara, 2007). Concurrently, the HIV/AIDS epidemic propelled the emergence of a plural social movement that also called for non-discrimination on the basis of sexuality (Paiva, Pupo and Barboza, 2006).

The 1988 constitutional reform enshrined the principles of dignity, equality and non-discrimination for all. As the 1988 Constitution did not include a clause on the right to life since conception, the space remained open for proposals on legal abortion, as in the case of the 2012 Supreme Court decision allowing for termination of pregnancy in the case of anencephaly. Although the text did not specify sexual orientation, its principles have been used subsequently to ground state and municipal laws prohibiting discrimination against LGBTI persons and to support court cases on the right of same-sex couples to health insurance, pensions and adoption. In 2011, the Supreme Court issued a positive decision on same-sex civil unions, since which time judicial administrative procedures have been approved that allow same-sex marriage.

Post-democratization Brazilian diplomatic positions on sexual matters contributed to the international human rights commitments reached at the 1990s UN conferences and related arenas on human rights, gender equality and sexuality itself, as illustrated by the resolution on sexual orientation and human rights tabled by Brazil in 2003. And these international debates and norms have also positively influenced national policy formation. Under the impact of ICDP, for example, in 1998, the Ministry of Health adopted a protocol for provision of abortion in the two cases permitted by law (rape and risk to the woman's life)

(Villela and de Oliveira Araujo, 2000). Beijing definitions on rape as a human rights violation led to partial reform, in 2009, of the 1940 Penal Code, which saw the title of the section on rape and other forms of sexual violence changed from 'crimes against morals' to 'crimes against sexual dignity'. The reform also defined non-coital infringements of bodily integrity as violations of sexual dignity, regardless of gender.

Although these gains are yet to be appraised, they have not translated easily into reality in daily life. Furthermore, the effects of legal and policy change vary sharply across the spectrum of claims pertaining to sexual and reproductive rights. As has also happened in many other Latin American countries, legal changes regarding same-sex unions and marriage have moved faster and are more widely accepted than are demands for legal abortion. Most importantly, moral conservative forces, visible since the early days of democratization, have decidedly become increasingly influential. This is illustrated by the setback to a 2004 proposal made by the executive to legalize abortion (Corrêa, 2006); and, most significantly, by the 2010 presidential campaign, whose dynamics were to a large extent determined by flare-up around abortion and same-sex marriage (Corrêa, 2010).

Since 2010, dogmatic religious forces have become particularly aggressive at Congress and societal levels, making sequential proposals on the rights of the unborn, the 'curing' of homosexuals and the criminalization of clients involved in commercial sex. Under the Roussef administration, on four occasions the federal executive branch has censored sex education materials, including three campaigns launched by the HIV/AIDS department (de la Dehesa, 2013). In June 2014, the Minister of Health, under strong conservative pressure, repealed the ordinance it had issued only a few weeks earlier in relation to legal abortion in the case of rape, risk to a woman's life and anencephaly.

Normative complexities and inconsistencies with respect to human rights and sexuality also need to be highlighted. For instance, law number 12015/2009 on rape has kept intact the six- to ten-year prison term, defined in the 1990 heinous crime law – a penalty greater than that for first-degree murder. This should be a matter of concern for those committed to human rights in a country where the number of prison inmates has tripled in the last thirty years and where the effective application of criminal justice remains highly selective in both race and class terms. The same reform raised the penalty for rape resulting in pregnancy or the transmission of sexual disease – a definition that, in practice, criminalizes HIV transmission, which goes against the long-standing rights-based premises of the national HIV/ AIDS response.

A compelling lesson from this winding road is that legal and policy reform, though indispensable, is wholly insufficient. History in Brazil and elsewhere shows that realizing human rights in the realm of sexuality requires unending struggles within the social fabric itself. Progress also depends, importantly, on dialogues and solidarity among the various constituencies advocating for sexual freedom and non-discrimination, and on sustained work to overcome class, race and other social hierarchies and inequalities that intersect with sexuality and human rights.

REFERENCES

Corrêa, S. (2006) *Interlinking Policy, Politics and Women's Reproductive Rights: A Study of Health Sector Reform, Maternal Mortality and Abortion in Selected Countries of the South,* DAWN Sexual and Reproductive Health and Rights Program, Quezon City.

Corrêa, S. (2010) 'Brazil: Abortion at the Frontline', *Sexuality Policy Watch Newsletter 8,* www.sxpolitics.org/wp-content/uploads/2010/10/brazil_-abortion-at-front-line.pdf.

de La Dehesa, R. (2013) The End(s) of Activism? Sexual Rights and the Brazilian Workers Party, *Fletcher Forum of World Affairs* online, www.fletcherforum.org/2013/09/30/deladehesa/ (accessed 25 October 2013).

Paiva, V., L.R. Pupo and R. Barboza, (2006) The Right to Prevention and the Challenges of Reducing Vulnerability to HIV in Brazil, *Revista de Saúde Pública* 40, pp. 109–19.

Vianna, A.R.B., and S. Carrara (2007) 'Sexual Politics in Brazil: A Case Study', in R. Parker, R. Petchesky and R. Sember (eds), *SexPolitics: Reports from the Front Line,* Sexuality Policy Watch online, pp. 27–51; www.sxpolitics.org/frontlines/book/pdf/capitulo1_brazil.pdf (accessed 25 October 2013).

Villela, W.V., and M.J. de Oliveira Araujo (2000) 'Making Legal Abortion Available in Brazil: Partnership in Practice', *Reproductive Health Matters,* vol. 8, no. 16, pp. 77–82.

PART V

Frontier challenges: building nation-states and social movements

CHAPTER 11
The state of states

CLAIRE SLATTER

This chapter considers the state of states in the South in relation to social contracts and the enlargement of citizenship rights for women. It considers the political and economic legacies of colonialism that have had a bearing on state–citizen relations, noting colonial and post-colonial continuities in political authoritarianism, the dysfunctionality of states in war zones and other places riven by long-standing conflict over resources, and the relatively recent citizenship gains for women in many Southern states attained through judicial rulings, more recent democratic transitions, and the global extension of human rights. It reviews some of the mainstream discourses on the state that have emerged in the era of economic globalization and the 'war on terror', the ideological justifications they respectively provide for restructuring the state, redefining state–citizen relations and, more recently, for big power military intervention in breach of the Westphalian principle of sovereignty. It concludes by reiterating the need for feminist activists in the fierce new world to (re)claim the state irrespective of its failings, and to continue working to both remake national social contracts and secure new modalities of global governance that are genuinely multilateral and that bring international human rights norms to bear on both economic/trade laws and interstate relations.

Contextualizing social contracts in the South: colonial and post-colonial continuities

Despite their common history of colonization, Southern states had markedly different experiences of imperialism and colonialism, attained independence in different periods, and by varying means, and followed distinct political trajectories following independence. These differences, shaped by the era in which they were colonized, their differing resource endowments and geo-strategic significance, and the survival (or not) of pre-existing socio-political systems and their supporting ideologies, had strong bearing on post-colonial state formation, founding constitutional contracts, political stability and development prospects, as well as on the possibilities for enlarging citizenship and rights, especially for women.

A common feature of all colonial states was their authoritarian nature. This was reflected in colonial laws, legislative and judicial systems, bureaucracies and, not least, the coercive apparatuses on which the colonial state ultimately relied to maintain political order and control. For most states that attained independence by negotiated settlement in the post-World War II period, the first 'democratic transition' occurred only on the eve of political independence (Nwauwa 2003; Naidu 2006). Variants of the liberal democratic state that had emerged in parts of Europe – based on parliamentary government, electoral competition between parties and an established opposition – were hastily transplanted to replace long-established authoritarian colonial state systems. The democratic foundations of the post-colonial state were thus quite shaky from the start, and, without the experience of the historical struggles and ideological challenges that had resulted in the evolution of the democratic state in Western Europe, it was hardly surprising that Southern political elites that inherited power at independence tended towards the more familiar form of governance – authoritarianism. Part of the colonial heritage, authoritarianism or dictatorship became the leitmotif of post-colonial state–society relations (Davidson, 1992; Bernstein, 2000; Potter, 2000; Nwauwa, 2003).

In the decades that followed post-war transfers of power from colonial rulers to leaders of nationalist or independence movements, gaining and/ or retaining control of the state, its bureaucratic-military apparatus and the national resources at its disposal (most often for personal enrichment) increasingly became the primary objective of male-dominated electoral competitions (where elections continued to take place), as has been documented for sub-Saharan Africa (Jha, 2006: 154). In many states, the signifiers of formal democracy (elections, opposition parties) were dispensed with early on, along with constitutions, as elected governments and electoral-based political systems gave way to even more distinctly masculinist one-party states,[1] or fell to military dictatorships. In many cases, the democratic social contract that independence constitutions represented was breached by the very nationalist political leaders (e.g. Jomo Kenyatta, Kwame Nkrumah, Sekou Toure, Kenneth Kaunda) who had negotiated them before taking power at independence, through constitutional amendments to extend their terms of office or make themselves Presidents for Life (Sklar, 1983; Nwauwa, 2003). Although he held power for twenty-four years under one-party rule, Julius Nyerere distinguished himself both by the ethical foundation of his (African) socialist model of development (Ujamaa), and by retiring gracefully from political office and facilitating a peaceful leadership transition in Tanzania. Entrenched regimes that have survived for several decades, such as those in the Middle East, Burma and Zimbabwe, have largely been able to do so by repressing their citizens. Countries with the richest natural resources tended to become more authoritarian than others (Jensen and Wantchekon, 2004).

Struggles for the control of natural resources intensified in the post-colonial period. Countries with rich natural resources were plagued for decades by vicious conflicts and wars. In these bloody resource conflicts, states were often pitted against local insurgents, the latter frequently armed and financed by external forces with direct interests in the resource (Tabb, 2007; Le Billon, 2002; Alley, 2003). In the cold war years, ideological offensives against the evils of 'godless communism' provided a convenient cover for engagements in resource wars that were often fought by proxy. In other instances, resource wars were masked by their outward manifestation (or representation) as domestic inter-tribal or inter-ethnic conflicts.[2] Since the state was often all that stood between contending external interests and access to lucrative resources, a weak state was the next best thing to a pliable, comprador one. The imperialist political project of toppling governments and undermining the state was usually covert, and often CIA-inspired or -backed.[3] In other instances, coups were planned and executed by mercenaries acting in collusion with business interests.[4]

Between the end of the cold war and 2000, sub-Saharan Africa experienced widespread civil–military tensions and a succession of civil wars: Angola (1989–94, 1998–99), Burundi (1998, 2000), Chad (1990), Congo

(1997–99), Democratic Republic of Congo (1997–2000), Ethiopia/Eritrea (1989–91; 1998–2000), Guinea Bissau (1998), Liberia (1990, 1992), Mozambique (1989–92), Rwanda (1991–92, 1998), Sierra Leone (1998–99), South Africa (1989–93), Somalia (1989–92) and Uganda (1989, 1991) (Fraenkel, 2004). A World Bank study of the economic causes of civil war (Collier Hoeffler, 1998), based on a survey of 98 countries (27 of which had experienced at least one civil war), found a high share of primary exports in GDP (or high natural resource endowment) to be one of four factors predisposing countries to civil war, but did not appear to correlate this factor with external interests in these resources. Resource wealth (or 'resource curse'[5] as it is frequently and more aptly termed) impeded democratic transitions in post-cold war Africa and created severely disabling environments for the fulfilment of social contracts by post-colonial states.[6]

That women and children suffer the worst in political conflicts and wars is indisputable – they comprise 50 per cent of the world's stateless people, refugees and internally displaced persons.[7] Women are the most vulnerable where law and order have broken down. In inter-ethnic and inter-religious wars, women's bodies are boundary markers, and the rape of women and girls signifies more than horrific acts of violence and domination, as it constitutes an insidious form of ethnic cleansing. Ongoing hostilities and the effective partition of states into rebel-held and government-held areas make nonsense of the notion of citizenship, since no one, least of all women, can enjoy or be guaranteed physical security and protection of life, let alone enjoyment of other rights and freedoms that might be inscribed in national constitutions. Economic and political insecurity and war have also sent unprecedented numbers of people across national boundaries in search of jobs and safety, triggering a backlash of racist xenophobia in receiving countries in both the North and the South.

Outside of war and conflict zones and refugee camps, where states are undermined and weakened, competing power centres often arise to fill the vacuum. Fiefdoms run by drug lords or commandants of other lucrative, albeit illicit, economies proliferate in many regions of the South, often functioning as states within states, providing services that states no longer provide, and subjecting citizens within their domain to their own laws and justice systems. Under these regimes, as in the theorized 'state of exception',[8] women live with daily oppression and abuse. However, neither the internal breakdown of state–citizen relations, nor the voluntary or forced migration of persons from one state to another, absolves any state from its fundamental responsibility to fulfil rights and afford protection to all residing within its territorial borders.

Even today, resource struggles involving foreign interests and related geopolitical machinations usually lie at the heart of political instability, eruptions of political conflict and war in Southern countries and impact on women in severely harmful ways, although these facts are rarely acknowledged in international media coverage of such events. The US funding of fundamentalist camps in Pakistan against the Russians during the cold war years, for instance (which was not unrelated to private US interests in both oil and, as more recently divulged, mineral wealth in the region[9]), spawned the Taliban, whose terrorization of women, evidently in reaction to the freedoms afforded them by the Najibulah regime, ranged beyond the borders of Afghanistan.[10] Struggles over the control of resources also clearly lie behind the so-called 'clash of civilizations' (Huntington, 1993) or of 'liberalism versus conservatism' highlighted in contemporary discourses on the war on terrorism. Yet the seizing of control of Iraq's oil wells and other forms of profiteering by US companies during and since the war are far less subjected to scrutiny or commented on in these discourses.[11] Post-9/11, 'evil regime' profiling and state-media collusion in disinformation marketing have also provided 'legitimate' pretexts or covers for war, plunder, regime change, and lucrative reconstruction work in resource-rich Southern states, on terms laid down by what some would unhesitatingly call imperialist victors.

Less well-endowed states marked by other legacies of colonialism such as ethnic and social class cleavages were not necessarily spared conflict either, as illustrated most tragically by Rwanda. The bedrock of mutual distrust created by colonial divide and rule strategies in multi-ethnic and multi-religious states usually encouraged identity politics and extremism, seriously impeding nation-building and the evolution of a sense of citizenship (Naidu, 2007).

The post-colonial state and women's citizenship

Except where women's traditional political role was deliberately eroded by colonialism, the gender systems underlying traditional social, economic and political arrangements appeared to survive the political transition to modern state forms virtually intact. The subordination of women as subject citizens across all ethnic and class categories in the post-colonial social contract was often quite explicit. Constitutions adopted at independence typically framed fundamental rights and freedoms in supposedly gender-neutral terms while at the same time enshrining patriarchal ideas and principles, such as the principle of patrilineal descent in citizenship provisions and customary land rights, thereby conferring on women fewer entitlements as citizens than men. Not only were women's rights and entitlements under inherited colonial laws usually circumscribed by Western patriarchal values, women's assigned place in the new nations was often also influenced by the sexual politics of nationalist movements – protection of the nation from rapacious outsiders was equated by nationalist leaders with protection of women from male colonizers. As Van der Veer has argued in the case of India, 'nationalist discourse connect[ed] control over the female body with the honour of the nation' (1994).

As such, apart from gaining the right to vote under independence constitutions, citizenship for women in post-colonial states often held little meaning. Even where constitutions provided broad guarantees of equal rights and opportunities for men and women, as India's 1949 Constitution did (Article 14), prohibiting discrimination on the grounds of sex (Article 15), permitting affirmative action in favour of women (Article 15 (3)), guaranteeing men and women equal pay for equal work (Article 39(c)), obliging citizens to renounce practices derogatory to women (Article 51A(e)), and covering the reservation of seats for women in elected bodies (Article 243D(3)), the fulfilment of rights guaranteed by the supreme law of the land usually required subsequent legislative enactments.

These deficiencies in the social contract aside, in the early post-independence period, post-colonial states generally played a significant role in economic and social development as well as in developing communications and physical infrastructure. This developmental and social provisioning role was inspired as much by the early successes of socialist states as by post-war colonial development and welfare policies, and even more significantly by the radical visions and development agendas of nationalist independence movements. While women were certainly beneficiaries of state-led development, their disadvantage within existing gender systems mostly remained ignored and unaddressed. Nonetheless, as the vehicle through which the nationalist promise of development would be delivered, the early post-colonial state enjoyed strong legitimacy, and discourses on the developmental state in the 1970s so legitimated the model of state-led development that it became the orthodoxy.

Where independence was won through a war of liberation, the resulting revolutionary order in many instances did bring about a significant transformation of the gender order by enabling women's leadership as well as representation, guaranteeing women's equality with men in the workplace and providing support for childcare, although these were largely instrumental measures aimed at expanding economic production and growth. Cuba stands out for its early introduction of constitutional and legal guarantees of equality for women in all spheres, including the workplace, home, family and marriage, and, after 1965, for its guarantee of women's reproductive rights (www.cuba-solidarity.org.uk).

Outside of the socialist world, major victories for women in post-colonial states have mostly been achieved since the 1980s. These have resulted from legal petitions or lawsuits filed by women or women's advocacy for law reforms, from constitutional changes during more recent democratic transitions, or in consequence of general advances in understanding and realizing human rights across the globe, as illustrated by the following examples:

- Both the African Charter on Human and Peoples' Rights, adopted in 1981 by member states of the Organization for African Unity (OAU) and recognized as a model regional human rights instrument, and the Optional Protocol on the Rights of Women in Africa, adopted in 2003 by the OAU's successor, the African Union, were milestone political gains in the advancement of women's equality in Africa.
- A major victory for women's equality was won in Botswana in 1992 when the High Court ruled in favour of Unity Dow, who sought a Court ruling that Section 4 of the Botswana Citizenship Act violated her fundamental rights and freedoms under Chapter 11 of the Constitution. The ruling confirmed the right of women in Botswana to enjoy the same right as Botswana men to pass on Botswana citizenship to their children, irrespective of paternal nationality (Seng, 1993).

- An amendment to India's Penal Code in 1983 made domestic violence a criminal offence, and a subsequent amendment in 1986 (304B.3) introduced stiff penalties for persons convicted of causing 'dowry deaths', defined as the death of a woman by burns, bodily injury or other than normal causes, that occurs within seven years of marriage where there is evidence of her subjection to cruelty or harassment by a husband or his family in connection with a demand for dowry.

- The state of Kerala amended the Hindu Succession Act in 1976 to give women equal inheritance rights, and other states followed suit: Andhra Pradesh in 1986, Tamil Nadu in 1989, and Maharashtra and Karnataka in 1994 (Roy, 2008). Also in Kerala, a landmark Supreme Court ruling in 2010 in the eight-year-long case of Mary Roy, who sued her brothers after her father's death, extended equal inheritance rights to Christian women (*India Today*, 30 October 2010).

- In 1993, constitutional amendments reserved 30 per cent of seats in elected village councils (panchayats) in India for women, overnight bringing more than 1 million elected women into local-level political leadership.

- Argentina's return to democracy in 1994 ushered in a new constitution that incorporated all international human rights treaties and instruments adopted or ratified by Argentina and gave equal opportunity for men and women to elective and political party positions and constitutional standing to the National Women's Council (which monitors CEDAW implementation), providing for its direct reporting to the president.[12]

- The landmark ruling of the Supreme Court in Nepal in 2010 in support of women's reproductive rights and equal access to safe abortion came in response to a public interest case filed in the Court in 2007 by Lakshmi Dhikta (who was forced to carry an unwanted pregnancy to term because of her inability to pay for an abortion), five other plaintiffs and an NGO. The judgment gave effect to the fulfilment and equal enjoyment of women's reproductive rights, recognized under Nepal's Interim Constitution of 2007 as fundamental rights, by ordering both the enactment of a comprehensive abortion law to guarantee safe and affordable access to legal abortion services for all women, and the establishment of a government fund to meet the cost of abortion for poor women (http://reproductiverights.org/en/our-issues/abortion).

Victories similar to those cited above have been won elsewhere in the South, aided by global advocacy to advance human rights, and provide cause for celebration. Although some states have recently backtracked, breaking the social contract and the advancement of women's rights through women's agency by returning to military rule,[13] recent popular uprisings against long entrenched (and dynastic) regimes are opening opportunities for unprecedented democratic transitions in which women citizens should expect to secure increased rights – although these will not be won without sustained and strategic negotiations. Ironically, the project of advancing women's rights within some post-colonial states appears to have attained urgency. Among the USA's justifications for bombing Afghanistan and waging war against Iraq (two strategic, resource-rich states), was a pretended concern to liberate the women of these 'enemy states' from repressive regimes. Similar pretensions to saving women from the barbarism of death by stoning for the 'crime' of adultery could well pave the way to military strikes against Iran.

The celebrated inclusion of gender equality in the new social contracts forged as part of the reconstruction of Afghanistan and Iraq may prove a pyrrhic victory for women in these states, as it has come at a very high price. It is at risk of backfiring given its tainted origins under US occupation, and, with the unravelling of state and society as a result of continuing civil war in both states, may have very little real meaning. Rwanda's new parliament, the first in Africa to reflect gender equality, while conceived in the aftermath of a horrendous genocidal war as part of a post-conflict settlement and reconstruction agreement, gives greater cause for hope and lasting peace, arising as it has in the context of inter-nationally supported criminal court processes to bring at least some of those responsible for genocidal crimes to justice. Even here, how secure these gains for women are remains to be seen. The intolerance for dissent and opposition already being demonstrated in the reformed state of Rwanda is a worrying indicator.[14]

In the fierce new world, only feminists appear to see the parallels among the various forms of fundamentalism or neoconservatism that have emerged across the globe, in both the North and South, East and West, and to recognize the threat to women's rights and interests posed by the mobilization of right and extreme-right or neo-fascist political forces, whatever their ideological cover. While those who sow the wind of fundamentalism do reap the whirlwind, as Gita Sen has observed,[15] citing the cases of both the US nurturing of the Taliban and their suspected subsequent involvement in the 9/11 attacks, and Indira Gandhi's support for Sikh fundamentalist Bhindranwale in the Punjab and her later assassination by Sikh extremists, countless others, not least women, are made to suffer in the process.

Current challenges in discourses on states and governance

Theorization of the developmental state, sometimes termed 'developmental state capitalism', characterized by state-led economic planning and strong regulation of and intervention in the economy to support the realization of nationally defined goals, was inspired by the 'Japanese Miracle' (Johnson, 1982). It was further validated by the spectacular growth levels achieved between the mid-1980s and mid-1990s in the so-called Asian Tiger economies of Southeast Asia, namely Hong Kong, Singapore, Taiwan and South Korea, and subsequently Thailand, Malaysia and Indonesia. The devastating impacts of the 1997 financial crisis on the Southeast Asian NICs, caused not by excessive regulation but by ill-advised financial liberalization and weakened monetary and fiscal governance, took their toll on these showcases for the developmental state. Together with the conceptual refurbishing of the state under the influence of neoliberalism and criticisms of the anti-democratic nature of the developmental state, they succeeded in dampening interest in this model, although it is now enjoying a comeback, notably in discourses on the state and poverty reduction.

Leftwich (2008), for instance, argues that, whether democratic or not, only developmental states are capable of developing the institutions needed to support poverty-reducing growth and associated welfare regimes, since these depend on political will and processes.[16] The developmental state is also being conceptually refurbished (e.g. as the democratic developmental state) for application in Africa (Mkandawire, 2010), as well as favourably cited in an analysis of CARICOM as the 'equivalent at the regional level' of the developmental state for the Caribbean (Payne and Sutton, 2007). While the developmental state certainly remains important as the heterodox alternative to the neoliberal state, its principally authoritarian character makes it problematic for feminists and the enlargement of women's citizenship and rights.

Ng's (2006) study of Malaysia, a developmental state which formally practises parliamentary democracy, but which has been variously described by scholars as 'repressive', 'quasi-democratic' and 'authoritarian' as well as critiqued for its ethnicized political system, is illustrative. Ng examines the Malaysian state's engagement with the women's movement in relation to the Beijing Conference, noting the opportunity presented by the UN World Conferences on Women and their processes to feminist activists within developmental states to secure gains in women's citizenship and rights. She illustrates well the clear limits to the responsiveness of the state to feminist demands and concludes that feminist engagement with the Malaysian state is 'fraught with tensions and ambiguities'.

Discourses on the 'effective state' have been part of the broader discourse on institutional reform of the state. In *Marketisation of Governance*, DAWN observed that this project, which led to a form of political conditionality imposed on Southern states, had emerged from critiques of the state from both ends of the political spectrum. The left critique of the state as 'alienated from people, corrupt, and promoting a new elite with vested interests in maintaining the status quo' provided useful supporting arguments for the right's roll-back, deregulation and liberalization policies, strengthening neoliberal arguments about bloated public bureaucracies, inefficiency and waste (Taylor, 2000: 12–13). In an earlier work,[17] DAWN had sought to differentiate its critique of the state from that of the international financial institutions, highlighting that DAWN's motivation was to make the state more accountable to ordinary citizens, to bring about more transparent, open, participatory processes and to strengthen institutional, and civil society, checks on executive power – not to destroy the state's legitimacy, its institutions and its capacity to check runaway capitalism. DAWN feminist critique of the state was closely tied to the project of reclaiming the state, and remains so.

State roll-back policies, on the other hand, were rationalized by the World Bank in its 1997 World Development Report, *The State in a Changing World*, by the argument that neither transition states nor post-colonial states could deliver on their development promises and therefore had to make a 'wrenching shift' from state-led central planning and face the 'failure of state-led development strategies' respectively. While the state's role was demonstrably key to achieving economic growth, as illustrated by the East Asian miracle economies, what was required according to the World Bank was an effective state, one that plays 'a catalytic, facilitating role ... [by enforcing] the rule of law to underpin market transactions ...and civil society more broadly', a government that 'plays by the rules itself, acting reliably and predictably and controlling corruption', and one that 'encourages and complements the activities of private businesses and individuals' (World Bank, 1997: iii).

The World Bank's effective state assigned a role to the state that fitted with neoliberal economic principles, which prize above all else free enterprise or the private, wealth-accumulating economic activities of individuals and corporate groups. The ideal state is thus a limited state, with the principal role of ensuring freedom of competition. In an analysis which essentially elevates the market above the state, and privileges entrepreneurs above other citizens, the Bank identifies the 'fundamentals' of the state's role: establishing and enforcing the rule of law; protecting property rights from theft, violence, other acts of predation and arbitrary government actions; ensuring macroeconomic stability; avoiding price distortions; liberalizing trade and investment; providing basic services and infrastructure; and protecting the vulnerable and the environment (World Bank, 1997).

This effective rewriting of the liberal democratic social contract, inherited in one form or another by newly independent states across the South, had more negative implications for women than the original social contracts, which had largely excluded them as it deprived them, among other things, of subsidized education, health and other services, and of regulated wages and conditions. Moreover, while the introduction of political conditionality by international financial institutions in support of what the World Bank termed good governance put pressure to reform on unaccountable, undemocratic governments in the South, its primary concerns were to support neoliberal economic reforms, through financial accountability, efficiency, transparency in government processes (particularly procurement processes), the rule of law, and respect for human rights, evidently narrowly conceived as civil and political rights, since neither the right to economic self-determination nor the right to development is encompassed in the good governance agenda. Despite its welcome anti-corruption and accountability strengthening thrust, the marketized, neoliberal state holds little promise for the enlargement of women's citizenship and rights.

Lastly, discourses on 'fragile', 'failed' or 'failing', 'rogue', or 'non-viable' states may appear to converge with strong critiques from the left of dysfunctional or perverted democracies, but they are not motivated by concerns to either strengthen or deepen democracy. They mostly appear to function to discredit or discipline unfriendly regimes in resource-rich states or ineffective or recalcitrant resource-poor states, and/or to justify intervention in such states, supposedly in the interests of wider, regional or global security.

The most recent, and globally witnessed, example of US-led interventionism in a resource-rich state occurred in Libya in March 2011 following an unprecedented media-supported call for big power enforcement of a no-fly zone, ostensibly to protect unarmed anti-Gaddafi demonstrators from annihilation by Gaddafi's air forces. The enforcement of the no-fly zone, presumably under cover of the UN Responsibility to Protect principle,[18] escalated within hours to a brutal air, sea and land assault by American and European submarines, warships and fighter planes, targeting military installations and facilities, airports, roads, ports and oil depots in support of what had metamorphosed overnight into armed rebel forces, and turning into another externally triggered civil war, with civilians the main casualties. The intensity, scale and speed of the US and NATO attacks on Libya and the confidence with which this brutal offensive was beamed to millions of television viewers across the globe were unprecedented and flew in the face of the Westphalian principle of sovereignty.

It could be argued that sovereignty has been under challenge for some time in the corporate-driven global economic order established by the international financial institutions and the World Trade Organization, as evidenced by the straitjacketing of states through imposed economic and governance reforms and binding trade laws, and the drive to secure investment agreements entitling corporations to sue states. In belittling discourses on small island states by neoliberal economists the sovereignty of resource-poor Small Island Developing States (SIDS) in the Pacific has effectively been questioned. One such scholar suggested that states with populations of less than 100,000 are non-viable sovereign political entities, do not merit international representation or a vote equal to that of larger states within the United Nations, and should be federated with other small states (Hughes, 2003).[19] Pacific and Caribbean SIDS which have resorted to unorthodox and unacceptable schemes such as offshore banking to raise revenue have been subjected to disciplinary controls.[20] Post-9/11, however, micro-Pacific states that were formerly US 'strategic trust territories' in the Northern Pacific and that continue to host US military bases and missile test sites have been restored to high levels of budgetary support from the USA, making them effective beneficiaries of the 'war on terror'. Larger Pacific Island states have meanwhile been tagged weak or failing states in an 'arc of instability', warranting, in the case of the Solomon Islands, Australian military intervention/occupation to restore law and order and oversee economic and political restructuring (Kabutaulaka, 2004).

Conclusion

Full and equal citizenship remains an unfulfilled promise for an over-whelming majority of women in today's fierce new states in the South, marked as they variously are by facades of formal democracy and actually thriving authoritarianism; by genuine citizens' movements for democratic reforms and human rights amid creeping political extremism by neo-fascist forces of one form or another; by state complicity in intensified resource plunder and amassing of private wealth amid grinding poverty; by civil wars and resultant humanitarian crises; by the reality of dys-functional states and day-to day rule by warlords, druglords, traditional chieftains or modern-day dons; and, last but by no means least, by the persistence of seemingly intractable gender systems.

We celebrate the incremental gains in women's citizenship and rights wherever they are won across the South, precisely because this is the longest revolution. Full and equal citizenship will surely be the goal of the brave women in Egypt who protested in the streets, shoulder-to-shoulder with their men, to oust a long-entrenched and repressive regime, despite being confronted in the aftermath of the struggle by bullying males intent on enforcing cultural norms to keep them subjugated and out of the public sphere. Their struggle will surely resonate elsewhere in the region and far beyond, encouraging other democratic transitions and human rights gains for women.

As we witness intensifying struggles and more violent wars over the control of non-renewable natural resources, it seems imperative and urgent that we redouble our feminist advocacy efforts to remake national social contracts so that full and equal citizenship is constitutionally enshrined, promote global citizenship and multilateralism, and secure more ethical modalities of global governance and global trade that do not conflict with international human rights norms, laws and processes. The survival of Planet Earth and the fulfilment of basic human rights for the countless millions of people who continue to live in worsening conditions of poverty, insecurity and distress in states across the South demand it.

NOTES

1. Akinrinade (2000) summarizes the arguments that were commonly used in support of one-party political systems, namely that it was more conducive to the task of nation-building than competitive, adversarial politics, especially given pre-existing ethnic and tribal divisions. He records that for most of the cold war period, only Botswana and the Gambia continued to 'practice democratic politics' in Africa.

2. See Malloy, 2001.

3. For a damning critique of US foreign policy of interventionism, see William Blum, *Rogue State* (2000). Blum turns the derogatory label of 'rogue state', used mostly by the Bush regime, to describe states it regarded as authoritarian, anti-human rights and pro-terrorism on the USA itself, and Israel.

4. In a more recent example, the businessman son of former British prime minister Margaret Thatcher was convicted in 2005 for his involvement in a coup attempt against the government of President Teodoro Obiang Nguema Mbasogo in oil-rich Equatorial Guinea.

5. Togolo, 2006.

6. According to Jensen and Wantchekon (2004) only resource-poor countries like Benin, Mali and Madagascar were demonstrating successful democratic reforms by 2004.

7. See www.unhcr.org/pages/49c3646c1d9.html and www.womensrefugeecommission. org/programs/women-peace-and-security/918–ada-williams-prince-remarks-gender-aspects-of-statelessness.

8. See Giorgio Agamben, *Homo Sacer* (1998), for an elaboration of the concept of the 'state of exception' – where the state, in a supposed time of crisis, 'legitimately' increases its power and operates outside of the norms of law, diminishing citizenship and human rights.

9. Risen, 2010; Foster, 2008.

10. A suspected Taliban-supported group in Kashmir that issued an edict saying that all Muslim women must veil themselves or risk having acid thrown on their faces had the effect, within a short time, of veiling all women in Srinagar. In Pakistan and India, low-caste women have had acid thrown on them for not behaving in ways appropriate to their caste.

11. Tabb (2007) cites Ted Koppel's response (*New York Times*, 24 February 2006) to the Bush regime's 'touchiness' over suggestions that oil was the reason the USA was in Iraq: 'Now that's curious. Keeping oil flowing out of the Persian Gulf and through the Strait of Hormuz has been bedrock American foreign policy for more than half a century.'

12. A 1999 amendment to Argentina's Penal Code, however, subjects women to an age-old patriarchal system of 'justice' based on male honour, by exempting rape offenders from punishment for rape if they marry their victim.

13. Fiji's model constitution, adopted in 1997 in a democratic settlement following the 1987 military coup, was abrogated after the 2006 coup, and feminist opponents of the coup were detained, harassed and subjected to threats of sexual violence. Decrees issued by the military government deny media freedom and prohibit political parties, trade unions and women's organizations from meeting without a permit, but make domestic violence a punishable offence and legalize abortion where pregnancies result from incest or rape.

14. For a different reading of the pre-election crackdown on opposition in Rwanda, see Clark, 2010.

15. Analysis shared during a DAWN Steering Committee meeting.

16. Leftwich, 2008.

17. See DAWN, 1995: 38–9.

18. The Responsibility to Protect principle was adopted by the UN at the 2005 World Summit, in paras 138 and 139 of the World Summit Outcomes Document, but was first given expression in the founding charter of the African Union in 2005, following the genocide in Rwanda in 1994.

19. Far from receiving special consideration for their smallness, isolation from markets, vulnerability to natural disasters (not to mention man-made ecological crises, such as climate change/sea level rise), as they did in 1995 at the UN Conference on Small Island Developing States, SIDS are today subjected to one-size-fits-all neoliberal economic policy prescriptions that take little account of their vulnerabilities, and are forced to comply with a rules-based multilateral trading system based on principles of 'non-discrimination' and 'reciprocity' that severely disadvantage them. See Naidu, 2008; Slatter and Underhill-Sem, 2009.

20. Nine out of thirteen of the offshore 'non-cooperative states' listed in 2000 by a task force headed by the Bank for International Settlements were small states and territories. James A. Paul points out that while millions of dollars have flown into small states and territories, the primary beneficiaries of offshore banking are 'expatriate bankers, lawyers and financiers' (Paul, 2000).

REFERENCES

Agamben, G. (1998) *Homo Sacer: Sovereign Power and Bare Life*, Stanford University Press, Stanford CA.

Akinrinade, S. (2000) 'Single or Multi-Party System: What Option for Africa?', *Africa Economic Analysis*, www.afbis.com/analysis/party.htm.

Alley, R. (2003) Blood for Diamonds – the African Situation, *Pacific Ecologist* 5, Autumn/Winter, http://pacificecologist.org/archive/blooddiamonds.html.

Bareiro, L. (2000) 'The State, Women and Politics throughout Latin American History', in *About Women's Powers and Wisdom: Debates on Political Restructuring and Social Transformation*, DAWN REPEM, Montevideo.

Bernstein, H. (2000) 'Colonialism, Capitalism, Development', in T. Allen and A. Thomas (eds), *Poverty and Development into the Twenty-first Century*, Open University, Oxford University Press, Oxford, ch. 11, pp. 241–70.

Blum, W. (2000) *Rogue State: A Guide to the World's Only Superpower*, Zed Books, London.

Clark, P. (2010) 'Rwanda: Kagame's Power Struggle', *Guardian*, 5 August; www.guardian.co.uk/commentisfree/libertycentral/2010/aug/05/rwanda-kagames-power-struggle.

Collier, P., and A. Hoeffler (1998) 'On Economic Causes of Civil War', *Oxford University Papers* 50, pp. 563–73.

Davidson, B. (1992) *The Black Man's Burden: Africa and the Curse of Nation-State*, Times Books, New York.

DAWN (1995) *Markers on the Way – DAWN's Platform for the Fourth World Conference on Women*, Development Alternatives with Women for a New Era, DAWN, Beijing.

Foster, J. (2008) 'A Pipeline through a Troubled Land: Afghanistan, Canada, and the New Great Energy Game', Foreign Policy Series, *Canadian Centre for Policy Alternatives*, vol. 3, no. 1, June.

Fraenkel, J. (2004) 'The Coming Anarchy in Oceania? A Critique of the "Africanisation of the South Pacific" Thesis', *Commonwealth and Comparative Politics*, vol. 42, no. 1, pp. 1–34.

Hughes, H. (2003) 'Aid Has Failed the Pacific', *Issue Analysis* 33, Centre for Independent Studies, May.

Huntington, S.P. (1993) 'The Clash of Civilisations', *Foreign Affairs*, vol. 72, no. 3, pp. 22–50.

Jensen, N., and L. Wantchekon, (2004) 'Resource Wealth and Political Regimes in Africa', *Comparative Political Studies*, vol. 37, no. 7, September.

Jha, P.S. (2006) *The Twilight of the Nation State – Globalisation, Chaos and War*, Pluto Press, London.

Johnson, C. A. (1982) *MITI and the Japanese Miracle: The Growth of Industrial Policy 1925–1975*, Stanford University Press, Stanford CA.

Kabutaulaka, T.T. (2004) '"Failed State" and the War on Terror: Intervention in the Solomon Islands', *Asia Pacific Issues: Analysis from the East West Centre*, no. 72, March, EWC, Honolulu.

Le Billon, P. (2002) 'The Political Economy of Resource Wars', www.iss.co.za/pubs/books/Angola/3LeBillon.pdf.

Leftwich, A. (2008) *Developmental States, Effective States and Poverty Reduction: The Primacy of Politics*, UNRISD Project on Poverty Reduction and Policy Regimes, Geneva.

Malloy, I. (2001) *Rolling Back Revolution: The Emergence of Low Intensity Conflict*, Pluto Press, London.

Mkandawire, T. (2010)'From Maladjusted States to Democratic Developmental States in Africa', in Omano Edigheji (ed.), *Constructing a Democratic Developmental State in South Africa – Potentials and Challenges*, HSRC Press, Cape Town, pp. 59–81.

Murunga, G.R. (2002) 'A Critical Look at Kenya's Non-transition to Democracy', *Journal of Third World Studies*, Fall.

Naidu, V. (2006) 'The State of the State in Fiji: Some Failings in the Periphery', in S. Firth (ed.), *Globalisation and Governance in the Pacific Islands*, ANU Press, Canberra, pp. 297–316.

Naidu, V. (2007) 'Coups in Fiji Seesawing Democratic Multiracialism and Ethno-nationalist Extremism', *Devforum* 26, pp. 24–33.

Naidu, V (2008) 'A View on Contemporary Development Issues from the South Pacific: Where's the Level Playing Field ?', in A. Thornton and A. McGregor(eds), *Southern Perspectives on Development: Dialogue or Division?*, Devnet/University of Otago, Dunedin, pp. 15–28.

Ng, C. (2006) 'An Unholy Alliance? Women Engaging with the State', paper produced for DAWN's analysis on Social Contracts.

Nwauwa, A.O. (2003) 'Concepts of Democracy and Democratization in Africa Revisited', paper presented at the Fourth Annual Kent State University Symposium on Democracy, Kent OH.

Paul, J.A. (2000) *Small States and Territories*, www.globalpolicy.org/nations/state/microindex.htm#links.

Payne, A., and P. Sutton (2007) 'Repositioning the Caribbean within Globalisation', *Monthly Newsletter* No. 132, July, Caribbean Paper No. 1, www.iadb.org/intal/articulo_carta_new.asp?tid=5idioma=ENGaid=284cid=234carta_id=561.

Potter, D. (2000) 'The Power of Colonial States', in Tim Allen and Alan Thomas (eds), *Poverty and Development into the Twenty-first Century*, Open University, Oxford University Press, Oxford.

Risen, J. (2010) 'US Discovers Vast Mineral Riches in Afghanistan, *New York Times*, 13 June, www.nytimes.com/2010/06/14/world/asia/14minerals.html?pagewanted=2&th&emc=th.

Roy, S. (2008) 'Female Empowerment through Inheritance Rights: Evidence from India', London School of Economics, London.

Sen, Gita (2006) 'Feminist Politics in a Fundamentalist World' [Keynote address to the 2002 KIT Conference on Governing for Equity: Gender, Citizenship and Governance in Kochi, Kerala], *Minerva* 30, pp. 16–18.

Seng, M.P. (1993) Notes on Unity Dow Case – Botswana Court of Appeal, *Toledo Law Review* 24, Spring, p. 563.

Sklar, R.L. (1983) 'Democracy in Africa', *African Studies Review*, vol. 26, no. 3–4.

Slatter, C., and Y. Underhill-Sem (2009) 'Re-claiming Pacific Island Regionalism: Does Neo-liberalism Have to Reign?', in K.L. Koo and B. D'Costa (eds), *Gender Global Politics in the Asia–Pacific*, Palgrave Macmillan, New York, pp. 195–210.

Tabb, W.K. (2007) 'Resource Wars', *Monthly Review*, vol. 58, no. 8, January; http://monthlyreview.org/2007/01/01/resource-wars.

Taylor, V. (2000) *Marketisation of Governance: Critical Feminist Perspectives from the South*, DAWN, Suva.

Togolo, M. (2006) 'The "Resource Curse" and Governance: A Papua New Guinea Perspective', in Stewart Firth (ed.), *Globalisation and Governance in the Pacific Islands*, Australian National University EPress, Canberra.

Van der Veer, P. (1994) *Religious Nationalism – Hindus and Muslims in India*, University of California Press, Berkeley.

World Bank (1997) *The State in a Changing World*, World Development Report, Washington DC.

BOX V.1 **ICTs: efficient exploitation or feminist tool?**

CAI YIPING

Media issues have played an important role in global feminist politics, but mass media never became public resources or public service providers towards gender equality, regardless of their ownership and structure – state, public or privately owned.

The Big Six media companies – General Electric, Disney, NewsCorp, Time Warner, Viacom and CBS – own the television, radio, print, film and electronic media that have global reach. They control the flow and availability of information, and are largely responsible for popularizing the images that shape world opinion. They have created unidirectional media flows from the developed to the developing world, potentially drowning out cultural and linguistic diversity (Jensen, 2010).

New Information and Communication Technologies (ICTs) do not seem to be too different. While the user-generated content is more diverse and interactive on the web than in the mass media, the big platform and service providers (Facebook, Twitter, Google, 3G mobiles, wifi, broadband etc.) are also commercial enterprises. Web 2.0 and other new communication tools are owned by concentrated capital and have the power to engage in propaganda.

ICTs have led to tremendous changes in ways of organizing and mobilizing in women's and other social movements towards the transformation and democratization of societies, catalysing and strengthening online-based civil journalism, including community and independent media. From the Green Movement in Iran, where for days after the June 2009 elections scores of people went into the streets to protest the results and accuse the administration of vote-rigging, to recent revolutionary movements in Middle East countries, digital and social media have powerfully demonstrated how essential information – via mobile phones, blogs, online social networks, satellite TV, wikis, and user-generated news and pictures – is able to reach people who otherwise would have been disenfranchised.

Despite the growing number of women Internet users, the online world is far from a gender-neutral or women-friendly space. Some sites are a sexist's paradise (Valenti, 2007) and in addition there is electronic violence against women (eVAW) – defined as using information and communication technology (ICT) to track and harass someone, causing emotional distress and fear for their personal safety, which can include unauthorized recording, reproduction and distribution of videos and image and ICT-mediated violence such as rape and assault by text or chat and online gaming. The user-generated content is more diverse and interactive on the web than in the mass media, but the big platform and service providers are commercial enterprises that finance themselves like mass media. The rapid and uneven pace at which new ICTs develop continues to divide societies into the information-rich and information-poor, creating a digital divide that cuts across class, nation, age, race, ethnicity and gender.

Security and surveillance threaten cyberspace democracy. Social media sites such as Facebook have been blocked in Pakistan, China and Bangladesh, since they are considered threatening to the regimes. For example, the One Million Signatures Campaign that since 2007 has been calling for the end of discrimination against women in Iran is consistently blocked in the country.

How can feminists and human rights advocates claim and reclaim this space as it has been and continues to be controlled and censored by the state, on the one hand, and monopolized by mainstream and commercial media, on the other?

That is why initiatives such as the Take Back the Tech! Campaign, a collaborative effort to end eVAW during the annual 16 Days Activism against gender-based violence, and MXit, a counselling space on a popular mobile phone chat service for children, are so important. They amplify the voices of women and children and create more positive cyberspace for them. In China migrant workers are using theatre and music to mobilize around and raise public awareness of workers' rights. Lesbian Bisexual and Transgender (LBT) groups in the Philippines have launched their own radio programme and online uploads to reach a larger audience.

Traditional communication tools such as radio, theatre, print and face-to-face discussion are still the most effective means to reach out to women at the grassroots. Face-to-face communication remains the most important tool for building the movement (de Vela and Ofreneo, 2008). The comparison is between a cyber-campaign with 10,000 supporters and a street demonstration of 2,000 people.

The convergence of traditional communication tools and new ICTs such as the combination of community radio and the Internet allows women to transcend the status of passive collective recipient to become active producers of information while empowering themselves and their communities to advocate for women's rights and resisting the challenges of neoliberal globalization, militarism, forms of intolerance, discrimination and fundamentalisms.

REFERENCES

de Vela, T., and M.A. Ofreneo (2008) *People's Communications for Development*, Isis International, Manila.

Jensen, H. (2010) 'Global Feminist Politics Concerning Media and ICTs: Past Lessons and Present Challenges', *Women in Action* 1.

Valenti, J. (2007) 'How the Web Became a Sexists' Paradise?' *Guardian*, 6 April; www.guardian.co.uk/world/2007/apr/06/gender.blogging.

CHAPTER 12

Religious fundamentalism and secular governance

AMRITA CHHACHHI

The fiercest face of the world today is the growing strength and power of religious fundamentalist groups deploying terror to hold our lives to ransom. From being a phenomenon that occurred somewhere else – the borderlands – it has entered our daily lives and now each of us faces the threat of annihilation anytime and anywhere in the world. The media feed us with images of the fundamentalist as the bearded man/Arab/Muslim/barbaric individual – all of which equate to 'terrorist'.

The scale and brutality of 9/11 marked the critical turning point, but for many of us this terror has been creeping up over a period of a few decades. The images that we link with 9/11 are similar to the images of the demolition of the Babri Masjid mosque in India in the 1990s and the subsequent escalation of violence, the pogrom against Muslims in Gujarat in 2002, and the continued bombing of trains, hotels and marketplaces in India as well as in many other parts of the world.

Alongside these violent incidents, we receive almost normalized reports of targeted violence against women who are seen as transgressive in Nigeria, Malaysia and Iran, and of attacks by Christian fundamentalists in the USA unleashed through Operation Rescue and by Hindu fundamentalists on young women in Bangalore, India.

Insidiously, vigilantism, bans and censorship are becoming the forces of civil and political governance of everyday life. These, combined with the 'war on terror' with its technologies of panoptic surveillance and racial profiling, are leading to a deepening sense of generalized ontological insecurity, signalling a profound shift as a number of certainties become shaky. We need to understand the unleashing of these forces, which seem, at first glance, to be beyond control.

One certainty has been the counterposition of religious fundamentalisms and secular governance. Such a framing implies that religious fundamentalism is the problem and secular governance the solution. I question this assumption by deconstructing these concepts, and elaborating on what they mean in practice within the women's movement, concluding with some issues for reflection.

Towards the end of the 1980s the women's movement began working on a definition of religious fundamentalism from a feminist perspective. Questioning the standard dictionary definition, which holds that 'religious fundamentalism is a strict maintenance of traditional orthodox religious beliefs such as an inerrancy of scripture and literal acceptance of the creeds as fundamentals of protestant Christianity' (*Concise Oxford Dictionary*) and posits it as the opposite of liberalism and modernism, the women's movement evolved a broader conceptualization of religious fundamentalism. Rather than limiting the definition to a specific historical context wherein the term 'fundamentalism' was originally used to refer to the formation of the World Christian Fundamentalist Association by American Protestant churches in 1919, the women's movement *pluralized* the term to refer to the global phenomena of specific kinds of Christian, Hindu, Jewish, and Islamic political movements which had emerged or expanded in the last century.

'Religious fundamentalism' is itself a contested term. Some argue that its use should be restricted to the historically specific Christian/Western phenomenon. Another strong objection points to the way in which the term has been deployed in US security discourse, substituting the 'red devil' (the communist threat) with the 'green devil' (reference to Islam), wherein religious fundamentalism is equated with terrorism and forms part of the attitude characterized as 'Islamophobia'. This strategic deployment reduces Islam to terrorism while simultaneously elevating the West as the site of moderation and rationality. This implies an inevitable 'clash of civilizations' à la Huntington and provides a rationale for war between the rational moderates in the civilized West and the darker threatening religions and civilizations of the East.

Given this conflation of Islam and fundamentalism, some feminists have argued for identifying the heterogeneity of religions as well as the specific nature of each religious movement (Corrêa, Petchesky and Parker,

2008). In addition, the term 'religious fundamentalism' is seen as a misnomer since it seems to imply authenticity (i.e. is fundamental); many believers feel under attack by the use of the term. Scholars who argue that 'religious fundamentalism' is too broad a term prefer to use more specific characterizations such as 'Islamism',[1] 'nationalism', 'populism' and 'religious extremism' (Bayat, 2005). The phrase 'new religious politics' has been proposed (Keddie, 1998), since it refers to contemporary movements, highlights their political content, and is neutral.

Despite this ongoing debate, the women's movement still widely uses the term 'fundamentalism', since it effectively describes the commonality of both ideological content and methods employed by the various kinds of religious fundamentalism. In certain arenas, there has even been an ideological convergence, particularly around issues of reproductive health and rights, as noted during the 1994 Cairo Conference on Population and Development and subsequent conferences. 'Religious fundamentalism', it is argued, is a politically potent term while alternatives such as 'populism', 'nationalism' or even 'religious extremism' tend to sanitize and dilute the authoritarian and fascist impulses of these movements. Every movement is 'exceptional' since it is located in a particular context, and specificities as well as changes and shifts in organizations and movements clearly need to be brought out.[2] However, from the perspective of the women's movement what remained critical for analysis and strategy was the global emergence of religious fundamentalisms as political movements that used religion to consolidate power and extend social control over the state and civil society. Distinguishing religion, religiosity and spirituality from what was meant by religious fundamentalism, the women's movement stresses that what are being asserted as fundamental basic religious principles are in fact a very selective interpretation, which is in turn linked to a broader political project.

Rather than quibble over definitions it is important to identify common features that characterize these religious fundamentalist movements. A key feature is selectivity in interpretation of 'the fundamentals' and the imposed homogeneity of that interpretation. The fundamentalist discourse is framed in terms of dislocation, disruption and infection, hence rationalizing the need for boundary maintenance. Within the boundaries, there is a profound sense of being under siege and of the breakdown of social order, particularly of the family. In all such discourses, there is an emphasis on the erosion of 'family values' and calls for a restoration of order. In the face of moral decay caused by supposed deviations from tradition, blamed on modernization and secularization, a selective retrieval of and a return to the 'sacred text' is undertaken. The selectivity takes various forms, such as defining permissible sexual behaviour and dress codes as well as other theological interpretations.

The second significant feature is the fabrication of a glorious past and invention of a 'tradition'. In this process of reinvention and re-narrativization, there is very little distinction made between canonical texts and specific cultural practices. A select set of beliefs, rituals and practices are given transcendental validity and abstracted from their respective histories – the differences between culture and institutionalized religion are collapsed.

Integral to the fundamentalist project is a process of 'othering' and intolerance, the third shared feature. The construction of 'imagined identities' is based on a selective strand of broader pluralist cultures. This pluralism is crushed outside the frame, as well as within – some of the most virulent attacks have been against members and institutions of the same religion, as seen in Taliban attacks on Sufi shrines and Ahmediyas in Pakistan. The legitimation for this behaviour is derived from 'divine will', while the political form it takes is the construction of a singular, homogenous 'national' or 'religious' culture. Authority is sacralized, so whoever challenges it is a traitor, blasphemous and eligible for death. Exclusion is hence built into the construction of the community/nation.

The fourth feature – and this is the aspect that the women's movement has focused on – is control exercised over women and the redefinition of gender relations. There are normative prescriptions for men and women, particularly the control and disciplining of women's bodies, in response to the sense of dislocation and the need for boundary maintenance due to a perceived invasion by the outside world. The denial of reproductive and sexual rights goes hand in hand with the denial of the right to work, the right to mobility and the right to education. There have been horrific instances of sexual violence by fundamentalist groups; in this context, sexual violence has to be understood as 'productive' inasmuch as it is not only punitive but also delivers a pedagogic message. 'Teaching a lesson' creates terror, thereby solidifying boundaries and communities, furthering the process of othering.

Fifth, these fundamentalist movements have a clear, articulated, political project. For instance Nawaz (n.d.), who was recruited to such an organization, was told that Islam is not a religion but an ideology that seeks to establish the Caliphate. Some clearly want to capture state power; others work to capture institutions, particularly cultural and educational organizations. Other fundamentalist movements are outside the state but align themselves with state policies. The Christian right, for instance, influenced Bush's domestic as well as foreign policies. Karen Armstrong mentions in her analysis of Christian fundamentalism that the crackdown in Palestine was motivated in part by Bush's personal agenda to be there at the time of 'rapture' as the 'chosen one' (Armstrong, 2005).

Sixth, such movements are anti-democratic, authoritarian and hierarchical male-dominated organizations. Some openly maintain paramilitary wings, like the Hindu fundamentalist Rashtriya Swayamsevak Sangh, while others are organized as militias, witness the Taliban. Women rarely hold leadership positions.

Finally, these movements are not irrational or medieval. They are modern movements and have grown not in opposition to but as a way of accommodating capitalism. They do not reject technology, weapons or political power. Like the image of a donkey carrying a missile launcher, the vehicle is traditional but the content is contemporary.

This understanding was the basis for feminist activism against fundamentalisms – both fundamentalist states and fundamentalist movements globally. Central to the analysis at that time was that women are victims. Even if women were involved in fundamentalist movements, we saw these women as coerced or manipulated and, at best, deluded by false consciousness. Things have radically changed over the last decade. There is a need to revisit this characterization as well as take into account new developments and analysis. We need both political economy and culture to understand contemporary religious fundamentalisms.

First, it is extremely important to apprehend the moment of emergence and consolidation of transnational religious fundamentalist political formations. Al-Qaeda is one such example, for it has become a generic term for a vast range of family-related organizations. These organizations are de-territorialized – members come from various locations, including Afghanistan, Chechnya, Pakistan, Central Asia, Nigeria, the Middle East, the UK, the USA and Europe. Similarly the export by Saudi Arabia of Wahabism across the world does not require territorial control. Likewise the Hindu fundamentalist network is also global, with groups from the diaspora involved in funding and supporting the project of Hindutva (Sabrang/SACW, 2002).

What we need to think about is how these political formations dislodge traditional ideas of sovereignty, or disrupt the operations of sovereign territories. These organizations are not restricted to the nation-state and can only be partially addressed by the understanding of modes of governmentality that describe the dynamics of what are largely liberal-democratic nation settings (Bhatt, 2007). Furthermore, such formations cannot be understood simply in terms of the logic of capital accumulation, whether it is through dispossession or extended accumulation or capture of territory. They relate to what Bhatt calls modes of 'hyper governance'. Running concomitantly with the process of McDonaldization wrought by socio-economic globalization is a process of reconstitution and reinvention of identities and subjects through the ideological interventions of transnational religious fundamentalist political projects.

Second, a corollary to the development of 'global fundamentalisms' is the worldwide nexus between the armaments and drug industries and the ways in which militarization and narco-terrorism have been fostered for geopolitical agendas, by governments as well as non-governmental actors. The open market in arms and the establishment of heroin labs in Pakistan were a consequence of the supply of arms by the CIA to the ISI-Afghan mujahideen in the 1980s. It is not just fundamentalist groups that benefit from the global trade in drugs but also other interest groups such as organized crime, intelligence agencies and businesses, with a large share of the multimillion-dollar revenues being laundered through Western banks.

A third dimension is the link between these fundamentalist movements and neoliberalism. Neoliberalism informs fundamentalist projects even as they draw support from people suffering from its outcomes. The failure of the state to deliver services, increased poverty, high levels of unemployment and increasing inequality have propelled large numbers of the marginalized and the disfranchised to join these groups. The discourse on decadence is critical since it resonates with the disenfranchised and is linked to the experience of inequality. In particular, with the rise of male unemployment, the primary marker of masculine gender identity – the male breadwinner – is being eroded. There is a resultant crisis of masculinity, which takes different forms. Attempts to reconstitute and reassert hegemonic masculinity can take violent forms at the individual and personal level; for instance a rise in sexual violence has been noted. In addition there are political formations that provide spaces for the construction of exclusive communities with legitimate and compensatory practices and actions for the reconstitution of this hegemonic masculinity in a collective way. Support for fundamentalist ideologies often comes from classes directly affected by neoliberalism, both the new middle classes with an investment in liberalization and those disenfranchised through unemployment.

The political economy of religious fundamentalisms needs elaboration. There are often complexities. For instance, even as Hindu fundamentalists in their discourses and policies support liberalization, they also invoke *swadeshi* (self-sufficiency) to protect local manufacturing and avoid the consumption of foreign goods.

Fourth is the identity of the fundamentalist. Contrary to the image in some Western media of the fundamentalist as the mad mullah, the leaders and ideologues of both the Islamic fundamentalist groups and the Hindutva groups are highly educated, belonging to middle-class or upper-middle-class families. The mass following they enjoy is explained in part as a response to the effects of neoliberalism, whereby unemployed youth find a forum within which to express their dissatisfaction, but it is also linked to alienation, racism, loss of identity and a legitimate anti-imperialism. In addition many fundamentalist organizations are very active in welfare and humanitarian aid and are the first to respond when there is a natural disaster. Most of the young female and male suicide bombers in Lal Masjid in Pakistan were orphans from the recent earthquake; they were recruited by the fundamentalists, who provided them with support, shelter and ideological training.

Another idea that needs debunking is that madrasas are the breeding ground of fundamentalists or terrorists. Recent studies have shown that in Pakistan, for instance, state schools are equally responsible. Similarly in India, the controversy over history textbooks published for all schools in Madhya Pradesh, a state governed by a Hindu right-wing party, revealed attempts to institute ideological training within the state system.

Women and fundamentalism today

There was a tendency to see women primarily as victims, but increasingly women are being seen as participants and perpetrators of violence in the cause of religious fundamentalism. There is now a better understanding of women's participation. Women are involved in these organizations not simply because they are coerced, manipulated or forced. On the contrary, they find that participating is a form of entry into the public sphere. They can get involved in politics and talk equally with men because it is legitimized by religion. The pressure to get married is lifted since they are now 'working in the service of God'. In other cases allegiance to the religious community is a 'forced identity' (Chhachhi, 1991), not in the sense of coercion or manipulation but as a choice women make in a context of communal/racial discrimination and violence. In other words, these movements and organizations seem to provide women opportunities for agency.

What this tells us is that such political formations offer a lethal mix of welfare and identity which cannot be deduced one from the other. If the problem of poverty is resolved, it doesn't mean that the problem of identity will go away. It is the coalescence between the two that is crucial to the successful expansion of fundamentalist political formations.

Can secular governance be the answer, in light of the preceding discussion of religious fundamentalism? The meaning of secularism is also itself a subject of debate. Hingeing on the separation of church and state, the policing of the boundaries between the state and religion has taken many forms. There are many differences, for instance, between the United States' conception of mutual exclusion wherein 'neither the state nor religion is meant to interfere in the domain of the other' (Bhargava, 2011) and that of France's one-sided exclusion of religion based on a 'wall of separation' between the two institutions. The Indian conception is yet another variant, which calls for equal treatment of all religions and allows state intervention in cases of discrimination or violation/injury to 'religious sentiments'

(Bhargava, 2010). In no instance has a complete, 'pure' separation been achieved. Consequently, there is no actually existing fully secular state. The subtext of European secularism was revealed by the attempt to write Christianity into the EU Constitution. Hence, just as it is more appropriate to talk of fundamentalisms in the plural, it is likewise best to speak of secularism*s*.

Given its ambiguities in practice, many have rejected the utility of the concept of secularism. It is argued that the historical emergence of secularism in the context of the Western experience of Enlightenment makes it inapplicable elsewhere. Another objection raises the role of secularism in the neoliberal imperial project. For Mahmood, 'Secularism, as a principle of liberal state governance, has entailed not so much the abandonment of religion but its ongoing regulation through a variety of state and civic institutions' (Mahmood, 2006, 2008). She elaborates on how some of the 'constitutive assumptions of secularism enable the distinction between enlightened religiosity and its more backward/dangerous forms' which 'underwrite the current U.S. government's attempts to intervene politically and strategically in the Muslim world'. The project to identify moderate Islam implies that Islam is inherently extremist and immoderate.

These very contradictory processes need to be properly understood. Even as there are calls for secular governance, there is an ongoing process of the de-privatization of religion. Multiculturalism in Canada and in the UK, for instance, reconstructs religious communities as the basis for demanding rights as well as resources. The World Bank proposes the strengthening of the zakat system, a religiously mandated charity tax, as one of the most important safety-net programmes for social protection in Pakistan. However, a religious-based system of social security does not satisfy any of the normative principles of social justice. Apart from upholding a paternalistic relationship with beneficiaries, the power of the mullah as spokesperson for the 'community' and the controller of resources is solidified, which reinforces women's subordination in religious gender hierarchies (Chhachhi, 2009).

Secularism does not by itself ensure minority or women's rights. A classic example is the secular Nazi state. The universal conception of citizenship that underpins the concept of secular governance is patriarchal and heteronormative. This ignores the lived experience of multilayered citizenship (Yuval Davis, 1999). We are not just citizens in relation to the state but are also members of communities and households. For women in particular, relations with the state are often mediated through these other collectivities. In addition these other layers of citizenship – community and family – also provide members with entitlements that may be informal or formalized in customary law. Very often entitlements derived from these other layers of collectivities can be lost when individual rights are asserted. For instance, the demand for women's individual right to land in Africa has raised critical issues. There is general agreement that customary laws discriminate against women, but some do provide women with collective entitlements to the commons. Codification of customary laws and marketization of land have eroded these rights. The demand for individual land titles can often backfire. There are cases in Africa where, after fighting for independent and individual rights to land within the framework of secular governance, women were the first to sell since they did not have the resources to cultivate the land productively. The demand for individual rights to land has to be seen in the context of the recent World Bank recommendation for large-scale land acquisition as a means of poverty reduction and the aggressive grabbing of huge swathes of land, especially in Africa, by transnational companies (Zoomers, 2010). This manifests clearly the sometimes occluded link between a neoliberal model of development and secular governance.

A further crucial element of the critique of secularism is that it is not, despite popular belief, an onward march of rationality devoid of coercion and power struggles. It involves a notion of governmentality which binds together state and civil society transforming and creating particular subjectivities, as expressed in Foucault's analyses of the imbrication of pastoral power in modern techniques of government. Secularism is also not the only realm of reason. Religious fundamentalist groups, for instance in Latin America, oppose sexual and reproductive rights by invoking the authority not only of the Bible but also of scientific discourse and reason, with the claim that 'God is harmonized with reason'.

There are, furthermore, a number of contradictions inherent to the practice of secularism. One such is that between the individual and the collective, between individual rights for women and the rights of the collective, who are often minority communities that are being persecuted

and marginalized. From a feminist perspective we look at both, identifying the need for women's rights but also recognizing other forms of
marginalization and social exclusion. The long struggle for a uniform
civil code and the scrapping of religious-based family laws in India is
illustrative of the dilemmas such a contradiction creates. Every time
the women's movement raises this demand, minority groups stand up
and claim that the demand for a uniform civil code is a threat to their
identity. Sections of the women's movement then seek reform within
customary law. In the last decade, Hindu fundamentalist groups have
taken up the demand for a uniform civil code as part of their project of
a homogenized nationalism. The appropriation of the demand from the
women's movement led to a process of silencing and forced a withdrawal
of the campaign. A way forward began with a refusal to be caught between
majoritarianism and minoritarianism, between Hindu fundamentalism disguised as secular governance and identity politics. The women's
movement has tried to overcome these by putting forward the idea of
universal citizenship-based rights which also recognized other layers of
citizenship in collectivities (WGWR, 1996). This perspective asserts that
a person born into a nation is entitled to a whole charter of rights that
cover areas of the family as well as rights at work and the right to education, among others. This charter of rights is a birth entitlement. This
approach reversed the current option whereby every Indian is actually
born into a religious community and religious laws govern the rights to
inheritance, marriage, divorce and custody, but individuals could choose
to opt out of the community and apply secular law. Very few do this
because opting out of the community can also mean the loss of certain
rights as well as isolation in a communalized context. The movement
argued that women had a birthright entitlement to the secular charter of
rights, but, recognizing the importance of minority rights, felt that the
option to live subject to religious family law must also exist. This added
a third approach to the two positions held in the women's movement,
namely to continue to demand a uniform civil code or to work for reform
within religious laws. This third approach, the 'reverse option', tried to
accommodate both positions in a politically sensitive way. However it
was heavily criticized. Secular feminists argued that it was a betrayal of
citizenship and secularism, while others maintained that it ignored the

threat to minority communities. There has been no resolution, and the dynamic has resulted in a silencing of voices. There remain possibilities, but a purely secular governance approach is problematic, given that it must take into account political contexts.

Another contradiction has emerged in strategies adopted by the women's movement to oppose the new transnational religio-political formations. State complicity in the fostering of many of these formations has been documented, yet when it comes to confronting them it is the state that is appealed to. There is an even greater contradiction in opposing military solutions while at the same time acquiescing in the military's actions to wipe out religious fundamentalists, as is happening in Pakistan and Afghanistan. A similar position was taken in Algeria where the military crushed the Islamist forces, accompanied by claims that on occasion the military can play a progressive role. In contexts where the military and intelligence services in effect form a shadow state, is such a position a viable and principled one?

A major contradiction from a feminist perspective involves the public and the private spheres. Feminists have long fought to bring certain private activities into the public realm. An example here is rape, including marital rape, which has successfully been brought out into the open. Secularism, however, places religion in the private sphere. In doing so, it marginalizes those feminists who define themselves with Islam but are struggling for the reinterpretation of family laws. This creates contradictions and imposes a kind of secular moralism. Perhaps religion should not be located in the private sphere but instead brought into the public sphere and made a subject of public debate. In this way, the variety and multiplicity of interpretations and interdenominational differences can become transparent.

In conclusion, moving forward would mean a discussion of the process of secularization and the development of secularity, along with the process of democratization. Secular governance is a loaded and static concept that presupposes a state that fails to deal with the dimensions raised here. Key is the process of democratization, rather than secularism as such; this must involve the creation of subaltern counter-public spheres for collective deliberation. The basis of fundamentalist groups cannot be undermined by military solutions. What is needed is the initiation of a process of democratization, recognition of multiple identities and redistributive measures ensuring universal access to public goods. This would facilitate the transformation of internal power hierarchies within communities and the forging of a new social compact with the state.

The term 'religious fundamentalism' needs to be revisited. In 2007 the Association of Women in Development (AWID) undertook a survey among feminist activists: 51 per cent used the term 'religious fundamentalisms' in their work, while the other 49 per cent were either not sure or rejected the term. AWID continues to use the term for movements that exhibit the following features or practices: scripturalism, radicalism, extremism, exclusivism, militancy and the idea of a 'radical patriarchalism' (AWID, 2008).

Imam and Yuval-Davis (2007) express the dilemma when they say 'we continue to speak of fundamentalisms because there has not been an alternative term that covers the same range of political and social phenomena and intuitively conveys the message'. The message is indeed significant since it distinguishes these movements from others, not just in stressing that they are essentially political but that they couch their claims in religious terms, which evokes a different kind of control and deference. Rather than employ a static label, we need to use the term 'religious fundamentalisms' also as an analytical tool to interrogate the ideological content and practice of organizations with the features noted here and map changes. The transnational religio-political formations, extreme right-wing militarized political movements, are only one end of a continuum that includes less militarized or physically violent groups which nonetheless exhibit the features of religious fundamentalist movements identified above. This would also enable evidence-based evaluation of possible shifts and changes. These are issues raised in the ongoing discussion on internal tensions within the recent democratic movements in the Middle East.

Finally, there is a need to broaden frameworks beyond straightforward human rights. The human rights regime has proved to be an important frame for making claims. Indeed, feminists have fought hard to extend the boundaries of this framework to include rape, forced marriage and domestic violence. At the same time the human rights framework itself has serious limitations. Human rights are part of a regime of law that is invested in the modern state. Another paradox presents itself here. Though state discourse is couched in universal terms, the state always has its own particular interest. Despite talk of the indivisibility of rights, it is the civil and political rights which address the state that have been enforced or are being struggled for, while social and economic rights that would imply claims also on capital are hardly ever raised. In Development Studies today everyone is talking about rights-based development, from the World Bank and DFID to the social movements, and all are using the language of voice, agency and rights. Yet there are different meanings and agendas at work.

In the political arena there is another serious dilemma: on the one hand the United States-led 'war on terror' is leading to the suspension of human rights and increased surveillance over the body politic, and the discourse of human rights is being appropriated by the US/NATO alliance to legitimate imperialism. On the other hand the discourse is also being appropriated by organizations that espouse extremist and violent forms of identity-based politics, and some human rights organizations are extending their support to them. The space for a position that challenges both of these stances is shrinking, and human rights are becoming hostage to broader authoritarian political agendas.

A broader social justice vision needs to be developed which incorporates the issues of redistribution, recognition and representation (Fraser, 2008), because it is only through these combined concepts that the women's movement can challenge that mix of welfare and identity that is offered by religious fundamentalist groups.

NOTES

1. Bennoune (2010: 644) argues that 'fundamentalist' is more accurate than this term, which is 'both potentially derogatory of Islam itself and privileges "Islamist" claims of authenticity'.
2. Scholars have tried to characterize Hindu fundamentalism as 'exceptional', resulting in a range of labels, including 'Hindu nationalism', 'Hindu fascism', 'the Hindu right' – the last being the most commonly used.

REFERENCES

Armstrong, K. (2005) 'Christian Fundamentalism in the US', lecture at the American University in Cairo, 12 December.

Bayat, A. (2005) 'Islamism and Social Movement Theory', *Third World Quarterly*, vol. 26. no. 6, pp. 891–908.

Bennoune, K. (2010) 'Remembering the Other's Others: Theorizing the Approach of International Law to Muslim Fundamentalism', *Columbia Human Rights Law Review*, vol. 41, no. 3, Spring, pp. 635–98.

Bhargava, R. (2000) *Secularism and Its Critics*, Oxford University Press, New Delhi.

Bhargava, R. (2011) 'States, Religious Diversity, and the Crisis of Secularism', *Open Democracy*, 22 March, www.opendemocracy.net/rajeev-bhargava/states-religious-diversity-and-crisis-of-secularism-0.

Bhatt, C. (2007) 'Frontlines and Interstices in the Global War on Terror', *Development and Change*, vol. 38, no. 6, pp. 1073–93.

Chhachhi, A. (1991) 'Forced Identities: The State, Communalism, Fundamentalism and Women in India', in D. Kandiyoti (ed.), *Women, Islam and the State*, Macmillan, London, pp. 119–34.

Chhachhi, A. (1991) 'The State, Religious Fundamentalism and Violence against Women in South Asia' in G. Lycklama (ed.), *'Towards Women's Strategies in the 1990s: Challenging Government and State*, Macmillan, London, 1991, pp. 16–50.

Chhachhi, A. (2009) 'Democratic Citizenship or Market-based Entitlements? A Gender Perspective on Social Protection in South Asia', ISS/Erasmus Working Paper 485, December.

Corrêa, S., R. Petchesky and R. Parker, (2008) *Sexuality, Health, and Human Rights*, Routledge, New York.

Fraser, N. (2008) *Scales of Justice: Reimagining Political Space in a Globalizing World*, Polity Press, Cambridge.

Imam, A., and N. Yuval-Davis (2007) 'Introduction' in *Warning Signs of Fundamentalisms*, WLUML Publications, London.

Keddie, N. (1998) 'New Religious Politics: Where, When and Why Do Fundamentalisms Appear?', *Comparative Studies in Society and History*, vol. 40, no. 4, October, pp. 696–723.

Mahmood S. (2006) 'Secularism, Hermeneutics, and Empire: The Politics of Islamic Reformation', *Public Culture*, vol. 18, no. 2, Spring.

Mahmood S. (2008) 'Is Critique Secular?', *The Immanent Frame*, http://blogs.ssrc.org/tif/2008/03/30/is-critique-secular-2.

Mahmood S. (2009) 'Religious Reason and Secular Affect: An Incommensurable Divide?', *Critical Inquiry*, vol. 35, no. 4, Summer, 'The Fate of Disciplines', ed. James Chandler and Arnold I. Davidson, pp. 836–62.

Mullick, F., and M. Yusuf (2009) *Pakistan: Identity, Ideology and Beyond*, Quilliam Foundation, London.

Nawaz, M. (n.d.) *In and Out of Islamism*, Quilliam Foundation, London.

Sabrang Communications Pvt. Ltd (India)/SACW (France) (2002) 'A Foreign Exchange of Hate: IDRF and the American Funding of Hindutva', 20 November, http://stopfundinghate.org/sacw/index.html.

Sahgal, G., and N. Yuval-Davis (2001) *Refusing Holy Orders: Women and Fundamentalism in Britain*, WLUML London

Vaggione, J.M. (2008) *Shared Insights: Women's Rights Activists Define Religious Fundamentalisms*, ed. S. Gokal and S. Zuberi, Association for Women's Rights in Development, Toronto, Mexico City, Cape Town.

WGWR (Working Group on Women's Rights) (1996) 'Reversing the Option: Civil Codes and Personal Laws', *Economic and Political Weekly*, vol. 31, no. 20, May 18, pp. 1180–83.

Yuval-Davis, N. (1999) 'The "Multi-Layered Citizen": Citizenship in the Age of "Glocalization"', *International Feminist Journal of Politics*, vol. 1, no. 1, pp. 119–36.

Zoomers, A. (2010) 'Globalisation and the Foreignisation of Space: Seven Processes Driving the Current Global Land Grab, *Journal of Peasant Studies*, vol. 37, no. 2, pp. 429–47.

Zuberi, S (2013) *Understanding Religious Fundamentalisms for Activists*, Association for Women's Rights in Development, Toronto, Mexico City, Cape Town.

BOX V.2 **Case study of engagement and responses by women's groups in the face of violence in Gujarat**

The March 2002 riots in Gujarat were a watershed for many rural women's groups. Soon after the riots, the priority of all women's groups was to provide relief in the camps where displaced families were housed. While this was a long and arduous process, even bigger challenges came when families moved back to their villages and slums. Women working with communities were faced with the break-up of their groups in areas where violence had occurred. Hindu and Muslim women refused to come together and sit with each other. In villages, the forced apartheid scared the Hindu women away, while Muslim women experienced both fear and insecurity. Sanctions imposed by village Hindu power elites were another deterrent. In urban slums, although the conditions were different, hostility prevented women coming together.

A major problem was finding a physical space to meet. There were several hurdles. When women made attempts to meet at the local *anganwadi*, the state-sponsored child development centres, the teacher, a Dalit, faced a number of pressures and had to resign. Upper-caste Hindus complained that illegal activities involving Muslims were being held. When women tried to meet in a local village school, they faced the same obstacles. Anyone willing to rent a room to the group was threatened. Finally, after many attempts, a Muslim family who had rebuilt their house offered a room.

Those working among the Tribal populations on community development issues, such as water and micro-credit, faced much probing and soul-searching over the meaning of 'development' work, when the basic rights of one community were constantly put under threat and where an outbreak of violence could undo years of work by women's groups. The citizenship rights of Tribals cannot be advanced at the expense of the total suspension of civil, political, socio-cultural and economic rights of another community.

The group that started working for relief and rehabilitation among Muslims also faced problems. First there was a threat from the Hindu groups of the Sangh Parivar: 'We will do [to you] what we did with the Muslims ... we will burn your office.' This threat destabilized the staff members of the women's organizations, who temporarily stopped going to work. A series of meetings was held among the staff to face up to this new challenge of whether development work can be divided along religious lines.

Through a long but enabling process, the group decided that they just couldn't act like ostriches burying their heads in the sand at this critical juncture, and work with only one group of people, the Tribals. This religious divide was not just superficial but meaningless when larger issues working against the grain of citizenship were confronting them, and social breakdown affected the very core values on which their work was based. The context had changed radically and required new approaches, so they decided to work among Muslims as well. 'We are a women's group ... we have to stick together and stand by each other ... we are learning to manage diversity and work towards this. How do we learn to say we are "different" ... this need not be resolved through violence alone.'

Both groups used religious symbols and festivals of both communities as a way to cement ties. Group one used a festival called *raksha-bandhan*, which means literally a 'bond for protection'. Hindus celebrate this once a year, where a sister ties a thread to her brother, symbolizing his duty to protect her. One women's group strategically inverted this ceremony. In their version, Hindu and Muslim women tied the thread, as sisters promising protection to each other. The same group, which has more than 130,000 women members and derives its identity from mobilizing working-class women who do marginal and menial jobs, strongly emphasizes and reinforces the identity of women as workers in a bid to forge a sense of unity among Hindus and Muslims. It is these women's livelihoods that are first threatened in riot situations, which can have ripple effects over the rest of their lives.

In a peace process initiated in the urban slums where they have members, women's groups called Shantaben and Ektaben, which means 'sisters for peace' and 'sisters for unity' respectively, work to bring women from the two communities together through a series of sessions dealing with the schisms in their neighbourhoods. In one area, when the threat of violence flared up into a riot between Muslims and Hindus, the sisters for peace and unity lay down on the road in protest. This instant mobilization by the women led to a lessening of tension. By the time the police had arrived the problem had been resolved: 'We sent a message to the police, saying it's our problem, not yours' (a member of Ektaben).

Women's groups in Gujarat are positioning themselves as arbitrators in post-riot conflicts and negotiations between Hindus and Muslims in an attempt to rewrite the social contract around peace and security.

CHAPTER 13

Reframing peace and security for women

KUMUDINI SAMUEL

Changing terrains of security

Two unprecedented critical processes – the 'war on terror' and global financial crises – have so far marked the opening decades of the twenty-first century. In consequence, we have seen the growth of nationalism and fundamentalisms in every part of the world. National security doctrines undermine democratic frameworks and heighten militarization; social inequity, poverty and unemployment are increasing, accompanied by a collapse of economic systems focused on economic growth at the cost of human development. The concept of human security, defined by the United Nations Development Programme (UNDP) to mean the ensuring of both freedom from fear and freedom from want for the individual (UNDP, 1994), has been marginalized through these processes. The public policies that have emerged out of this context have had an immediate and usually negative effect on the lives and rights of ordinary citizens in almost every country in the world. In the process, issues of livelihoods, poverty, human rights, freedom of expression and mobility, identity and sexuality have been reshaped and changed radically, creating multiple forms of new in/securities for women.

In the 1980s, DAWN defined 'the crisis of reproduction' in its analysis of the debt crisis (Sen and Gowen, 1987). This crisis has today evolved into 'a crisis of human in/security' that has different impacts on women and men. Gendered in nature, it includes the 'informalization and feminization of employment; the lengthening and intensification of women's labour time, an increase in the "reproductive tax", increased burden on the care economy; [and] "the crisis of masculinity" as men can no longer maintain the myth of male breadwinner' (Truong, Wieringa and Chhachhi, 2006).

The crisis of human in/security has also intensified, as the nature of conflict has shifted from inter-state to intra-state, with its casualties being mainly women and children. Contemporary wars occur in the sites of the most severe social divisions, concomitantly generating multiple forms of crisis (Petchesky and Laurie, 2007). Militarization reinforces armed conflict and is also integrally linked to systemic violence. The heightening of insecurity in all aspects of the daily lives of civilian populations has therefore played a major role in shaping and changing women's lives. The crisis of reproduction is thus exacerbated by conflict and overlaid by the crisis of in/security.

These crises are also embedded in a changing global security archi-tecture. The end of the cold war shifted debates within the United Nations (UN) to a focus on establishing democracies, improving relations between East and West and the imperatives of market economies. Political foci shifted from inter-state to intra-state armed conflict. By the early 1980s, there was a proliferation of internal conflicts. The enemy of national sovereignty and security was increasingly identified not as an external force, but rather as persons or organizations in civil society wanting to change the dominant structures of power (Taft, 2001). These conflicts and attendant militarization are reinforced by juridical situations that suspend the normal rule of law with the introduction of emergency powers and repressive legislation. They create a 'state of exception' in which citizens are reduced to 'bare life', or stripped of the ordinary rights of citizenship (Agamben, 1998), which in turn impact adversely on democratic rights such as the freedom of expression, association, mobility and so on. In such militarized environments, law and order and accountable governance are suspended for military ends and a state of exception is instituted as the norm.

In the 1990s, the Balkan wars and NATO's unilateral air strikes in Kosovo, the genocide and UN inaction in Rwanda, and the Gulf War (1991) brought about new definitions in security and in the role of the UN Security Council in ensuring world peace. It also resulted in a number of UN interventions in peacekeeping and humanitarian operations that challenged the principles of state sovereignty and non-interference in internal domestic affairs.

For women the insecurities of war and conflict take on a particular gendered dimension. They are compounded by the diversity of contemporary conflict, which ranges from identity-based conflicts to occupation and civil unrest; and by the roles played by a range of state and non-state actors in conflict and its resolution. Women and girls also play multiple and diverse roles in conflict and transitions, from armed combatants to single heads of household to peacemakers. They are displaced, become refugees, migrants or stateless and are forced into roles that are outside traditional familial ones. They face marginalization and challenges to varying degrees in terms of access to resources and decision-making processes based on their political, ethnic, caste, class, religious or other status and identity. Women also face violence, often as a continuum through periods of conflict, transition and post-conflict. They are subject to sexualized violence used as a weapon of war, which leads to social, economic and cultural disempowerment during transition and in post-conflict settings. Women are also often impeded from seeking the appropriate methods of redress or reparations for war-time crimes. Further, in the context of globalization and the interconnections of geopolitics, trade, business and aid, conflict settings inevitably involve far more actors than the state in which hostilities are geographically located. These range from external states to UN entities and international financial institutions, resulting in particular gendered in/securities for women.

Linking women to concerns of peace and security at the UN

It is in the context of these changing security imperatives that women achieved the adoption of UN Security Council Resolution 1325 (UNSCR 1325) in October 2000. The resolution was made possible by the determined advocacy of an informal network of women/feminists from local to global NGOs, human rights and peace constituencies, representatives of government, UN agencies, academics and activists. It also involved skilled lobbying of complicated UN mechanisms and processes of power-broking (Cockburn, 2011; Strickland and Duvvury, 2003; Naraghi-Anderlini, 2001).

The UN has traditionally compartmentalized women's issues in its social and development departments. The adoption of UNSCR 1325 succeeded in finally bringing about the recognition of women's concerns in relation to international peace and security, from the domains of soft policy into those of the UN's political departments and inter-governmental bodies dealing with matters of peace and security (Whitworth, 2004).

UNSCR 1325 was the first resolution to link women to concerns of peace and security. It acknowledges the effects of war on women as well as the role of women in conflict prevention, resolution and peacekeeping as critical for international peace and security (UNSCR 1325, Prefatory Paragraphs 5 and 10), placing these in the context of the Security Council's responsibility for ensuring peace and security globally (Cockburn, 2011; Chenoy, 2009; Bell and O'Rouke, 2010). It has three broad domains: *protection* – the recognition of women's rights, the meeting of gender specific needs, the protection of women from sexual violence; *participation* – the recognition of women's role in peace-building and peacemaking and the inclusion of women at all levels of decision-making, including in high-level posts at the UN and in peace processes; and the inclusion of a *gender perspective* in UN peacekeeping operations and DDR (disarmament, demobilization and reintegration) processes post-war. Unanimously adopted, the resolution was expected to have political as well as normative force. However, its implementation has been slow and uneven, and it has no mechanism that can hold states accountable for its enforcement (Whitworth, 2004). For many women, too, the principles embedded in UNSCR 1325 are too abstract, and, increasingly at the global level, the discussion on security and peace is reduced to a simplistic framing around a narrow understanding of UNSCR 1325 (DAWN, 2012).

Peace and security for women: a resolution mired in contradiction

This essay seeks to identify some of the substantive gaps in Resolution 1325 while accepting the determinants that continue to influence its implementation. Among them are developments in International Relations, internal processes within the UN, geopolitical realities and the normative frame of the resolution. As critical are the inherent contradictions entrenched in the resolution.

AMBIGUITY IN LANGUAGE

In UN parlance, Resolution 1325 is a 'thematic resolution'. Such resolutions adopted under Chapter VI (non-coercive measures) carry normative imperatives intended to influence the behaviour of member states. They use persuasive language such as 'urges', 'encourages', 'invites', 'calls', and so on, which is intended to be non-coercive in nature. In contrast, resolutions adopted under the authority of Chapter VII use the strong language of enforcement and are binding on states parties. Thematic resolutions therefore embody an inherent ambiguity. The low priority given to the implementation of UNSCR 1325, it is believed, may be due to this contradiction and may well account for the lack of interest and slow implementation of the resolution in the decade of its existence.

STATE-CENTRIC SECURITY

Another major contradiction and fundamental problem with the resolution is that its articulation and understanding of security is state-centric. Security can be interpreted in different ways – realists conventionally define it in one-dimensional terms – as the protection of the territorial state from external or internal enemies. When understood as such, the maintenance of security is directly linked to the creation and maintenance of militaries or 'security' forces and the securing of borders and territorial boundaries. This conception is inevitably predicated on militarism, in terms of its policies as well as its practice. In practice, security has essentially been a male preserve, with men in positions of political power and decision-making. Security in this context has been a preoccupation of the patriarchal state bent on preserving national interest, particularly in times of war or internal conflict (Enloe, 2000; Mohsin, 2001; Bunch, 2004; McKay, 2004; Chenoy, 2009). This same conception becomes a key consideration in defining processes of conflict resolution and peacemaking in post-conflict and transitional situations. In 1994, the UNDP articulated the concept of human security, seeking to broaden the frame of security to include a range of threats, from economic to social, political, personal, community, health and environmental factors, and making the referent of security the individual rather than the state.

Cynthia Cockburn, an initial proponent of UNSCR 1325, relates how feminists, particularly those in peace movements, sought to redefine security by critiquing militaristic conceptualizations and supporting an inclusive understanding of human security beyond the UNDP articulation, giving it gender specificity and framing it in the context of unequal patriarchal power relations. She avers that this was the meaning feminists gave to the word 'Security' in the title of UN Resolution 1325. She notes, however, that in today's political context organizations such as NATO manipulate the concept of security in the furtherance of militarization and war, and UNSCR 1325 can thus well be ab/used in this project (Cockburn 2011).

MITIGATING CONFLICT

Most of the countries developing national action plans to implement the resolution are from the global North. They are not countries in conflict (despite large mobilizations of discontent and riots) but are countries supporting and maintaining a global arms industry often with large defence budgets. Conversely, they contribute to 'mitigating' conflict, by contributing troops for 'peacekeeping'. The USA is a case in point. It has now moved towards developing a National Action Plan (NAP) on Resolution 1325, bringing defence contractors and senior officials of the Pentagon together with the peace constituency to build a 'community of practice'. However, America's promise of US$44 million for this work is miniscule in comparison to its colossal defence budget of $693 billion for 2010. In addition, as the Department of Defense controls one-fifth of foreign assistance funding, for Americans the line between military and development assistance is increasingly blurred. The Department of Defense is the main contractor for jobs, which go to defence contractors, consultants and firms-for-hire, who perform much of American security work at home and abroad. The Department of Defense is therefore not in the business of ending war (Thompson, 2010).

MAKING WAR SAFE FOR WOMEN

Another contradiction inherent in the resolution is the equality dilemma in feminism (Cockburn, 2011). Interestingly the resolution in its text is careful not to call for more women in militaries, but rather urges an expansion of 'the role and contribution of women in United Nations field-based operations, and especially among military observers, civilian police, human rights and humanitarian personnel'. However, in practice

282 THE REMAKING OF SOCIAL CONTRACTS

NATO, together with many troop-contributing countries, has begun to promote the inclusion of more women in militaries as a means of modernizing and professionalizing contributing armies, and indeed as a means of preventing sexual and gender-based violence or making the reporting and investigating of violence against women gender-sensitive. While supporting the principle of formal, or quantitative, equality on the basis of justice and free choice, Cockburn stresses that the struggle for equality must always be pursued in concert with the unrelenting struggle for transformative change in gender and other power relations, and therefore the sole objective of increasing women's representation in coercive institutions such as militaries defeats the objective of justice (Cockburn, 2011).

CO-OPTATION BY MILITARISM AND PATRIARCHY

Despite the fact that the Security Council's core responsibility under its charter is to maintain international peace and security, the women drafting the resolution were dissuaded from incorporating language critiquing militarism, militarization and the pursuit of war by member states. In a self-critique of this failure, Carol Cohen states: 'Protecting women in war, and insisting that they have an equal right to participate in the processes and negotiations that end particular wars, both leave war itself in place… [1325 is not] an intervention that tries either to prevent war, or to contest the legitimacy of the systems that produce war – that is, "to put an end to war"' (Cockburn, 2011). This leaves in place the conventional realist logic that a state is invested with the power to defend as well as avenge itself, and the use of violence in this task is legitimized (Chenoy, 2002). This legitimizing is inscribed on the conscious and the unconscious through militaristic imagery, thought and emotion, where the resolution of conflict becomes inconceivable without resorting to force. Conversely, security in the context of peacemaking must engage with conflict resolution through inclusive and democratic processes. Peacemaking therefore cannot be controlled by patriarchal states or the custodians of their coercive power apparatus (Manchanda, 2010; Samuel, 2010; Banerjee, 2008). In not challenging the war system but merely allowing women a role in its structures, Resolution 1325 does not allow for the making of sustainable peace.

WOMEN'S ACTIVISM AND AGENCY IN TIMES OF CONFLICT

Feminists and peace activists conceptualized UNSCR 1325 specifically to address the impact of war on women and women's contributions to conflict resolution and sustainable peace. In order to achieve its full potential, the resolution should bring about a shift in global perceptions relating to women, peace and security and lead to the development of a political framework for addressing the gendered nature of war and peace with a nuanced understanding of the in/securities of women. To overcome the barriers to implementation of the resolution, there has to be an understanding of 'where normative standards might make a difference, where their effect may be limited, and what the negative trade-offs for women may be' (Bell and O'Rourke 2010:2).

Women's experiences allude to the complexity of conflict and its transformation for women, where peace often is a nebulous and abstract category and the in/securities experienced are based on myriad interlocking factors that span the spectrum from the personal to the political. To secure transformative peace and ensure economic, social, political and personal security for women there has to be an understanding of the complexity of conflict and of peace. The interpretation and exercise of UNSCR 1325 need to take these complexities and experiences into account.

SECURITY/INSECURITY AND RISK

For women the experience of security in everyday life is mediated through a range of constantly changing social structures that include culture, religion, family, identity and gender. The recognition of a continuum of violence against women is also now central to feminist conceptualization of peace, human rights and security. All forms of this violence, whether interpersonal, in the family or the community, or perpetrated by state/non-state actors, are interrelated; and this violence continues into times of transition and post-war, posing a continuum of threat to women in space, time and location (Cockburn 2001; Baines, 2008; Chenoy, 2009).

The referent of security is not merely the individual but also the social relations that mediate human life (Truong, Wieringa and Chhachhi, 2006). In wartime, women's sexuality is controlled through the withholding of access to contraception or the criminalizing of abortion. This reflects the global/local processes that coalesce to create 'plural forms of gender power and control' over women. This also shapes 'new risks and forms of insecurity for women and their communities' (Truong, Wieringa and Chhachhi, 2006). The defending of women's human rights both in time of conflict and during the transition to peace has brought about new risks for women, leading to increased domestic and sexual violence as well as the victimization of women as witches by state and non-state actors (DAWN, 2012).

These gendered risks for women are also manifest in times of conflict and transition in the dislocation of everyday life and the increase in women's burden in the domain of care, in the brutalization of the body and impunity in the domain of violence, and in women's exclusion from decision-making in the domain of political agency.

CONTINUED IMPUNITY FOR SEXUAL CRIME

Women's bodies and their sexuality are markers of culture, tradition and family and are constantly subject to institutional and interpersonal contestations of power, control, regulation and surveillance. In times of conflict, this contestation is overtly expressed as a part of the broader struggle where women's bodies, and sometimes the bodies of men, become virtual battlefields (Truong, Wieringa and Chhachhi, 2006).

Other violent forms of human rights abuse are also meted out on women, particularly on account of their role as frontline human rights defenders, in its more traditional manifestation of custodial torture, disappearances and extrajudicial executions, which also have specific gendered implications for women. Violence against women, particularly sexual violence, is not an aberration of wartime, however. It has been argued that institutionalized male dominance is itself a form of violence and that such dominance is justified and perpetuated through the threat and use of violence against women at all times (Coomaraswamy and Fonseka, 2004). This is made possible by the subordination of women to hegemonic masculine and heteronormative culture that articulates women's status as the property of men and condones violative practices such as incest, rape, female genital mutilation and other forms of coercive sexual violence as means of controlling women's sexuality (Meintjes, Pillay and Turshen, 2002).

In periods of transition it is imperative that sexual crimes committed during armed conflict are recognized and punished effectively. Feminist analysis of and concerted campaigning against conflict-related gender violence has focused attention on sexual violence and resulted in some forms of such violence being classified as war crimes and crimes against humanity (ICC, 1998).

The judgments of the Ad Hoc Tribunals set up for the former Yugoslavia and Rwanda, recognition of the struggle of the 'comfort women' in Korea and Japan, and the setting up of the International Criminal Court reflect the success of such efforts (Coomaraswamy, 1999). International war crimes tribunals have made important inroads into dealing with impunity in relation to sexual crimes, but only a few countries are covered by their jurisdiction. The International Criminal Court also sets in place fundamental standards recognizing sexual crimes as grave breaches of the Geneva Conventions, war crimes and crimes against humanity. These are expected to inform standards of domestic jurisprudence. However, despite this recognition, sexual violence in times of war is often perceived as a crime against 'honour', and continues to receive much less attention and is committed with impunity around the world. It also receives very little attention in times of transition and is rarely dealt with in mechanisms set up to facilitate transition. For example, the legislation creating the Truth and Reconciliation Commission (TRC) in South Africa made no mention of rape; when rape did surface in testimonies, it had to be dealt with under the heading 'severe ill-treatment' (Krog, 2001).

This has led feminists to question the possible collusion between masculine institutions of law enforcement and justice and the patriarchal power politics that condone the control of women's sexuality. The links between dominant notions of masculinity, war and militarization converge in both the control of women's sexuality and the abuse of women's sexuality during wartime. Conventional wisdom defines war as a male affair that excludes women, and militarization foregrounding war draws on the most violent and aggressive features of masculinity (Sideris, 2002). It provides men with a heroic identity. This, coupled with real experiences of courage and conviction, gives soldiers and militants alike a sense of meaning and direction, and of playing a special role in society (Sideris, 2002: 151). This construction of the hero justifies or condones many infringements or abuses committed by men during war, including killing, torture, rape, sexual slavery, enforced prostitution and so on. The reluctance to prosecute crimes of rape and sexual torture is a direct result of this nexus.

Understanding agency

From situations of conflict to post-war transition and post-conflict, women express an agency that goes beyond the essentialist stereotyping of victimhood. In some instances, women become militant and use violence as a means to a common end, while in others they engage in conflict mitigation or resolution (DAWN, 2012). They express an agency, therefore, that 'attributes to the individual actor the capacity to process social experience and to devise ways of coping with life even under the most extreme forms of coercion. ... for women as much as men, the experience of violent conflict and migration, as with social life, is not built upon a single discourse. As social actors, they form multiple ways of formulating their objectives, however restricted their resources' (Moser and Clark 2001: 5).

Women thus create new spaces for political engagement that often defy the formal and the conventional and offer an emancipatory potential to post-conflict and post-war political restructuring and social transformation. Discussing the transversal spaces for dissident activism along the Burma–Thai borderlands, O'Kane notes that 'distinctions between public/private, politics/survival, mother/activist, freedom fighter/ illegal alien collapse, and become inseparable experiences' (O'Kane, 2006: 236), resulting in shifts and transformations in women's identities. In Sri Lanka, the exigencies of protracted conflict and the traumatizing experience of being captive in a site of brutal conflict have impelled women to cross public–private boundaries and dare to give voice to dissent and claim rights, albeit in initial and minute ways. These include the continued search for the disappeared, the choice to give evidence before the Lessons Learnt and Reconciliation Commission and the claiming of land rights post-war (DAWN, 2012).

The reality is that in wartime many frontline human rights defenders are women, expressing political agency when it is dangerous and impossible for men to do so. From the Madres of the Plaza Del Mayo in Argentina to the Women in Black in Palestine to the Mothers' Front in Sri Lanka and the Women Human Rights Defenders in Nepal, women use diverse strategies to move from the margins of exclusion to political visibility.

These experiences suggest that women's agency is never completely muted. While women, and men, may not be allowed the right to 'bear rights', they continue to find ways and means to subvert their subjugation, defying conventional power relations to express a complex agency. Refusing to accept Agamben's 'rigid binary that divides humanity into political life (citizenship) and bare life (no rights, nonparticipation)', these women display 'a crucial spectrum of ambiguous and interstitial practices mounted by the abject – mediating between the two extreme ends of political and nonpolitical – that actually extends and reanimates the life of citizenship from the very margins of abjection' (Lee, 2010).

Understanding the complexity of peace and security

The complexity of conflict and peace makes it patently apparent that there is no clearly defined post-war moment (DAWN, 2012). Rather, women's experience suggests

> a continuum of conflict, expressed now in armed force, now in economic
> sanctions or political pressure. A time of supposed peace may later come
> to be called the 'pre-war' period. ... A time of post-war reconstruction,
> later, may be redesignated as an inter bellum – a mere pause between wars.
> (Zarkov and Cockburn, 2002: 10)

As critically, the significance of structural violence, long-term oppression and impoverishment, which is often part and parcel of 'peacetime', cannot be ignored. As such economic oppression continues, so does the continuum of violence faced by women before, during and after war, and the relation of violence against women to sexual control, political control and the allocation of resources (Meintjes, Pillay and Turshen, 2002).

These many experiences of women living in conflict or in transitions to peace have in common the brutalization of the body and impunity in the domain of violence – sexual, gender-based, military and existential. However, the common experience is that while international feminist advocacy has enabled recognition of the gendered nature of peace and security, redress is mired in 'the complexity of the operation of power within and across categories of gender, ethnicity and generation' (Truong, Wieringa and Chhachhi, 2006: xiii). It is also dependent on the nexus between militarism, patriarchy and hegemonic masculine and heteronormative culture that controls women's sexuality and status in society.

Another vital consideration is that it is too late for women to begin the transformation of gender relations post-war. Post-war rhetoric of democratization or political restructuring often masks the reconstruction of patriarchal power relations and the reinstating of the gender status quo. However, 'social transformation is not just about conditions and structures, but also about internal processes of consciousness, of creating words and language' (Meintjes, Pillay and Turshen 2002: 8) that will challenge the old order and create 'new democratic institutions and practices' that will be sustained in the aftermath of conflict. This process of democratization must include participatory and consultative decision-making processes and the affirmation of the principles of equality and non-discrimination. It must also include state and security-sector reform and inclusive constitution-making. Such a reframing of security must also ensure a transformative peace that challenges existing structures of patriarchal power and dominance. Peace must therefore not be limited to the mere absence of war but must also result in the absence of social and political violence, as well as violence within the domestic sphere. This is the true meaning of peace and security for women, and these are the nuanced complexities that must be taken into account for the realization and implementation of UN Resolution 1325.

REFERENCES

Agamben, G. (1998) *Homo Sacer: Sovereign Power and Bare Life*, Stanford University Press, Stanford CA.

Baines, E. (2008) *Is Canada's 'Freedom from Fear' Agenda Feminist?*, www.ligi.ubc.ca/sites/liu/files/Publications/JRP/RethinkingWomenWorkingPaper.pdf.

Banerjee, P. (2008) *Women in Peace Politics*, Sage Publications, New Delhi.

Bell, C., and C. O'Rourke (2010) 'Peace Agreements or Pieces of Paper? The Impact of UNSC Resolution 1325 on Peace Processes and Their Agreements', *International and Comparative Law Quarterly* 59, October, pp. 941–80.

Bunch, Charlotte (2004) 'A Feminist Human Rights Lens on Human Security', *Peace Review*, vol. 16, no. 1, p. 4.

Chenoy, A.M. (2002) *Militarism and Women in South Asia*, Kali for Women, New Delhi.

Chenoy, A.M. (2009) *The Gender and Human Security Debate*, Institute of Development Studies, Special Issue on *Transforming Security and Development in an Unequal World*, vol. 40, no. 2, March, pp. 44–9.

Cockburn, C. (2001) 'The Gendered Dynamics of Armed Conflict and Political Violence', in C. Moser and F.C. Clark (eds), *Victims, Perpetrators or Actors? Gender, Armed Conflict and Political Violence*, Zed Books, London.

Cockburn, C. (2011) 'Snagged on the Contradiction: NATO, UNSC Resolution 1325, and Feminist Responses', contribution to the Working Group on 'Feminist Critiques of

Militarization, No to War – No to NATO' annual meeting, Dublin, 15–17 April, www.wloe. org/fileadmin/FilesEN/PDF/no_to_nato/women_nato_2011/NATO1325.pdf.

Coomaraswamy, R. (1999) 'A Question of Honour: Women, Ethnicity and Armed Conflict', Third Minority Rights Lecture, Geneva.

Coomaraswamy, R., and D. Fonseka (eds) (2004) *Peace Work: Women, Armed Conflict, and Negotiation*, Women Unlimited, New Delhi.

DAWN (2012) *Women Transforming Peace Activism in the Fierce New World: South and South East Asia*, ed K. Samuel, Development Alternatives with Women for a New Era.

Enloe, C. (2000) *Maneuvers: The International Politics of Militarizing Women's Lives*, University of California Press, Berkeley.

ICC (1998). *Rome Statute of the International Criminal Court*, A/CONF.183/9, International Criminal Court, Rome.

Krog, A. (2001) 'Locked into Loss and Silence Testimonies of Gender and Violence at the South African Truth Commission', in C.O.M. Moser and F.C. Clark (eds), *Victims, Perpetrators or Actors? Gender, Armed Conflict and Political Violence*, Kali for Women, New Delhi.

Lee, C.T. (2010) 'Bare Life, Interstices, and the Third Space of Citizenship', *Women's Studies Quarterly* 38, pp. 57–81.

Manchanda, R. (2010) *States in Conflict with Their Minorities: Challenges to Minority Rights in South Asia*, Sage, Delhi.

McKay, S. (2004) 'Women, Human Security, and Peace-building: A Feminist Analysis', in *Conflict and Human Security: A Search for New Approaches of Peace-building*, IPSHU English Research Report Series No. 19, Hiroshima University, Hiroshima.

Meintjes, S., A. Pillay and M. Turshen (eds) (2002) *The Aftermath: Women in Post-Conflict Transformation*, Zed Books, London.

Mohsin, A. (2001) 'Governance and Security: The Experience of Bangladesh', in P.R. Chari (ed.), *Security and Governance in South Asia*, Manohar, Delhi.

Moser, C.O.N., and F. Clark (eds) (2001) *Victims, Perpetrators or Actors? Gender, Armed Conflict and Political Violence*, Zed Books, London.

Naraghi-Anderlini, S.B. (2001) *Women, Peace and Security: A Policy Audit*, International Alert, London.

O'Kane, M. (2006) 'Gender, Borders and Transversality: The Emerging Burmese Women's Movement in the Thailand–Burma Borderlands', in N. Behera (ed.), *Gender, Conflict and Migration*, Sage, New Delhi.

Petchesky, R.P., and M. Laurie (2007) *Gender, Health and Human Rights in Sites of Political Exclusion*, Women and Gender Equity Knowledge Network, WHO.

Samuel, K. (2010) *The Centrality of Gender in Securing Peace: The Case of Sri Lanka*, Women in Security, Conflict Management and Peace (WISCOMP), Delhi.

Sen, G., and C. Gowan (1987) *Development, Crises, and Alternative Visions: Third World Women's Perspectives*, Monthly Review Press, New York.

Sideris, T. (2002) 'Rape in War and Peace: Social Context, Gender Power and Identity', in S. Meintjes, A. Pillay and M. Turshen (eds), *The Aftermath: Women in Post-Conflict Transformation*, Zed Books, London.

Strickland R., and N. Duvvury (2003) *Gender Equity and Peace Building: From Rhetoric to Reality*, International Center for Research on Women Washington DC.

Taft, E.I. (2001) *Integrating a Gender Perspective into Conflict Resolution: The Columbian Case*, in I. Skjelsbaek and D. Smith (eds), *Gender, Peace and Conflict*, Sage, London.

Thompson, L. (2010) 'War and 1325: Principles or Diversity Checkbox?', 18 November, www. opendemocracy.net/5050/lyric-thompson/war-and-1325-principles-or-diversity-checkbox.

Truong, T.D., S.E. Wieringa and A. Chhachhi (eds) (2006) *Engendering Human Security: Feminist Perspectives*, Zed Books, London, and Women Unlimited, New Delhi.

UNDP (United Nations Development Programme) (1994) *Human Development Report 1994*, UNDP, New York.

Whitworth, S. (2004) *Men, Militarism, and UN Peacekeeping: A Gendered Analysis*, Lynne Rienner, Boulder CO and London.

Zarkov, D., and C. Cockburn (eds) (2002) *Postwar Moment: Militaries, Masculinities and International Peacekeeping*, Lawrence & Wishart, London.

BOX V.3 **LBT rights and militarization in post-conflict context**

JAYANTHI KURU-UTUMPALA

For the past thirty years – my entire lifetime – the government of Sri Lanka (GOSL) has been engaged in a civil war with the Liberation Tigers of Tamil Eelam (LTTE), who have been fighting for a separate state in the north and the east of the island. This conflict has claimed more than 70,000 lives and displaced thousands. In May 2009, the GOSL militarily defeated the LTTE after a brutal attack in which a further 40,000 Tamils were killed and nearly 60,000 injured.

HIERARCHY OF RIGHTS

One of the key challenges faced by sexual rights advocates is the argument that the violation of rights relating to sexual orientation and gender identity (SOGI) is never as important as human rights violations that occur during conflict or post-conflict situations. Sri Lanka criminalizes adult consensual same-sex relationships. Two key legal provisions enable this: the first is under Section 365A of the Penal Code of 1883, which follows the archaic British Sodomy Law; the second is under the Vagrants Ordinance of 1842, whereby anyone 'deemed to be loitering in public' can be arbitrarily arrested. Under the latter provision, therefore, sex workers, especially transgender sex workers and non-stereotypically feminine women, are harassed by the police and other state authorities.

A hierarchy of rights is implied, wherein SOGI-related rights are considered only a trivial matter when compared with 'larger, more serious' human rights violations. When issues of sexuality have been raised, this has been done within a heteronormative framework, mostly dealing with violence against women, rape and reproductive health services for women affected by the conflict. It is not only lesbians, bisexual women and transgender people who are excluded, but also adolescents, single women, and other women who choose to live outside the heterosexual matrix.

POST-CONFLICT NATURE OF THE VICTORIOUS STATE

Immediately after the military defeat of the LTTE by the GOSL, the government adopted a victorious attitude, underpinned by Sinhala Buddhist nationalism. Cultural values restricting women's sexual autonomy became more strongly manifest. In July 2010, for example, nearly 300 heterosexual couples were arrested by police for holding hands on the grounds of 'public indecency'.

During this period, television advertisements valorized a militarized masculinity. The armed forces were portrayed as heroes and, therefore, ideal husbands for young women, implying the promotion of a particular type of masculinity, a type reserved for biological males. Valorizing one type of masculinity inhibits what Judith Halberstam calls 'female masculinity', which she distinguishes from 'masculinity' in the male domain. Thus, in post-conflict Sri Lanka the space for women to perform masculinity or express themselves in non-feminine ways is limited.

ENTRENCHED MILITARIZATION

During the conflict, military checkpoints were established throughout the island, most of which were strategically placed along access points into and out of the capital city of Colombo. Movement required the showing of identity cards. Harassment followed those identified as Tamils, particularly women. Harassment was also experienced by trans-men and trans-women, as their chosen gender identity differed from those indicated on the cards.

Restrictions to freedom of association and organization have also increased. Organizations that have called for an international investigation of human rights violations are viewed by the government as a threat. Consequently there is now increased scrutiny of NGOs and their sources of funding. Those working on sexuality rights operate under a convergence of anti-NGO sentiments with criminalization of homosexuality. LBT activists have therefore been compelled to use HIV, health, reproductive rights and sex work as entry points to working on sexuality.

ECONOMIC AND ECOLOGICAL JUSTICE

Military personnel have been able to impose severe restrictions on Tamil women's mobility and access to basic resources. Some women have been forced to barter sexual favours in return for financial aid or food rations. If women are affected to such an extent, one can only imagine that consequences must be worse for LBT women, who often remain invisible.

In the post-conflict scenario, lands and irrigation systems that were used for paddy cultivation have been ravaged and destroyed. Landmines must be cleared before there can be redistribution to internally displaced persons. Since government assistance and compensation are also linked only to the heteronormative family unit, land redistribution is not accessible to LBT women because their relationships are not recognized or accepted by the state.

ACTION FOR LBT RIGHTS

For LBT rights activists it is impossible to work in isolation. It important to link up with the women's movement and look to them for support and solidarity. A case in point is a recent experience within the CEDAW reporting process when Sri Lanka was due for a review in February 2011. As their first engagement, the Women's Support Group submitted a separate NGO 'Shadow Report' to the

CEDAW committee that dealt specifically with the status of lesbian, bisexual and transgender people (see Women's Support Group, Sri Lanka 2011). This was in part a response to the CEDAW Committee General Recommendation No. 28, Article 2, released in 2010, to include discrimination based on sexual orientation and gender identity. The Women's Support Group also lobbied mainstream women's NGOs to include their concerns in the main 'Shadow Report'. As a result of these efforts, CEDAW's concluding comments urge the state party to 'decriminalize sexual relationships between consenting adults of the same sex, and abide by the obligation of non-discrimination under the Convention' (para. 25g). LBT rights activists advocating for sexuality rights to be recognized as women's rights need to work with the women's movement in order to move forward and grow stronger.

REFERENCES

Halberstam, J. (1998) Female Masculinity, Duke University Press, Durham NC and London.
Women and Media Collective (2011) 'Sri Lanka Shadow Report to the Committee on the Elimination of All Forms of Discrimination Against Women'; www2.ohchr.org/english/bodies/cedaw/docs/ngo/WMD_SriLanka48.pdf (accessed 21 January 2012).
Women's Support Group, Sri Lanka (2011) 'The Status of Lesbians, Bisexual Women, and Transgender People', NGO Shadow Report to the Committee on the Elimination of All Forms of Discrimination Against Women; www2.ohchr.org/english/bodies/cedaw/docs/ngos/WSG_SriLanka48.pdf (accessed 21 January 2012).

CHAPTER 14

Feminist activisms for new global contracts amidst civil indignation

JOSEFA FRANCISCO AND PEGGY ANTROBUS

The first decade of the twenty-first century was a living theatre of re-sistances and citizens' collective actions. Waves of mass mobilizations included the anti-globalization and anti-war rallies associated with the World Social Forum, the national struggles for democracy and justice in the Arab world, the protests for jobs and welfare in Spain, Greece and elsewhere in Europe, and more recently the Occupy movements that first emerged in the United States but have now become a global phenomenon. Protest actions by citizens, mainly young and aided by social media, demanding change from national, regional and global institutions, stand side by side with the older struggles against hunger exploitation and marginalization in the economic South.[1]

The simultaneous explosions of instabilities and threats across geog-raphies of poverty and affluence – North, East and South – diminished the ability of elites to comfort the public with their orthodoxy, amidst the devastating global repercussions of their reckless behaviours. The dramatic proportion of families and communities destroyed through tyrannical rule, militarisms, financial meltdowns and corporate-induced climate change could no longer be denied. Across the globe, there are amplified calls for governments to save humanity and the planet from the greed of industrial/finance corporations and from traditional political elites that provide the authoritative, legal and military mantle for capital accumulation and large corporations.

Given this backdrop of a world capitalist system in crisis and transition, this essay is an examination of persistent and new demands on women's movement politics and feminist political actions. In so doing it touches on familiar questions about the relationship of women's movements with the

United Nations; the interaction between feminist movements and social justice movements; forms of feminist organizing; challenges for resource mobilization; and feminist leadership for inter-generational movement-building. We engage with these questions as feminists rooted in our specific activist contexts in the economic South, who are at the same time members of a global women's movement for which a key battleground is the United Nations.

Feminist activism in a dysfunctional multilateral system

Women's movements and feminists are globalized transnational actors, with distinctive issues, political projects, strategies and histories of struggle for rights and equality on the planet.[2] This international women's movement has had a rich and sustained experience of constructing and defending the United Nations agreements on development and human rights of the 1980s and the 1990s wherein women's rights, including sexual and reproductive rights, and the linkage between economic justice and gender justice, were inscribed.[3] Organized women in the South, DAWN included, have used the United Nations to name and shame governments that have broken global social contracts around development, women's rights and gender equality. This multilateral space, however, is an area where disputes regularly occur over global norms and rules. An oft-repeated scenario is the practice of ghettoizing women in 'soft' development issues and in the 'add women and stir' approach to engendering agreed text. In more recent deliberations, feminists were alarmed and fought hard to prevent some governments from pushing back hard-won international commitments to women's rights and more just and equitable development.[4] The struggle is expected to intensify leading up to and during the ICPD+20 Review that will take place in 2014.

For feminists, the United Nations has been a complicated but necessary global site for waging important political struggles to gain support for human rights and equitable development from governments. Although the relevance of the United Nations is now under severe attack by those who see the institution as increasingly ineffective, unwieldy, expensive and unable to face new risks from globalization,[5] many women's rights advocates have not completely abandoned the platform. Why? The answer is simple: there ha been no other inter-governmental space in which an overwhelming number of states are represented. Feminist activists have learned hard political lessons while engaging in a field marred by unequal power among member states, as well as by political differences on a range of issues among civic groups of women and progressives. Modalities for access by and inputs from civil society organizations during negotiations remain in place and there have been occasions when these have been utilized effectively by feminists. Without feminists in these spaces, other more conservative women's organizations and non-governmental organizations would have monopolized the attention of government negotiators and, as a result, captured global social contracts. Even among like-minded feminists from North and South, tensions exist around how exactly to engage within the United Nations. However, feminist activists have also constructed mechanisms for horizontal debates and discussions around advocacy positions and lobbying strategies, as shown in the next section. Indeed, pragmatic politics and adaptive challenges from global indignation continue to link feminists and women's rights activists to the United Nations, where all issues facing feminists can be tackled in an integrated way by most nation-states.

Within a highly interconnected world, the limits posed by a global governance complex that is based on the Westphalian nation-state model has faced extreme scepticism and severe contestation from all sides – governments, civil society, academe, even business. Key actors in the protest movements associated with the World Social Forum, who are advancing a radical concept of planetary citizenship, and other activists are demanding that the United Nations institute an accountability mechanism to the peoples of the world as a counterbalance to the decision-making by state authorities that has resulted in neoliberal policies.[6] The challenge with regard to reform of the United Nations is to find ways to address the need for a more democratic, plural and accountable multilateral body that is at the same time able to respond immediately to major and unexpected economic, financial and environmental crises in a way that can resolve these long-term systemic issues.

On the question of whether civil society organizations, social movements and feminists ought to abandon advocacy in the United Nations even before these demands are met, positions differ widely. Some organizations believe it is both wise and practical to invest time and energy in newer sites of contestation where real alternatives can be tested and developed.[7] Others, like DAWN, have sustained their engagement in the United Nations, citing the need to secure its central role in economic governance in the face of the pre-eminence of the Bretton Woods institutions and the World Trade Organization. In addition, the need for frequent multilateral contacts and joint responses to global emergencies and crises has underlined the importance of informal but extremely powerful groupings of governments such as the G8, the Organization for Economic Cooperation and Development (OECD), and now the G20.[8] These exclusive spaces are made up of traditionally powerful, rich countries joined by the newly emerged, influential BRICS.[9] The non-transparent nature of these organizations is considered a huge challenge to global governance by feminists/women's organizations and social movements that are demanding more accountable, democratic and human rights-respecting global leadership.[10]

Is the United Nations untouched by the widespread protests? Recent events show that the spirit of radical change has found its way into formal inter-governmental debates and negotiations. In the midst of the sidelining of the United Nations in economic governance issues, some representatives from developing-country member states have sought to bridge the silos of trade and development that exist in a fragmented multilateral system. They have also used the opportunity to stage a learning encounter between the protestors from organized movements that look favourably on the United Nations rather than the World Trade Organization and government delegates in the United Nations itself. This dramatic intervention took place in the leadup to the United Nations Conference on the World Financial and Economic Crisis and Its Impact on Development in 2009,[11] when progressive government representatives from Latin America invited well-known personalities from the globally linked resistances against neoliberal trade policies. This marked the first time that a high-profile panel of known anti-WTO activists was convened in the General Assembly. As the panellists spoke one after the other, they invoked radical proposals for moving away from the requirements of the global market and clipping the powers of corporations. The event was a rare opportunity that was a notch above the usual activist tactic of hiving into the halls and corridors of the United Nations and approaching individual country representatives. However, the panel generated negative reactions from some country delegates who were unused to the language of protest reverberating in the halls of the United Nations, where the rules and protocol of diplomacy hold sway.

In its continuing assessment of advocacy aimed at inter-governmental negotiations and meetings, DAWN has identified several fault lines that currently plague the United Nations:[12] (a) the continuing grip of developed countries on the Security Council; (b) turmoil in the Human Rights Council in regard to women's human rights and sexual rights; (c) the breakdown of secular states, which paves the way for the influence of neoconservatives in inter-governmental negotiations; (d) easier access to the United Nations by big business and multinational corporations through philanthro-capitalism; (e) continuing pressure from the Bretton Woods Institutions and governments that push free-trade agreements; and (f) the sidelining of the human rights of lesbian and bisexual women and trans people.[13]

Politics of solidarity and joint global actions

It is generally recognized in books about feminist activism and women's movements that feminist activists from the economic South advocating for the interlinked issues of gender and economic justice had previously been involved in political struggles, social movements and left-wing political parties. When they formed distinct and autonomous women's movements, they continued to engage with their former comrades and co-activists around transformative political and cultural projects. For instance, feminists working with grassroots organizations on social justice issues have stood alongside men in seeking broader political restructuring and social transformation, mostly at local and national levels but increasingly at the global level. Feminists have made sure that equality issues and rights that they have managed to secure as part of global agreements were brought into social justice and development agendas.[14] DAWN, for one, sustained its political work on confronting the structures of gender and economic injustices, building on its earlier analysis of adverse and gender-differentiated impacts of structural adjustment programmes on poor women's (and men's) development in the economic South.[15]

Male activists, for their part, supported feminists in their advocacy for a more equitable system of benefit sharing and responsible governance, especially among poor women and men in the South, and of late in countries that are in a process of political reform. Some more than others have also raised issues of diversity that go beyond the narrow confines of a dualist gender framework and support the visibility of gays, lesbians and trans people within women's rights and other social movements. However, these political projects have often encountered mixed responses, including generating homophobic reactions from some activists. Even when successful, they have been unable to guarantee the prioritization of equality and diversity issues and demands, or the visibility of diverse agents, within oppositional or official government sites.

The power of women's movements and feminist encounters and the need for them to interconnect horizontally with other social justice movements were made particularly evident in the open space of the World Social Forum (WSF).[16] Predictably, and notwithstanding rhetoric to the contrary, this has not always been an easy dialogue or partnership. Like all political relationships, this one is marked by permanent tensions arising from the processes of interlinking diverse priorities around common struggles. The complexities of such plural resistance spaces within which women's movements debate, including through the formation of the Feminist Dialogues in the World Social Forum, are discussed in greater detail elsewhere by the present authors.[17] As with feminist struggles inside the United Nations, there have been gains as well as reversals, temporary unities amidst permanent tensions, an elaborate complex of old and new issues, and continuing transactions and negotiations to ensure that power is dispersed as equally and democratically as possible given the shifting relations among diverse groups.

In the flux of activisms that weave in and around simultaneous shifts in every imaginable sphere, the World Social Forum, despite logistical problems, has remained the only space where diverse groups of social movements and peoples' organizations regularly aggregate and debate proposals for an alternative to a neoliberal world.[18] Of late, World Social Forum events have been dispersed across various countries, localities and thematic foci, where the Forum's rejection of mainstream world-views and short-term solutions are creating sparks closer to where they matter

– on the ground. Similarly, feminist movements and struggles can be seen dotting the political terrain but nevertheless interconnecting with other struggles. There are, at least for the moment, fewer images of the vibrant, imaginative all-women street mobilizations for rights, equality and development. Instead we see colourful, creative citizens' mobilizations wherein feminist political projects and mass actions articulate inter-sectorally and/or transnationally with other social movements around struggles for regime change, freedom, justice, welfare and sustainable development. We witness this melding of peoples and movements in the protests around G8 or G20 meetings and at anti-dictatorship and anti-capitalist mobilizations in major capitals across continents. Even in the United Nations, women's groups and feminists increasingly work with other movements around joint NGO statements and advocacy. With political manifestations taking on a more plural face, the aggregation of feminists and women's rights activists increasingly takes place within larger sites of inter-movement encounters or as a step in the process of joint global reflections and actions by non-governmental organizations. The launching of the DAWN Development Debates in the Fierce New World, of which this book is one of the outcomes, was an attempt by one network to bring together the intellectual and political energies of inter-connecting analyses and advocacies on gender, sexuality, human rights, development, conflict and global governance.[19]

Importantly, feminists are engaged in another stream that interweaves with actions and reflections they undertake with other non-governmental organizations and social movements in protest and advocacy contexts. They continue to aggregate as a distinct social movement in several spaces and forms, using each opportunity to recall histories of feminist struggles; to take stock of gains, losses, issues, dilemmas and contra-dictions; and to network around specific issues. One of these spaces continues to be that of the United Nations. In the 1990s women's cau-cuses were formed and actively engaged in advocacy at various major United Nations conferences. This mechanism was at work again when women's organizations came together to engage collectively with the review of the Monterrey Consensus on Financing for Development,[20] and when a global campaign brought several women's organizations together around common proposals for the new UN Women entity.[21] By then the environment had changed. Within the United Nations system, debates on its political relevance, mandate and capacity to respond quickly to global emergencies had generated intense political dynamics among member states, which were made more complex by the fact that they also had to deal with an ongoing organization-wide reform. In the larger environment, chaos could be felt everywhere as the latest financial crisis engulfed the entire world, radically affecting all facets of development and putting into question a quarter of a century of international responses to peace and development. At the time of writing, women's caucuses are beginning to reactivate around two upcoming global events. One is the effort around and through the institutionalized Women's Major Group mechanism in preparation for feminist advocacy aimed at recovering and moving forward the lofty content of Agenda 21 to counter Malthusian and market-based arguments at the Rio+20 conference in 2012.[22] The other is bringing together an inter-generational group of women to prepare for a strong presence at the 2014 Cairo+20 review where sexual and reproductive rights are expected once again to be a point of controversy.[23]

In addition, there are the recurrent global events that provide women's rights organizations and individuals an open space in which to congregate, celebrate and debate. These generally welcome all forms of feminist expressions and ideological persuasions, are not primarily defined in relation to specific people's resistances and protests, and are invigorated by the broadest reach of diversity and plurality of feminisms. Among these are academic gatherings, such as the International Inter-disciplinary Conference on Women; Women's Worlds convened by the International Sociological Association; the annual International Association for Feminist Economics meeting; and the international forum of the Association for Women's Rights and Development, held every four years, which attracts a huge number of younger women.[24] In addition, smaller meetings of an inter-regional nature are still held for joint strategizing, reflection and training. Some feminist activists are able to constantly and easily traverse these spaces, formal inter-governmental platforms and protest sites.

Where perhaps a strong single issue or gender-identity-based movement can be seen constantly reverberating is on the Internet, a powerful form of feminist cyber-activism that has been enabled by the information technology revolution. An exponential increase in the number of networked sites and blogs, run mainly by younger feminists but also by long-time women's rights and feminist organizations, is keeping the global feminist/women's movement alive and felt everywhere through a cultural revolution. There is an almost nonstop cyberspace criss-crossing of feminist conversations and interconnections, whether through listserv, Facebook, Skype, chatrooms, emails or sms messaging. But even here, the link between Internet activism and on-the-ground resistances is inextricably tight and obvious. Various sites and blogs regularly post video streams of protest actions in places where the media have been strongly censored and of women calling for people to go out into the streets, such as in the cases of the Syrian and Egyptian uprisings. Signing up to statements issued by women's rights organizations, such as condemning the repression of feminists and sexual rights activists in Fiji or Papua New Guinea or South Africa, has become a constant source of awareness-raising and action-taking on the part of many young women and men.

Today's major crises have forced upon our diverse and plural humanity the need to bond together for a collective re-visioning of how a new world may be possible. The call for solidarity has been reignited by people's organizations and social movements. Unlike in the past, when the politics of solidarity was confined to a single ideology, today's call is founded on plural and diverse ideas that have been generated by an increased civic awareness of the systemic nature of issues that tear apart people's lives. Women's rights activists who have benefited from historical and contemporary political relationships between feminist movements and social justice movements have much to contribute to the realization of solidarity across struggles. This is true of those who have been in long-time struggles for political, economic and gender justice, and is also true of younger feminists engaged in struggles for personal choices, freedom and autonomy as they take part in larger social causes, where they constitute a member of a plural constituency. Speaking of the critical need for interlinking struggles at this conjuncture, DAWN's Gita Sen says:

> We are at a time of massive economic and political instability, all occasioned
> by the fact that we are actually in the moment of shifting from one
> hegemonic power to another in the global economy. These are moments
> of greatest danger, when instabilities are greatest. And we don't have a

history of human rights alone being able to tame the world in that kind of situation... We have to do something to bring together in a more fruitful way the language and discourse of social justice and the language and discourse of human rights. Our big challenge is, I feel, if we're not able to bring those two together in much more intrinsic ways – to see how they are interlinked, and the complexities of that – we're not in a shape to move forward.[25]

Survival and demise in a financially distressed environment

Acquiring resources in support of women's rights advocacy, including at official spaces such as the United Nations, has today become a huge concern among women's rights organizations and social movements. which have long been dependent on development assistance for their political work. The prolonged financial crisis in traditionally rich countries has meant more prudent spending and gift-giving on the part of donors, public and private alike. Both business and governments have incurred massive losses from the huge financial market crash and its aftermath. Money meant for development assistance suddenly became scarce, pooled, targeted and increasingly linked to the regime of aid effectiveness.[26]

The tsunami-like impact of the financial crunch has been quick and devastating. Northern-based women's rights organizations and international non-governmental organizations (INGOs), whose women's programmes had for years generously supported feminist activism across the global South and East and in international spaces, have had to cut back drastically on staffing and programmes, with some organizations completely shutting down operations or relocating to the economic South, where overhead costs are lower.[27] Meanwhile, across the economic South, the advocacies and organizing work of some local and national-level women's non-governmental organizations (NGOs) have been interrupted. With institutional funding suddenly drying up, several organizations have precariously sustained their activities on a shoestring of short-term project funding. Even vertical funds, such as for HIV/AIDS, that were generously endowed have been fraught with difficult dynamics among various beneficiaries, women's rights organizations included, competing for much-needed resources.[28]

The uncertain funding environment is forcing social activists to shift their approaches and strategies in resource generation and utilization.

From discussions with other feminists and women's organizations, DAWN learned of some of these new ways. There are now more collaborative undertakings among women's rights organizations as well as between them and other social movements and non-governmental organizations.[29] Direct fundraising from the public in support of direct actions, either through on-site or web-based donations, has become more familiar. Accessing funds from national governments, either through government ministries/agencies or embassies of donor countries, is now more vigorously explored, as compared to the past when fundraising in the national sphere was less favoured due to possible political strings attached to the money. Moreover, smaller donors such as women's funds and private family-owned foundations have started to engage in more regular strategic discussion towards complementation in funding priorities and targets.

Accompanying these new ways of working together are tensions that have re-emerged in regard to the ethics, politics and values around funding. How far do we go in accessing the wealth of the '1 per cent'? Will this involve compromises that weaken our agenda or will they lead to new understandings? While inclusion, plurality and diversity must be respected, we should also make sure that critical processes of political debate and reflection towards clear principles and unities guiding political practices are kept alive.

Feminist leadership for movement building in precarious times

The struggle for more democratic global institutions and rights-based and just social contracts remains one of the key millennial challenges for feminists. To remain strategic protagonists in the re-imagination and re-creation of alternative global rules and mechanisms, feminists and the global women's movement need to become more politically prepared to take on risks and seize the opportunities thrown up in an uncertain and rapidly changing environment. As chaos swirls around us, there is a need to focus attention on the dominant as well as the aberrant in the environment. We should be able to understand what is crumbling away and what is emerging, for not all of what is old is bad and needs to go away and not all that is new is good and hence should be valorized.

Following our feminist visions of alternative worlds, our analysis must be able to pinpoint and understand both the generative and the degenerative prospects arising from heightened civic restlessness and indignation, enact shrewder opposition to fundamental changes, and recognize a dysfunctional multilateral system. One aspect that needs to change is that 'feminists will need to move away from exclusively heteronormative perspectives, and locate our analyses within more plural grounding of gender-sexual orders and their interactions with economic and other social forces shaping personal and social histories.'[30]

Exercising feminist leadership amidst confusion further requires the creation of opportunities for transversal feminist analyses and advocacies (a) vertically across formal inter-governmental sites, such as the United Nations, and local/national sites of protests and aggregation of people's movements, and (b) horizontally across a range of alternatives and visions that cut through plural feminist and social movements politics. For women's rights advocates and activists who have had to constantly traverse various sites of resistances – personal and political, production and social reproduction, local and global – moving from site to site and altering and expanding relations are not completely novel, but the context in which this needs to happen is dangerously unstable. The acceptance of the necessity for multiple strategies, including locking arms with progressive men even while we remain vigilant of residual and/or resurgent patriarchal attitudes, is important as choices are made to work in one sphere/level or the other. Having the astuteness and commitment to exploring avenues for interlinkages, be it through organizational collaboration, issue-based alliances and/or sustaining creative tensions through debates and global conversations, is a must. It is difficult to construct another world and more difficult to ensure that what has been built is not swept away overnight. We must be courageous, creative and strategic.

Feminist leadership recognizes the fundamental value of women's solidarity as a basis for organizing around issues that affect all people at once but also differentially across class, race/ethnicity, caste, religious affiliation, country, sexual orientation and other social markings. These issues concern principally vulnerability to discrimination, violence, poverty, disempowerment and the tension between responsibility for others and for the self.

Indeed, negotiating new social contracts in a context that is antithetical to social justice requires a special type of leadership.

> We ... need a concept of leadership that goes beyond the formal definition of leadership to include women at every level, and one that understands leadership as facilitating rather than directing [change]. (Antrobus, 2004)

Ultimately, feminist leaders who will make a difference are those who are in touch with their own sources of power, understanding its paradoxes and limitations in the feminist struggle along with others in the shaping of the new post-capitalist epoch; who engage in collective inspirational and empowering projects with other feminists and activists so that all are able to exercise their own agency while committed to broad human rights and social transformations; and who are self-reflective and open to learning from mistakes, growing in self-understanding and in relation to others, and ready to pass on as well as to accept leadership of feminist organizations and women's movements for inter-generational movement-building. Let us keep the fire of feminist political struggles burning through and beyond the fierce new world of the twenty-first century!

NOTES

1. This essay draws from the writers' insights in ongoing feminist activisms and reflections as members of the Development Alternatives with Women for a New Era (DAWN), a global network of feminists from the economic South.
2. Antrobus, 2004. See also Eschle, 2010.
3. Sen, 2005.
4. The Plus Five Reviews of the ICPD are always an occasion for some conservative governments to introduce language that would pull back commitments to sexual and reproductive health and rights.
5. See, for example, Evans, 2007.
6. Rikkilä and Patomäki, 2002.
7. For example, some feminist organizations in Latin America partly disengaged from global processes and prioritized engagement in the regional construction of democratic processes and institutions that were led by progressive governments in the region.
8. Established in 1975, the G8 is a forum of governments from major industrialized countries. The OECD was established in 1961 for industrialized countries to share info and coordinate in order to promote growth in markets and cooperate in providing development assistance. The G20 was formed in 1999 in response to the 1997 Asian financial crisis. It is made up of the finance ministers and central bank governors of twenty important countries along with the World Bank and the International Monetary Fund.
9. BRICS stand for Brazil, Russia, India, China and South Africa.
10. See Statement of the WWG on FFD to the G20 Summit in Pittsburgh, 2009, www.dawnnet.org/uploads/documents/WWG_September%202009.pdf; and Civil Society Statement Calling on the G20 to Embed Human Rights in Financial Regulatory and Climate Change Decisions, 2011, www.coc.org/files/Statement%20with%20signatures.pdf.

11. The panel was hosted by the Bolivian ambassador to the United Nations, Pablo Solon, and supported by the Nicaraguan ambassador and later president of the General Assembly, Miguel d' Escoto. See United Nations Conference on the World Financial and Economic Crisis and Its Impact on Development, 24–26 June 2009, www.un.org/ga/econcrisissummit/background.shtml.

12. DAWN, 2010.

13. In December 2011, the United Nations issued a report recognizing the human rights of LGBT persons and seeking their protection from discrimination and violence. See DAWN statement www.dawnnet.org/uploads/documents/website_pressrelease_sogi_2011–Dec-19.pdf.

14. Some examples of global formations with feminists and women/gender caucuses are Social Watch; GCAP; Trade–Finance Linkages; Reflection Group on Alternative Development.

15. Sen and Grown, 1987.

16. The World Social Forum is a network-based process linking progressive forces that are united against neoliberalism, fundamentalisms and militarism. See Aguiton, 2005.

17. Francisco and Antrobus, 2011.

18. See Immanuel Wallerstein on the WSF: www.iwallerstein.com. the-world-social-forum-egypt-and-transformation.

19. DAWN Development Debates in the Fierce New World took place in Mauritius, Africa on 18–20 January 2010. See www.dawnnet.org/resources-news.php?id=91.

20. The Women's Working Group on Financing for Development was formed among women's organizations that engaged in difficult debates on Financing for Development in the United Nations platform at a time when another more heavily funded global discussion on aid effectiveness was rolled out by the Organization for Economic Cooperation and Development (OECD). See WWG on FFD archives at www.dawnnet.org.

21. The Global Gender Equality Architecture Reform (GEAR) Campaign is led by a Working Group composed of global and regional focal points; see www.gearcampaign.org.

22. See the intervention on behalf of Women's Major Group by DAWN's AnitaNayar at the 2nd Intersessional on/ro+20 at the United Nations-New York, www.uncsd2012.org/rio20/index.php?page=viewnr=653type=230menu=38.

23. See 'Our Rights, Our Lives: Women's Call to Action Toward Cairo+20', issued by the International Women's Health Coalition, RESURJ and DAWN, at www.dawnnet.org/advocacy-appeals.php?signon=180id=180.

24. A description of the forum may be found at www.forum.awid.org/forum12/about.

25. Gita Sen speaking at the DAWN Panel on Development Debates in a Fierce New World, NGO Forum of the Commission on the Status of Women Meeting, New York, 2010; see www.dawnnet.org/advocacy-un-ny.php?id=78.

26. See FundHer reports published by the Association of Women's Rights in Development at http://staging.awid.org/About-AWID/AWID-Initiatives/Where-is-the-Money-for-Women-s-Rights.

27. At the time of writing, some non-governmental organizations and charities that have been undertaking long-time work on women's rights have issued appeals for donations from other women's organizations or announced cut-backs and temporary work stoppages.

28. See Box IV.3 above.

29. It is widely known that several proposals received by the Dutch government that sought funding from their FLOW grant of 2011 covered collaborative programmes and projects to be undertaken by several organizations.

30. Francisco, 2011.

REFERENCES

Aguiton, C. (2005) 'Mapping the Movement', *Development*, vol. 48, no. 2, June, pp. 10–14.

Antrobus, P. (2004) *The Global Women's Movement: Origins, Issues, and Strategies*, Zed Books, London.

DAWN (2010) 'The Beijing Platform for Action 15 Years After: Surviving Multilateral Dysfunctionality in a Fierce New World', DAWN Statement at the 54th Session of the Commission on the Status of Women, New York, www.dawnnet.org/advocacy-un-ny.php?id=75.

Eschle, C., and B. Maiguaschca (2010) *Making Feminist Sense of the Global Justice Movement*, Rowman & Littlefield, Lanham MD.

Evans, A. (2007). 'A New Global Leaders' Forum? Comparing and Evaluating Recent Proposals', New York University Center on International Cooperation, New York.

Francisco, J. (2011) 'Feminist Knowledge Production within Social Activism', posted on ICAE Working Group on Education Virtual Exchange 'Education in a World in Crisis: Limitations and Possibilities with a View to Rio+20', December.

Francisco, J., and P. Antrobus (2011) 'Women's Movements Negotiating Social Contracts in Multilateral Inter-government and Trans-national Inter-movement Spaces', in G. Di Marco and C. Tabbush (eds), Feminisms, *Democratization and Radical Democracy: Case Studies in South and Central America, the Middle East and North Africa* (in English and Spanish), UNSAMEDITA, Buenos Aires.

Rikkilä, L., and K. Sehm Patomäki (eds) (2002) 'From Global Market Places to Political Spaces', Network Institute for Global Democratization, Helsink, www.reformwatch.net/fitxers/50.pdf.

Sen, G. (2005) *Neolibs, Neocons, and Gender Justice: Lessons from Global Negotiations*, Occasional Paper Number 9. UNRISD, Geneva.

Sen, G., and C. Grown (1987) *Development, Crises, and Alternative Visions: Third World Women's Perspectives*, Monthly Review Press, New York.

BOX V.4 **The promise and pitfalls of UN Women**

NICOLE BIDEGAIN PONTE

UN Women, the United Nations entity for gender equality and empowerment of women, was born in July 2010 after several years of negotiation within the UN regarding the importance of having a special agency capable of accelerating progress for gender equality and women's empowerment.

Its creation is framed within the reform of the UN system and is also the result of a global campaign by the women's movement. UN Women has an important goal but is part of an institution that has challenges ahead. In the grip of the drawn-out global economic crisis, the United Nations has been told it must be more efficient. There are criticisms regarding the effectiveness of UN peacekeepers, about the time it is taking to reform the composition of the Security Council, and of the weak outcomes in international UN conferences. The emergence of the G20 as a mechanism of global governance to tackle the international financial and economic crisis adds to the critical situation for UN legitimacy.

MORE THAN THE SUM OF ITS PARTS

UN Women consolidated all four UN bodies working on gender equality: the UN Division for the Advancement of Women (DAW), the International Research and Training Institute for the Advancement of Women (INSTRAW), the Office of the Special Adviser on Gender Issues and Advancement of Women (OSAGI) and the United Nations Development Fund for Women (UNIFEM). The aim was to have a stronger agency at a higher level in the UN. However, there still appears to be a clear division between the normative and the operational functions, which need to work together more organically to create synergy between the two (DAWN, 2011). UN Women's strong foundation built on the previous experience of its component bodies require an integrative and long term approach especially if it hopes to provide strong leadership in global forums to fulfill its mandate. Also, if UN Women is to define its niche and step out of the shadows of previous entities and agencies, it has to keep its agenda inclusive and transformative, especially as the women's agenda has always been at the forefront of exposing and addressing gender-based exclusion, discrimination, vulnerability, deprivation and poverty (DAWN, 2011).

UN Women began its operations in January 2011 by focusing on five priority areas: increasing women's leadership and participation; ending violence against women; engaging women in all aspects of peace and security processes; enhancing women's economic empowerment; and making gender equality central to national development planning and budgeting. While seemingly comprehensive, these priority areas are not clearly linked to the development debates around poverty and inequality, macroeconomics and finance, that often define the global agenda. If there is no analysis or proposal to transform global economic imbalances and tackle the lack of regulation of the financial- ized global economy, it will not be possible to secure sufficient funds and policy space to achieve gender equality at the national level. 'UN Women needs to take leadership in policy analytics and influence at the national and global arenas, the more challenging and substantive role navigating the inter-linkages of gender with the economy, environment, peace and human dimensions, which are the expert areas and mandates of other UN entities, including other development institutions' (DAWN, 2011: 30).

Besides working within the UN agencies to ensure gender mainstreaming, UN Women needs also to engage in dialogue with the Bretton Woods and other global institutions to challenge restrictive economic policy frameworks that hinder the advancement of social development and gender equality worldwide. This needs strong leadership, sound analysis and research, as well as convincing arguments to overcome gender blindness and break down political resistance. Former Chilean president Michelle Bachelet, the first under-secretary-general and executive director of UN Women, is attempting to do just this. One vital consideration is to ensure that UN Women is properly funded; agreement has yet to be reached on its proposed budget of US$500 million per year. An adequate level of funding will minimize the likelihood that UN Women would need to approach the international financial institutions with a begging bowl.

Civil society participation through multiple and meaningful processes is key to strengthening the legitimacy, transparency and projection of the entity. Feminist and women's organizations should be ready to be the major critical counterpart in mechanisms of accountability.

These challenges are key to any future assessment of the impact of UN Women. We are moving towards a polycentric world, where Brazil, Russia, India, China and South Africa – collectively known as BRICS – are assuming global leadership. The legitimacy of the UN, and of the leadership of UN Women within it, will depend to a great extent on whether the BRICS choose to enhance multilateralism and reposition the United Nations at the centre of global economic and social governance.

REFERENCES

DAWN (2011) 'What is the Women's Agenda in Asia?' background paper prepared for Towards Advancing the Women's Agenda in Asia, workshop, 11–13 June, Bangkok.
DAWN (2011) 'DAWN Statement at the Launch of UN Women', www.dawnnet.org/ feminist-resources/content/csw-dawn-statement-launch-un-women.

BOX V.5 Young people: shattering the silence on sexual and reproductive health and rights

JENNIFER REDNER AND FADEKEMI AKINFADERIN-AGARAU

The lives and environments of many young people have changed dramatically since the 1994 International Conference on Population and Development (ICPD). While early and forced marriage persists at unacceptable rates, girls generally are marrying later, attending school longer, and have greater access to information and technology in a globalizing world. Nevertheless, high rates of unemployment (ranging from 9·0 per cent in East Asia to 27·9 per cent in North Africa (ILO, 2012)), inequality, and poor sexual and reproductive health (SRHR) outcomes persist for both young women and young men.

Concerned about inequality and inadequate investments in health, development and human rights, and recognizing that achieving SRHR is necessary for a healthy, educated, safe and empowered life, young people are using both older and newer models of advocacy and activism. While the diversity (by age, ethnicity, location, sexual orientation, gender, language, socio-economic status, among others) and the magnitude of youth movements vary across countries and regions, social mobilizing by young people in many countries is one of the most notable developments since ICPD.

Young activists have recognized that international political processes provide significant opportunities, and are increasingly organizing to influence regional and global intergovernmental negotiations on SRHR, population, environment and development. Recent examples include significant contributions to the outcomes of the UN Commission on Population and Development (2012), and the regional meetings in Asia (UNESCAP), Africa (UNECA), Europe (UNECE), Latin America (ECLAC) and Western Asia (ESCWA) for the UN's assessment of two decades of ICPD implementation ('ICPD Beyond 2014'). Young people, shattering expectations of silence as a requirement of respect for their elders, have clearly articulated their priorities in these and other fora, such as the 2012 Bali Global Youth Forum, where they achieved a landmark declaration with very strong SRHR content (ICPD Beyond 2014 Global Youth Forum, 2012).

Youth activists are, inter alia, demanding: universal access to comprehensive sexuality education and to sexual and reproductive health services, including safe abortion, that respect their rights to privacy and confidentiality and are easily accessible; elimination of violence, coercion and discrimination on the basis of sexual orientation and gender identity; prevention and mitigation of all forms of violence against girls and women, including early and forced marriage; protection and fulfilment of all sexual and reproductive rights; and concrete actions to ensure young people are represented as equal stakeholders in all decisions and processes that impact their lives.

Migration, social media, and other factors are shifting cultural and national identities and moving young people to question and transform deeply entrenched norms and attitudes about SRHR, including the priorities articulated above.

The central challenge, now and in the future, is strengthening, through strategic investment, young people's capacity, especially young women's capacity, for consistent and influential engagement with their national governments, bilateral donors and other decision-makers, in order to generate national policies and programmes that implement the international agreements they have helped to achieve. For example, many young activists do not yet know whom they should contact to influence their governments, how to translate global commitments into national policies and programmes, or how to monitor government actions.

Fulfilling the global commitments to youth SRHR, and engaging a diverse group of young people as equal partners in a non-tokenistic way, requires that adults with power, resources and access take sustained and concrete actions. Actions include the following. First, strengthening of the knowledge and skills that young people need in order to influence national and international political processes, and to participate in designing, implementing and evaluating effective and evidence-based policies and programmes. Second, inviting youth groups to participate, ensuring they have the necessary information and documentation, including government position statements and commitments, as well as time to consult, formulate positions and present them. Third, funding and otherwise ensuring the sustainability of advocates and youth-led organizations to participate, influence and articulate their voice and perspective within various movements and national and international processes. Fourth, assisting youth activists to mentor new cohorts of young people and to be able to continue to work with and on behalf of young people's SRHR as adult allies. Finally, ensuring equal access to participation within youth movements, and in the processes in which they engage, to challenge persistent inequalities among young people and develop youth movements that have diverse members, spokespersons and leaders.

Such investments and actions will, among other benefits, help to ensure that the ICPD Beyond 2014 and the UN's post-2015 global agendas prioritize the perspectives, opportunities and rights of today's adolescents and young people, as well as those who come after them, for the benefit of all.

REFERENCES

ICPD Beyond 2014 Global Youth Forum (2012) Bali Global Youth Forum Declaration, http://icpdbeyond2014.org/uploads/browser/files/bali_global_youth_forum_declaration.pdf (accessed 5 November 2013).

ILO (International Labour Organization) (2012) Global Employment Trends for Youth (2012) International Labour Office, Geneva.

Contributors

BARBARA ADAMS is a member of the Reflection Group on Global Development Perspectives and co-author of its report *No Future without Justice*. Her many publications include *Accounting for Africa at the United Nations: A Guide for Non-Governmental Organizations* and *Putting Gender on the Agenda: A Guide to Participating in UN World Conferences, Reclaiming Multilateralism: For People, Rights and Sustainable Development* and *Whose Development, Whose UN?*

FADEKEMI AKINFADERIN-AGARAU is co-founder and executive director of Education as a Vaccine, an organization dedicated to improving the health and development of young people in Nigeria. She holds a B.A. in Chemistry and Molecular Biology and Biochemistry from Wesleyan University and a Master's in Public Health from the Mailman School of Public Health, Columbia University.

PEGGY ANTROBUS is a founding member of DAWN; she was general coordinator 1990–96. In 1975 she established the Jamaican Women's Bureau and in 1978 the Women and Development Unit (WAND) at the University of the West Indies. She has contributed to many publications. *The Global Women's Movement: Origins, Issues and Strategies* was published by Zed Books in 2004.

NICOLE BIDEGAIN PONTE is a Uruguayan feminist activist and sociologist. A member of the Executive Committee of DAWN since 2012, she has worked in networks such as the Latin American and Caribbean Youth for Sexual and Reproductive Rights, Social Watch, the International Council for Adult Education and the Center for Interdisciplinary Studies for Development in Uruguay (CIEDUR). She holds a Master's degree in Contemporary Latin American Studies from the Universidad Complutense de Madrid and the Universidad de la República, Uruguay.

DIANA BRONSON is a Montreal-based political scientist and sociologist. She worked with the international technology watchdog ETC Group as a programme manager from 2009 until 2012, focusing primarily on geoengineering. In 2012, she joined Food Secure Canada as Executive Director. For the past twenty-five years, she has been involved in researching, writing and organizing around international trade and investment, human rights, climate change and many related issues.

CAI YIPING is a DAWN Executive Committee member currently based in China. Previously she was the executive director of Isis International and was an associate professor at the Women's Studies Institute of China. She was a journalist for *China Women's News* for ten years, and participated actively in women's NGOs after the UN 4th World Conference on Women held in Beijing in 1995.

ALDO CALIARI is director of the Rethinking Bretton Woods Project at the Center of Concern, Washington DC, where he has worked since 2000. He has a Master's in International Policy and Practice from George Washington University, and a Master's in International Legal Studies from the Washington College of Law, American University.

AMRITA CHHACHHI is Assistant Professor, Gender, Labour and Poverty Studies, at the International Institute of Social Studies, Erasmus University, The Hague. She has written several books and papers on gender, labour, poverty and social policy, religious fundamentalism and social movements. She is on the editorial board of *Development and Change* and involved with peace, feminist and labour networks in South Asia.

LICE COKANASIGA is DAWN campaign assistant and a member of the DAWN GEEJ Pacific network. She is a postgraduate student in Diplomacy and International Affairs at the University of the South Pacific, Suva. Her work revolves around research on trade liberalization and its impacts in the Pacific, as well as solidarity work involving the impact of extractive industries in the Pacific.

SONIA CORRÊA was DAWN's research coordinator for sexual and reproductive health and rights between 1992 and 2009. She is presently a research associate at the Brazilian Interdisciplinary Association for AIDS, Rio de Janeiro. She co-chairs Sexuality Policy Watch, a global forum on trends in sexuality-related policy and politics. Her publications include *Population and Reproductive Rights: Feminist Perspectives from the South* (Zed Books, 1994) and *Sexuality, Health and Human Rights*, co-authored with Richard Parker and Rosalind Petchesky (2008).

MARINA DURANO was a member of DAWN's executive committee from 2008 to 2011, working on gender issues in financing for development, including international trade policies. She was a post-doctoral fellow at the Women's Development Research Centre (KANITA) of the Universiti Sains Malaysia and is now an Assistant Professor at the Asian Center of the University of the Philippines–Diliman. She has a Ph.D. in economics from the University of Manchester.

JOSEFA FRANCISCO is general coordinator of DAWN. Gigi, as she is fondly known, is chair of the International Studies Department in the College of International Humani-tarian and Development Studies in Miriam College. She has an M.A. in International Studies from Miriam College, and is pursuing a Ph.D. in organizational development at the Southeast Asia Inter-Disciplinary Development Institute.

ALEXANDRA GARITA is the Executive Coordinator of Realizing Sexual and Repro-ductive Justice (RESURJ), a transnational feminist alliance seeking to influence national, regional and global policies and programmes to realize women's and young people's sexual and reproductive rights.

FRANÇOISE GIRARD is President of the International Women's Health Coalition and a highly regarded advocate for women's rights and sexual and reproductive rights and health. She is regularly consulted and has played a key advocacy role at UN conferences on population and development, women's rights and HIV/AIDS. She has contributed to journals including *Science, Health and Human Rights, International Family Planning Perspectives* and *Reproductive Health Matters*.

YAO GRAHAM is coordinator of Third World Network–Africa, a pan-African research and advocacy organization based in Accra, Ghana. He has written and campaigned extensively on African development issues. He is the Africa editor of the *Review of African Political Economy* (ROAPE) and co-edited *Africa and Development Challenges in the New Millennium* (Zed Books, 2006).

JAYANTHI KURU-UTUMPALA is a feminist activist and scholar with over ten years' experience in women's human rights in Sri Lanka. She has an M.A. in gender studies from the University of Sussex with a focus on queer theory. She has advocated for the decriminalization of adult, consensual, same-sex relationships in Sri Lanka before CEDAW. She currently works with men/boys to address gender-based violence in Sri Lanka.

RODELYN MARTE is a feminist activist from the Philippines. 'RD' has worked in national and regional women's health and rights, and in HIV and AIDS programmes. She has also worked in the Philippines, India, Nepal, Bangladesh, Pakistan, China, Indonesia, Vietnam, Cambodia and Laos in the areas of advocacy and community capacity development.

ANITA NAYAR, a feminist activist and scholar, is engaged in research on the social and ecological consequences of commercializing indigenous medicine in India. She has worked with women's movements, governments and UN agencies to bring a gender perspective on ecological, social and economic issues to bear on inter-governmental negotiations and agreements, and national and local policies.

ADEBAYO OLUKOSHI is Research Professor of International Economic Relations at, and currently director of, the UN African Institute for Economic Development and Planning (IDEP), headquartered in Dakar, Senegal, and interim director of the Africa Governance Institute, also located in Dakar. He previously served as executive secretary of the Council for the Development of Social Science Research in Africa (CODESRIA).

MAGALY PAZELLO is a Ph.D. candidate at the Federal University of Rio de Janeiro School of Social Work. She is a researcher of EMERGE, the Research and Project Center on Communication and Emergence, and an independent consultant on gender and ICTs.

ROSALIND P. PETCHESKY is Distinguished Professor Emerita of Political Science at Hunter College and the Graduate Center, City University of New York. She is a long-time participant in many transnational social movements. With Sonia Corrêa and Richard Parker she co-authored *Sexuality, Health and Human Rights* (2008). She has many other publications on sexual and reproductive rights as they link to issues of militarism, disaster and economic, racial and gender justice.

ZO RANDRIAMARO, a human rights and feminist activist from Madagascar, is a development sociologist. She has served as an expert for international organizations and UN agencies, and was a former Executive Committee member and Training Coordinator for DAWN. She is currently a DAWN Associate and the Coordinator of the Research and Support Center for Development Alternatives – Indian Ocean. She has authored several publications on the gendered dimensions of economic, trade and global governance issues.

BHAVYA REDDY is an M.P.H. candidate at the Department of Maternal and Child Health, Gillings School of Global Public Health, University of North Carolina at Chapel Hill. Formerly a Research Associate with the Gender and Health Equity Project, Indian Institute of Management, Bangalore, her interests include gender-based violence, women's health, and sexual and reproductive health and rights.

JENNIFER REDNER has worked in Washington DC for over ten years, including as senior program officer for the International Women's Health Coalition. She has worked for the Population Council and the International Center for Research on Women, assisting with programmes related to women and young people. She has an M.A. in International Development from the American University, Washington DC.

KUMUDINI SAMUEL is an executive committee member of DAWN based in Sri Lanka, and director of the Women and Media Collective. She was a member of the subcommittee on gender issues advising the plenary of Sri Lanka's peace process. She has a Master's in Women's Studies from the University of Colombo. She publishes on peace, security, human rights, governance and women's activism.

STEPHANIE SEGUINO is Professor of Economics at the University of Vermont, and a past president of the International Association for Feminist Economics. She served as an economist in Haiti for several years. She is currently a professorial research associate at the School of Oriental and African Studies (SOAS), London, and a research scholar at the Political Economy Research Institute, working on the relationship between inequality, growth and development.

GITA SEN is Adjunct Professor of Global Health and Population at the Harvard School of Public Health, and was Professor of Public Policy at the Indian Institute of Management, Bangalore. She has been for many years a feminist analyst, activist and advocate on the political economy of globalization, and on sexual and reproductive health and rights. She is a member of DAWN's Executive Committee.

CLAIRE SLATTER is a development expert and university lecturer with an M.A. from Australian National University and a Ph.D. from Massey University. She has been a consultant with a number of international development agencies on issues around gender equality, economic security and human rights. She is chair of the DAWN board, and was DAWN General Coordinator, 1997–2004.

FATOU SOW holds a doctorate in sociology from the University of Paris–Sorbonne, and a habilitation from the University of Paris–Diderot. She has worked as a sociologist at the Cheikh Anta Diop University in Dakar, Senegal, and at the University of Paris–Diderot. She was DAWN Regional Coordinator for Francophone Africa for a decade, editing several DAWN publications, and is currently the International Director of the Women Living under Muslim Laws network in London. She has co-edited *Engendering African Social Sciences, La Recherche féministe francophone: langue, identités et enjeux* and *Le Sexe de la mondialisation.*

ERIKA TRONCOSO is an anthropologist at the Universidad de los Andes, Colombia, with a Master's in Population Studies from the Facultad Latinoamericana de Ciencias Sociales, Mexico, and a pre-doctoral fellowship at the Hewlett Foundation at the University of California, San Francisco. Her publications concern health-sector reforms, sexual and reproductive health and rights, gender, and public–private collaborations in Mexico.

OSCAR UGARTECHE holds a Ph.D. in Philosophy and History from the University of Bergen and an M.Sc. from the London Business School. He is currently a senior researcher at the Instituto de Investigaciones Económicas of the Universidad Nacional Autonoma de México, and a member of the SNI /Conacyt system, working on regional financial cooperation and the international financial crisis. He was a visiting professor at the Freie Universität Berlin in 2011 and was Santander Visiting Scholar at Newcastle University. He has published widely on financial and political issues.

HIBIST WENDEMU KASSA is a feminist activist and DAWN Associate. She holds B.A. and M.Phil. degrees in Political Science from the University of Ghana. She is currently a Ph.D. candidate at the Centre of Social Change in the University of Johannesburg, where she is undertaking a comparative study on gender, mine labour and mining communities in South Africa and Ghana.

Index